THE DOCTRINE OF
THE HOLY SPIRIT

THE DOCTRINE OF THE HOLY SPIRIT

George Smeaton

The Banner of Truth Trust

THE BANNER OF TRUTH TRUST
3 Murrayfield Road, Edinburgh EH12 6EL
P.O. Box 652, Carlisle, Pennsylvania 17013

*

First published 1882
Second edition 1889

First Banner of Truth Trust reprint taken
from the 1882 edition 1958
Reprinted 1958 and 1961

Fourth Banner of Truth Trust reprint taken
from the 1889 edition 1974

ISBN 0 85151 187 2

*

Printed in Great Britain by Offset Lithography by
Billing and Sons Ltd., Guildford and London

FOREWORD

George Smeaton was ordained to the ministry of the Church of Scotland at Falkland in the Presbytery of Cupar in 1839. He was among those hundreds of ministers who came out at the Disruption in 1843 to form the Free Church of Scotland. Later he was appointed by his Church to be professor in her College at Aberdeen (1854) and in 1857 he became professor of Exegetics in the New College, Edinburgh. He died on the 14th April, 1889. He was one of the brilliant galaxy of men on the staff of the Free Church College in Edinburgh a century ago. Principal John Macleod describes Smeaton as "the most eminent scholar of the set of young men who with McCheyne and the Bonars sat at the feet of Chalmers". This volume of Smeaton on the Holy Spirit Dr. Macleod declares to be "invaluable within its own range", and adds of him that "next to Principal William Cunningham he stood as our foremost student of the history of Reformed theology". Smeaton had a thorough grasp of the historical development of the great Christian doctrines, such as the doctrine of the Atonement and the doctrine of the Holy Spirit. In this field, as Dr. Macleod informs us, he did "very fine work indeed". Dr. Macleod adds: "Dr. Smeaton was the master of a very clear and unobtrusive style of expression. . . . He was as modest and unassuming as he was thorough and painstaking. A man can take his word in regard to any theme that he handles as soon as that of any writer on theological subjects. His talented colleague, James Macgregor, said that Smeaton had the best-constituted theological intellect in Christendom". The late Dr. Alexander Stewart of Edinburgh esteemed Smeaton as "perhaps the most learned theologian in the Free Church and a man of deep and unaffected godliness".

Smeaton was a close friend of Dr. Hugh Martin and of that doughty champion of the faith, Dr. James Begg. When Dr. Begg died in 1883, the funeral sermons in his church at Newington were delivered by two of his oldest friends—Dr. John Kennedy of Dingwall and Dr. George Smeaton of Edinburgh.

Of Smeaton's work on the Holy Spirit, Dr. Caspar Wistar Hodge, Junior, of Princeton Seminary, had a very high opinion, and Dr. Hodge was no mean judge. He recommended it as the best work on the subject. It is surely high time for a fresh edition.

W. J. GRIER

Belfast,
Northern Ireland.
November 1st, 1957.

PREFACE.

———o———

I FOUND it necessary in the preparation of this Course of Lectures to travel over a field of vast extent. The subject has on this account taken shape in my hands as a survey of Theology from the view-point of the doctrine of the Holy Spirit. To this course I was shut up by the fact that attention could not be limited to one or two departments of the subject, and because a selection could not well be attempted. I have endeavoured, therefore, to take a survey of the doctrine of the Holy Spirit from the various points of view commended to our attention by the testimony of Scripture on the one hand, and by the results of theological discussion, as well as by the history of the doctrine, on the other. This has given a threefold division to the work.

To bring out these three aspects of the topic, it seemed necessary, IN A FIRST DIVISION, to survey the Biblical testimony in the Old and New Testament, or to furnish such a sketch as would show that the doctrine of the Holy Spirit was exhibited and apprehended from the first dawn of Revelation, though fully displayed only on the day of Pentecost. Then follows, IN A SECOND DIVISION, a brief outline or sketch of the positive truth accepted by the Church, or the form in which the Church dogmatically holds the doctrine. This is contained in the six Lectures which required to be formally prepared. As this was still felt to be incomplete without a Historical survey of the discussions connected with the doctrine of the Holy Spirit, I have subjoined, IN A THIRD DIVISION, a condensed history of the doctrine from the Apostolic age to the present time.

May the Holy Spirit, whose personality and work this treatise is intended to exhibit, condescend to accept and bless it to the glory of a Three-One God.

GEORGE SMEATON.

PREFACE TO THE SECOND EDITION.

——o——

I RESPOND with pleasure to the call for a Second Edition of this Volume. The additions interspersed here and there, with a view to make it more full on several points, leave the great body of the work as it was.

One of the most hopeful signs of the times is the growing interest in the doctrine and work of the Holy Spirit. This is evinced by the religious conferences, by the concerts for prayer, and by the desire for further statements and expositions on the great theme. If this new edition shall in any measure tend, by God's blessing, to satisfy the interest and guide the inquiries of many Christian minds, I shall be very thankful.

EDINBURGH, *February* 1889.

CONTENTS

THE DOCTRINE OF THE HOLY SPIRIT.

FIRST DIVISION.

THE topic on which we enter is by no means superfluous at this time. We may safely affirm that the doctrine of the Spirit is almost entirely ignored. The representatives of modern theology, it is well known, have almost wholly abandoned it. Many of them deny the Spirit's personality in the most open and undisguised manner. Some affirm that a dogma on this topic is not essential either to religion or theology, and that we may altogether dispense with it. On the contrary, wherever Christianity has become a living power, the doctrine of the Holy Spirit has uniformly been regarded, equally with the atonement and justification by faith, as the article of a standing or falling Church. The distinctive feature of Christianity, as it addresses itself to man's experience, is the work of the Spirit, which not only elevates it far above all philosophical speculation, but also above every other form of religion.

In this day it is impossible to divest the mind of the impression that, among those who take religion in earnest, a disposition exists, in no small measure, to pass over the supernatural agency of the Holy Spirit, and to speak and write upon religious truth as if the gracious intervention of the Son of God came more impressively home to men's business and bosom when disencumbered of any reference to another Person as the great Applier of redemption. In many cases

that tendency may rather be called a sentiment than a
formal dogma; with others it is a system.   But in either
case it betrays the most defective views of the relations of
the Trinity.   By maintaining silence on this doctrine, one of
the grand provisions of the gospel for meeting the wants
of mankind is omitted.

But it may be asked, not without reason, can any man in
the nineteenth century from the entrance of Christianity be
in any doubt as to the Personality, Deity, and work of the
Holy Ghost ?   Does not the Church declare her belief in it
as an elementary and fundamental truth in every administration
of the ordinance of baptism ?   Is it not inserted in all the
Church-creeds ?   Have not theologians discussed and vindicated it from Patristic times and since the Reformation so
copiously, that many pages might be filled with a mere
enumeration of the writers' names, and with the titles of their
works ?   The answer is : Unsettled opinion and doubt prevail
upon this point, to a surprising degree, abroad and at home,
even among those who profess to accept as authoritative the
words of prophets and apostles, and the sayings of our
Lord.   One explains them in one way, and another explains
them in a different way, in order to exclude this doctrine.

No one, it is true, has attempted, in reference to the
doctrine of the Spirit, to show that the Lord's own teaching
differed, in essential points, from that of His apostles.   The
harmony is so unquestionable and so obvious, that it gives to
all a sufficient ground of confidence.   Moreover, less is said
than formerly of accommodation ; for reverent minds are ready
to admit that deception, however subtle and refined, is still
deception ; and that this is an element which is not to be
endured in a divine revelation.   Theological opinion has
taken a forward step in this respect, though not much is
really gained, while the language of Scripture—which a
natural interpretation would make conclusive as to the
personality and work of the Spirit—is explained away as

figurative, or as a mere personification, by many modern divines.

To set forth the doctrine of the Spirit EXEGETICALLY, according to the programme which I have sketched, is not an unnecessary task in the present state of theology ; and, in carrying out this undertaking, my object is truth, and truth alone, without the bondage of any artificial system, past or present. So far as the outline of Scripture testimony is concerned, I shall largely content myself with the results of investigation, and often hold the statement of the process in abeyance. And where the word is silent, I shall accept its silence as well as its declarations without hesitation or reserve. The Jewish Church was formed by a special education to receive Christianity when it should come. It was the issue of a long development, meant to lead them to comprehend the import of Christ's instruction.

As we come in contact, in the course of this discussion, with the doctrine of the Trinity at every point, it may be fitting to refer to that great theme at the outset, so far at least as concerns the relation which essentially belongs to the Holy Spirit. This will pave the way for the consideration of the other doctrines which we have to discuss. Though every attempt to comprehend or to unfold the mystery of the Trinity has failed, and must fail, from the ineffable nature of the subject, we may affirm that in the five following propositions the faith of the Church is satisfactorily exhibited, viz. :—

1. That there is one God or divine essence.
2. That the same numerical divine essence is common to three truly divine Persons, who are designated Father, Son, and Holy Ghost.
3. That between these three divine Persons there obtains a natural order of subsistence and operation : that the first Person hath life in Himself (John v. 26); and that the second and third Persons subsist and act from the first.

4. That this order of the divine Persons belongs to the divine essence prior to, and irrespective of, the covenant of grace.

5. That this natural order of subsistence and action is the ground and reason of the several names, Father, Son, and Spirit; the Son being begotten of the Father, and the Spirit by spiration proceeding from both.

And as to the divine WORKS, the Father is the source FROM WHICH every operation emanates (ἐξ οὖ), the Son is the medium THROUGH WHICH (δι' οὖ) it is performed, and the Holy Ghost is the EXECUTIVE BY WHICH (ἐν ᾧ) it is carried into effect.

The Christian Church, from the beginning, believed in the doctrine of the Trinity with unhesitating faith. It was not a conclusion formed gradually in the consciousness of the Christian community, partly by reflection, partly by Biblical inquiry. The Church found in the baptismal formula an emphatic allusion to Father, Son, and Holy Ghost, and simply accepted it as her doctrine of the Trinity. It was brought within the scope of every Christian mind, learned and unlearned, as the fundamental and the primary truth, of which no Christian disciple could plead ignorance. The substance of the doctrine is, that God is one, and that the Persons are distinct; and after all the investigations that have confounded and fatigued the acutest understanding, we only return to the same simple formula of baptism, which is level to the capacity of the humblest.

The doctrine of the Trinity is not so much a point among many as the very essence and compendium of Christianity itself. It not only presents a lofty subject of contemplation to the intellect, but furnishes a repose and peace which satisfies the heart and conscience. *To explain this mystery is not our province.* All true theologians, who have trained their minds in the right school, whether in expounding positive truth or in combating erroneous views, have uniformly accepted it as their highest function simply TO CONSERVE THE MYSTERY, and to leave it where they found it, in its inscrutable sublimity, or, as the poet expresses it, " dark though excessive bright." Leibnitz happily said, If we could bring it within the terms of any humanly constructed definition, it would be a mystery no longer. The zeal and erudition of the Fathers, accordingly, were mainly employed to retain and preserve the mystery.

And when we look at the doctrine from the practical point of view, a belief of this great truth is absolutely essential to the Christian man and to the Christian Church. Without it, Christianity would at once collapse. As this doctrine is believed on the one hand, or challenged on the other, Christian life is found to be affected at its roots and over all its extent. Every doctrine is run up to it; every privilege and duty hang on it. It cannot escape observation that scarcely a heresy ever appeared which did not, when carried out to its logical results, come into collision with the doctrine of the Trinity at some point. Through the whole history of opinion, the ever-recurring fact presented to us is, that however a man may begin his career of error, the general issue is that the doctrine of the Trinity, proving an unexpected check or insurmountable obstacle in the carrying out of his opinions, has, to a large extent, to be modified or pushed aside ; and he comes to be against the Trinity because he has found that the doctrine of the Trinity was against him.

The attacks on the Trinity, menacing though they might be for a time, have commonly been the occasion of real benefit to the Church. The Church might have been less on the alert than was found to be imperatively necessary when asked, for instance, by the Sabellian to allow within her pale a mere modal distinction in the Trinity, or when asked by the Arian to give a certain amount of liberty to such as questioned or denied the supreme Deity of the second or third person of the Trinity. By varied discipline and experience, she has been schooled to apprehend the doctrine of the tri-personal God, or the threefold personality in unity, as the most funda-

mental, vital, and practical of doctrines ; that it forms the
ultimate ground of every truth; that it is absolutely intertwined
with the essential provisions of the gospel ; and that the plan of
salvation cannot be left standing entire, if this great doctrine,
the keystone of the arch, is either loosened or displaced.

The Church, accordingly, has always posted herself here
as in the Thermopylæ, where her last stand is to be made.
She knew that, without this doctrine, the Creed would have
no coherence, nor her members have any solid peace. The
enlightened Christian in this field neither expects nor wishes
to find that which will not baffle his comprehension by its
vastness, nor dazzle him by its splendour. Nay, the appeal
to the ADORING WONDER of the finite mind becomes more
powerful when its limited capacity fails to comprehend the
theme in all its magnitude. We cease to comprehend and
begin to adore. The Christian Church, feeling that she has to
believe what God has condescended to declare, is alive to the
fact that there is no loyalty greater than the loyalty of the
intellect ; and she calls for the submission of the finite
reason. Hence every one feels the force of these beautiful
words of Gregory Nazianzen in reference to the Trinity. In
his sermon on Baptism he says : οὐ φθάνω τὸ ἓν νοῆσαι καὶ
τοῖς τρισὶ περιλάμπομαι· οὐ φθάνω τὰ τρία διελεῖν, καὶ εἰς τὸ
ἓν ἀναφέρομαι. " I cannot think of the ONE but I am immediately surrounded with the splendour of the THREE; nor can
I clearly discover the three, but I am suddenly carried back
to the One."

The objection to the Trinity on the ground of the unfathomable mystery, has been repeated in every successive
age. And it may not be out of place to say that if there
had been no mystery, an opposite objection might not improb-
ably have emanated from the very same parties. Had there
been no inscrutable doctrines beyond the sounding line of
man's reason, no profound mysteries in the revealed account
of God's Being, purposes, and works,—if such a thing were

conceivable in a revelation communicated from God to man, — the objectors might have decried and depreciated it from a wholly different point of view as a stale, flat, and unprofitable message, which had nothing in it worthy of the claims which it made on men's minds, because it had nothing beyond the discovery of the human understanding. When we reach the manhood of our being, we may understand what we cannot now fathom. Addison and Swift both conjectured, not unwarrantably, in connection with these very mysteries, that new faculties might be given in the life to come to apprehend what is now incomprehensible and unknown.

I shall endeavour to bring out the testimony of Scripture to the doctrine of the Holy Spirit as contained in the Old and New Testaments. As my object in this division is to set forth the place which the doctrine of the Spirit occupies in contrast with the modern Sabellianism, I shall rather state the cumulative import of the Scripture testimony, than launch into a full or exhaustive exegesis of all the passages. And in fulfilling this task it will be my aim, except where some elucidation is necessary, to mix with it as little of my own as possible, lest foreign elements should invalidate the evidence which is so conclusively furnished by the harmonious testimony of the Scripture itself from first to last. I shall try to evolve what the Scriptures say; and for that end transplant myself into the circumstances in which the writers of the different ages were placed. To penetrate, as far as possible, into the teaching of inspired prophets before the coming of Christ, and of inspired apostles subsequent to His resurrection, it will be necessary to bring out, in a condensed outline, their scope and harmony.

That the Scripture testimony about to be adduced in reference to the Holy Spirit may also be readily applied to the refutation of modern errors, it may not be out of place to mention the Sabellian postulate, and the deduction from it to which Schleiermacher has given expression in this century. According to the view stated by Schleiermacher in his own ingenious way, all that is intimated by the names SON OF GOD and SPIRIT OF GOD did not exist before the work of redemption, and before the founding of the Christian Church respectively. It was held by him that God is Father as He creates, Son as He redeems, and Holy Spirit as He unites Himself to the Christian Church, but without the personality which the Church doctrine ascribes to each of them. Sabellianism was always at a loss to explain the Biblical truth that all things were created by God through the Son and the Holy Spirit; for the divine Persons must manifestly have existed before they could act. That was the argument which of old the Patristic writers adduced with invincible force against the Sabellian theory; and neither Sabellius in former days, nor the Schleiermacher-school in recent times, have done anything to meet or answer it. The Jewish Church, though carefully trained, failed at the decisive moment, from this same Unitarian bias which had come to predominate in it. And many have, in all ages, been engulfed by opinions which impugned the Spirit's personality on the one hand, or questioned His supreme Deity on the other. Of those who deviate from Church-doctrine in our day, the majority are led by a strong Sabellian bias, which, while it admits that predicates of Deity are undoubtedly ascribed to the Spirit, interprets these allusions as descriptive of a mere influence or energy, or as attributes and manifestations of Deity without the personal distinction in any form. This Sabellian view is at present a theological current of immensely greater force and wider diffusion than is commonly suspected by theological readers in this country.

We shall endeavour in the present dissertation, introductory to the six dogmatic lectures afterwards given in proper form, to give an outline of the Biblical testimony to the doctrine of the Holy Spirit. This will supply an exegetical foundation.

INTRODUCTORY DISSERTATION.

We shall first keep the Old Testament doctrine of the Spirit full in view; and in tracing the stream of history, we shall consider (1) the testimony to the spirit of prophecy in the Books of Moses and Job; (2) in the time from Moses to David; (3) in the period from David to the Exile; (4) from the Exile to the close of the Old Testament. But underneath this mere chronological division, we shall have occasion to notice the Spirit's operations in nature and in grace; in the supernatural gifts conferred upon gifted men, and in the prophecies relating to the Messiah prior to the Pentecostal economy.

THE BOOKS OF MOSES AND JOB.

"*The Spirit of God moved on the face of the waters*" (Gen. i. 2). The term Spirit (*Ruach*) denotes a BREATH, a WIND, and also an intelligent thinking Being. The designation "the Spirit of God," denotes two persons—God and the Spirit of God, like the analogous title "the Son of God." It implies distinct personality, and indicates that He is from God, or of God. The action here ascribed to Him, in connection with the creation of all things, seems to be a metaphor taken from the incubation of a bird, and sets forth how the Spirit, dove-like, sat brooding o'er the dark abyss, and made it pregnant.[1]

"*By His Spirit He garnished the heavens*" (Job xxvi. 13). He is called God's Spirit ("His Spirit") to show that He is of the same essence with God and from Him. When it is said that He who garnished the heavens is the Spirit of God, we are not warranted to interpret the words in any other way than as a declaration that the personal Spirit —elsewhere called the finger of God and the power of God —adorned the heavens, and framed them to display the divine glory.

[1] Milton, i. 21 and vii. 233.

" *The Spirit of God made me*," says Elihu, "*and the breath of the Almighty hath given me life*" (Job xxxiii. 4). The reference to a personal agent standing in a unique relation to God—that is, from God, but personally distinct—is too express to be evaded by any subterfuge.

" *Thou sendest forth Thy Spirit, they are created; and Thou renewest the face of the earth*" (Ps. civ. 30). There the Psalmist speaks of God's manifold works according to their order. He shows that God gives the animals their food; that He hides His face and they are troubled; that He takes away their breath and they die; that He sends forth His Spirit, and a fresh succession or race of animated beings is created. The title "Thy Spirit" distinguishes between the uncreated and the finite Spirit, and proves that the Spirit of God is the fountain of life; and that creation, amid all its necessary changes, receives from Him its renovating or rejuvenating power. The blossom and decay of vegetation; the succession of races on the earth's surface; the bias impressed on various minds; the skill in arts; the manifold gifts which hold society together,—are all the workmanship of the Spirit.

MAN MADE TO BE THE TEMPLE OF THE HOLY GHOST.

We come to the indwelling of the Spirit in primeval man, which may be called the deep ground-thought of all right anthropology, as appears from these words: " *The Lord God formed man of the dust of the ground, and breathed into his nostrils the breath of life*" (Gen. ii. 7). When God breathed into man the breath of LIFE (or LIVES, for it is plural), we must understand life in the Holy Spirit as well as animal and intellectual life. Calvin, and the mass of commentators since his day, have interpreted the words of the physical life, as if they intimated nothing more than the animation of the clay figure. The Patristic writers, Athanasius, Basil, Ambrose,

and Cyril, refer the words to the occasion when God communicated the Spirit, the breath of the Almighty, the giver
of the HIGHER as well as of the lower form of life. If further
proof of the correctness of this interpretation were necessary,
it is furnished by the contrast of DEATH threatened in the
penalty, which certainly cannot be limited to natural death.
Adam had the Spirit in the state of integrity, not only for
himself, but for his seed ; and he walked after the Spirit as
long as he stood in his integrity. I must here refer a little
more fully to the Spirit's work in connection with the first
Adam.

From the narrative of creation, brief but suggestive, which
is given in Genesis, the great thought is derived that, according to the constitution which God was pleased to give to the
first man among the creatures of His hand, not only was a
federal unity assigned to him as the head of the race, but a
relation to the whole Trinity which comes to light, in his
being made in the image of God. That he not only bore a
likeness to God's perfections in his mental, moral, and religious constitution, but that he was placed in a peculiarly
CLOSE RELATION TO ALL THE PERSONS OF THE TRINITY,—nay,
in a conscious personal relation to all the divine Persons,—
is clearly intimated in the words : " Let US make man in our
image, after our likeness " (Gen. i. 26). The use of the plural
number in the pronoun US is not to be reduced, according to
the evacuating principle of Rationalism, to a mere mannerism
in style. Dr. Owen has well remarked that God, having
manifested by other parts of creation His existence, nature,
and perfections, designed in the creation of man to manifest
Himself in a trinity of persons ; a remark setting forth a
momentous truth only too little pondered. For the right
interpretation of many passages of Scripture in their coherence and meaning, it is necessary to take this thought
along with us.

The question now raised in theological circles in reference

to man is: Did he, as God's creature, realize in any measure His idea? And was he the object of divine complacency not only as the partaker of a pure nature, but as a Son who was then replenished, just as redeemed men are again replenished, with the Holy Spirit? Or, on the contrary, was he, according to the Rationalistic theory, formed in a low and rude condition, though capable of advancing in an ascending scale, and necessarily requiring even in his creation-state some further intervention to make him correspond to His idea? On exegetical grounds as well as on the ground of analogy, we must hold that man as he was formed not only corresponded to His idea as a Son within the sphere of creaturehood, but was the temple of the Holy Ghost. This is a view so essential to all right conceptions of our primeval relationship, that without it no sound anthropology can be maintained. The deep ground-thought presupposed by Christianity is, that Adam had the divine image and life from the Spirit of Life. It follows, accordingly, that the elements were already deposited in him by which he was in a position to reach the full perfection of his being, as he was. He needed only to have further developed that which was already in him, and to abide the probation under which he was placed.

The advocates of the Rationalistic conception of man— however variously it may be modified, and however imposing some aspects of it may at first sight appear—describe man's original state as commencing with a low grade or type, and rising to a higher. But of all the forms in which this baseless theory has been presented, by far the most attractive is the novel theory supported, in our day, by many able men, that an incarnation would have entered to complete the idea of man even though no sin had ever entered to disturb the harmony of the universe. This favourite speculation [1] of modern German theologians has no Biblical

---

[1] See Dorner's *Doctrine of the Person of Christ ;* Liebner, Martensen, Ebrard.

ground, but has a tendency to introduce a wholly different conception of man's original state. It gives a false idea of his original integrity or perfection. According to this theory, they postulate the necessity of an incarnation to make man correspond to His idea; and what does that supposition involve? It necessarily implies imperfection in his very constitution, and in the adaptation of the means to the end designed. It reflects on the perfection of that nature in which our race was made. Assuming that man was formed by the Creator in an imperfect and rude state,— that is, without the elements that would have unfolded themselves in the full efflorescence of his being,—it takes for granted that the ideal of creation, without a new intervention from above, must have remained unrealized; that with all his natural powers exerted to the utmost, and with all the aids provided for him in his original sphere, he could not have completed his destiny without an intervention wholly new and supplementary. If there still remained a further extraordinary interposition to carry forward to completeness the act of creation which, by the supposition, was left imperfect—or, at least, unfinished—in kind as well as in degree; if nature required no mere development within its assigned sphere into the perfection of its capacities, but was left defective in its structure or mental conformation from the first,—then everything most confidently accepted by inspired and uninspired men from the beginning is seen in a cross light and through a distorting medium. If imperfection, at least in the sense of incompleteness, attached in such a degree to creation in its normal state, — in other words, if it did not correspond to its idea,—reason would be staggered. The moral problem of responsibility—arduous enough as it is—would in that case be insoluble. We could not speak of all as "very good" in its primordial state, nor could we vindicate the ways of God to men. On the contrary, the representations of man from a Biblical point of view are to the effect that he had, from the first, realized and formed within him the divine idea to such an extent that he needed nothing more than the required probation in order to his being confirmed, and then exalted to an immensely higher degree, according to the promised reward.

We naturally ask whether *the first Adam had the Holy Spirit at his creation.* This must be affirmed whether we look at the exegetical grounds, which we hold to be conclusive (Gen. ii. 7), or at the analogy of the Second Adam. This has not been denied in any quarter entitled to respect, Patristic or Protestant. Bishop Bull has proved in his sermons, by quotations from the Fathers, that they believed firmly on the warrant of Scripture, that Adam along with the principle of natural life received also the grace of the Hóly Spirit. This is a point that has never been taken up in earnest by any divine of note, with the single exception of Howe, whose *Living Temple* proceeds upon it as a postulate. The explanation of that omission, from which not only anthropology but the doctrines of grace have suffered not a little, may be the following. In a treatise which long passed under the name of Augustin, there was a formal denial of the position that Adam in his state of integrity was in the possession of the Spirit. The great influence of Augustin's name, thus supposed to have pronounced a different judgment, seems mainly to have had the effect of repressing due inquiry, and of blunting statements which might otherwise have been at once clearer, ampler, and less reserved in the direction to which I have referred. That treatise, ascribed to Augustin,[1] contains, however, so many gross mistakes and errors on many different points, and even on the doctrines of grace, on which the views of Augustin were the most pronounced, that any man might have detected the injury done to him by attributing such an unworthy composition to his pen. It is now with a general concurrence

---

[1] *Vid. Quæst. ex utroque Testamento,* Quæst. 123.

of opinion rejected as spurious, and replete with views which Augustin did not hold. The arguments from analogy which go to prove that Adam had the Spirit are conclusive.

The doctrine that man was originally, though mutably, replenished with the Spirit, may be termed the deep fundamental thought of the Scripture-doctrine of man. If the first and second Adam are so related that the first man was the analogue or figure of the second, as all admit on the authority of Scripture (τύπος τοῦ μέλλοντος, Rom. v. 12–14), it is clear that, unless the first man possessed the Spirit, the last man, the Healer or Restorer of the forfeited inheritance, would not have been the medium of giving the Spirit, who was withdrawn on account of sin, and who could be restored only on account of the everlasting righteousness which Christ brought in (Rom. viii. 10). Sin separated between the soul and God; and, according to the tenor of God's just and holy moral government, the Spirit was of necessity withdrawn at the moment when Adam lent an ear to the tempter's glozing words. And the privation to which man's nature was subjected, as the term FLESH clearly shows (Gen. vi. 3), implies that he had forfeited that fulness of the Spirit which he once possessed, and which, but for sin, would have descended as an inheritance to his posterity.

The arguments against the view that Adam had the Spirit are wholly destitute of Biblical ground, and have no validity or weight. One ill-understood text has been adduced to prove that Adam was not replenished with the Spirit, viz.: " the first man Adam was made a living soul; the last Adam was made a quickening Spirit" (1 Cor. xv. 45). That is the main argument in the spurious treatise ascribed to Augustin. But that passage, when closely examined, is no absolute antithesis; for the apostle aims to show that there is a natural body and a spiritual body, the one before the other; the one inherited from the first man, the other received from Him who is the quickening Spirit. But the apostle says

nothing against Adam being replenished with the Spirit—
nothing in favour of the notion which it was adduced to
prove. On the contrary, it is clear that man must have
realized his idea, for God pronounced all very good; and he
had only to undergo the necessary probation, which implied
that his nature, from the first, was so perfect that it might
certainly have come out unhurt. Why, in fact, was there any
probation at all, if man at his creation was left without the
Spirit to guide and animate him? and how could he be tried
if he did not answer his idea, as one supplied with all that was
requisite for the trial, the successful issue of which would
have placed him amid the glory and incorruption of the
resurrection state?

There are two conclusions to which we must come:
(1) Man as a creature, but with a certain standing as a son
in the beloved Son, was the object of the divine complacency,
though mutable; (2) His soul was inwardly irradiated with
the supernatural presence of the Holy Spirit, which might
have been retained. That man stood at first related to all
the persons of the Trinity, and bore the image of God, though
mutably, upon his soul; that the Spirit of Life filled him for
a service of holy love, may be accepted as a postulate in all
our investigations — a postulate which Christianity, as a
restorative or remedial economy, will not permit us to ignore,
although it has never received the place to which it is
entitled in any system of anthropology—Patristic or Protestant. But it may be affirmed, on the ground of the
analogy between the two Adams, that Christ would not have
been the medium of giving the Spirit, if the first man had not
possessed the Spirit. The Spirit departed from the human
family when Adam gave ear to the tempter's seducing words;
and the restoration by the second man implies the possession
of the Spirit by the first. No one, in fact, can read the
action of Christ on the first evening after His resurrection,
and consider the symbolic breathing on the disciples, and the

words which fell from Him in conveying a new gift of the Spirit, without an impression that *these two acts were counterparts*—the one the original gift, the other the restoration of what was lost.[1]

THE HOLY SPIRIT LOST BY THE FALL.

The Fall involved three things which must be regarded as presuppositions to the whole doctrine of the Spirit which we are now discussing:—

(1.) The withdrawal of the Holy Spirit from the human heart as one of the penal consequences of sin. Man, destitute of the Spirit, is now called flesh (Gen. vi. 3); and they who live the life of sinful nature are designated "earthly, sensual, *having not the Spirit*" (Jude 19). The Holy Spirit, in consequence of the Fall, departed from the human heart, which was once His temple, and the frame of which sufficiently proves that it was at first a fit habitation for the divine presence. Only the ruins can now be traced.

(2.) The Fall involved our captivity to Satan, which he maintained by right of conquest. The evil spirit entered the heart when the Holy Spirit withdrew, and continues to lead men captive, *working* in the children of disobedience (Eph. ii. 2).

(3.) The image of God, in which Adam was created, was replaced by the entire corruption of man's nature (John iii. 6). His understanding had been furnished with a true and saving knowledge of his Creator and of spiritual things; his heart and will had been upright; all his affections had been pure; and the whole man holy: but, revolting from God by the temptation of the devil, the opposite of all that image of God became his doleful heritage; and his posterity derive corruption from their progenitor, not by imitation, but by the

[1] See Basil on the breathing upon Adam and upon the apostles (*Against Eunomius*, v. 119).

propagation of a vicious nature, which is incapable of any saving good. It is prone to evil, and dead in sin. It is not denied that there still linger in man since the Fall *some glimmerings of natural light*, some knowledge of God and of the difference between good and evil, and some regard for virtue and good order in society. But it is all too evident that, WITHOUT THE REGENERATING GRACE OF THE HOLY SPIRIT, men are neither able nor willing to return to God, or to reform their natural corruption.[1]

THE RESTORATION OF THE SPIRIT BY A REMEDIAL ECONOMY.

In view of the Fall a covenant or method of restoration had been formed, according to which we find the persons of the Godhead acting their proper part on man's behalf; for no covenant could have been directly formed between God and fallen sinners. The agreement, pact, or covenant was, that the Father, holding in His hands the rights of God, should send the Son as the one Mediator between God and men; that the incarnate Son, as the second Adam, should fulfil the law and bear our sins in His own body; and that the Holy Ghost should then return with a plenitude of grace and of power to be forfeited no more.

No sooner had sin entered than we find the Mediator carrying out by His Spirit the provisions of the remedial plan by announcing the gospel, viz. that the seed of the woman should bruise the serpent's head, and putting enmity between the seed of the serpent and the seed of the woman. There THE WORD AND THE SPIRIT are already in conjunction—the one filling the mind with truth, the other filling it with spiritual life. From the first we have brought before us the ruin and the remedy; then the two opposite families; then a marked revival in the days of Enos; then as marked a declension. We hold it as antagonistic to all Biblical doctrine to

[1] See Articles of Dort.

represent the first man, as the Rationalistic theory uniformly represents him, as originally made on a lower platform, and as always mounting higher.

"*My Spirit shall not always strive with man, for that he also is flesh*" (Gen. vi. 3).——With whatever shade of meaning the word rendered *strive* may be connected, the general import unquestionably is, that the forbearance long exercised was about to close, that the antediluvians had rejected the testimony of the Spirit, addressed to them by inspired or Spirit-filled men, and despised every call to repentance and faith. *He who thus speaks of His Spirit is undoubtedly Christ.* This we learn from Peter, the inspired commentator on the words in Genesis, who says that Christ by the Spirit went and preached to these antediluvians or spirits in prison, who were alive when Noah preached to them, but were spirits in prison or hell when Peter wrote his Epistle (1 Pet. iii. 19). The Spirit of Christ speaking by Enoch and Noah was about to leave that corrupt generation to its doom. The Messiah, having received the Spirit by anticipation for the purposes of His kingdom, on the ground of the coming atonement, preached the gospel to them by the mouth of Noah, and the message was impiously rejected. The Spirit of Christ, who filled and animated all the prophets, not only summoned them to repentance, but testified beforehand the sufferings of Christ and the glory that should follow (1 Pet. i. 11).

THE COVENANT MADE WITH ABRAHAM.

We come next to Abraham, who was called to leave his country and kindred. The God of glory appeared to him (Acts vii. 2), and vouchsafed to him no fewer than eight theophanies or manifestations of Himself. After the days of Noah we find no new revelations till it pleased God by the call of Abraham to work a new thing in the earth, to separate a single family from the rest of the nations, and thus in reality to institute a Church, which should serve God apart. This call was accompanied with another great proclamation of the gospel, similar to what had been given to our first parents in the garden. The first promise by which multitudes had been saved was that *the woman's seed* should bruise the serpent's head. The word now announced was that in Abraham's seed all the families of the earth should be blessed (Gen. xviii. 18, xxii. 18). Momentous and suggestive as this promise was, we cannot discuss all its elements. The point that demands attention in connection with our theme is that the blessing of Abraham, according to the interpretation of the Apostle Paul, includes in it THE PROMISE OF THE SPIRIT (Gal. iii. 14). To make this plain, we have only to notice that when God gives a blessing, it is given in free and unmerited grace to sinful men (Rom. iv. 5). The apostle, by divine inspiration, reads into that ancient promise the two things undoubtedly contained in it when the blessing was announced, viz. that faith on the promised seed was counted for righteousness, and that he should receive the promise of the Spirit by faith. Through faith on the promised seed of Abraham, who came in the fulness of time, the Gentiles also are justified by faith as Abraham was, and receive the promised Spirit in all the amplitude of His gifts and grace. All this was in the promise given to Abraham, according to the apostle's authoritative interpretation, and not a jot has failed of its accomplishment.

It may be added that Abraham was called a prophet, and therefore he had the Spirit (Gen. xx. 6). The three patriarchs, indeed, who are called the first-fruit and root of the covenant people (Rom. xi. 16), evinced in many ways, and especially at the close of life, the Spirit of prophecy. In Joseph we see the same gift continued, and it was made the means of preserving the Old Testament Church ; for the language of Pharaoh in reference to him was plainly borrowed from Joseph himself, when he said : " Can we find such a

man as this — a man in whom the Spirit of God is?"
(Gen. xli. 38).

THE LAW OF MOSES.

It seems hard to find the doctrine of the Spirit when we
turn our thoughts to an Economy where we meet at the very
threshold more of law than promise, more of the letter and of
the shadow than of grace. The line between the Abrahamic
Covenant and the Mosaic Economy, it must be owned, has
not always been well or rightly drawn. Nay, the widest
difference of opinion has prevailed both among Churches and
individual divines. But we may put all these divergences on
one side, and content ourselves with Biblical ideas. We find,
according to the Pauline description of this difference, that
the promise made to Abraham was irrevocable; that the legal
Economy could not disannul it; and that it entered only as
an intervening and temporary dispensation, the scope of which
was to convince men of sin, and make them repair to the
great promised Seed of Abraham (Gal. iii. 15–19). The
underlying covenant with Abraham, on which it rested,
supported the whole. The blessing of Abraham and the
promise of the Spirit were never awanting to them that
believed. The Spirit, indeed, was more sparingly imparted;
and there were elements of law before every mind, and a
covering veil over all.

In reference to Moses, we find explicit statements that he
was raised up and qualified by the Spirit of God for his great
commission. When the Lord, to relieve his heavy burden,
associated seventy elders to bear rule along with him, He said:
"I will take *of the Spirit* that is upon thee, and put it upon
them" (Num. xi. 17). We see from that memorable narrative that the Spirit rested upon them as the spirit of prophecy,
a fact which accredited their commission. The incident connected with Eldad and Medad made that donation of the
Spirit all the more remarkable. Moses was directed to take

Joshua, a man *in whom was the Spirit*, and to lay his hand on him (Num. xxvii. 18 ; Deut. xxxiv. 9). Many passages in like manner speak of the Spirit of God coming upon men in a supernatural way, that they might be equipped for official service. The Spirit's work in this period is seen in many spiritually-minded men, as well as in the supernaturally gifted few. The miraculous gifts which at times were copiously given were but a sign, and might be withdrawn, while the Spirit of Life remained. The same spirit of faith and the same new nature were always found in a remnant forming the true Church of God, in reference to which God said by Jeremiah : " I remember thee, the kindness of thy youth, the love of thine espousals, when thou wentest after me in the wilderness " (Jer. ii. 2). The presence of the Spirit appeared in the drops from heaven accompanying the Sinai Covenant, which, with all its sternness and shadows, was a mode of administering the covenant of grace (Ps. lxviii. 8).

The Spirit is seen also in inspiring Moses to commit to writing the word of God, the great outward means for promoting the spiritual good of the children of men. We see the Spirit's work, moreover, in all the theophanies and audible voices, in all the prophecies and types outwardly given ; but we see it also in that spiritual illumination of multitudes of true believers, which is far different from the inner consciousness of which our modern divines are fond of speaking. There are two noteworthy passages which refer to the comforting power of the Spirit during the wilderness sojourn, and which apply to the Church at large, and not to the supernaturally gifted few : (1) " Thou gavest also Thy *good Spirit* to instruct them, and withheldest not Thy manna " (Neh. ix. 20); (2) " Where is He that put His Holy Spirit within him ? " (Isa. lxiii. 11); " As a beast goeth down to the valley, *the Spirit of the Lord* caused him to rest" (ver. 14).

From the Time of Moses to David.

The Spirit of God is not mentioned in the whole Book of Joshua. Joshua himself, indeed, was full of the spirit of wisdom (Deut. xxxiv. 9). After the elders who outlived Joshua had passed away, we find the indications of a great change.

In the Book of Judges, which ushers us into a period of declension, repeated allusion is made to the fact that the Spirit of God came upon men supernaturally gifted, and who were raised up for the deliverance of Israel. The people from time to time did evil in the sight of the Lord; they were delivered into the hand of some of the neighbouring nations; they repented and cried to the Lord—an alternating state of things which we find pervading the entire book; and then a bold leader was raised up by the Spirit of God to deliver them. Thus the Spirit of the Lord came upon Othniel, and he judged Israel (Judg. iii. 10); upon Gideon (vi. 34); upon Jephthah (xi. 29); and upon Samson, a very mixed character, with strong faith, but with equally great personal defects all too marked (xiv. 19). Then war was waged successfully on the nations which had oppressed them. The Spirit of God, the author of all those gifts which they received, intellectual as well as spiritual, kindled in them intrepid valour; for God was King of the Theocracy, and it redounded to His glory to break the yoke of the oppressor, when the purposes of discipline were served. One hero after another, endowed with extraordinary courage, patriotism, and zeal, was raised up by the Spirit of God to deliver Israel.

After the unquiet times of the judges, a period of marked revival appears in the days of Samuel, the last of the judges. Next to Moses, Samuel, who walked with a reformatory zeal and power in the steps of the former, may be regarded as the greatest benefactor of the nation, which, in the interval between the two, had forgotten the law, lost true conceptions of God, sensualized His worship, and become enfeebled by irreligion and vice. In a higher sense than could be affirmed of any other of the judges, Samuel was a deliverer of the nation; for he delivered it from irreligion, ignorance, and vice. This was a transition-period to the flourishing times of the Israelitish kingdom. When the Spirit came upon Samuel at that time, God imparted to him one theophany after another, and a new state of things was introduced. The spirit of prophecy filled Samuel in a peculiar way (1 Sam. x. 20); and from his time downwards an order or school of prophets arose. A whole line of prophets, not in lineal succession like the priesthood, but in a succession of a higher order, appeared to guide the future history of Israel. We are thus supplied with a true idea of the nature of prophecy, on which we can cast only a passing glance, because a full description of this remarkable institution would demand a far more many-sided inquiry than either our aim or our limits will permit.

The prophet requited for the duties of his function the inspiration and guidance of the Holy Ghost. He personally represented the cause of God, and viewed historical events of every class, as they occurred, in relation to Jehovah and His law. Hence his message was largely the proclamation of warnings and menaces, or the burden of the Lord, which the ungodly often turned into ridicule. He was the organ of the Holy Spirit; and it was the impulse imparted by the Spirit of God that animated and enlightened him. The Lord Jesus by the Spirit, whom He dispensed by anticipation for the purposes of His kingdom, on the ground of the future atonement, revealed Himself to their spirit, moving them to speak and act, and also to write when an addition was to be made to the Old Testament canon. It was not according to their will that they either spoke or continued silent. Like a musical instrument which gives out its tones only as it is struck, they simply obeyed as the Spirit acted on each prophetic mind at His pleasure, using all those peculiar gifts or

aptitudes with which He had endowed the different individuals for the end He had in view, and which were called
into activity only so far as they were moved by the Holy
Ghost (2 Pet. i. 21); and hence they acted as God's servants, or as His mouth, whenever they spoke the words of
God (Ex. iv. 16; 2 Kings ix. 7). The prophet, accordingly,
is described as a man of the Spirit, who felt himself apprehended by the Spirit (Hos. ix. 7); and a discretionary
commission was never entrusted to him. God never deposited
the gracious supplies of His Spirit in Churches, ministry, or
ordinances, to be dispensed at man's discretion or caprice.
Nor did it run counter to this undoubted truth when Elisha
asked and obtained a double portion of Elijah's spirit. The
request amounted to nothing more than this : that the same
Spirit that dwelt in the departing prophet might by the
dispensation of God's free gift dwell in a large measure also
in him : much like the arrangement according to which the
first-born got a double portion of the inheritance.

The influence wielded by these Spirit-filled men was great.
They were watchmen and shepherds (Isa. xxi. 11; Zech.
xi. 3). As contrasted with what was merely political, they
represented the spiritual elements of the kingdom of God ;
and as contrasted with the frequently secularized priests, with
their outward forms and sacrifices, they laid emphasis on the
fear of God and the spiritual elements of true religion (Isa.
i. 11–15; 1 Sam. xv. 22). Again, as compared with the
kings, who often leant on an arm of flesh, the prophets, men
of the Spirit, uniformly counselled trust, not in confederacies,
but in the God of Israel (Isa. viii. 12).

Into the mode of giving them the gift of prophecy it is
needless to inquire; for it was simply miraculous, and therefore inscrutable. They who received this gift had an
intimation of the divine will, and therefore received something that they had not before. They performed what was
competent only to those who were inspired, and therefore

announced something not directly communicated to the rest of the people. No prophet alleged that he obtained from God the gift or the aptitude of intimating the divine will, or of foretelling future events at his discretion. That power or capacity was never given to them. Thus Jeremiah expressly said that he knew not that they had devised devices against him (Jer. xi. 18). Daniel denied that he knew the dream or the interpretation by any wisdom of his own ; and it was in answer to prayer that the secret, which no wise man or astrologer could ever have discovered, was made known to him (Dan. ii. 19, 30). It is clear that the prophets never wished it to be understood that they gave forth their predictions as the result of their own wisdom. On the contrary, they declared that God alone knew future and contingent events ; and that He claimed this knowledge as His absolute prerogative (Isa. xlii. 9). The word of the Lord, moreover, came only at certain times. The prophets never supposed, nor did the Israelites believe, that the power of prophecy was possessed by any man as a constant or uninterrupted gift. This sufficiently shows that the writers of the Old Testament understood that the Spirit of God was a personal agent, that He was very God.

When we put all these facts together, it is clear that the Spirit of God is something distinct from the prophet's mind, and apart from any natural capacity with which he was endowed. We nowhere read that God first revealed something to the Holy Spirit as if He were not consubstantial with God Himself, and then charged Him to convey the communication to the prophet. On the contrary, while there is a certain order of subsistence and operation in the Godhead, the Spirit of God is always spoken of as possessing divine intelligence, omnipotence, and omnipresence ; and all the prophecies are uniformly spoken of as the immediate act of God Himself. The personal Holy Spirit, or the Prophetic Spirit, is called " The Spirit of God " in the Books of Samuel.

The result of our investigation up to this point demonstrates that the Spirit of God is not, as the modern thought
alleges, a virtue or excellency of the human spirit which is to
be sought and obtained from God. That theory of the
modern theology [1] is utterly baseless. In the very oldest
books of Scripture, and in all the stream of history downwards, THE SPIRIT OF GOD is always introduced as the Personal
Creative Spirit of God.

FROM THE RISE OF DAVID TO THE EXILE.

The number of sacred books which appeared during this
period is large. They include the Psalms in good measure,
the writings of Solomon, Hosea, Joel, Micah, Isaiah, in all
which we have express allusions to the Holy Spirit. And in
tracing out the doctrine in these books, we shall not permit
ourselves to be swayed by that evacuating criticism which
either breaks up the books into parts and fragments, or takes
no account of the light reflected on the record as a whole by
the supplementary and authoritative teaching of Christ and
His apostles.

When David was anointed by Samuel to be king, we read:
" *The Spirit of the Lord came upon David from that day forward* " (1 Sam. xvi. 13). His soul was so filled with the
consciousness of his high destiny, and with the animating
power and presence of the Spirit of God, that he became a
different man. He was not only filled with the office-gifts
necessary for rule, but was faithful to the principles which
devolved on him as the subordinate or under-king of a divine
Theocracy. The same Spirit that ennobled and guided him
abandoned Saul.

---

[1] By a perversion of all sound exegesis, DIEHL., in the *Jaarboeken voor Weten-
schappelijke Theologie*, 1850, and KLEINERT, in the *Jahrbücher für Deutsche
Theologie*, 1867, in this Sabellian way explain away all these texts. So also do
VON CÖLLN, STEUDEL, etc., in treating of Old Testament theology.

Nor must we forget the inspiration given to him. "*The Spirit of the Lord spake by me, and His word was in my tongue*" (2 Sam. xxiii. 2). He received divine communications, intelligible enough to him as a prophet (Acts ii. 30), as to the birth and sufferings, the death, the resurrection, and glory of his greater seed, or offspring,—all which are wrought into the Psalms. He refers in that closing utterance to the prophetic Spirit which had rested on him, and he virtually announces: "All my Psalms were composed by the inspiration and guidance of the Spirit of the Lord."

But while these allusions to the Spirit are of a more public and official character, there are others in which we trace the Spirit's operations upon himself as a regenerate and sanctified man:

"*Whither shall I go from Thy Spirit? or whither shall I flee from Thy presence?*" (Ps. cxxxix. 7). In this psalm, which may have been prepared before he ascended the throne, the omnipresence and omniscience which are affirmed of God are also declared to be equally the attributes of the Spirit of God. The psalm sets forth a gracious and beneficent omnipresence. It is only learned trifling, all too plainly betraying an unchristian bias, when it is expounded as meaning: "Whither shall I go from Thy stormy wind." The allusion is to the personal Spirit—"Thy Spirit"—graciously omnipresent in all the universe to the believing mind. This is not a flight of imagination.

In the 51st Psalm also David prays: "*Take not Thy Holy Spirit from me*" (Ps. li. 11). David had grievously sinned, and in that psalm, which contains the expression of his repentance, he penitently prays that the Holy Spirit may not be taken from him. Previous to his fall he must have tasted the joy of God's salvation, and possessed that free Spirit, when he pleads with such a vehement desire for the Spirit's restoration. Here, for the first time, we have the epithet HOLY connected with the Spirit of God. He is not only the Spirit of wisdom and the Spirit of power, but the Holy Spirit. And in another psalm He is designated the GOOD Spirit.

"*Thy Spirit is good: lead me,*" or "*let Thy good Spirit lead me into the land of uprightness*" (Ps. cxliii. 10). He prayed that the same good Spirit that had always led him might lead him still. We cannot depart from the usual meaning of the expression "THY SPIRIT," as alluding to the personal Holy Ghost.

The unction and fragrance of the Spirit with which the Psalms are replete lead me to notice, before leaving this portion of our survey, that it is an utter misconception to represent the Old Testament religion as more fed by mundane hopes than by the influence of the Holy Spirit. It is to lose sight of all the numerous expressions of joy, rapture, and praise with which the Psalms abound from the first to the last, and to pervert the plainest evidence, to affirm, as Cocceius and his school affirmed, that there was neither sonship nor the spirit of adoption in the Old Testament Church. That is to ignore the Abrahamic Covenant, and Christ's divine presence with His Church, and merely to fix all attention upon the intermediate and transitory Sinai Covenant. But the Psalms to which we are adverting, when considered as the actual expression of praise for the Israelitish Church, as well as a legacy handed down to us in the Christian Church, sufficiently refute that view. No book of a similar kind was prepared for the New Testament Church. The Holy Spirit, replenishing the sweet singers of Israel with spiritual truth and holy love, anticipated in this way much of the necessity that should be felt in Christian times. I am not here discussing the important, though still debated point as to the use of psalms in the Christian public worship. My object is to show the spirituality of the Israelitish Church as evinced by its inspired and invaluable psalms. They describe the eternity and omnipresence, the majesty and condescension, the justice and mercy of God in a strain of the most fervid devotion. They sing of repentance and faith, of joy in God and delight in God's law, with an ardour beyond which it is impossible to go. They depict Christ's royal reign and His union with His Church; the anointing with the oil of gladness (Ps. xlv. 7); the receiving of gifts for men (Ps. lxviii. 18); and the supreme dominion with which Christ was to be invested by the Father with a tenderness, unction, and joy to which no other words are equal. And those psalms which are called "new songs" anticipate the full millennial glory.

To reason back from effect to cause, the power and presence of the Spirit in ample fulness must have been graciously conferred to produce these psalms, and to use them fitly when prepared. We trace the power of God's Spirit in turning the captivity of Israel, and in filling them with penitence. Not only so: the apostle, when adducing the quotation from the Psalms, "I believed, therefore have I spoken," prefixes, " *We having the same spirit of faith*—we also believe and therefore speak" (2 Cor. iv. 13; Ps. cxvi. 10). The language of the apostle affirms that he and the Church had the same faith and the possession of the same Spirit. From this fact, and from the whole series of quotations made from these Psalms, it is evident that the experience of the Church was the same in both economies, though complexional varieties attached to each. But these varieties, as Calvin [1] well remarks, describe the Church more in its CORPORATE character than in the experience of the individual members. The true Church in the Old Testament, whatever might be the character of the nominal adherents, cannot be said to be unspiritual when we trace a faith and a knowledge of God, a fidelity and courage, an endurance and self-denial in all that great cloud of witnesses that fill us with astonishment, and leave us conscious that we are practically far behind (Heb. xi. 1–40).

[1] See Calvin's admirable remarks on Gal. iv. 1, etc.

When we peruse the sacred writings which came from the hand of Solomon, we find not only evidence of the Spirit's illumination, but the most express reference to the Spirit in connection with the preacher's words: " *Turn you at my reproof: behold, I will pour out my Spirit unto you* " (Prov. i. 23). He means the graces of the indwelling Spirit, which were enjoyed then as well as now.

THE TESTIMONY IN THE PROPHETS.

We come now to the writings of the PROPHETS expressly so called. And in these we find many allusions to the Spirit of God. If we classify them, we may say, (1) that some of them refer to the time then present, and to the way in which the Spirit helped the prophets to fulfil their office ; (2) that some refer to the great effusion, when the Spirit should be poured upon the Church from on high ; (3) that some refer to the unction awaiting the Messiah, which was the great central thought of the Jewish religion, as it is of all revealed religion.

HOSEA, the oldest writing prophet perhaps, and placed at the head of the minor prophets, speaks of " the man of the Spirit " (Hos. ix. 7). Whether, with many expositors, we refer the words to the boastful language of the false prophets, or refer them to the perplexity of the true prophets in a time of apostasy, such as Hosea encountered among the ten tribes, they bring out the general notion entertained in regard to the prophets, that they were men of the Spirit.

JOEL, sent about the same time to Judah, gives the prediction respecting the great outpouring of the Spirit which was reserved for the last days: " *and it shall come to pass afterward, that I will pour out my Spirit upon all flesh* " (Joel ii. 28). The Spirit, called by the divine speaker " my Spirit," is the Holy Spirit promised in connection with Messianic times. According to the New Testament quotation (Acts ii.),

there is a shade of meaning not to be lost in the words
" of my Spirit " (ἀπό), distinguishing between the measure
vouchsafed to men and the inexhaustible fulness in the
resources of the fountain.   The expression : " *I will pour out,*"
can refer only to the Lord, from whom the Spirit proceeds,
and by whom He is sent.   The Lord God, who dwelt in the
midst of His Church, promised that He would amply compensate it for the reproach of barrenness by imparting the
copious supply of His Spirit.   There is one party who sends
and another who is poured out, personally distinct, but not
different in essence.   And this gracious promise as to the
outpouring of the Spirit, when read in the full light of New
Testament times, must be regarded as historically fulfilled at
Pentecost ; and the blessing must be viewed as dispensed by
the MESSIAH, the Son of God.   This is to be ascribed to the
incarnate Son, in whom all fulness dwells ; and the effusion
itself consisted in the communication of the Holy Spirit by
His gracious presence and operation.

Plainly we are to understand the ordinary as well as the
extraordinary gifts of the Spirit.   The effects flowing from
that effusion of the Spirit were prophetic gifts to be conferred on the New Testament Church as well as on its
several members ; one and the same Spirit distributing to
every one severally, according to His will.   Joel divides
the gifts into three classes—prophecy, dreams, and visions.
There are various interpretations of these three promised
gifts ; but the allusion is to different forms of revelation.
As to PROPHECY, it is either taken more generally for an
intimation of the divine will, or more strictly for the
prediction of future events by the aid of the Holy Spirit.
As to DREAMS, they were certain images presented to the
mind in sleep, and understood by the Spirit's interpretation
in such a way that no doubt was entertained either as to
their import or their origin.   As to VISIONS, they were
appearances submitted to the eye or to the cognitive

faculty, and must be understood as immediate revelations while the seer was asleep or awake.

But neither are we to exclude the ordinary and sanctifying gifts of the Spirit. This appears, beyond dispute, from the fact that, according to the intention of the supreme Dispenser of them, that shower of heavenly gifts, which filled the mind of those to whom they were promised, was meant to lead them to a true invocation derived from faith, or to " call on the name of the Lord." They were converting and sanctifying gifts, such as faith, hope, love, and invocation. They were also ministerial gifts for awakening and edifying the mind of others.

We need specially to consider what is intimated by the ALL FLESH, on whom this gracious effusion of the Spirit was to be conferred. When we ask what was meant by Joel's prophecy that the Spirit was to be poured upon ALL FLESH, the allusion cannot be, as Grotius held, to worthy Israelites. Nor can it be limited, as Origen limits it, to Churches gathered from the Gentiles. Another interpretation is that the term ALL is sometimes used in Scripture to denote classes; and hence Chrysostom, Luther, Gerhard, refer it to classes of individuals, but they restrict it to the display of SUPERNATURAL gifts at the commencement day of the New Testament Church. In this sense it will mean that men of every sort were replenished at Pentecost with the extraordinary gifts of the Spirit, viz., every age, sex, and condition. But the promise CANNOT BE LIMITED TO THAT DAY, nor to the miraculous gifts then communicated. This appears from the Apostle Peter's commentary when he said : " Repent and be baptized every one of you, and ye shall receive the gift of the Holy Ghost " (Acts ii. 38),—where the reference is plainly to the sanctifying gifts of the Spirit and to His gracious inhabitation. And the apostle added that the promise was to them, and to their children, and to all that were afar off. Others, as Glassius, make it men of every class in all nations. While the MIRACULOUS GIFTS, specially given to organize and found the Church, must be regarded as, in part, the accomplishment of Joel's prophecy, THE SAVING AND SANCTIFYING GIFTS must also be included down to the latest times. The phrase "upon all flesh" implies all nations, without distinction: for God was to pour out His Spirit on all nations, without distinction of Jew and Gentile, the partition-wall being taken down. No distinction was to be made, either in SOCIAL CONDITION or in NATIONALITY, as was intimated by the promise that the gifts should descend on old men and young, on sons and daughters, on servants and handmaids.

A question here arises: Are we to conclude that Joel's prophecy was fulfilled on the day of Pentecost, or was that outpouring of the Spirit but the symbol and dawn of another fulfilment yet to come? That it was fulfilled on Pentecost, ought not be doubtful to any one who reads Peter's sermon at the descent of the Spirit. "This is that which was spoken by the prophet Joel" (Acts ii. 16): and there is no indication here or elsewhere that this Dispensation shall ever be replaced by another. It was the opening of the river of the water of life which will flow on for ever. Where should we find a proof of Christ's Messiahship, or of the Christian Church,—as contrasted with the Israelitish community still adhering to the covenant at Sinai,—if the fulfilment of Joel's prophecy did not take place, as Peter declared it did, on that Pentecost immediately following the Lord's ascension? That was not A MERE TRANSITORY EVENT or TYPE OF ANOTHER FULFIL-MENT. For neither Joel nor any other prophet speaks of any more definite fulfilment. Besides, Peter expressly pointed to this as the fulfilment. But the fulfilment is A GERMINANT FULFILMENT, which takes in all subsequent times. The effusion was not an abruptly terminated fact. It was not a type: for shadows and types have ceased. It is the issuing forth of the river of the water of life, which will flow on till it cover and fertilize all lands (Ezek. xlvii. 1).

ISAIAH and MICAH, contemporary prophets in the days of Jotham, Ahaz, and Hezekiah, refer, in various passages, very emphatically to the Spirit of God. I adduce Micah first in order. He had to combat the false prophets who made the people err, and who cried peace (iii. 5); for false prophets appeared among the people, and were permitted, for holy ends, to try the faithfulness of Israel in the course of God's moral government (2 Pet. ii. 1). And the princes, as well as the people, were swayed by their flattering words. Hence the princes sometimes enjoined silence on the true prophet, saying, Prophesy not (Mic. ii. 6). When it is said: "*Is the Spirit of the Lord straitened ?*" (Mic. ii. 7), that was the prophet's stern answer to those who would silence him. He intimates: Is the Spirit of the Lord so weakened and straitened that He dare not reprove you, or does He fail of resources to make His voice and authority felt? Will the divine Spirit yield to your presumptuous will? And when he says: "*I am full of power by the Spirit of the Lord, and of judgment, and of might, to declare to Jacob his transgressions*" (Mic. iii. 8), that is an announcement in the same tone. The prophet, with power and courage derived from the Spirit of the Lord, declares to the nation its sin; and though the nation resents the reproof, and would avoid, if possible, the summons to hear the stern tenor of his message, it must be compelled to hear it. The prophet, moved by the Spirit of the Lord, compels attention to his words. The Spirit and power are conjoined as cause and effect, but distinguished. The prophet was also full of judgment by the same Spirit, that is, with the capacity of discerning the evil and the good in human actions, full of might or resolute perseverance also by the same Spirit.

ISAIAH has scattered throughout his prophecies allusions to the Spirit so manifold and various, in express descriptions and in brief turns of phrase, that it might not be difficult to put together, from his words, the complete doctrine of the

Spirit.   I shall briefly glance at the outline which he gives.

(*a*) He speaks of the Holy Spirit more generally.   In the past history of Israel which he gives, the prophet shows that the nation in their wilderness - life was graciously supplied with the Spirit, and that He dwelt among them and gave them rest (Isa. lxiii. 11 and 14) ; but they rebelled against Him, and vexed His Holy Spirit (ver. 10).   Events occurring in the moral government of God—such as the gathering of the vultures to their prey—are also ascribed to the Spirit *as the executive of all the divine purposes :* " My mouth it hath commanded, and HIS SPIRIT it hath gathered them " (Isa. xxxiv. 16).   The purging of Jerusalem from defilement and blood is also ascribed to the Spirit of judgment and burning ; that is, to the Spirit of God acting as the author and cause of all these effects, which are not penal, but gracious (Isa. iv. 4). Sinners taking counsel, but not of God, that they may take their own way, are said to cover with a covering — or to shelter themselves under a shelter and protection—which is not of GOD'S SPIRIT ; that is, they ran counter to the dissuasives and warnings which the prophet addressed to them (Isa. xxx. 1).

(*b*) Isaiah's allusions to the Spirit's work as the anointer of the Messiah with the necessary unction for His office are particularly noteworthy.   He introduces the Servant of the Lord saying : " *And now the Lord God has sent me and His Spirit* " (Isa. xlviii. 16).   This is a much preferable translation to that of the Authorized Version, which is here faulty.   The rendering we have accepted is preferable, and has been followed by some of the best exegetes, such as Cocceius, Vitringa, and Lampe.   One conclusive argument which may be adduced against the Authorized Version is, that the mission of Christ is never ascribed to the Spirit ; and that the Persons of the Trinity, who are all referred to in the passage, invariably act according to their order of subsistence in the Godhead. The Spirit is here said to be sent along with the Son, and indissolubly conjoined with the Son from the moment of the incarnation. In pre-Christian times the same order prevails by anticipation.

There are several passages in Isaiah which vividly set forth the large measure of the Spirit, which was to be shed upon the Christ from the time of His coming in the flesh. This was prefigured by various anointings introduced into the typical economy. And it appears especially in the name MESSIAH, THE ANOINTED, given to the promised One who should come into the world.

"*The Spirit of the Lord shall rest upon Him, the spirit of wisdom and understanding, the spirit of counsel and might, the spirit of knowledge and fear of the Lord*" (Isa. xi. 2).

"*Behold my Servant, whom I uphold; mine elect, in whom my soul delighteth; I have put my Spirit upon Him*" (Isa. xlii. 1).

"*The Spirit of the Lord God is upon me; because the Lord hath anointed me to preach good tidings to the meek*," etc. (Isa. lxi. 1).

I have put these three passages together because they refer to the unction with which the Lord Jesus was to be anointed for His threefold office as Mediator between God and man; and though couched in the words of prophecy, no clearer language could possibly have been used to delineate the accomplished fact. The gift of the Spirit to replenish Christ's humanity was not to supersede the necessity of His higher or divine nature, for these supplies of the Spirit flowed from the hypostatic union. The Spirit Himself was to REST upon Him, which implies something far greater than a temporary visit, or a mere creature's privilege. Then follows a vivid description of the effects of that unction in six definite predicates, or three pairs,—the Spirit of wisdom and understanding, the Spirit of counsel and might, the Spirit of understanding and fear of the Lord; graces of which the Spirit of

God is the sole author, and which are found only in their perfection and ample fulness in the Messiah. The graces of the Spirit there enumerated are *six :* but the general designation, " the Spirit of the Lord shall rest upon Him," with which the promise commences, is the common name for the SPIRIT OF PROPHECY, as appears from the seventy elders, who received the spirit that was on Moses, and also from other instances. We may be warranted to number, then, the spirit of prophecy first, and say that the number SEVEN is preserved. Lampe, in commenting on this passage, gives perhaps undue rein to his fancy when he supposes that the first pair was given at the nativity, the second at His baptism, the third at His exaltation ; and he thinks that the Spirit of knowledge and fear of the Lord must be regarded as poured out upon His Church. He appears to have adopted this ingenious but unnatural view of the last pair, from the groundless idea that the fear of the Lord could not fitly be ascribed to the Lord Christ.

These three passages which we have put together delineate and foretell that unction of the Holy Spirit with which the Messiah was to be equipped for all His offices. The second passage is applied to Christ by Matthew (chap. xii. 18). The third is quoted and applied by Christ Himself (Luke iv. 17). The three passages, by a memorable variety of expression, set forth that the Spirit should *rest upon Him*, should *be put upon Him*, should *be upon Him* as the anointing oil. The human future of Christ was thus to be anointed with the plenary supply of the Holy Spirit for the discharge of the mediatorial function : for it was predicted as the necessary unction of the Servant of the Lord.

(c) Another class of passages in Isaiah refers to the gift of the Spirit to the Church. How far the prophet was able to trace the connection between the gift of the Spirit to the personal Messiah and the gift of the Spirit to the Church, or to follow the order of events by which the one paved the way for the other, we do not presume to decide.

But the more we compare the prophetic testimony with the apostolic testimony, we are the more disposed to hold that it was sufficiently known to the Old Testament Church, that the Messiah should not only be anointed with the Spirit, but also BESTOW the Spirit. But that the Spirit was to be plenteously conferred on the Church in Messianic days, is repeatedly and explicitly affirmed by the prophet. Thus the pouring out of water and the pouring out of the Spirit are synonymous: " I will pour water on him that is thirsty, and floods upon the dry ground: *I will pour my Spirit upon thy seed, and my blessing upon thine offspring* " (Isa. xliv. 3).

Two other passages may here be quoted,—one showing how the Spirit resists the enemy, the other how he abides with the redeemed Church. (1) " When the enemy shall come in like a flood, the Spirit of the Lord shall lift up a standard against him " (Isa. lix. 19). (2) " My Spirit that is upon thee, and my words that I have put in thy mouth, shall not depart out of thy mouth, nor out of the mouth of thy seed, nor out of the mouth of thy seed's seed, saith the Lord, from henceforth and for ever " (Isa. lix. 21).

FROM THE BEGINNING OF THE EXILE TO THE END OF THE OLD TESTAMENT CANON.

To this period belong not a few books which are of a historical and prophetic character,—viz. Ezekiel, Daniel, Haggai, and Zechariah, the Books of Chronicles, and Nehemiah. In these we find many allusions to the Holy Spirit.

There are two prophets, indeed, in this period, where the expression " Spirit of God " does not occur,—viz. Jeremiah and Daniel. JEREMIAH, as a man, is described as sanctified from the womb; and, as a prophet, he received some of the most definite revelations ever communicated, particularly the revelation of the New Covenant, with all its spiritual pro-

visions and blessings (Jer. xxxi. 31). Yet we do not find in
him the precise phrase which we have here been making it our
object to trace out. The same thing holds true of DANIEL.
Though we cannot fail to perceive the Spirit's agency in all
his interpretations of dreams, in all his visions of the future,
and in all the allusions found in him to the anointing of
Christ the Most Holy (Dan. ix. 24), yet the phrase " Spirit of
God " is not found in him.

In the writings of EZEKIEL, the expression, " the Spirit,"
" the Spirit of God," or " my Spirit," very frequently occurs.
Thus the prophet says : " The Spirit entered into me " (ii. 2) ;
" The Spirit entered into me, and set me upon my feet, and
spake with me " (ii. 24); " The Spirit lifted me up, and took
me away " (ii. 14); " The Spirit brought me in the visions
of God to Jerusalem " (viii. 3) ; " Afterwards the Spirit took
me up, and brought me in a vision by the Spirit of God into
Chaldea, to them of the captivity " (xi. 24). And all the
great promises announced by Ezekiel have very express reference to the converting and sanctifying grace of the Spirit
promised to Israel in connection with their restoration to the
divine favour. Whether all is still future, or whether the
promise to put the Spirit within them was fulfilled on their
return from Babylon, has long been a point on which conflicting views prevail : " *I will sprinkle clean water upon you, and
ye shall be clean : from all your filthiness, and from all your
idols, will I cleanse you. A new heart also will I give you, and
a new spirit will I put within you : and I will take away the
stony heart out of your flesh, and I will give you an heart of flesh.
And I will put my Spirit within you, and cause you to walk in
my statutes, and ye shall keep my judgments, and do them* "
(Ezek. xxxvi. 25–27). Grotius, Greenhill, and others incline
to the opinion which connects the fulfilment of the prophecy
with the simple restoration of the remnant who came back
from their seventy years' exile in Babylon ; others absolutely
connect the prophecy with the future. Perhaps it may best

be regarded as a germinant prediction, having a partial or incipient accomplishment, and a full and complete accomplishment. It certainly sets forth the justification or cleansing of their persons, and the Renovation of the Holy Ghost. As a consequence of the cleansing which should be given, and of the Spirit which should be put within the Israelitish Church and nation, it depicts a remarkable change of disposition, character, and manners which should be produced. The promised sprinkling with clean water is the reality of what was typified by the water mingled with the ashes of the heifer, and sprinkled upon persons and things to purify those who were defiled, and to render them clean and holy in the eye of the law (Num. xix. 2). The inward renewing of the people from moral and spiritual defects, indissolubly connected with the former, though distinguished from it, is emphatically ascribed to the irresistible grace of the Spirit of God. The agency used in taking away the insensibility of the stony heart, and making it a heart of flesh, susceptible and tender, is expressly ascribed to the Holy Spirit, called " my Spirit," within them.

Two other memorable prophecies denote the same thing, though couched in highly figurative language, and given in the form of vision,—the reanimation of the dry bones in the valley of vision, when the prophet was commanded to prophesy to the Spirit (Ezek. xxxvii. 1) ; and the rapid outflow of waters, swelling into a river, from under the threshold of the house of God (chap. xlvii. 1), which seems elsewhere to be called the river of the water of life (Rev. xxii. 1).

After the Babylonian Exile.

The prophecy of HAGGAI announced, for the comfort of the Israelitish Church, that though the external glory of the second temple should be inconsiderable as compared with the first temple, they were to entertain no fear, because THE

SPIRIT should remain among them, a help in their infirmities, as well as the source of grace, of light, of comfort, and of holiness (Hag. ii. 5).

In the prophet ZECHARIAH we find two explicit allusions to the Spirit's agency,—one for the time of the prophet, another for the remote future of the chosen people. Amid discouragements which might otherwise have depressed Zerubbabel -the ruler, the prophet was commissioned to show— (1) that the maintenance of the Church was not dependent on the resources of worldly kingdoms, but on God's Spirit: "*Not by might, nor by power, but by my Spirit, saith the Lord of Hosts*" (Zech. iv. 6). And this assurance was fortified by the significant and suggestive vision of the candlestick and of the two olive trees. (2) Another promise of the Spirit was in connection with the memorable prophecy of Israel's repentance, unexampled mourning, and return to the crucified Messiah. The titles given to the Spirit in this passage are full of significance. He is called THE SPIRIT OF GRACE, which implies that He is not only given to us in the exercise of the free love of God, but that He is the cause of all the grace by which we are at once accepted in the Beloved and regenerated at the time of our first conversion, as well as the author of the assurance or certainty that we have found grace in God's sight. He is also called THE SPIRIT OF SUPPLICATION, because He is the author of all the prayer which individual Believers and the Church pour out before the Father through the merits of the crucified Saviour. The promise in the prophet was to the effect that He should be the Spirit of grace and supplication to the house of David in the latter days, and effect the national conversion of the people amid the deepest expressions of sorrow and mourning (Zech. xii. 10).

We only further notice the allusions to the Holy Spirit in NEHEMIAH and in the Book of CHRONICLES. In Nehemiah it is said, with special reference to the way in which the Jewish nation vexed the Spirit during their day of merciful visitation : " *Many years didst Thou forbear them, and testifiedst against them* BY THY SPIRIT *in the prophets*" (Neh. ix. 30). The passage means that the Holy Spirit moved the prophets, and spoke by them as organs whom He condescended to employ in the revelation of His mind and will. The allusions to the Holy Spirit in the Book of Chronicles record two historical occasions when the Spirit, coming on the prophets Jahaziel and Zechariah, prompted them to declare the mind of God. The one was a great crisis, when Jahaziel awakened the people's courage and confidence in God in the immediate prospect of a great battle (2 Chron. xx. 14). The other was an equally great crisis, when the prophet Zechariah, filled with the Spirit, was commissioned to reprove the people for their sins, but fell a victim to their fierce and fiery resentment (2 Chron. xxiv. 20).

All these memorable instances in the history of Israel which we have surveyed, disclose to us the Holy Spirit in the work of imparting the superhuman gift of prophecy to a few, and the comforting power of the Spirit to the many. The Old Testament Church was in many respects different from the New Testament Church ; the former being more occupied with externals, the latter being privileged to have a worship which may be described as more in Spirit and in truth. But the divine personality of the Spirit, as we have clearly seen, was not less known and not less recognised in the one economy than in the other. He who spoke by holy men from the beginning was in every age recognised as a DIVINE PERSON.

THE TESTIMONY TO THE SPIRIT IN THE GOSPELS AND BOOK OF ACTS.

A long pause ensued from the last of the prophets to the time when the Spirit of God again spoke by revelation. After an interval of nearly four hundred years the long-expected time of fulfilment arrived, and we no sooner take up the evangelist's narrative of the incarnation than we find, as was to be expected, the same important place occupied by the Holy Spirit. We shall endeavour here again to give an outline of the Scripture testimony in the same historical way.

It will be found, on examination, that the Holy Spirit is referred to more or less copiously by every New Testament writer. Not only so ; there is not a single New Testament book drawn up as a public document for the Church which does not contain a marked, though often brief, allusion to the Holy Spirit, and very frequently, if not always, in connection with the main design or scope which the writer had in view. The only exceptions are found in the three small Epistles of a more private nature,—the Epistle to Philemon, and the Second and Third Epistles of John. In every book more specially prepared for public and ecclesiastical use, the allusion to the Spirit is most explicit. It will be my object, without attempting a commentary on all these passages, which would carry us over too vast a field, to put together the cumulative evidence which they supply. Except in some passages which cannot be passed over without fuller elucidation, a few words of comment will for the most part suffice.

All the evangelists refer to the Holy Spirit in connection with the birth, baptism, and temptation of our Lord. Of all the New Testament writers, next to Paul, Luke most frequently reverts to it. We should be disappointed, however, if we sought in him a full explanation of the nature and properties of the Spirit, when his principal object was to sketch the supernatural and miraculous works of the Spirit in the first founding of Christianity. There was no denial and no dispute at that time as to the divine personality of the Holy Spirit.

We find that the doctrine of the Spirit taught by the Baptist, by Christ, and by the apostles, was in every respect the same as that with which the Old Testament Church was familiar. We nowhere find that their Jewish hearers on any occasion took exception to it. The teaching of our Lord and His apostles on this topic never called forth a question or an opposition from any quarter,—a plain proof that on this subject nothing was taught by them which came into collision with the sentiments and opinions which up to that time had been accepted and still continued to be current among the Jews. The fundamental idea connected with the Messiah, that He SHOULD BE ANOINTED WITH THE SPIRIT, was still an undoubted doctrine ; nor were the apostles ever compelled to meet doubts or to disarm opposition in the Jewish mind on this point.

The title CHRIST or MESSIAH was given to the Redeemer from the peculiar unction of the Spirit conferred on Him, which was unique in nature and in degree. The different servants of God who were filled with the Spirit, but in a far other way, illustrate this remark by contrast. To begin with, the promise which the angel Gabriel gave respecting the Baptist. He was to be filled with the Holy Ghost even from his mother's womb, and go before the Lord Jesus in the Spirit and power of Elias (Luke i. 15–17). The words mean that he should be FILLED and immediately directed by the Spirit in the discharge of his prophetic function, and that though he did not work miracles like Elijah, for obvious reasons, he was supplied with gifts of wisdom and courage, holiness, zeal, and power, for the purpose of proclaiming the law and gospel to a corrupt and self-righteous generation. Of Elizabeth, Zacharias, and Simeon, we read that they were FILLED with the Holy Ghost, and gave forth inspired announcements of the divine will (Luke i. 42, 67, ii. 25). But with Christ it was wholly different. The infinite fulness of the Spirit which was given to Him was constant and uninterrupted, and the result of the hypostatic union—that is, was the effect of humanity being assumed into personal union by the only-begotten Son. The Baptist, going before Him in the Spirit and power of Elijah, combined the two thoughts when he announced a Person pre-existent and divine, who was before him (John i. 15), and one not merely receiving the absolute fulness of the Spirit, but DISPENSING THE SPIRIT. The Messiah, according to the Baptist, was to baptize with the Spirit and with fire (Matt. iii. 11), which places Him in a different category from the Old Testament judges and prophets. That authority to give the Spirit was the culminating point of Christ's exaltation. It has been alleged by Schmid [1] that this prediction of the Baptist was a thought unknown to the Old Testament prophets, and that it wholly transcended their range of view. It might have been difficult for any one to find this truth in the language of the prophets, apart from the light reflected upon them by the New Testament statements. But we may affirm that it was there, to the satisfaction of those who could see it or should use aright the key when it should afterwards be given to them; for the Messiah was to receive gifts for men (Ps. lxviii. 10), and to be anointed with the oil of gladness above His fellows (Ps. xlv. 7); nay, that He should pour out the Spirit of grace and supplication (Zech. xii. 10). And that this could be none other than the Messiah is evident from the addition: "And they shall look upon me, whom they have pierced, and they shall mourn." The baptism with the Spirit and with fire, which John contrasts with his own baptism, implies that the Spirit should be dispensed by the hand of the Messiah, and that He who had this power must be an accepted Mediator as well as a divine Person. But it also intimates an abundant communication of the Spirit's extraordinary and sanctifying gifts.

THE SAYINGS OF OUR LORD ON THE SPIRIT.

We come next to THE SAYINGS OF JESUS on the doctrine of the Spirit, and it is worthy of notice that on several points, and especially on the inscrutable relations of the Trinity, we

[1] See C. F. Schmid's *Biblische Theologie des N. T.* p. 164, Stuttgart 1859.

find, as was to be expected, disclosures from His lips more definite and ample than are expressed by any of His servants, whether prophets or apostles. In His last discourses, spoken in the midst of His disciples (John xiv.–xvi.), He set forth for their comfort and for the Church's instruction the essential as well as economical relations in which the Holy Spirit stood to Him, and also the mission of the Spirit for the guidance of apostles and the application of redemption, in a manner more full and ample than we find in any other part of Scripture. He shows (1) that the Father should send the Holy Spirit IN HIS NAME (xiv. 26), a statement which implies that the Spirit, previously forfeited and withdrawn from mankind in consequence of sin, should, on the ground of His merits and intercession as the Mediator, be sent by the Father for all the purposes of His redemption. He shows (2) that the Spirit should be dispensed or given by His hand. This He repeatedly announced, and much more explicitly than was ever done by the Baptist.

We find that there are two principal divisions of our Lord's sayings on the subject of the Spirit,—those which describe the Spirit's work in conversion, and those which describe the Spirit's work on the mind of apostles and of the Church in general.

Those sayings which describe the Spirit's work in conversion, will be most fitly adduced afterwards (Lect. IV.).

Christ also promised the Holy Spirit to His believing disciples as rivers of living water : " *If any man thirst, let him come to me, and drink. He that believeth on me, as the Scripture hath said, out of his belly shall flow rivers of living water. But this spake He of the Spirit, which they that believe on Him should receive : for the Holy Ghost was not yet given ; because Jesus was not yet glorified* " (John vii. 37–39). We have to notice first Christ's saying, and then the apostolic commentary appended to it. While water is in certain passages the element of cleansing, it is introduced here and

elsewhere (Isa. lv. 1) as the element of quenching thirst.
They who are said in a religious sense to thirst have a painful
feeling of want, and desire relief in the only way in which
they can attain it.   Two things are included in the invitation.
They are desired TO COME, which simply means to believe, as
is evident from the alternated expression employed in another
passage (John vi. 35), implying a misery from which they
escape, and a fountain, that is, the Saviour, to which they are
invited to repair; and they are desired to DRINK, for in no
case can the sense of thirst be removed by merely looking at
the fountain.   The terms thus conjoined, COME and DRINK,
mean faith, but are no mere tautology.   They are the
incipient, and the enlarged or continued exercise of the same
grace of faith.

And it is promised that from the heart of this believing
disciple there should well up or flow out rivers of living
water, which intimate precisely the same thing as Christ said
to the woman of Samaria (John iv. 14).   The meaning is not
that the Spirit flows from one disciple to another,—for none
can so give the Spirit,—but that the Spirit as a flowing river
quenches the thirst and satisfies the desires, so that the soul
no longer thirsts for any other object.   The promise is not to
apostles alone, for that ulterior promise following faith in
Christ is made definite : *He that believeth on me.*   But this by
no means presupposes that the believing disciple has, by his
own self-determining power, produced this faith without the
teaching of the Father (John vi. 45), the drawing of the Son
(xii. 32), of the life-giving power of the Spirit (vi. 63).

The terms of the apostolic commentary subjoined are very
significant.   They show that Christ meant the Spirit, and that
all the inward satisfaction, rest, peace, joy, and assurance
flowing into the soul and quenching its thirst, are the result
of the Spirit's operation.   When John says that Christ spoke
of the Spirit which believers should receive, he explains why
Jesus used the future tense and not the past : *rivers of living*

water shall flow. But the apostle adds that "the Spirit was
not yet," because Christ's glorification had not yet arrived.
He does not mean that the Spirit did not yet exist,—for all
Scripture attests His eternal pre-existence,—nor that His
regenerating efficacy was still unknown, — for countless
millions had been regenerated by His power since the first
promise in Eden,—but that these operations of the Spirit
had been but an anticipation of the atoning death of Christ
rather than a GIVING. The apostle speaks comparatively, not
absolutely, as is always done when the old and new economy
are contrasted.

Christ's testimony to the Spirit contained special reference
to the Comforter (John xiv. 16–xvi. 7). As further allusion
will be made to these promises, it may here suffice to
enumerate the passages and give their scope. For wise
reasons, the Lord reserved His special teaching on the Holy
Spirit to His last evening on the earth, that the donation of
the Spirit might be connected in the mind of the disciples
with His vicarious sacrifice, and that He might be expected
as Christ's Deputy. We are reminded of this antecedent and
consequent when He speaks of sending the Spirit (John
xv. 26), of giving the Spirit (vii. 39), of *pouring out* the
Spirit (Joel ii. 28), of *kindling* a fire on the earth (Luke
xii. 49). The culminating point of Christ's exultation was to
have the authority or power of baptizing with the Holy Ghost,
as foretold by John the Baptist and announced by the Lord
Himself (Acts i. 5). The authority to give the Spirit was
assigned to the Son as the reward of His finished work.
That no one might suppose that the Spirit's dependence on
the Father is removed, Christ says: "Whom I will send to
you from the Father" (John xv. 26). And to show that this
was done at Christ's intercession and request, He says: "I
will pray the Father, and He shall give you another Comforter" (John xiv. 16); that is, to compensate them for their
great loss in losing the visible presence of their Lord.

To be convinced of the importance which Christ attached to the mission of the Spirit, we have only to recall the terms in which He four times refers to the Paraclete or Comforter. Whether we render the word TEACHER with some, or HELPER with others, or ADVOCATE and PATRON with others, or abide by the translation COMFORTER, with which we are most familiar, the tenor of the promise implies that He was to be sent at Christ's intercession, and to act as His Deputy.

A brief summary of the different operations of the Comforter may be set forth as follows. He was, after Christ's departure from the world, to take the Saviour's place, and in all cases of official duty or emergency to impart the necessary aid. He was to remind the apostles what Christ had taught them; He was to give them clearer and more extensive communications in reference to the doctrine of Jesus; He was to unfold to them what they did not comprehend when the Lord was with them. They were to be under the perpetual direction and superintendence of the Spirit, and supported by Him in the proclamation of the gospel wherever they should be sent, — promises which imparted to them the greatest calmness, and gave rise to the most joyful state of mind. Such a close union is represented as existing between the Son and the Spirit, that it almost seems from the passages which describe the indwelling of the Spirit as if they were identical. But that is only in appearance. For Scripture represents Christ as sending the Spirit to glorify Him,—to supply His place,—to lead the disciples into all truth, and to imbue the minds of the apostles with an immediate revelation of the divine will.

The Lord Jesus, in the evening of the first resurrection day, first began to GIVE THE HOLY SPIRIT to the apostles assembled in one place. And to make the occasion significant, He breathed on them, and said: " Receive ye the Holy Ghost." It has often been affirmed by expositors that this was but a pledge or promise accompanied with a symbolic action, and awaiting its accomplishment on the day of Pentecost. The words, however, must be accepted as they stand, and in their full significance. They intimate an actual donation of the Holy Ghost, not an allusion to the gift conferred fifty days afterwards. The atonement was already a completed fact, and accepted by the Father; the everlasting righteousness was actually brought in; every barrier to the communication of the Spirit was now removed; and the Lord did not deal in empty symbols or mere terms. He bestowed what the words imply when He said: " Receive ye the Holy Ghost " (John xx. 22).

This interpretation enables us to dispose of two misleading opinions which have obtained greater currency than could have been supposed. (1) It is held by not a few, such as Stier, Wardlaw, and others, that the apostles acted with undue precipitance in filling up the vacant apostleship, because the promised effusion of the Spirit was not received. The doubts raised by Stier against the steps taken to supply the place from which Judas by transgression fell, carry more serious consequences than the propounders of that interpretation imagine. It is of no avail to say, If the Spirit came in the room of Christ, it would have been more natural for Him to nominate the new apostle. The answer is, The Spirit was actually doing so through the Church. When it is said, Is it not possible that the apostles, with all their intellectual knowledge and childlike confidence, might err ? the answer is, That the Lord, in breathing upon them and imparting the Spirit, intimated that what they remitted or retained would be ratified in heaven ; and as for the comparison between Matthias and Paul, whom Stier refers to as alone filling the vacant place, it is sufficient to say that Paul calls himself " one born out of due time." The whole college of apostles, to whom the Lord said : " Receive ye the Holy Ghost," cannot be supposed to have erred in their interpretation of the psalm (Ps. cix. 8), or in the further step of publicly filling up the vacant office.

(2) Another error is the modern notion propounded by the Plymouth Brethren, that believers are not to pray for the Holy Spirit, because He was once for all given on the day of Pentecost, and that the Christian body may not pray for what is already possessed. That rash and presumptuous position, by whomsoever it is held, is discredited by the fact that the apostles who had received the Holy Ghost on the first resurrection day continued with one accord in prayer and supplication for the promise of the Father (Acts i. 14). They prayed for the Spirit though they had received the Spirit. They waited for more of the Spirit that they had, in compliance with their Lord's command. This is the true attitude of the Christian Church in every age. And the history of the apostles shows that not once, but on many occasions, they were made partakers of the baptism of the Spirit and fire.

THE EFFUSION OF THE SPIRIT ON PENTECOST.

The importance of the Book of Acts as the historic narrative of the public effusion of the Spirit cannot be over-estimated. It shows how the first disciples received the ascension gifts, and went forth equipped with them to found the Christian Church. We learn that the little company, obedient to the Lord's command, tarried in Jerusalem, not forming plans how they should appear in public, but wrestling in prayer till they were endued with power from on high. At length all that was comprehended in Christ's farewell discourses found its wonderful accomplishment when the day of Pentecost was fully come.

The significance of the Pentecost may be noticed in connection with the Passover, the one referring to the Redemption, the other to the New Covenant, as in the history of Israel. Pentecost, the fiftieth day from the Pass-over, and from the exodus out of Egypt, was the feast of First-fruits, and also, according to Jewish belief, the day when the Law was proclaimed from Sinai. Both facts have their proper import. Regarded as the feast of First-fruits, the Pentecost furnished the first-fruits of the world's con-version at the outpouring of the Spirit. Regarded as the commemoration day of the Sinai Covenant, which made the Jews a kingdom of priests, it was a fitting occasion for the removal of the old economy and the erection of the new, and to be the espousals-day of the Christian Church.

A new revelation from God to man must needs be inaugu-rated with supernatural signs and miracles. As the Sinaitic Covenant was set up in a miraculous way, it is obvious that when the time arrived for its abrogation the new economy that superseded it must be ushered in by similar miracles. As God came down on the mount in a supernatural way, so did He bear witness to the apostles by signs and wonders and divers miracles and gifts of the Holy Ghost (Heb. ii. 4) ; or, as some will have it, the glory of the Lord, the Shechinah or fiery pillar, again appeared.

The greatest event in all history, next to the incarnation and atonement, was the mission of the Comforter; for it will continue, while the world lasts, to diffuse among men the stream of the divine life. The Pentecost was the great day of the Holy Ghost, the opening of the river of the water of life. As Goodwin [1] says : " He must have a coming in state, in a solemn and visible manner, accompanied with visible effects as well as Christ had, and whereof all the Jews should be, and were witnesses." Not only so ; there must be a Church which at its commencement should give the clearest indica-tions of its heavenly origin. That was the great birthday of the Christian Church.

[1] Goodwin's Works, vol. vi. p. 8.

The Christian economy was inaugurated amid supernatural manifestations which could not be questioned. When the reality came, the shadow passed away. The Jewish economy gave place before that which was to comprehend all nations. Now the New Covenant founded on better promises began (Jer. xxxi. 31 ; Ezek. xxxvi. 25). The noise as of a rushing mighty wind intimating that the Spirit is the divine breath of life, and reminding them of the strong wind in Ezekiel's vision that made the dry bones live ; the flame of fire probably reminding them of the Shechinah ; and the cloven tongues like as of fire, significant of an inexplicable and miraculous power of speaking in every language, and of filling men's hearts with the glow of divine love, constituted the solemn and public consecration of Christ's ambassadors for the founding of a Church which should fill the whole earth, and into which all nations should flow. The fire from heaven testifying the acceptance of Aaron's and Elijah's sacrifice was even in the Old Testament an emblem of the Holy Spirit. God was well pleased with all that had been done. Thus the Pentecost was openly signalized as the day of the mission of the Comforter.

The apostles had some experience of the nature of their calling from the mission on which Christ had sent them while yet with them ; but now they came forth with a public testimony, not only to Christ's Messiahship, but to the great salvation purchased by His death. The Holy Spirit, as the promised Paraclete, took the place of Christ's corporeal presence. They were led by the Spirit into all truth, and the tongues were a conclusive proof that the persons to whom such gifts were imparted spoke by divine inspiration, and that it was not so much they as the Spirit that spoke the words.

The great effusion on the day of Pentecost did not mean a religious mood of mind or a pious enthusiasm, but that THEY WERE FILLED with the personal Holy Ghost. Though some have a difficulty in accepting the literal meaning of these terms, because they seem to imply a local limitation which, of course, cannot be applied to the omnipresent Spirit, it may be proper to remark that they have no more difficulty than that the Spirit made, preserves, and governs the soul of man. The meaning is, that they received a rich measure of the Spirit to fill the human faculties, and such communications, gifts, and operations as were needed to prepare them for their work. They were filled according to their capacity and mental conformation, but in such a way that there was not only ample variety, but room for increase and enlargement of the earthen vessel. Nor does the expression refer only to extraordinary communications. *The ordinary sanctifying gifts are not to be excluded.* One thing they all had to perform— to confess the truth; and courage was supplied by the Spirit. The transforming power of the Spirit so filled them that the timid became bold, the selfish self-denied, the arrogant humble; the ambitious aspirants after distinction ceased to seek great things for themselves. They felt that all gifts were from the Lord and for the Church's welfare; and jealousy and envy vanished.

The effusion of the Spirit made a great change on all the powers of the apostles, whether we look at their heart or at their understanding. They received a knowledge such as they never had before of the great work which Jesus had finished for man's salvation, and betrayed no longer the perverse idea that the Messiah's kingdom was to be of a worldly nature. They perceived in His whole earthly obedience the grand ransom necessary to procure a spiritual redemption. And they were in full accord with the Lord's instructions on all the principal topics of religion.

But special reference must be made to those extraordinary gifts conferred by the sovereign gift of Christ on the day of Pentecost, which continued all through the apostolic age, and which were not only very various, but wholly distinct from the ordinary sanctifying or ministerial gifts which continue in the Church through all her history. The supernatural or extraordinary gifts were temporary, and intended to disappear when the Church should be founded and the inspired canon of Scripture closed; for they were an external proof of an internal inspiration.

In describing them we shall follow the enumeration given by Paul (1 Cor. xii. 8–11). Of all the miraculous gifts the chief and highest was THE GIFT OF PROPHECY, which was intended—whether we look at the Old Testament or the New—to be more of an official than personal nature, for revealing the divine counsels for the edification and comfort of the Church. The gift of prophecy and the field it covered —whether we look at it simply as prediction, or as the revelation of the divine will in general—forms so vast a theme, that we can do no more than refer to it. What manifold and various communications were made by the prophets previous to the completion of the canon, how they revealed the present and future counsels of God, and how they spoke as they were moved by the Holy Ghost, are points known only to the Lord, who gave them their commission and message.

Another supernatural gift was THE GIFT OF TONGUES, the power of speaking in foreign languages which had never been acquired;—a great work of the Holy Ghost, which gave a sort of visibility to the inward inspiration by which their mind was guided and controlled. Peter unaided could only speak his Galilean dialect, which easily betrayed him, as we see in Pilate's judgment hall; but now he could, in company with his colleagues, command without difficulty the attention of educated hearers, who heard them speak in their own tongue the wonderful works of God. Many, interpreting the narrative of Acts in the light of the peculiar allusions to the gift of tongues referred to in the Epistles to the Corinthians, put another construction on the phrase. They interpret the expression in the latter case as a speaking in ecstasy. That is the modern German speculation, devised to escape the full admission of the extraordinary miracle. But it is a mis-interpretation, and a violence to the terms used in all the passages. The gift was wholly miraculous. The apostles at the moment of inspiration received the extraordinary endowment which qualified them to utter new words, wholly unknown before, and to express by means of them sentiments and doctrines which arrested, convinced, and enlightened the mind of those whom the Holy Ghost was leading to the Saviour. Whatever difficulties we in this age may have in understand-ing the mode by which the operation was accomplished, there can be no doubt that amid a conflux of people from remote lands, no more appropriate or powerful means could be employed to extend the gospel than that use of foreign languages,—intimating as it did that the gospel, unlike the limitations of Judaism, was not for one people, but for all people. It filled the hearers with amazement and admiration. To speak a new language by the sudden influence of the Spirit exceeded all the powers of nature, and afforded a sure testimony to the presence and omnipotence of the Holy Ghost. But in the Church it had comparatively little value ; for tongues were for a sign not to them that believed, but *to them that believed not* (1 Cor. xiv. 22). The apostle, therefore, when he heard that this gift was coveted for the mere purpose of ostentatious display, took occasion to reprove the Corinthians for that perversion (1 Cor. xii. 20–32).

An allied gift was the INTERPRETATION OF TONGUES, differing from the former only in this, that these interpreters, not having the gift of tongues, were enabled by the same Spirit to understand and explain the languages which were used. They thus possessed in interpretation what they wanted in utterance. In certain cases these related gifts were conjoined (1 Cor. xiv. 5).

The WORD OF WISDOM, the first named among the gifts,

must not be reckoned an ordinary gift (1 Cor. xii. 8).   Without accepting the ingenious definitions which have been propounded, it may be affirmed that as wisdom, in the ordinary acceptation of the term, is that mental endowment by which one regulates his life and plans most surely to gain the ultimate end; so wisdom, as an extraordinary gift, differed from the former only in this, that it was bestowed on the gifted persons by the immediate effusion of the Holy Spirit. But as the apostle calls it not only wisdom, but THE WORD OF WISDOM, we must understand a singular faculty of pointing out the way of wisdom, both by their counsels and their life, to those who were of weaker judgment and capacity.   And the same thing holds true of those who are in the same verse represented as endowed with the WORD OF KNOWLEDGE by the same Spirit.   As the apostles, from the nature of their office, could not long reside within the bounds of any single city or congregation, and as they deemed it enough to lay the foundations of Christian doctrine as to repentance, faith, and the like (Heb. vi. 1), an extraordinary gift of illumination was given to certain members of the Church, in order that the new-born babes, as they are termed by Peter, might grow and increase in knowledge.

Next to these the apostle enumerates the GIFT OF FAITH. We need scarcely remark that by that expression we are not to understand saving faith, the like precious faith common to all believers, but the extraordinary faith, or faith of miracles, relating to those displays of divine power which tended to the glory of God.   It may be considered also as a display of confidence or world-overcoming faith in the presence of dangers peculiar to themselves or to others.   There seems also to have been a certain counteracting or repelling power which, in imminent perils from demons, noxious animals, or the elements of nature, deprived them of the power to injure (Mark xvi. 18 ; Acts xxviii. 5).   Faith was often needed to confront dangers with a confident mind.

Allusion is next made to GIFTS OF HEALING and working of MIRACLES by the same Spirit (ver. 9). The apostle distributes his classification of the extraordinary gifts in this way, because they were not all in the hand of any one man, but divided according to the Spirit's sovereign pleasure. Though the apostles seem to have possessed all the supernatural gifts, it does not follow that this held true of other disciples. As to the working of miracles by a power far transcending man's energy or skill, we need not make a special enumeration of the many operations of that nature. They are said to be by the same Spirit,—one and the same Spirit distributing these miraculous operations to each man severally as he pleased. They were sometimes called *wonders* (τέρατα), from the effect of those astonishing interventions, and *signs* (σημεῖα), because they indicated an efficient cause which was alone adequate to work such prodigies and to lead men to God their Creator.

Another supernatural gift was the power of DISCERNING SPIRITS, which, for wise reasons, was conferred on many in the primitive Church to unmask Satan's devices (ver. 10). The adversary, incessantly active in sowing tares, never failed to send the blighting influence of false teachers, who ceased not to deceive others, and might themselves be deceived. Great evils, as the Scriptures everywhere testify, resulted from this to the Church. To obviate these perils, the Spirit imparted to certain members of the Church the gift of discerning spirits; in consequence of which these gifted disciples, in a way far transcending human wisdom, were enabled to warn the Church.

Such were the supernatural gifts of the Holy Ghost with which the disciples were amply supplied and adorned. And as is clearly indicated by Paul's exhortations to Timothy, they might be either stirred up and increased, or neglected (1 Tim. iv. 14 ; 2 Tim. i. 6). They were not possessed by all, but distributed among those who possessed them by a sovereign disposal, and probably according to the mental conformation which each one had received by nature. Nor were they invariably confined to true disciples; for we find undoubted allusions to the fact that these extraordinary gifts were sometimes wielded by temporary disciples, such as Judas, to whom at last the Lord shall say: " I never knew you " (Matt. vii. 23). The power of the Spirit is seen in that agency that acted on the day of Pentecost. We trace the action of the Holy Spirit in uniting a company of disciples in prayer and supplication, and in animating them to continue waiting for the promise of the Father. And the action of the disciples in all times and countries is analogous.

Not only so; the instruments by whom the Spirit works are prepared for service in an analogous way, that is, with the sole exception of the supernatural and extraordinary accompaniments. They are Christians first, then called to labour. This is brought under our notice in the most impressive manner, when we consider how the first disciples were prepared for service. Their gifts were there so far as these were natural endowments; but they knew them not themselves; and they were required to wait for the Spirit in the attitude of humble suppliants till they were endued with power from on high; a preparation so necessary, that had they precipitately proceeded to work without that power, they would have accomplished nothing. To evince the greatness of the change to be wrought upon them, we have only to recall the ignorance and darkness which covered their minds, notwithstanding the instructions which they had received.

The Book of Acts narrates the operations of the Spirit. When persecution at length broke out, the disciples, pouring out their united prayers, were all filled with the Holy Ghost (iv. 31). The terrible discipline displayed on Ananias and Sapphira for an act of attempted deception, which proceeded on the supposition that they could overreach the omniscient Spirit that dwelt in the apostles and spoke in them, filled the whole community with awe, and vindicated the honour due to the Holy Ghost. And we see the Church after a time of persecution walking in the fear of the Lord and in the comfort of the Holy Ghost (ix. 31).

Without tracing the history of the Spirit's operations, let me succinctly state the general scope of the Book of Acts. It sketches the movements of the kingdom of God; it exhibits men full of the Holy Ghost and wisdom (vi. 3, xi. 24); it narrates the appointment of the labourers, and the disposal of their services. It shows, as Luther happily remarks, that the Holy Spirit was given, not by the law, but by the hearing of the gospel. We trace how men were summoned to serve God, and were owned as well as guided and controlled in the prosecution of their work. The sovereign Spirit, as a personal agent, directed the Church at Antioch to send forth Barnabas and Saul, saying: " Separate to me Barnabas and Saul for the work whereto I have called them." We see the Spirit prompting Philip to join himself to the eunuch's chariot, and directing Cornelius to send for Peter, as well as directing Peter to go and receive the first Gentile into the Church. We see the Spirit prompting at one time and hindering at another (Acts xvi. 6).

THE TESTIMONY TO THE SPIRIT IN THE APOSTOLICAL EPISTLES.

The apostolic testimony to the Holy Spirit was given according to a fivefold type—that of Paul, of Peter, of James, of Jude, and of John. The allusions in the Epistles, and especially in the whole compass of Paul's teaching, are so numerous that they must rather be put together than expounded at length.

One preliminary remark may be made. The apostles take for granted, with full consent, the general corruption of man's nature, and refer to the Spirit as the originator and source of all the saving, sanctifying, and comforting influences which

Christians experience (Eph. iii. 16 ; Rom. xv. 13).   How the renewing of the Holy Ghost is harmonized with the freedom of the will, they stopped not to inquire, as if these points were no part of their concern.   But the fact of men's responsibility along with the proclamation of converting grace and the renewing of the Spirit, is set forth with a solemnity and urgency to which the solution of these questions, if it were possible to solve them, could add no further weight.

THE TESTIMONY OF THE APOSTLE PAUL.

In none of the apostles do we find so many allusions as in the Epistles of Paul to the Spirit's work in the full extent of His saving and sanctifying operations.   Besides other reasons which might be mentioned, this may be ascribed to the fact that Paul had not known Christ after the flesh (2 Cor. v. 16), and received his revelations more in the way of inward communication by the Spirit than by outward intercourse with his Lord, though he also received the latter. And accordingly, in the memorable passage where he says : " Now the Lord is that Spirit " (2 Cor. iii. 17), the close con- nection in which he places Christ and the Spirit shows how fully he apprehended their joint mission, and how emphati- cally he intimates that Christ is never to be conceived of apart from the Spirit, nor the Spirit conceived of apart from Him.

To the impartial inquirer who only seeks the truth, the Apostle Paul conveys, with sufficient evidence, a testimony to the divine dignity of the Spirit, when we find him saying in the Book of Acts, that the Holy Ghost spoke by the prophet Isaiah (Acts xxviii. 25) ; that the Spirit testified from city to city, that bonds and imprisonment awaited him (xx. 23) ; when he declares that the Holy Ghost sustained him in his ministry (Rom. xv. 19) ; when he appeals to the Holy Ghost, and calls Him to witness (Rom. ix. 1) ; when he uses the same expression, SENT FORTH (ἐξαπέστειλεν), to describe the mission of the Spirit that he employed to describe the mission of the Son (Gal. iv. 4–6). But we shall find, as we proceed, other proofs even more express.

When we survey the names or titles of the Spirit in Paul's Epistles, they are numerous. Thus He is called the Spirit of God (Rom. viii. 9), the Spirit of His Son (Gal. iv. 6), the Spirit of Christ (Rom. viii. 9), the Spirit of Him that raised up Christ from the dead (Rom. viii. 11). If we look at the economy in virtue of which the Spirit is sent, He is said to be shed on us abundantly through Jesus Christ our Saviour (Tit. iii. 6). If we survey His titles as derived from the benefits and blessings which He confers, and of which He is the immediate author, He is called the Spirit that dwelleth in us (Rom. viii. 11), the Spirit of grace (Heb. x. 29), the Spirit of wisdom and revelation in the knowledge of the Lord Jesus (Eph. i. 17), the Spirit of adoption (Rom. viii. 15), the Spirit of life (Rom. viii. 2), the Spirit of meekness (Gal. vi. 1), the Spirit of power, and of love, and of a sound mind (2 Tim. i. 7).

The commencement of the Christian life, as contrasted with the previous sinful life, is uniformly ascribed by the apostle to the Holy Ghost. Thus he says : " No man can say that Jesus is the Lord, but by the Holy Ghost " (1 Cor. xii. 3) ; and again : " He saved us by the washing [laver] of regeneration and renewing of the Holy Ghost " (Tit. iii. 5). Whether we refer this expression : *the laver of regeneration,* to baptism or not, certainly the last term, the renewing of the Holy Ghost, must be construed as referring to the active operation of the Spirit at the commencement of the Christian life. As it is the shedding or pouring out of the Spirit (ἐξέχεεν) to which salvation is traced, this cannot be referred to mere doctrine. The personal Spirit is mentioned as the producing cause. If it is asked in what sense can men be said to be saved by the renewing of the Holy Ghost, when the salvation is in Christ, the answer is obvious. There is a series of truths of which no link can be awanting. We are saved by the divine purpose, for God hath chosen us to salvation; we are saved by the atonement as the meritorious ground of all; we are saved by faith as the bond of union to Christ; we are saved by grace as contrasted with works done; we are saved by the truth as conveying God's testimony; and we are saved, as it is here expressed, by the renewing of the Holy Ghost, as producing faith in the heart. The special work of the Spirit in conversion is thus proved to be as essentially necessary and indispensable as any other link in the chain. The apostle further speaks of saving blessings which eye hath not seen nor ear heard, revealed to us by the Spirit (1 Cor. ii. 10); and he adds that we receive not the spirit of the world, but the Spirit which is of God, that we may know the things that are freely given to us of God (1 Cor. ii. 12). When the Spirit is called "the Spirit of faith," that is, the AUTHOR or producing cause of faith (2 Cor. iv. 13), according to the uniform meaning of that formula, there can be no more conclusive proof that the commencement of the new life must be ascribed to the Holy Spirit.

There are three Pauline Epistles which are very full and definite in the elucidation of the doctrine of the Spirit,—viz. the Epistles to the Corinthians, to the Galatians, and to the Romans. I shall first refer to their testimony, but by no means in a minute or exhaustive way, in the above-mentioned order.

One principal topic found in the EPISTLES TO CORINTH has reference to the personality and work of the Holy Ghost. It was particularly necessary to call the attention of the Corinthian Christians to the personality and presence, the influence and operations, of the Spirit, because they were counteracting his work by attaching undue importance to human wisdom, and pluming themselves on the possession of various supernatural gifts which they owed absolutely to the Spirit, but which were given for a different purpose than display.

They dishonoured the Spirit, partly by self-complacency, emulation, and contentious partisanship ; partly by their readiness to think lightly of the old licentious tendencies and feelings for which Corinth had only been too notorious, and which all too plainly threatened to return.

By the Holy Spirit the apostle did not mean, as some have thought, a mere title of God or of Christ. He meant and taught the personal Holy Ghost, distinct from the Father and the Son, but partaker of the same numerical divine nature. He referred to the Spirit sent forth on His mission as the guide and teacher of the Christian Church, whose fellowship as a divine person was invoked in the apostolic benediction (2 Cor. xiii. 14) as the great gift of the Christian Church. He reminded the Corinthians, who were so favoured with a supply of supernatural endowments as to come behind in no gift, that they were the temple of God and inhabited by the Spirit (1 Cor. iii. 16), and then subjoins a warning against defiling it (ver. 17).

In the most conclusive way, but without formal proof, the apostle introduces the PERSONALITY AND OMNISCIENCE of the Holy Ghost when He says : " The Spirit searches all things, yea, the deep things of God " (1 Cor. ii. 10). He is thus referred to as personally distinct from God ; for He searches the deep things of God. And He who can fathom the plans, the purposes, and deep things of God, must be distinct in person, yet divine in essence. The same divine personality is brought out in connection with the rich profusion of extraordinary gifts with which the Christian Church was endowed (1 Cor. xii. 4–6) : " Now there are diversities of gifts, but the same Spirit : and there are differences of administrations (or ministries), but the same Lord : and there are diversities of operations, but it is the same God who worketh all in all." The Spirit, the producer of the gifts, is thus distinguished from the gifts. But He is also distinct from God, the author of the operations, and from the Lord Jesus, the author of the ministries. The import is to the same effect as that which the apostle elsewhere expresses, when he speaks of one God the Father, and one Lord Jesus Christ, and one Spirit who unites Christians in the closest bond of union (1 Cor. viii. 6 ; Eph. iv. 4–6). A personal will is ascribed to Him ; for He divides His gifts to every one severally as He will (ver. 11). To the subject of spiritual or miraculous gifts, which occupies a most important place in these Epistles, I need not refer, after the elucidation already given, except to say that they illustrate the peculiar economy of the Holy Spirit.

Other passages not less clearly teach the special action of the Spirit in the whole application of redemption. To some of these we shall now allude.

(a) "*Such were some of you : but ye are washed, but ye are sanctified, but ye are justified in the name of the Lord Jesus, and by the Spirit of our God*" (1 Cor. vi. 11). The three verbs : WASHED, SANCTIFIED, and JUSTIFIED, have such an affinity to each other that they must all be put in one category, as referring to the absolution, sacrificial acceptance, and judicial justification of the Corinthians, compared with their former state as one of guilt, exclusion from God's presence, and just condemnation. One and the same thing, says Calvin, is expressed by different terms. How far these Christians corresponded individually to their high calling we forbear to inquire. But what we desire to place prominently before our mind is that these saving blessings are referred, first, to the name or merits of Christ as the procuring cause, and then to *the Spirit of our God*, who made the Corinthians partakers of them by His own effectual application. Plainly this operation of the Spirit is distinguished from the preaching of the gospel. The latter may be, and probably is, included in the phrase : "*the name of the Lord Jesus*," which certainly intimates His merits, and may take in the further thought of the preaching of His merits. But manifestly something more than moral suasion is intimated as to the application of redemption. A power immeasurably greater—that is, the Spirit of our God—is referred to as enlightening their mind and leading them to embrace the great salvation, and to be assured that they were washed, sanctified, and justified.

(b) " *The natural man receiveth not the things of the Spirit of God : for they are foolishness to him : neither can he know them, because they are spiritually discerned* " (1 Cor. ii. 14). Here the apostle, after noticing the unsearchable glory of revelation, and tracing it up to the Spirit of God, sets forth, in the subsequent part of the chapter, that the spiritual discernment and saving reception of it are not less from the Spirit of God than the revelation itself. As to the title NATURAL MAN, it is not difficult to apprehend its meaning, if we are content to interpret Scripture by Scripture, without being encumbered by the language of philosophy. They who are so called are simply those having the animal and rational elements of man without the Spirit (Jude 19). The point of the expression, whether we suppose extreme depravity or not (Jas. iii. 15), is the privation or absence of the Spirit ; and where this is, men *do not* receive the things of the Spirit,—that is, the atonement and all the saving provisions of the gospel,—and they *cannot* know them. I shall not efface the angles of this expression to make it less emphatic, nor apologize for the expression being used ; for I am only an interpreter ; and with that my duty ends. The *natural* man is he who is not occupied by the supernatural power of the Spirit. The phrase : " *to receive the things* " of the Spirit of God, as applied to the word of truth, is a common New Testament expression,—meaning that through grace the word is not only viewed as true, but assented to as good (Acts xvii. 11 ; 2 Cor. xi. 4 ; 1 Thess. i. 6). That word the natural man does not receive. But when it is added: " neither can he know them," expositors and divines in general, of the modern type, transmute the words into *will not know them*. Heumann and others adduce as corroborative proof for this sense: "He could there do no mighty work because of their unbelief" (Mark vi. 5, 6). But it is a mistaken interpretation. The unbelief of Christ's townsmen at Nazareth was such that they neither brought their diseased and helpless friends to receive His miracles, nor came themselves to hear His wisdom; thus limiting or curtailing His opportunity of conferring benefits. Or if we refer the words to the moral obstruction interposed by the unbelief itself, and suppose that Jesus, from a regard to the declarative glory of God, would not proceed to work miracles which were only to be met with scorn and rejection, there is as little warrant for transmuting the apostle's *cannot know* into *will not know*.

Why the natural man neither receives nor knows the things of the Spirit of God is next subjoined. The way of salvation by the cross, described as "the things of the Spirit of God," appears to him absurd; for they are foolishness to him. Though the propositions, as such, in which the doctrines are expressed can be sufficiently apprehended by the natural understanding, he receives them not, neither can he know them, without a supernatural discernment, taste, or relish for them imparted by the Spirit of God. The apostle makes no concealment of the malady, and draws a broad distinction between one who has the Spirit and one who has not the Spirit.

(*c*) This leads me to notice some of those significant expressions scattered over the Epistles where the Spirit receives express titles from the work which He performs in the application of redemption, especially this title: the Spirit of faith.

"*We having the same Spirit of faith, according as it is written, I believed, and therefore have I spoken; we also believe, and therefore speak*" (2 Cor. iv. 13). The title SPIRIT OF FAITH intimates that the Holy Ghost is the author of faith; for all men have not faith; that is, it is not given to all, and does not belong to all (2 Thess. iii. 2). The designation means that the producing cause of faith is the Holy Spirit, who produces this effect by that invincible call and invitation which accompanies, according to the good pleasure of His will, the external proclamation of the gospel. The faith, therefore, of which He is the author, is not effected by the hearer's own strength or by the hearer's own effectual will (John vi. 44, 45; Eph. ii. 8; Phil. i. 29). But it is also a fruit of Christ's merits; for, apart from the merits of the Saviour, no benefit can be conferred or can actually take effect upon condemned men (Eph. i. 3). And though the mode in which the Spirit produces faith cannot, in all its outlines, be fully comprehended by believers in this life, of one thing there can be no doubt: He takes out of the heart every hindrance and obstruction, pleasantly persuades the judgment, and gently binds the will—nay, works in us both to will and to do; or, to put it into the words of Jesus, " Every one, therefore, that hath HEARD AND LEARNED of the Father cometh unto me " (John vi. 45). The word of truth and the regenerating work of the Spirit are fully distinct, but always concurrent. The special operation of the Spirit inclines the sinner, previously disinclined, to receive the invitations of the gospel; for it is He alone, acting as the Spirit of faith, that removes the enmity of the carnal mind to those doctrines of the cross which, but for this, would seem to him unnecessary, or foolish and offensive.

The apostle, in a profound passage in the Second Epistle to the Corinthians, delineates the difference between the Jewish and Christian economy as two different modes of administering one and the same covenant of grace. He contrasts the two in the great points of antithesis between them. But what we have to consider here is their relation to the gift of the Holy Spirit. One important topic bearing on the difference of the two economies, is the supply of the Spirit in the New Testament as contrasted with the Old. This is fully elucidated by the apostle (2 Cor. iii. 6–18). The New Covenant contrasted with that of Sinai is called THE MINISTRATION OF THE SPIRIT (2 Cor. iii. 8), because it was a formally different economy. The New Covenant is called THE SPIRIT, not the letter, because accompanied with the mission of the Comforter and with the powerful operations of the Spirit in a measure and manner unknown before. Among its distinctive privileges, the supplies of the Holy Spirit, which were of old promised by the prophets, are conferred in a wholly new way, and with a copiousness not conferred before.

The antithesis between the Old and New Covenant is expressed in the striking proposition, which is not without its difficulty: "the letter killeth, but the Spirit giveth life" (ver. 6). This may be taken as a general proposition; and when so taken, it will be akin to the words: "It is the Spirit that quickeneth; the flesh profiteth nothing" (John vi. 63). If, on the other hand, it refers to the difference of the economies, which seems clearly to be the design of the apostle, the meaning must be, that the former, as a legal and national covenant, largely left men without the quickening Spirit; or that the Spirit of life was not dispensed by that economy. When it is said, with special reference to the New Covenant: "the Spirit giveth life," the import is that the Spirit of life is now communicated in full and abundant measure; that is, that Christ's words are spirit and life (John vi. 63), as compared with that shadowy dispensation which has passed away.

A brief explanation will serve to remove the difficulty which expositors have found in the passage. Some have thought that the Sinaitic Covenant was simply a covenant of works, wholly different in character from the covenant of grace. That supposition cannot be accepted, for the law is not against the promise of God (Gal. iii. 17). The apostle very often speaks of a matter in a certain respect; that is, not absolutely, but in a certain respect (*secundum quid*), and the statement here made must be so understood. The Sinaitic Covenant, so far as founded on the law of rites and apart from the covenant of grace, which involved the promise of the Holy Spirit, was A KILLING LETTER, not only diverse from the New Covenant, but leaving men in a state of bondage and death, and imparting no relief.

A twofold view may be taken of the Sinaitic Covenant. It may be taken *more largely* or *more strictly*,—a distinction to be applied as a key to solve many difficulties in the Pauline Epistles. Taken more largely, the Sinaitic Covenant, or the Old Testament type of religion, contains the patriarchal gospel, or the Abrahamic Covenant, based upon Abraham's seed, in whom all the families of the earth were to be blessed, and thus as comprehending the promise. Taken more strictly, the Sinai Covenant—a subsequent dispensation of which the patriarchs knew nothing—was a *national* transaction between God and Israel, and *conditional* in its character. The immutable moral law, which existed before its promulgation and exists since its abrogation, was its core. The nation was specially bound to the law of a carnal commandment, to a shadowy priesthood, to innumerable rites and ceremonies, which were but the letter, without any supply of the Spirit, and which were enforced with strictness and severity. The whole design looked to the end of the shadow in the atoning work of Messiah. Strictly taken, the Sinai Covenant is letter and shadow,—national, transitory, conditional, and burdensome in the whole character of its arrangements. Such was the distinction between the two. But it is necessary to add that it presupposes the Abrahamic Covenant, because God could make no covenant with sinful man but in a relation of grace. He could not have made a covenant at Sinai unless with a certain respect to grace, and having the covenant of grace as its basis and support.

When it is called " *a killing letter*," and contrasted with the Spirit which giveth life, the meaning is, that the Sinai Covenant, strictly taken, or used as the mere letter, did not give the Spirit of life.   But the apostle's words do not imply that there was no Holy Ghost operating on the saints of the Old Economy, or that there were not millions of saved men under it trained to eminent holiness and wisdom.   There were countless numbers of regenerate men in the Old Economy distinguished for a faith and wisdom, a holiness and self-denial, a courage and zeal, redounding to the declarative glory of God, such as far surpasses all modern examples.   But it must be noted that none of them received the regenerating grace and the Spirit of life which they possessed from the Mosaic law, or from the letter sundered from the promise. All who had the Spirit of life received it by faith upon the promise of a Saviour, and not from the Sinai Covenant.   For under all economies, salvation and the supply of the Spirit were by faith.   The measure of the Spirit, under the Old Testament, was comparatively limited, like the first-fruits ; and it was given by anticipation.   In comparison with the numbers composing the Old Testament Church, only a few were made partakers of the gift of the Spirit, while the vast multitude had no eye to see nor ear to understand.   On these grounds the apostle calls the one economy the letter, and the other the Spirit.

In the Second Epistle to the CORINTHIANS, the apostle gives expression to Christian experience in many particulars. The Spirit is adduced as a pledge of salvation, and as giving an assurance of the participation of God's love.

"*Now He who establisheth us with you in Christ, and hath anointed us, is God ; who hath also sealed us, and given the earnest of the Spirit in our hearts*" (2 Cor. i. 21).   That the efficacy of the Spirit is something distinct from the preaching of the gospel, is clearly indicated in this and in similar passages.   The theory which identifies them finds no coun-tenance from these words ; for there is an influence of the Spirit on the heart of Christians, apart from the mere moral

influence of the word. The apostle, as the founder of the
Corinthian Church, speaks of being united with them in Christ,
and of their being anointed as a royal priesthood to make
a common confession of Christianity. The previous allusion
to Christ as the Anointed One, seems to have led him to
describe THEM AS ANOINTED, which implies something more
than mere instruction through the word : It is unction for
priestly service. He adds, " who hath also sealed us," implying that they bore A SEAL or impress from God, by which
they not only were themselves assured, but marked as belonging to God, who put a seal on them as His property. Not
only so : God gave them *the earnest of the Spirit* in their
hearts. The term EARNEST (ἀῤῥαβῶν), three times applied in
the New Testament to the Holy Spirit, denotes a certain sum
in hand, as a pledge of something further to be conferred ;
and it was a security that they should not be put to shame.
Paul speaks of the Holy Spirit as producing these effects on
the heart. For we cannot expound the term EARNEST merely
of the miraculous gifts of the Spirit, which accompanied the
first proclamation of the gospel as a proof of its divine origin.

" *Ye are declared to be the epistle of Christ ministered by us,
written not with ink, but with the Spirit of the living God*"
(2 Cor. iii. 3). The Church of Corinth, a large flourishing
community, was an emphatic proof of Paul's apostleship, and
of the success with which his zealous efforts had been crowned
in spreading the gospel. They were an epistle, written not
with ink, but with the Spirit of the living God,—where we
cannot fail to notice two persons,—the living God and His
Spirit, by whom he acted at first, and continued to act, on the
heart of these Corinthians. By the Spirit we cannot there
understand revelation, or the divine origin of Christianity ; for
comments of that nature only betray an adverse bias, and are
not worthy of serious refutation. Plainly, the apostle distinguishes his ministry from the writing of the Spirit. He refers
to the efficacious effect of his ministry, and ascribes it to the

Holy Spirit. Nor does he appeal to miraculous gifts, but to the Spirit's influence in effecting the spiritual renovation of the heart, as contrasted with the Old Covenant, which was written on tables of stone.

" *He that hath wrought us for the selfsame thing is God, who hath also given us the earnest of the Spirit* " (2 Cor. v. 5). The Spirit is here again called " the earnest ; " and the longing for the heavenly glory is connected with His operation.

In the Epistle to the GALATIANS, the apostle's doctrine on the entire economy of the Spirit is peculiarly full. This was due to circumstances which made it necessary.

The gospel, as preached by Paul among the Galatians, had found a ready acceptance, and had been accompanied with the miraculous ministration of the Spirit, and with the most arresting displays of His power (Gal. iii. 5). The Galatians, it is said, had begun in the Spirit (iii. 3). Before much time elapsed, the recently-formed churches were subjected to the test of false teachers. Emissaries from the Pharisaic party demanded that Christians from the ranks of the Gentiles should observe the Jewish rites as necessary to justification before God. In a word, these ceremonies, along with the doctrine of Christ, were to be retained as essentially necessary. The apostle, in writing this Epistle, assails that fundamental error with all his energy, refuting it from central truth and from their own experience in the past.

He shows that they had *not received the Spirit* by the works of the law, but by the message or preaching (ἀκοή) of faith (iii. 3). This is the Holy Spirit, with all His gifts, as promised by the prophets to the Church. The ordinary saving gifts of regeneration and holiness, as well as the supernatural gifts, are here included. These were not received by the performance of any actions of the ceremonial or moral law, which could only have filled their mind with a knowledge of sin and a fear of wrath. On the contrary, they had received the Spirit by the message of salvation or grace received by faith.

We are next taught that the promised Spirit was procured by nothing less than the vicarious death of Christ. This argument completely exploded the legalism of the false teachers. The donation of the Spirit is thus connected with the atonement: " Christ hath redeemed us from the curse of the law, being made *a curse for us*, that (*ἵνα*) the blessing of Abraham might come upon the Gentiles, *that we might receive the promise of the Spirit through faith* " (iii. 14). The meaning of these words is : the death of Christ was the meritorious cause or purchase of this great gift—the promised Spirit. The final particle (*ἵνα*) leans on the words which describe the sacrifice of Christ. It is the connection of merit and reward, of cause and consequence.

To show, moreover, that works of law are wholly excluded, and that the great donation of the Holy Spirit, which was given to the Galatians at the founding of the Church among them, was not to be traced to doing on the part of man, but to simple reliance on the merits of Christ, the apostle adds, " That we might receive the promise of the Spirit (or the promised Spirit) *through faith.*" The Spirit of the Son— in other words, the Spirit of adoption—is further described by Paul as given only to those who are sons by faith, and partakers of the atonement (iv. 6). The proof is thus complete, that the Holy Spirit was not received by the works of the law.

The last part of the Epistle displays the work of the Spirit in another light. The former allusions were made more to the Christian's privileges. The two closing chapters set forth the graces of the Holy Spirit and the Christian's fruitfulness. The same apostle who was solicitous in the first part of this Epistle to assert the liberty of the Christian, and who bids us stand fast in it, is not less solicitous to set forth in the second part the Spirit's renewing and sanctifying influence. Thus, with respect to Christian HOPE or patience, he puts it in causal connection with the Spirit's operation in these terms: we *through the Spirit wait* for the HOPE of righteousness by faith (v. 5). The distinction between flesh and spirit, nature and grace, is next described in such a way as proves the momentous importance of drawing a strict line between the two, of apprehending it in the Christian's consciousness, and following it out in the Christian's walk: " I say then, walk in (by) the Spirit, and ye shall not fulfil the lust of the flesh " (v. 16, 17). He adduces it as a proof of their liberty from the curse of the law, that the Christian is led by the Spirit (v. 18). Then, after enumerating the works of the flesh, he specifies as the *fruit* of the Spirit—" love, joy, peace, long-suffering, gentleness, goodness, faithfulness, meekness, temperance " (v. 22). He calls these *the fruit* of the Spirit, as if they grew on a living, fruitful tree ; and he adds that against such persons—for the allusion is to persons (κατὰ τῶν τοιούτων)—there is no law (v. 23). From living by the Spirit he argues the duty of walking by the Spirit (v. 25), and he concludes these duties by referring to the duty of sowing to the Spirit (vi. 8).

The Epistle to the ROMANS gives an outline of the doctrine of the Holy Spirit in an experimental, not in a controversial way. This Epistle was meant not so much to smooth differences or unite parties, as to confirm the Church in true doctrine. On the subject which engages our attention, the Epistle to the Romans contains very marked allusions which distinguish the Holy Spirit's work from the operation of Providence on the one hand, and from the objective presentation of truth on the other. The Epistle shows another influence distinct from the word though connected with it, in producing faith, and in leading Christians in whom faith already exists. To this I refer the more readily, because the celebrated Griesbach in two University-programmes laboured to prove that the term SPIRIT in the eighth chapter means nothing more than Christian character and disposition; and because many others, paralysed by these objections, have been in the habit of affirming that there are few passages where the sense of the word "Spirit" is more difficult. We shall find that it does not occur in more senses than one, and that it neither means influence nor Christian disposition, but the Holy Spirit.

This appears beyond dispute when it is said that the Gentiles were made obedient by word and deed, through mighty signs and wonders, by the *power* of the *Spirit* of God (Rom. xv. 19). That the miracles wrought by Paul are there attributed to the Spirit, is beyond dispute. The agent and the power which the agent puts forth are both mentioned in alluding to these miracles. The conversion of the Gentiles, in like manner, or the offering up of the converted Gentiles as an acceptable sacrifice, is ascribed to the Holy Ghost (xv. 16).

On the economy of the Spirit, in connection with Christ's Sonship, there is a noteworthy passage, though on almost all sides it is incorrectly referred to the divine nature of our Lord: "Concerning His Son Jesus Christ our Lord, who was made of the seed of David according to the flesh; and declared to be the Son of God with power, *according to the Spirit of holiness*, by the resurrection from the dead" (Rom. i. 3, 4). Plainly the apostle does not allude to the two natures of our Lord, as commentators generally expound it, but to THE TWO STATES OF humiliation and exaltation. And the expression: "Spirit of holiness," does not refer to the divine nature, but to the dispensation of the Spirit after His resurrection, which supplied the most conclusive evidence of our Lord's divine Sonship. The effusion of the Spirit on the apostles and on the Church terminated the controversy whether He was the Son of God. The communication of the Holy Spirit—a gift competent to no created being — proved Him to be the

Messiah and the Son of God, according to His own claim
(John v. 19).

"*The love of God is shed abroad upon our hearts by the
Holy Ghost which is given to us*" (Rom. v. 5).   These words
intimate that the Holy Ghost as a divine agent does a certain
work ; that He is given according to a divine economy ;
and that through His aid the redeeming love in God's heart
is shed abroad in our hearts ; that is, is tasted and enjoyed,
not only in the first stages of the Christian's experience, but
ever afterwards.   Plainly this is distinct from miraculous gifts
and from the proclamation of the gospel.   It intimates that
the Holy Ghost sheds abroad God's boundless, free, unchang-
ing love in our hearts, and that He is given to believers as
a perpetually indwelling guest,—reminding the Christian of
reconciliation, supplying the constant experience of the divine
love, and assuring him of its perpetuity as a gift never to be
forfeited.

It is in the eighth chapter, however, that we find the
doctrine of the Holy Spirit most fully developed, from
different points of view.   The apostle's object is to prove the
certainty of the believers' salvation from the fact that they
are led by the Spirit of God.   He demonstrates that they
enjoy the effectual operation of the Spirit as a blessing which
has its ground in the surety-obedience of Christ its procuring
cause (2–4).   The argument is, that they who are occupied
by the Spirit and who walk after the Spirit are exempt from
condemnation.   In other words, he argues that they who are
free from the service of sin through the Spirit of life are by
that fact proved also to be free from condemnation.   The apostle
had set in a clear light the inseparable connection between
justification and sanctification on the ground of Christ's
merit or purchase (vi. 1–13).   He here shows that the
spiritual life is secured by the effectual operation of the
Holy Spirit.   The entire section exhibits the Christian in
the highest stages of the divine life, and supplies a rule by

which the Christian teacher is to regulate his thinking and phraseology.

The apostle begins his discussion on the Spirit with these memorable words: "The law of the Spirit of life in Christ Jesus hath made me free from the law of sin and death" (Rom. viii. 2). The two laws — that of sin and death, already referred to in the seventh chapter (vii. 23), and a counterpart law of life in Christ—are again put in direct antithesis—that is, into the contrast of flesh and spirit, which we find pervading the whole Pauline theology. But why, it may be asked, is the Spirit called the law of the Spirit of life in Christ Jesus ? The entire expression is equivalent to this : the Spirit of life residing in Christ and dispensed by Christ is a law of irresistible power counteracting the law of sin and death. It is the law written on the heart, by which the regenerate man is step by step enabled to resist the power of sin and to follow holiness. It is the law of the life-giving Spirit in the fellowship of Christ Jesus.

The apostle next adverts to several operations of the Spirit which deserve the most attentive consideration singly and collectively.

1. The first thing to be noticed is the sequence of operations as described in the Christian's experience. There are three distinct expressions, which are introduced in this order: (1) They walk after the Spirit (viii. 4); (2) they are spiritually-minded (viii. 6); (3) they are in the Spirit (viii. 9). In the order of sequence the last-named, however, comes first, as follows :—They are in the *Spirit* by the act of regenerating grace ; they are *spiritually-minded*—that is, they mind the things of the Spirit when they are inwardly disposed, moved, and animated according to the mind of the Spirit ; they *walk after* the Spirit, which refers more to their inward and outward practical life. The sequence is such as proves that it is not sufficient to perform good works which challenge the attention of spectators, unless there be the inner change of

character and disposition, which naturally weans the heart from the objects to which natural bias disposes it.

2. The second thing mentioned in the passage is, that the Spirit DWELLS in the Christian (viii. 9). A running contrast between the flesh and Spirit is carried out through the entire section. And the indwelling of the Spirit of Christ is adduced as a conclusive proof that we are not in the flesh, but in the Spirit; for Christ, the second Adam, received the Spirit as a reward for the performance of His work of suretyship, that He might impart the Spirit to all believers. When the apostle subjoins : " if any man have not the Spirit of Christ, he is none of His " (ver. 9), it shows that the participation of the Holy Spirit is not universal ; and that only they who were from eternity given to Christ and redeemed by Him, enjoy the inhabitation of the Spirit in the Biblical acceptation of the term. In them He dwells, as in His habitation or abode, for ever. It is this inhabitation which imparts the spiritual mind, the mark by which the true disciple is distinguished ; for Christ and His people are anointed with the same Spirit.

3. The Spirit is LIFE because of righteousness (v. 10). Though the body is dead because of sin, this death is not regarded as a punishment or anything properly penal, but only as a consequence, still permitted to run its course, after Christ has fully satisfied divine justice. But the Spirit is life on the ground of Christ's imputed righteousness. As He gave life to all creatures at first, so does He give life immortal, incorruptible, and unfading to the new creature—that is, to all the redeemed of the Lord.

4. They who have the Spirit mortify the deeds of the body (ver. 13). They are debtors, not to the flesh, but to the Spirit. The flesh, or the deeds of the body, they mortify, because they are the cause of death. They cannot so kill it, indeed, that it shall stir no more ; but they, by the Spirit, weaken it and lop off its branches one by one.

5. They are led by the Spirit of God, and are thus evinced

to be the children of God (ver. 14). The expression: "led by the Spirit," refers to an inward prompting, impulse, and inclination, which so rules and guides them that they cannot omit duty or neglect privilege. It implies the helplessness of a child which cannot stand alone, but needs a strong supporting hand; for it is not in man that walketh to direct his steps (Jer. x. 23). The saints of God, to whom the expression applies, are not only ignorant of the way, but when they know it, their liability to stumble too readily betrays itself; and their natural reluctance must constantly be overcome. This LEADING is attributed to the Spirit of God, the master of the inclinations, of the will, and of the affections by which men are moved and animated, so that in due time they desire to do nothing but what they are prompted to undertake by the illumination from on high.

They are on this ground evinced to be the CHILDREN OF GOD; and this leads the apostle to describe the Holy Spirit as the author of adoption, and as prompting the believer to realize the privileges connected with this filial relationship. Philippi seems to me mistaken [1] in denying that the phrase SPIRIT OF ADOPTION can mean the Spirit who effects the Sonship or transplants us into the relationship of sons. The analogy of all the phrases of this description—such as the Spirit of love, the Spirit of wisdom, the Spirit of power, the Spirit of revelation, and the like — implies that He is the author or producing cause of the term following in the genitive. This is no exception to the uniform usage. The same Spirit produces the bondage to fear, and effects the adoption. On this great central blessing which is put in our possession by the Spirit, I shall not now enlarge, as it afterwards engages our attention in the dogmatic part of this treatise.

The other effects of the Spirit mentioned in this chapter

---

[1] He says, incorrectly : " Das πνεῦμα υἱοθεσίας kann nun nicht sein der Geist welcher die Kindschaft wirkt " (Rom. viii. 15).

are these : " Christians have the first-fruits of the Spirit," and
the Spirit helps them in prayer.

6. With regard to the FIRST-FRUITS, the apostle says : " We
ourselves also who have the first-fruits of the Spirit " (ver.
23). Speaking of the groaning universe waiting for deliverance, he adds, that Christians also who have the first-fruits of
the Spirit groan. Some, with Grotius, incorrectly limit these
terms to the apostles. James, indeed, speaks of the early
Christians as the first-fruits (Jas. i. 18). But the Apostle
Paul is not speaking OF PERSONS, but OF GIFTS ; and there is
only one tolerable interpretation—viz. that which refers the
first-fruits to the commencement of the communications of
the Spirit which are enjoyed in this life, but which are after
all but a foretaste or first-fruits of what awaits us, in all its
amplitude and fulness in eternity.

7. The other benefit is the Spirit's HELP IN PRAYER (ver.
26). When Christians know not what to ask, the Spirit
helps their infirmities, interceding IN THEM with unutterable
groanings, while Christ intercedes FOR THEM.

The only other passage which I shall adduce from this
Epistle is the prayer of Paul, that the Roman Christians
might be filled with faith and hope through the power of
the Holy Ghost. He ascribes both the origin and growth of
these graces to the Holy Spirit (xv. 13).

The Epistle to the EPHESIANS, amid the deep truths opened
up to a congregation which was specially prepared to take
them in, interweaves the doctrine of the Spirit in a way
which makes the train of the argument in the highest degree
practical.

The economy in virtue of which the Holy Spirit is dis-
pensed is thus exhibited in the prayer for the congregation :
" Making mention of you in my prayers, that the God of our
Lord Jesus Christ, the Father of glory, may grant unto you
the Spirit of wisdom and revelation in the knowledge of Him "
(Eph. i. 17). He asks the Spirit on their behalf from the

God of the Lord Jesus Christ, the Father of glory, the dispenser of the Spirit, on the ground of Christ's merits as the
procuring cause. The import of the words : " The Spirit of
wisdom and revelation in the knowledge of the Lord Jesus,"
comprehends a full discovery of what was planned and effected
by God in the work of man's redemption. We have here a
numerous and varied class of blessings of which the Holy
Ghost is the author or producing cause. It is what philolo-
gists call the genitive of the author. It must be added that
" The Spirit of revelation in the knowledge of Christ " is a
memorable title of the Spirit from the work which He performs upon the human mind (Eph. i. 17), in illuminating the
eyes of the heart, as it is here expressed, to behold a beauty
in divine things of which it had previously no conception.
Notwithstanding the lingering remains of the image of God
in reason, conscience, and the longing after immortality,
there was not before this in man one spark from which the
illumination of the understanding could arise—only darkness
and enmity (1 Cor. ii. 14 ; Rom. viii. 7). The Spirit
enlightens the understanding, which was previously alienated
from the life of God (Eph. iv. 18), to perceive the truth of
the gospel, as worthy of God and divinely adapted to human
wants, and especially to receive the truth relating to Christ's
atonement. Not that the natural man could not with
sufficient correctness grasp the thought in a speculative way ;
but it was much in the same way in which a blind-born
man thinks or speaks of colours. When the eyes of the
heart are opened, a glory is beheld in Christ's person and
work unknown before ; and a light is conveyed to the mind
which produces a transforming change on all its powers.

Another passage in this Epistle not less emphatic is :
" *Through Him* (Christ) *we both have access by* [in] *one Spirit
unto the Father* " (Eph. ii. 17). The apostle, speaking in the
person of the Church composed of Jews and Gentiles, says :
" We BOTH have access, or introduction, to the Father," and

he mentions the Mediator through whose merits that introduction is effected.   He adds that it is IN ONE SPIRIT, whom we possess as a Spirit of faith and love, infusing confidence on the ground of Christ's priesthood.   The *one Spirit* can only mean the one Holy Ghost, which men of all nationalities, without distinction, now enjoy ; and the force of the preposition: " IN one Spirit," is by no means to be stripped of its significance, as has too often been done by commentators.   The intention of the apostle was to bring out with precision the difference of the relation in which Christ and the Spirit stand to the Church,—the one as the meritorious Surety, the other as the life-giving agent who puts us in possession of the whole redemption.

In the use of a favourite expression, the apostle again calls the Spirit a SEAL and EARNEST.   " After that ye believed ye were sealed with that Holy Spirit of promise, who is the earnest of our inheritance " (i. 13).   To the same effect the apostle warns them not to grieve the Holy Spirit by whom they were sealed (iv. 30).   As to the order in which this sealing stands, it comes after believing—that is, next after faith ; and as to the SEAL itself, too much ingenuity has often been used in elucidating it.   Without appealing to classical or Hebrew examples, it may suffice to say that the impress of a seal implies a relation to the owner of the seal, and is a sure token of something belonging to him.   From the three passages where the term SEAL is expressly used, we gather that believers are God's inviolable property, and known to be so by the Spirit dwelling in them.   The sealing implies that the image engraven on the seal is impressed on the thing, or on the person sealed.   In this case it is the image of God impressed on the heart by the enlightening, regenerating, and sanctifying power of the Holy Spirit.   By that seal believers are declared to be the inviolable property of God (2 Tim. ii. 19) ; and they are sealed to the day of redemption as something which is known to be inviolably secure as God's property

(Eph. iv. 30). Not only so : there is a subjective assurance which they acquire as to their own gracious state and final glory; for the Spirit is also called an EARNEST ($\dot{\alpha}\dot{\rho}\rho\alpha\beta\hat{\omega}\nu$) as well as a seal—that is, a foretaste which is equivalent to the first-fruits of the Spirit, which are elsewhere mentioned (Eph. iv. 14).

The apostle prays in a second memorable prayer for the Ephesians, that they might be *strengthened with might* BY THE SPIRIT in the inner man, that Christ might dwell in their hearts by faith (iii. 16). The Spirit *strengthens* the believer by giving him a share in all the benefits and blessings which Christ procured, as well as by confirming faith and love, that the conscious indwelling of Christ may be realized ; the indwelling of Christ answering to the strengthening or confirmation of the Spirit.

When the apostle refers to the Church, he calls it an habitation of God in the Spirit (Eph. ii. 22), and, by another figure, one body and one Spirit (iv. 4). Nor does he stop at doctrine : while enforcing Christian duty, he introduces the Holy Spirit in many connections. When he warns the Ephesians against indulging angry passions and unworthy practices, he says: " Grieve not the Holy Spirit of God," implying that such things on the part of Christians grieve the Spirit[1] (iv. 30). When he exhorts them to prayer, he bids them pray with all prayer and supplication in the Spirit (vi. 18). When he warns them against intemperance, he immediately subjoins an exhortation, calculated in its exercise to exclude all tendency to the habit of intemperance by the spiritual joy and satisfaction which take possession of the Christian ; *but be filled with the Spirit* (v. 18); for the enjoyment of that fulness of the Spirit satisfies the soul, and leaves

---

[1] See the beautiful remarks of Rev. Robert Hall on this passage : " Vindictive passions surround the soul with a sort of turbulent atmosphere, than which nothing can be conceived more opposite to that calm and holy light in which the blessed Spirit loves to dwell " (vol. i, p. 410).

it no longer a prey to intemperance or any such desires.
But in what sense can the Christian be EXHORTED to be
" filled with the Spirit," when we call to mind that it is God
alone by whom the Spirit is bestowed ? The answer is easy.
It is of God's gracious gift when the Spirit replenishes any
soul. But it is also a subject of exhortation. This is of the
same nature with the exhortations in the Epistle to the
Galatians : "walk in the Spirit" (Gal. v. 16, 25). The
Father, in the covenant of grace, provided for the restoration
of the Spirit; the Son procured the Spirit by His satisfaction,
and lives to confer the gift; and we have only to receive and
make room for Him daily, neither resisting nor grieving Him
away from the heart, which is designed to be again the temple
of the Holy Ghost.

In the Epistle to the PHILIPPIANS several allusions to the
Holy Spirit are found, having reference partly to Paul's own
condition and partly to theirs. Errorists had not as yet
troubled the Church from within, but marked intimations and
warnings are given respecting them to this congregation, of
whom the apostle always speaks with the deepest affection.

After noticing the mixed motives of some who preached
the gospel of contention, not sincerely, the apostle adds : " I
know that this shall turn to my salvation through your
prayer, and THE SUPPLY OF THE SPIRIT of Jesus Christ "
(Phil. i. 19). According to his own declaration elsewhere, he
was persuaded that all this would work together for good.
Their prayer and the supply of the Spirit of Christ are not
put together as co-ordinate. He means that all would
redound to the victory of Christ's cause, and to his own
highest advantage, through the supply (ἐπιχορηγία) of the
Spirit, while their prayer would be no unimportant subordinate link in the chain. As to the words here used, the
Holy Spirit is called " the Spirit of Jesus Christ," not only
because He is from the Son as well as from the Father,
according to the eternal procession from both, but because the

gift of the Spirit is derived from Christ's merits. He procured by His obedience and satisfaction not only the restoration of the divine favour, but the gift of the Holy Ghost, who is thus rightly called the Spirit of Jesus Christ. The more copious effusion of the Spirit is referred to the action of Christ no less than to the action of the Father, who, according to the covenant of grace, gave to the Son the power of sending the Spirit, and of conferring all the benefits which were acquired by His death (Zech. xii. 10).

The apostle expresses his confidence that the cause of the gospel would be promoted by the aid of the Spirit of Christ, who would not only cause the truth to triumph over falsehood, but nerve him with necessary courage to seal, if need be, his testimony with his blood. But that no one might imagine that these results would be given to the indolent or lukewarm, the apostle links the supply ($\epsilon\pi\iota\chi o\rho\eta\gamma\iota a$) of the Spirit with the PRAYERS of believing men in the Church, to which he was writing; for he constantly asked prayer as a means of spreading Christian truth. Such is the weakness of human efforts, that we accomplish nothing unless the Holy Ghost is the guide and ruler of all our actions, and unless He is invocated, as it is here intimated that He should be invocated, by the Church, as alone able to bring help.

To ward off the danger of disunion and mutual alienation, of which there was no little fear (iv. 2), the apostle bids them stand fast in ONE SPIRIT (i. 27); and at the commencement of the second chapter, he bases one of his arguments for unity, love, and concord on the fact that they had received *the communication* (not fellowship) *of the Spirit;* for this communication evinces itself in unity and love.

Another passage referring to the worship of God in the Spirit is: "We are the circumcision who WORSHIP GOD IN THE SPIRIT, and rejoice in Christ Jesus, and have no confidence in the flesh" (iii. 3); the contrast being between worship in the Spirit and ritualistic tendencies. The apostle depreciates circumcision : he speaks of it as nothing better now than concision, and by contrast he says we are the circumcision, the spiritual Church. The next clause is : *who worship God in the Spirit,* as the result of regeneration, and as deduced from it. It is not to be resolved into the vague idea of spiritual worship, as commentators too commonly expound it, but to be viewed as worship in the power of the Spirit ; the term *Spirit* being plainly the echo of the promise : " I will pour out my Spirit on all flesh." The reference is not so much to sanctification—though that, too, is comprehended —as to the adoption of sons ; nor does the apostle stop there, for another equally important point is, that this worship of God in the Spirit discovers itself in the exercise of rejoicing in Christ Jesus—that is, *as not leading away from Christ, but to Christ,* and inducing a reliance on Christ's merits and offices, and His whole mediatorial work. And in that proportion men abandon or forego all confidence in the flesh. The whole is an anticlimax, the first clause in the natural order being " we have no confidence in the flesh."

The Pauline Epistles, which yet remain to be noticed, contain only a few additional allusions, and our survey of them may be brief.

The Epistle to the COLOSSIANS, written to anchor the Church in sound doctrine against erroneous views, contains but one express allusion to the doctrine of the Spirit, though the whole Epistle implies it. The apostle, referring to Epaphras, says : " Who also declared to us *your love in the Spirit* " (i. 8). The Greek exegetes, followed by not a few Protestants, throw this into the vague phrase : " spiritual love," as contrasted with ordinary love in the relations of life. The love was to be exercised toward Paul, who was absent, and not personally known to the Colossians ; and hence he calls it " your love in the Spirit," because the Spirit was its producing cause or author. The love to the Saints was a fruit of the Spirit, as is elsewhere described.

The Epistles to the THESSALONIANS contain the following allusions to the doctrine of the Spirit. When the apostle recalls their first reception of the gospel, he says : " Our gospel came not unto you in word only, but also in power, *and in the Holy Ghost,* and much assurance " (1 Thess. i. 5). Various interpretations have been given of these words, but they offer, really, little difficulty. The obvious meaning suggested by the antithesis is, that the gospel was accompanied with converting power ; and when it is added, " and in the Holy Ghost," Calvin makes the expression refer merely to THE AUTHOR of the previously mentioned power. Others refer the words to the gifts of the Spirit, especially the supernatural gifts conferred upon believers in the apostolic age to confirm the truth (Gal. iii. 2). Whether we accept the one view or the other, there was a full certainty ($\pi\lambda\eta\rho o\phi o\rho\iota a$), a complete and perfect satisfaction, from which all dubiety was removed. According to this interpretation, the terms do not refer to the power with which Paul preached, as many suppose, but to the experience of the Thessalonians who received the Spirit.

There are allusions also to the sin of despising the Spirit and of quenching the Spirit. As to the first, it is said : " He that despiseth, despiseth not man, but God, who hath also given to us His Holy Spirit " (1 Thess. iv. 8). This language seems to refer to the INSPIRATION and supernatural guidance given to the apostles in revealing divine truth. As to *quenching* the Spirit (1 Thess. v. 19), the allusion must either be to the supernatural gifts, as many interpret the passage, or to the testimony of the Spirit, which may be quenched through sinful practices, indifference, or neglect. It is best to understand it of the supernatural operation of the Spirit, as the following verse, containing a warning not to despise prophecy, seems to imply.

" *God hath from the beginning chosen you to salvation* THROUGH SANCTIFICATION OF THE SPIRIT *and belief of the truth* "

(2 Thess. ii. 13). The believing reception of the gospel was effected by the Spirit changing their hearts. The apostle, by the phrase " the sanctification of the Spirit," means the cause by which their effectual calling was begun and carried out. The Spirit produced a full separation in heart and tone of mind from an ungodly world, thus setting apart all who were included in God's gracious purpose or decree. He works faith in them as the Spirit of sanctification.

When we examine the two EPISTLES TO TIMOTHY, only two allusions to the doctrine of the Spirit call for special mention. In the first Epistle, He who was manifest in the flesh is said *to be justified in the Spirit* (1 Tim. iii. 6). Of all the explanations that have been attempted of this expression, only two deserve attention. The one is, that Christ had proclaimed Himself the Son of God, and been put to death as a blasphemer, and that He was now raised up by His own divine nature, and justified in all that claim. The other interpretation, which I prefer, is, that He was put to death as a public person, as the second Adam, under the charge of our imputed guilt, and that as our Surety He was justified by the Holy Spirit when He rose.

The SECOND EPISTLE TO TIMOTHY repeats the frequent expression : " the Holy Ghost that dwelleth in us " (2 Tim. i. 14), which may be taken indeed as the brief formula of all living Christianity. The charge to Timothy to keep the gospel doctrine committed to him, was to be carried out only by dependence on the Spirit, and in believing prayer for His influences : " Keep through the HOLY GHOST which dwelleth in us."

The EPISTLE TO THE HEBREWS, which, with the Greek Church, I accept as of Pauline origin, brings out several points in the doctrine of the Spirit. As to the person of Christ, it sets forth how the Redeemer, through the eternal Spirit, offered Himself without spot to God (Heb. ix. 14), and how God anointed Him with the Holy Ghost as the oil of gladness above His fellows as His reward (i. 9). The testimony to the work of the Spirit in the inspiration of Scripture is very emphatic, *e.g.* : the Holy Ghost says (Heb. iii. 7) ; the Holy Ghost signifying this (ix. 8) ; whereof the Holy Ghost also is a witness to us (x. 15). The vast array of miracles and supernatural gifts with which the preaching of the gospel or the New Economy was ushered in is described as the accompanying testimony of God, with signs and wonders, and divers miracles and GIFTS OF THE HOLY GHOST *according to His own will* (ii. 4). The two difficult passages which involve the apostasy of some professing Christians after being made partakers of the Holy Ghost (vi. 4), and where the parties have done despite to the Spirit of grace (x. 29), are instances of men receiving only the supernatural gifts,[1] not true grace.

THE TESTIMONY OF JAMES.

The Epistle of James, directed against a nominal Christianity, or dead faith which had begun to prevail in his time, draws a line between nature and grace through all life. James contrasts spiritual religion with that forgetful hearing which, under the empty form, neither keeps itself unspotted from the world, nor exhibits the honour, the love, the benevolence which the law written on the heart prompts. He described that hollow profession by the licence given to the tongue, and by the vain boast of wisdom on which it plumed itself. Though he only once mentions the Spirit, the entire Epistle takes for granted the necessity of the Spirit's renewing grace. He bids those who lack wisdom ask it of God by believing prayer (Jas. i. 5). He implies the Spirit's agency when he

---

[1] So Klinkenberg puts it ; compare Matt. vii. 22. If we take this view, which is every way preferable, we need not labour, as Owen and others have done, to meet the arguments of those who contend against the perseverance of the saints from this text.

says that every good gift and every perfect gift is from above
(i. 17). He assumes the Spirit's work of regeneration by the
word of truth as the foundation of all (i. 18). The tenor of
the Epistle implies that the Holy Spirit, the author of faith,
first enters the Christian heart as His habitation, and then
makes it a temple worthy of Himself. In the only passage
where he definitely names the Spirit, he emphatically expresses
this, viz.: "*Do ye think that the Spirit saith in vain, The spirit
that dwelleth in us lusteth to envy?*" This confessedly difficult passage is better translated: "Do you think that the
Spirit speaketh in vain? Doth *the spirit that dwelleth in us*
lust to envy?"[1] If we compare these words with the common style of the apostles, who speak of the Spirit as the great
Inhabitant of the Christian heart, no doubt can exist that the
allusion is to the Holy Spirit (Rom. viii. 9 ; 2 Tim. i. 14 ;
1 John iii. 34), who dwells in believers, and instructs, comforts, and sanctifies them. One of the most comprehensive
descriptions of a Christian is that he is a man in whom the
Holy Spirit dwells. The pointed inquiry of the Apostle
James to the envious and contentious men to whom he
addressed himself is: Can the Holy Spirit have His habitation in a heart replete with envy? And the emphatic
answer, tacitly implied, is: No. *But* (that is, on the contrary,
δέ) *He giveth more grace.* The meaning is: the Holy Spirit
makes the man in whom He dwells to cherish no envy at
another's welfare, but rather to wish their blessings augmented ;
and the same Spirit gives more grace to him who is thus
minded, or makes him the recipient of more grace. On that
man he confers richer communications of grace. As to the
interpretation of the passage, it is not without its difficulties,
as the quotation is not found in so many words in Scripture.
Some refer it to the antediluvians (Gen. vi. 3), others to the
Book of Proverbs (Prov. iii. 34). Not to mention far-fetched

---

[1] See an admirable dissertation by WITSIUS, *de Spiritu concupiscente* (Jas.
iv. 5, 6).

interpretations, it seems rather to refer to Moses' conduct in the matter of Eldad and Medad, when Joshua, from a desire for the honour of Moses, would have forbidden them to prophesy. But Moses said: *"Enviest thou for my sake?"* (Num. xi. 29).

THE TESTIMONY OF PETER.

On the day of Pentecost Peter expounded and applied the prophecy of Joel as to the pouring out of the Spirit in the last days, pointing to the stupendous display of supernatural phenomena and of spiritual gifts, and declaring: "This is that which was spoken by the prophet Joel" (Acts ii. 16). On another occasion he represented Jesus as anointed with the Holy Ghost and with power (x. 38). And as to the giving of the Spirit to the Gentiles, irrespective of all national distinctions, he answered expressly that God gave them the Holy Ghost, and put no difference between the Jews and them (xv. 8).

But let us more narrowly examine the Petrine Epistles. When we examine what titles Peter applies to the Spirit, we find the following: "the Spirit of Christ" (1 Pet. i. 11); *the Spirit of God*, intimating God and the Spirit who proceeds from God (iv. 14); "the Spirit of glory," resting like the Shechinah on the persecuted Christian (iv. 14). As to the ancient prophets, he says THAT THE SPIRIT OF CHRIST which was in them testified beforehand the sufferings of Christ and the glory that should follow (i. 11); in a word, announced the cross and crown of the Redeemer. That passage furnished a convincing proof that Christ had a divine pre-existence, and that His Spirit, prior to the incarnation, guided the inspired writers in all their predictions. Attempts have been made, indeed, to explain this away; and modern divines, such as Weiss, who deny Christ's pre-existence, put this construction on the statement: that the Messiah-Spirit, before He came, was working in the prophets. For such an evacuating comment there exists no ground; it is but a foregone Sabellian conclusion.

Nor are we to explain the expression which is applied to Christ: " Put to death in the flesh, but quickened by THE SPIRIT," in any other way than as an allusion to the Holy Ghost. It is neither Christ's human spirit simply, nor the divine nature of our Lord, though both interpretations have found almost equal favour with recent commentators. It appears from the following verse that we must rather think of the Holy Spirit in which, it is said, Christ went and preached to the spirits in prison—that is, by Noah as a preacher of righteousness. And we have only to compare this text with the passage previously expounded (1 Pet. i. 11), to be fully convinced that the reference is to the Spirit of Christ which was in the prophets. That the Redeemer was QUICKENED and raised up by the Holy Spirit is here affirmed by Peter, and is not obscurely intimated by the Apostle Paul (Rom. viii. 11). The same Spirit that formed Christ's human body and gave it life in His mother's womb, gave to Him the restored life when He rose from the dead. He who raised up Christ from the dead, indeed, is frequently mentioned as one of the Father's most memorable titles or designations ; and to prove that it was the Spirit who performed this work, we have only to recall the fact that the Holy Ghost is the executive in every divine operation (Rom. iv. 24, vi. 4).

To the Spirit also is ascribed the Christian's sanctification : " Elect, IN (ἐν) sanctification of the Spirit, TO obedience and sprinkling of the blood of Christ " (1 Pet. i. 2). The Holy Spirit, by the gospel, separates Christians, or sets them apart, in a peculiar way, from the common mass of men ; and the blessings enjoyed are the fruit of the Spirit's sanctify- ing power. As the prophets had the Spirit, so, Peter adds, the apostles, in like manner, preached with the Holy Ghost sent down from heaven (i. 12). In the second Epistle it must be noticed that the only allusion to the Spirit is in connection with the inspiration of the prophets, who are said to have spoken as they were moved by the Holy Ghost (2 Pet. i. 21).

THE TESTIMONY OF THE APOSTLE JUDE.

The EPISTLE OF JUDE was directed against a body of licentious errorists who had crept into the Church, and were corrupting it by their doctrines and practice. These were evil men, and there was no room to entertain doubts respecting their character. The apostle accordingly appeals, by way of warning, to some terrible instances of judgment recorded in Scripture — to the Israelites who were destroyed in their unbelief after coming out of Egypt (ver. 5); to the angels who kept not their first estate (ver. 6); to Sodom and Gomorrah and the neighbouring cities (ver. 7). Two references are made to the Holy Spirit within the compass of this small Epistle,— the one alluding to the errorists, the other to the Christians whom he exhorts.

1. "These are they who separate themselves, sensual ($\psi\nu\chi\iota\kappa o \acute{\iota}$), having not the Spirit" (ver. 19). The adjective rendered *sensual* here and in the Epistle of James (iii. 15) is elsewhere rendered *natural*, or the natural man (1 Cor. ii. 14). The expression means simply one in a state of nature, or unregenerate, and without the Spirit. This cannot be doubtful to any one who considers the antithesis in which it is placed by three apostles. Expositors have brought more superfluous learning to the elucidation of the term ($\psi\nu\chi\iota\kappa o \acute{\iota}$) than was necessary. What a natural man denotes is easily discerned by the antithesis in which it stands to *the spiritual* man, who is one that has received the Spirit. The natural man is one who has merely natural reason, not the Spirit,— that is, is the animal man, as Melanchthon expounds it,—one living according to reason, like Zeno or Saul, though not

necessarily in gross vices. As to the next phrase : *having not the Spirit*, it conveys the idea that the natural man has not the Spirit, and is the antithesis to what is said, that the true Christian HAS the Spirit. On the contrary, he who has not the Spirit is not Christ's (Rom. viii. 9). We must understand the Holy Spirit, and the apostle pronounces it an indisputable truth that natural men, whether addicted to the grosser vices, like those errorists, or practically exempt from them, *have not the Spirit*—that is, do not possess the Holy Spirit, who, as a divine inhabitant, occupies the heart of all believers, and sanctifies and renews them after the divine image.

2. The second reference to the Spirit in this Epistle, interwoven with other essential elements of the spiritual life, is : " But ye, beloved, building up yourselves on your most holy faith, PRAYING IN THE HOLY GHOST, keep yourselves in the love of God, looking for the mercy of our Lord Jesus Christ unto eternal life " (vers. 20, 21). This implies a life in the fellowship of the Holy Ghost, a life of prayer resulting from that fellowship. The Christians to whom the apostle wrote are exhorted to build themselves up on their faith, which implies all the objects of faith as a foundation. They are taught that they are not simply to be passive, but to some extent active in the process, and especially taught *to pray in the Holy Ghost*, who prompts the matter of all true prayer,—opening men's eyes to discover their poverty, and showing them the value of spiritual things,—exciting true faith,—and imbuing them with right affections. All true prayer is shown to be prayer in the Holy Ghost as well as in the name of Christ (John xiv. 13).

THE TESTIMONY OF THE APOSTLE JOHN.

On the subject of the Holy Spirit we find comparatively little in the Epistles of John—less, in fact, than every one expects to find when he comes to the examination of it.

The reason might be that the Gospel of John had set forth in the Lord's own words the most full and exhaustive delineation of the doctrine of the Spirit, and we are supposed to carry those disclosures of His Gospel with us in the perusal of the Epistle and Apocalypse.

Though the Epistle alludes more to the Spirit's work than to the personal relations of the Trinity, there are passages which show Him personally distinct from the Father and the Son. As often as the apostle speaks of the Spirit, he speaks of Him as communicated (1 John ii. 20), and as given to us (1 John iii. 24); and he plainly shows that he regards the communication as imparted to us by the Son. As to the names or titles given to Him, He is called the Spirit of God (1 John iv. 2), sent forth from God ($\dot{\epsilon}\kappa$ $\tau o\hat{v}$ $\Theta\epsilon o\hat{v}$, 1 John iv. 3); the Spirit of truth, because He opens the mind to truth, and teaches it to distinguish truth from error (1 John iv. 6). He is called the unction from the Holy One, who anoints the followers of Christ as He anointed Christ Himself (1 John ii. 20, 27).

It is said, the Spirit is truth (1 John v. 6); the meaning of which, in that connection, seems to be that one may securely rely on the testimony of the Spirit as an infallible witness, because He is the truth itself.

We have specially to inquire in what sense THE SPIRIT is said TO BEAR WITNESS in the much canvassed passage which refers to the THREE WITNESSES on earth (1 John v. 6, 8).[1] Without subjecting all the opinions to examination, it may suffice to say that the WATER and BLOOD first named cannot naturally be referred to the two sacraments, or to the blood and water which flowed from the pierced side of our Lord, though both opinions are maintained by eminent expositors. We rather understand by the first witness, Christ's baptism and the miraculous events connected with it, which clearly

---

[1] All text-critics and exegetes now let go 1 John v. 7 as no longer tenable. It was probably a mere note on the margin inserted in the text by a subsequent transcriber.

attested His Messianic commission.   We must understand by
THE BLOOD, His departure to the Father, or the termination
of His earthly task by the atoning sacrifice, which was
accompanied by the most striking miracles (Matt. xxvii. 51).
The THIRD WITNESS, that of THE SPIRIT, is none other than the
effusion of the Spirit, first given on the day of Pentecost, the
Spirit that spoke by the mouth of all the apostles, who
preached with the Holy Ghost sent down from heaven—the
Spirit who accompanied their oral testimony with stupendous
miracles, and who moved them in their writings.   The
apostle's words were accompanied with signs and wonders and
divers miracles and gifts of the Holy Ghost (Heb. ii. 4).   But
it was not all objective.   The Spirit's testimony was also
internal—that is, He made all internally efficacious and
available to the elect.

The apostle refers also to Christian assurance when he
says : " We know that He abideth in us by the Spirit which
He hath given us " (1 John iii. 24 and iv. 13).   As Paul
calls the Spirit the EARNEST, so John declares that the Holy
Spirit given to Christians gives them a knowledge and an
assurance of divine love.

I have now briefly to refer to THE APOCALYPSE, the only
remaining work of the Apostle John.   The salutation with
which the book opens contains an allusion to the Spirit, but
in a way peculiar to John.   Paul's manner in invocating
blessings on the several Churches to whom he writes was to
ask " grace and peace from God the Father and the Lord
Jesus Christ ; " and he does not name the Spirit, because
the Spirit was implied in the blessings which were communicated.   They were imparted by the agency of the Holy
Ghost, who applies redemption.   John, according to his
peculiar manner, invocates grace and peace from the whole
Trinity,—from the Father, called " Him who is, and who
was, and who is to come ; " FROM THE SPIRIT, represented as
the seven Spirits which are before the throne ; and from

Jesus Christ (Rev. i. 4). The seven Spirits in the plural indicate the manifold and various operations of the Holy Ghost in the application of grace, with a reference to the seven gifts mentioned in Isaiah (xi. 2), or with an allusion to the seven Churches. Throughout the Apocalypse this style of description is repeatedly used to represent the Spirit as resting on Christ for the great ends which were involved in the execution of the Covenant. Thus, in the third chapter, we read: "These things saith He that hath the seven Spirits of God and the seven stars" (Rev. iii. 1). In the fourth chapter the apostle describes a door opened in heaven, while the writer says: "Immediately I was in the Spirit" (iv. 2); and he adds: "There were seven lamps of fire burning before the throne, which are the seven Spirits of God" (iv. 5.) In the fifth chapter, the apostle describes what he beheld in connection with the book written within and without, and sealed with seven seals, which no man in heaven or in earth could open: "I beheld, and, lo, in the midst of the throne and of the four living creatures, and in the midst of the elders, stood a Lamb, as it had been slain, having seven horns and seven eyes, which are THE SEVEN SPIRITS of God sent forth into all the earth." The design of these passages was to set forth the communication of the Holy Spirit in the infinite supplies which Christ imparts, as the Spirit of wisdom and understanding, the Spirit of counsel and might, the Spirit of knowledge and of the fear of the Lord (Isa. xi. 2), and as all resting on Christ.

The apostle says at the beginning: "I was in the Spirit on the Lord's day" (i. 10). When Christ sends the seven Epistles to the seven Churches, He bids them hear what the Spirit speaketh to the Churches (ii. 7); for it is the personal Holy Ghost that speaks in and by the gospel, and that speaks in all the word of truth. And the book closes with the call: "THE SPIRIT and the Bride say, Come"—that is, the Church moved by the Spirit says, "Come."

SECOND DIVISION.

————

LECTURE I.

THE PERSONALITY AND PROCESSION OF THE HOLY SPIRIT.

I PURPOSE to discuss to-day the DIVINE PERSONALITY of the Holy Spirit. This is a point on which few doubts may be entertained by the vast majority of believing men among us. But it must not be passed over. Nor must attention be absorbed with the WORK of the Spirit so as to forget HIMSELF. All history proves, for instance, that to give exclusive prominence to the work of Christ while the personal Redeemer is left in the background, ends, for the most part, in placing a mere dogma where Christ Himself should be. The divine dignity of the Spirit demands, in like manner, that no obscuring influence shall come between the soul and the agency of the living person; and in the whole investigation on which it is necessary to enter, we must be upon our guard against being swayed either by the sound of words, which decide nothing, or by those refining speculations which are more shadowy than solid.

As to the divine personality of the Spirit, there are two modes by which we prove it. We prove it *a priori*, from the fact of the eternal procession, as we prove the divine personality of the Son from the fact of the eternal generation; for these immanent acts of God underlie respectively the personal distinctions in the Godhead. Or we prove it *a posteriori*

from the unquestionable evidences of divine personality which
are given in the sacred Scriptures in connection with His
works.   We shall begin with the latter, and proceed step by
step, taking up in order first the PERSONALITY, and then the
PROCESSION of the Spirit.

It is clear to every mind that, after His personality is
established, no further proof can reasonably be demanded to
show that such a Person must be God.   If He is not an influence or energy, but a personal agent, it follows on grounds
the most conclusive that He is not lower than Supreme God.
Hence the objections adduced in opposition to the doctrine
of the Spirit mainly turn at present against the proof of
His personality.   For to no created being can the actions
which are ascribed to Him be fitly or competently applied.

My object is to show that the Spirit of God is as truly a
Person as the Father or the Son,—a Person in whom mind
resides, and to whom men perform actions which are either
culpable or acceptable.   The divine personality is asserted
against two currents of opinion which agitated the Church in
early times,—the Sabellian and Arian heresies, which reciprocally evoked each other, and are ever ready to captivate
minds which miss the safe middle way.   The former is the
negation of the Spirit's personality, the latter the denial of
His Deity.   All who deviate in our day from the Church-
doctrine are led by a strong Sabellian bias to consider the
Holy Spirit as a mere influence or divine energy without personality,—a theory called the indwelling scheme by some,
but only a form of Unitarianism.   The Arian or Macedonian
opinion, which described the Spirit as a creature, is little
favoured at present, but may at any moment reappear, according to the strange vitality which is the accompaniment of
error.   At present Sabellianism is the error on the Trinity—
an error of wide diffusion and power ; and it is adopted by
many who come under the spell of German theology.   These
theologians evade the force of the Scripture proof by treating

the passages as rhetorical personifications or figures of speech, even while they dilate on the advantages of using only the grammatico-historical method of interpretation. They speak not of the Holy Spirit, but of the COMMON SPIRIT OF THE CHRISTIAN CHURCH, which, in fact, means nothing more than an *esprit de corps,* and detaches itself from all obligation to accept the doctrine of the personal Holy Ghost. How far modern theology is alienated from this entire domain of doctrine is known only to those whose special studies have led them to institute inquiries as to the German current of theological thought, and as to the multitudes in every land who have come under its influence. The personality of the Holy Ghost is treated by these divines as a dogma, for the acceptance of which no sufficient ground is found either in Scripture or experience.[1]

When Scripture alludes to the Holy Spirit, the personal terms conveying the idea of MIND, WILL, and SPONTANEOUS ACTION are so numerous that they may be regarded, not as the occasional, but as the general, nay, uniform and unvaried usage; and it is a usage observed by all the sacred writers, without a single exception. It is observed by the Old Testament writers and by the New Testament writers alike. It is retained as the natural expression of their thoughts, even in passages where the writers, without the slightest trace of emotion or elevation in their style, write and speak as simple narrators of historic facts (Acts ii. 15), or convey plain and practical instruction (Eph. iv. 30). To deny that there is any allusion to a person in such references to the Spirit, betrays either deep-seated bias and prejudice, or lack of exegetical aptitude and capacity.

[1] Dr. Kahnis says, in the preface to his work, *die Lehre vom Heiligen Geiste,* 1847, of which only a first part was published : "*was die neuere Theologie betrifft,* so sagt Baumgarten-Crusius (*compendium der Dogmen Geschichte,* ii. p. 189, Anm. 4), *dass der neuere Protestantismus die Persönlichkeit des Heiligen Geistes aufgegeben hat.* Das wenigstens ist wahr dass die strengkirchliche Dogmatik diese Lehre ziemlich unvermittelt hinstellt, *die Vermittelnde Theologie* der man Kirchlichen Grund und Boden nicht streitig machen kann, *meist negativ dazu steht.*"

To evade or explain away these proofs of personality, two modes have been adopted, having not even the semblance of probability. The one evasion is, that the expressions mean nothing more than AN ABSTRACT QUALITY; and the other is, that they are instances of TROPICAL LANGUAGE. It may suffice to reply, that few examples of rhetorical personification occur in any history written in simple prose, and that this holds true pre-eminently of the New Testament, where the writers of set purpose make use of a natural, popular style. In these perspicuous narratives, there was neither occasion nor scope in any of the allusions to the Holy Spirit for a highly figurative diction; and when a personal agent is referred to, it is out of keeping with the nature of their composition to understand the terms of a quality or influence. We must understand one in whom intelligence and will reside. It would be the most violent and far-fetched of all conceivable modes of interpretation, to lay it down as a rule—as this theory must do—that whenever the speakers or writers, either in the Old or New Testament, turned their mind toward the doctrine of the Spirit, they instantly abandoned all the plain and easy style familiar to them, and resorted to rhetorical personification, prosopopœa, and the most high-wrought figures which language can sustain, when their object was to be understood in the language which they used. To suppose such a thing is a sufficient refutation of that whole mode of interpretation. If Jesus and His apostles uniformly represented the Holy Spirit as a Person when He is not a Person, it would be the boldest personification ever found in any literature upon any subject.

Not only so; the apostles lived at a time when their assailants, the Gnostics, transmuted divine operations into emanations and persons. We may therefore, with Michaelis, pronounce it impossible—a thing, certainly, not to be believed —that the apostles should so frequently resort to rhetorical personification in reference to the Holy Ghost, and thus give occasion to regard Him as a Person, if, in the use of such terms, they did not think of Him as possessed of a divine personality.

It is not denied that there are passages where impersonal things are so described that at first sight they might seem to be taken as personal qualities. The two instances most frequently adduced are these : " The wind bloweth where it *listeth*," and " The blood of sprinkling that *speaketh* better things than that of Abel " (Heb. xii. 24). No man of ordinary capacity, however willing to weigh the force of the words, will for a moment doubt that these are figurative expressions, personifications which no man can mistake. The delineation of charity is so given (1 Cor. xiii. 1–8) that we may call it another instance of this personification. Every one sees that it is a vivid way of depicting the various activities of love in the whole conduct of a living Christian. But it is a wholly different case when we can show, in reference to the doctrine of the Spirit, that this mode of speaking is general, unvaried, uniform ; that it is adopted by all the sacred writers .with one consent ; and that it is retained even in the simplest passages where they narrate facts or give plain instruction.

It is common among modern theologians, swayed by a Sabellian bias, to allege that the name " Spirit of God " means no more than God Himself, without reference to a personal distinction which, indeed, they do not believe ; that Scripture contains such anthropomorphisms as the face of God, the name of God, the soul of God, as metaphors for God Himself ; and that the expression " Spirit of God " is therefore of similar import. To meet this misapprehension, it is not enough to show that the Spirit is possessed of divine properties, but that He is also personally distinct from the Father and the Son. The fact that the Spirit is named as occupying a co-ordinate rank with the other persons of the Godhead, supplies a valid argument against which no objection can be advanced.

It is also urged that the term PERSON is not Biblical, and is capable of being much perverted. But every thoughtful inquirer perceives that the term " person " is only used for convenience' sake ; that it is an ecclesiastical usage, like the words Trinity, Sacrament, and the like ; and that it became current in the Oriental as well as Western Church, simply because a generic term was found necessary to point out the three subsistents in the Godhead. It has at the same time been always admitted that the use of this particular term was adopted only to avoid circumlocution ; and that if a better term could be substituted for it with a general consent, no one would contend for it as indispensable. But with the doctrine underlying the expression the case is wholly different. That cannot be surrendered. Only remove from the use of the term every notion involving imperfection, as we do without difficulty when eyes, ears, or fingers are applied to God, from the mere lack of vocables to express the fit idea, and it must be admitted that in human language no term can be found better fitted to express the Church's meaning than the term PERSON. Because we must use intelligible language, no difficulty should be felt in calling the Holy Spirit a Person.

The evidence for the personality of the Holy Spirit, it may be remarked, though often indirect, is not less convincing. For the Scriptures were not written in such a way as to overbear those who challenge every statement till they are subdued by evidence, and who commonly find or make the stumbling - blocks which they wish to meet, but for true inquirers,—for receptive minds and honest hearts, which feel the need of redemption, and can be satisfied with a sufficient amount of evidence. The evidence consists in the uniform teaching of Scripture, and in the fact that no counter state- ments refute it. It amounts to this : (1) That the Spirit is not the Father or the Son, but distinct from both ; (2) that He is an agent possessed of intelligence and will, power and wisdom, which come to light in deeds performed with a design; (3) that the masculine pronouns applied to Him, and the nature of the mission on which He is sent, attest a Person.

The Scriptures distinctly recognise the Spirit as a Person. We have only to recall the language used in reference to THE COMFORTER to be convinced of this. To compensate for the loss incurred by the departure of the Lord Jesus to the Father, He promised that He would send another Comforter, who should take His place as their immediate Teacher, Helper, and Protector, and thus supply the want of His own presence, the anticipated loss of which filled them with trouble and dismay. When we look at the Persons referred to in that promise, it would be a perversion of language to suppose that a mere quality or influence is meant in any of the personal allusions. The sender is certainly different from the person who is sent: for we do not speak of sending a quality on an errand. Nor does ANY ONE SEND HIMSELF FROM HIMSELF, as the Sabellian [1] must put it when he interprets the words: " When THE COMFORTER is come, whom I WILL send to you FROM the Father " (John xv. 26). Whether we accept one rendering or another of the word Comforter, whether we make it TEACHER with Ernesti, or HELPER, or ADVOCATE, or PATRON with others, it is obvious to every mind that He who was to compensate the disciples and the Church, of which they were the first-fruits, for the loss of Christ's visible presence, was certainly a Person. The refusal to accept the Spirit's personality in that text compels the interpreter, if consistent with himself, TO DENY THE PERSONALITY OF CHRIST in whose room He came. That is the alternative before him which no ingenuity can evade. And the absurdity is not less obvious of identifying the title Comforter or Paraclete with the impersonal gifts which the apostles subsequently received. That such a comment is untenable, is clear from the explicit

[1] See e.g. Dr. Weiss' *Lehrbuch der Biblischen Theologie*, 1868 ; Grimm's *Wilke's Lexicon*, 1868,—both in a Sabellian tendency.

announcements that the Spirit should teach them all things (John xiv. 26); guide them into all truth (xvi. 13); bring all things to their remembrance (xiv. 26); glorify Christ by receiving of His and showing it to His disciples (xvi. 14). It is not possible more explicitly to distinguish a person from the works which he performs. Nor ought we to omit a note-worthy peculiarity in the THREE passages which refer to the Comforter. A change of gender in the use of the masculine demonstrative pronoun (ἐκεῖνος) forestalls the possibility of putting any other sense than a personal reference upon the words. Thus it is said: " The Comforter, the Holy Ghost, whom the Father will send in my name, He (ἐκεῖνος) shall teach you all things" (John xiv. 26); " When the Comforter is come, whom I will send unto you from the Father, the Spirit of truth who proceedeth from the Father, He (ἐκεῖνος) shall testify of me;" " Howbeit, when He (ἐκεῖνος), the Spirit of truth, is come, He will guide you into all truth: for He shall not speak of [better: from] Himself; but whatsoever He shall hear, that shall He speak, and He will show you things to come. He (ἐκεῖνος) shall glorify me" (xvi. 13, 14).

The unbiassed sense of unlettered men, who are beyond the influence of the theological currents, is alive to the fact that the meaning of many passages is lost, unless we think of the Holy Ghost as a Person, and not as a mere influence or energy. To lie to the Holy Ghost (Acts v. 3), to grieve the Holy Spirit of God (Eph. iv. 30), are expressions which, as every reflecting mind perceives, imply a Person who is pleased or displeased; and they cannot, with any propriety or fitness, be referred to what is impersonal.

The Book of Acts, specially prepared, as we have seen, to exhibit historically the Spirit's operations in the Church after the Lord's ascension, contains allusions to the personal leading of the Spirit on the mind of all Christ's servants, and in the formation of the various Churches. Thus He said to Philip, who had been directed to the way along which the chamberlain of the Ethiopian Queen was returning home: "Go near and join thyself to this chariot" (viii. 29); and after that mission was successfully accomplished, the Spirit of the Lord caught away Philip (viii. 39). To Peter, when the deputation from Cornelius arrived at Joppa, the Spirit said: "Behold, three men seek thee" (x. 19). When Saul of Tarsus was set apart to his great Gentile commission, which made him in a peculiar sense the apostle of the Gentiles, the Holy Ghost said to the prophets and teachers who were ministering to the Lord in the Church at Antioch: "Separate to me Barnabas and Saul for the work whereunto I have called them" (xiii. 2). When Paul and Timothy attempted to go into Bithynia, the Spirit suffered them not (xvi. 7). When the members constituting the council at Jerusalem gave forth the result of their deliberations for the guidance of the Churches in reference to the observance of the Jewish rites, they said: "It seemed good to the Holy Ghost and to us" (xv. 28)—language which could not have been used if the Holy Spirit were nothing but an influence. When He commissioned the apostles, and either directed or forbade them to do this or that according to His will, the language attests a free and sovereign agent, unless we are prepared to abandon the literal sense of words and the style of historic narrative. Fritzsche, in his learned treatise on the Spirit,[1] correctly maintains—though the treatise is unsatisfactory as a statement of ecclesiastical doctrine—that it is clear as noon-day that Scripture speaks of a Person or subsistence, not of a divine influence or energy; and the Christian Church from the beginning, notwithstanding the deflections of individuals, may be said to have asserted the Spirit's personality, and to have based it on the Scriptures. Collecting the evidence supplied by the survey of Scripture, we may put the arguments for the personality of the Spirit under the six following heads:—

[1] Dr. Christ. Fried. Fritzsche, *Nova Opuscula Academica*, 1846.

1. The personal actions ascribed to Him abundantly prove it (John xiv. 26 ; 1 Cor. xii. 11).
2. His distinction from the Father and the Son, and His mission from both, prove it (John xv. 26).
3. The co-ordinate rank and power which belong to Him equally with the Father and the Son prove it (Matt. xxviii. 19 ; 2 Cor. xiii. 14).
4. His appearance under a visible form at the baptism of Christ and on the day of Pentecost proves it.
5. The sin against the Holy Ghost implying a Person proves it.
6. The way in which He is distinguished from His gifts proves it (1 Cor. xii. 11).

The glorification of the Holy Ghost in connection with the Church is still future. Passage after passage might be adduced to show that He occupies a co-ordinate rank with the other Persons. But the completion of the Church opens a vista into the future. The appearance of Christ among men ushered in a full historical revelation of the Son in word and deed; and the abasement to which He stooped was followed by an equally conspicuous exaltation. With the Holy Ghost it is not so as yet. He dwells in redeemed hearts bought with a price. He occupies a co-ordinate rank. *But His work is still unseen.* The personality and Deity of the Spirit are, however, one day to be displayed in conspicuous glory in connection with His work upon the Church, when He shall have completed the marvellous transformation. The final issue in the glory reflected from every redeemed and perfected saint, and from the entire body of Christ now scattered over every country, and visited from hour to hour with new communications of wisdom, grace, and power, but then seen to be united to their glorious Head, will be worthy of the divine workman who is carrying on His transforming work, and raising up a temple in which the Godhead shall dwell for ever. At present the divine personality of the

Spirit is less perceptible, because it is not beheld in connection with the accomplished work. The redeemed are not yet perfect; the Church is not yet complete. There is still another stage of revelation, when the Spirit shall be glorified in connection with the work which He shall have finished and brought to its destined completeness.[1]

ON THE PROCESSION OF THE HOLY SPIRIT.

The words of Christ on which this discussion largely turns are these: "When the Comforter is come, whom I will send to you from the Father, even the Spirit of truth, who proceedeth from the Father" (John xv. 26). These three things challenge our attention: (1) The mission of the Spirit by Christ from the Father; (2) the essential relation prior to that mission, and on which that mission rests: "who proceedeth from the Father" ($\acute{o}$ $\pi\alpha\rho\grave{\alpha}$ $\tau o\hat{v}$ $\pi\alpha\tau\rho\grave{o}\varsigma$ $\acute{\epsilon}\kappa\pi o\rho\epsilon\acute{v}\epsilon\tau\alpha\iota$); the words "from the Father" corresponding to what is said of the generation of the Son, the Only-begotten "from the Father" ($\pi\alpha\rho\grave{\alpha}$ $\pi\alpha\tau\rho\acute{o}\varsigma$); (3) the present tense, "proceedeth," intimates an immanent ever-during present.

Some hold that the name HOLY SPIRIT refers exclusively to His office in man's salvation. But it is necessary to distinguish when truth and error are confusedly put together. The designation SPIRIT OF GOD is the distinctive name of the third person of the Godhead, denoting a divine subsistent, with intelligence and will, proceeding from another. The epithet HOLY, frequently conjoined with the term SPIRIT, gives us a nearer view of the Spirit's SPECIAL WORK in connection with man's salvation, and suggests an antithesis to every unholy spirit, whether human or Satanic. The procession of the Spirit is spoken of by our Lord in connection with a reference to the covenant of grace,[2] and doubtless the reason is

---

[1] This is well brought out in Schmid's *Biblische Theologie*, p. 167.
[2] See Lampe's Latin *Disputations on the Spirit* (vol. ii. p. 151 ff.).

to show that the natural order in the Godhead is also the order in the execution of the covenant of grace. Had we no other word of Scripture through which to think on this matter, the single title " THE SPIRIT OF GOD " shows the relation of two Persons, the one proceeding from the other, just as the title "the Son of God " proves the eternal Sonship. He is called—(1) the Spirit of the Lord (Isa. xi. 2) ; (2) the Spirit of God (Rom. viii. 9) ; (3) the Spirit that proceedeth from the Father (John xv. 26) ; (4) the Spirit of His Son (Gal. iv. 6) ; and we should grievously err if we believed that these phrases have no significance. We ascribe no such procession to Him as is in any way associated with the idea of imperfection. We acknowledge, however, something fitly represented by the analogy of respiration, for it would be irreverence to imagine that there is no analogy in the terms employed.

The more the matter is discussed, the more is Scripture found to warrant the position that, in the scheme of grace, the acts of the Persons of the Trinity are found to be according to their order of subsistence in the Godhead, and are but the visible manifestation of that order in the divine essence. The Spirit could not be called the Spirit of the Father, or the Spirit of Him who raised up Christ from the dead (Rom. viii. 11), unless He proceeded from the Father. He could not be called the Spirit of His Son (Gal. iv. 6), or the Spirit of Christ (Rom. viii. 9), because He replenished the humanity of Jesus. Nor does it appear how the Spirit could be sent by Him except upon the footing of that procession by which He is the Spirit of the Son as well as the Spirit of the Father, and which is eternally continued, without a past and without a future. The question is important in every respect, because it lies at the foundation of the MISSION OF THE COMFORTER. And as to its practical results, Church history informs us that it is in the last degree calamitous to ignore it.[1]

---

[1] See an excellent paper referring to the practical importance of this question, in Rudelbach's *Zeitschrift für Lutherische Theologie*, 1849, p. 45.

Some divines, in other respects orthodox, have recently taken exception to the eternal procession, as they also do to the eternal Sonship. Thus the author of an excellent work on the Spirit, while soundly Trinitarian as to the action of the three divine Persons in the covenant of grace, unhappily says: "The spiration, procession, or promanation of the Spirit from the Father, or from the Father and the Son, are phrases occupying no mean place in the theology of the early ages. Now, we humbly submit—whatever reverence may be due to holy synods and to learned men—that such explanations are founded on an erroneous principle, for they are *analyses of human thoughts or words*, not developments of divine realities" (p. 82).[1] They whose sentiments are thus re-echoed (viz. Roellius of Holland, Dr. Wardlaw, Prof. Moses Stuart, and the like) dismiss the subject of the procession with summary marks of impatience. But by so doing they cut themselves off from the Patristic literature, as well as from the Reformation, Puritan, and Anglican theology. The Scripture evidence in support of the procession is conclusive; and it is set forth in a mass of solid literature, from the earliest times to the present day. The question of the procession, analogous as it is in all respects to the question of the eternal Sonship, deserves and rewards a full investigation.

They who err in this article depart from the confession of a doctrine which the entire Church of God has taught and enforced from the days of the apostles. And the denial of this truth carries with it the most perilous consequences. (1) If there be no generation or procession, and if the names FATHER, SON, AND SPIRIT have respect merely to the covenant of grace, it would follow that these names are but official names, and have no essential relation underlying them. (2) It would follow that the Father could act in an isolated way without the Son and Holy Spirit, and that

[1] *The Work of the Spirit.* By William Hendry Stowell. London 1849.

they, again, could act from themselves apart from the Father
without any natural and necessary relation of the one to
the other.   (3) It would follow that the bond of unity
between the Persons 'was really subverted or overthrown.
These perilous consequences, especially the last two, may be
repudiated; and far be it from me to burden any man or
class of men with consequences which they do not themselves
accept and avow.   But the consequences which are admitted
are one thing, and the consequences which follow logically
from an opinion are another thing.   The consequences may be
of potent influence though neither suspected nor acknowledged.

The point to which we have adverted is at the foundation
of the unity and distinction in the Godhead.   The three
Persons have a natural relation to each other, both in
subsistence and action.   They are one in essence and in
operation.

The Biblical foundation of the doctrine that the Spirit is
FROM THE SON as well as from the Father is explicit.   Thus
it is said: "He shall glorify me: for He shall receive of
mine, and show it unto you" (John xvi. 14).   The import
is: HE SHALL, in the sphere of divine truth and revelation,
DELIVER ONLY WHAT I HAVE TAUGHT, and by so doing,
GLORIFY ME as a divine teacher; for it redounds to Christ's
glory that no other doctrine should be taught but that
which was derived from Him.   Christ had declared of His
own doctrine that it was not His, but the Father's who sent
Him, and that He taught nothing but what He had heard of
His Father—that is, *the Son received all from His Father in
the eternal generation* (John xv. 15); and the Spirit receives
all by procession from the Son in the same way as the Spirit
of the Son.

The same thing is elsewhere set forth as follows: "*For
He shall not speak of Himself* [better: *from Himself*] (ἀφ'
ἑαυτοῦ); but whatsoever He shall hear, that shall He speak"
(John xvi. 13).   As the Son said regarding Himself: "What

I hear, I speak," referring to His ineffable immanence in the Father, so the declaration that the Spirit should NOT SPEAK FROM HIMSELF, implies that He spoke nothing but what the Father and Son spoke by Him.   There is a certain order, but no isolation of the one Person from the other ; and the twice-repeated statement: " He shall receive of mine,"—united as it is with the declaration that the Son has the essence, attributes, and perfections that the Father has,—enables us to understand what is involved in this procession—viz. that the Holy Ghost receives the same numerical divine essence with the Father and the Son.

Such has been the belief of the Church from the first as set forth in all the creeds.   It must be accepted AS ESSENTIAL TO THE PERFECTION OF THE DIVINE NATURE that the Father have a Son, and that there should be a Spirit proceeding from them both.   The phrase : *who proceedeth from the Father*, in the present tense (ἐκπορεύεται), intimates an immanent, internal, ever-during act according to the unchangeable essence of the Deity.

THE DEITY OF THE HOLY SPIRIT BASED ON THE PROCESSION.

The SUPREME DEITY OF THE SPIRIT is clearly established by the procession of the Spirit.   The expression through which we think, whenever we direct attention to this doctrine, is the designation THE SPIRIT OF GOD.   Like the analogous designation " the Son of God," it sets forth a unique relation, or a personal distinction, before any work was done. And as we say that the only Son is supreme God, not although He is the Son, but *because* He was begotten of the Father ; so we say that the Spirit is supreme God, not although, but *because* He proceedeth from the Father and the Son.

The following fivefold line of proof, when carried out to its legitimate consequences, and all taking for granted the

procession from the Father and the Son, furnishes conclusive
proof of the supreme Deity of the Holy Spirit :—

1. The incommunicable acts of creation and providence
   ascribed to the Spirit.
2. Divine attributes ascribed to Him.
3. Divine honours and worship paid to Him.
4. The co-ordinate rank in which He is placed with the
   Father and the Son.
5. The name of God indirectly given to Him.

1. The creation and conservation of all things are attributed to the Spirit of God (Gen. i. 6 ; Ps. xxxiii. 6 ; Job
xxvi. 13).   He who summoned the world into being, with its
countless laws, adjustments, and concurrent adaptations, is
supreme God.   The conservation of the stupendous fabric by
what is tantamount to a sustained creation, the knowledge
necessary for a task beyond finite comprehension, the power
that never faints, and the vigilance that never slumbers, argue
the ever - present activity of supreme God.   *But all that
creative energy* which evoked the universe out of nothing, and
all the conserving Providence which sustains it, are *ascribed to
the Spirit of God.*   To speak of delegation, as the Arians have
done, is a hypothesis which needs but to be uttered to be
repudiated.   For to whom could such activity be delegated ?
Who could wield the perfections which such a task implies,
but He to whom these divine perfections naturally belong ?
The prophet Isaiah, as if to laugh to scorn the notion of a
delegated activity in such a sphere, thus exclaims : " Who
hath measured the waters in the hollow of His hand, and
meted out heaven with the span, and comprehended the dust
of the earth in a measure, and weighed the mountains in
scales, and the hills in a balance ?   Who hath directed *the
Spirit of the Lord*, or, being His counsellor, hath taught
Him ? "   A consideration of the universe with the light
which modern science has shed upon its laws, adjusted as
they are with the finest adaptation over all the realms of

nature, affords such a view of the wisdom necessary to plan, and of the power necessary to uphold them, that none but a divine hand was equal to the task. *But that hand was the Spirit's.* And the same argument applies to the great work of the Spirit in the RESURRECTION of our mortal bodies by His omnipotent power (Rom. viii. 11), and, in a word, to all the other omnipotent acts of the Spirit.

2. As to the DIVINE ATTRIBUTES ascribed to the Spirit, we may choose out of the great supply of materials furnished to our hand a few of the properties of supreme Godhead which He is said to possess, such as omniscience, omnipresence, and eternity.

We find OMNISCIENCE affirmed of the Spirit when it is said : " God hath revealed them to us by *His Spirit :* for the Spirit searcheth all things, yea, the deep things of God. For what man knoweth the things of a man, save the spirit of man which is in him ?   Even so the things of God knoweth no man, but the Spirit of God " (1 Cor. ii. 10, 11). The apostle says that he was in a position to unfold the purposes of God, because God revealed them to him by His Spirit : for the Spirit searcheth all things, yea, the deep things of God.   This is elucidated in the following verse by an illustration of a man knowing the things of a man by the spirit of man which is in him. .The term SEARCH, by analogy, transferred from man to God, does not mean that the Spirit inquires to learn, but that He intimately knows.   The language announces His perfect knowledge of the hidden counsels of God, and that the Spirit stands in the same relation to God that the soul of man does to man.   The knowledge which the soul has of man's hidden purposes and resolutions is compared with the Spirit's knowledge of the secret purposes of God.   For He is said (1) to know all things ; (2) to know the deep things of God ; (3) to have an intuitive knowledge with the precision and accuracy which the term *search* conveys ; (4) to know them with the intimate knowledge with which a man knows his own counsels.

With regard to the attribute of OMNIPRESENCE or immensity ascribed to the Holy Spirit, we find a vivid description of it in the psalm specially prepared to guide the Church's worship on this point: " Whither shall I go from Thy Spirit ? or whither shall I flee from Thy presence ? " (Ps. cxxxix. 7). The remark of the anonymous writer in the Greek CATENA on this psalm, that His Spirit intimates the Holy Spirit, and His face the only-begottten Son, is not without probability.[1] But the evidence of the Spirit's omnipresence is put beyond all doubt. And when we trace the Spirit's presence as the inhabitant and guide of the believing soul, and of the Christian Church in all lands at one and the same moment, it is evident that He is as truly omnipresent in essence as He is omniscient in knowledge. For a mere creature cannot be in two places at once, or act, at the same moment, in a great variety of ways in many lands. The attempt of the Socinians to blunt the force of this consideration by referring to Satan plucking away the seed sown in the heart of many hearers of the gospel, is not analogous, because it involves a multitude of evil spirits, and successive, not simultaneous action. To the other attributes we need not advert.

3. As to DIVINE WORSHIP paid to the Spirit, it is found in various religious exercises. It is the more necessary to put this matter in the proper light, because Arminian writers, with the concession too readily evinced by them, were in the habit of asserting, along with those who denied the doctrine of the Spirit, that we have neither example nor command in Scripture for the worship of the Spirit. That statement is groundless. Why it is not more frequently mentioned may, without difficulty, be ascertained. One reason why the Spirit is not more directly, as well as more frequently

---

[1] He uses the words: τὸ πνεῦμα αὐτοῦ φησὶ τὸ ἅγιον πνεῦμα, πρόσωπον δὲ τὸν μονογενῆ υἱόν.

addressed in prayer, is, that He is THE PROMPTER OF PRAYER,
and because no one can pray without the surrender of the
heart to Him, and without full dependence on His help
(Rom. viii. 26), who moulds within us the prayer which the
Son presents. But it is not true, in point of fact, that there
is no example of prayer to the Spirit. Of the texts which
fully evince it, let me adduce THE ORDINANCE OF BAPTISM performed in the name of the Holy Ghost. We have only to
consider the nature of the ordinance to perceive in it a
solemn act of worship, an expression of faith, a testimony
that He in whose name it is performed is our God, with a
heartfelt surrender to Him in an act of new obedience. That
all this is involved in it is clear from the words: " Were ye
baptized in the name of Paul ? " (1 Cor. i. 13). That these
three Persons cannot be put in any other category than entire
equality, is obvious from the fact that if any one of them
were not God, two irreconcilable opposites would equally be
the object of our faith, which is impossible.

Another proof of the same thing is THE INVOCATION OF
GRACE from the Spirit, as well as from the Father and from
Christ (Rev. i. 4). The words used are : " the seven Spirits
which are before His throne ; " but the allusion is not to
created spirits, but to the one Spirit of God, described in the
plural by the number SEVEN, to show the perfection of the
gifts, or to point out their sufficiency for the Church's
necessity and duties. That the reference is to the Spirit is
clear, because Christ is said to " have the seven Spirits of
God " (Rev. iii. 1) ; and there is no subordination in point of
essential glory when He is equally invoked as the fountain of
divine communications.

Another consideration evincing the DIVINE HONOUR to be
paid to Him is derived from the declaration that THE SIN
AGAINST THE HOLY GHOST can never be forgiven. On the
one hand, that could not be affirmed if He were not God ;
and, on the other hand, it by no means implies a superiority

to the other Persons from whom He is sent. It is to be
explained by the nature of the sin which rejects the testimony,
or quenches the operations of the Spirit, by which alone men
can be saved. The Holy Spirit is never represented as a
worshipper, but always as the object of divine worship.

4. THE CO-ORDINATE RANK in which the Spirit is placed
with the Father and the Son, is brought out in not a few
descriptive passages. We find the three Persons holding a
co-ordinate rank when we look at Christ's baptism (Matt.
iii. 16), or at the Pentecostal effusion of the Spirit (Acts
ii. 33), or at the Baptismal formula in the Christian Church,
or at the fact which the Apostle Paul so emphatically adduces,
that by Christ we have access in one Spirit to the Father
(Eph. ii. 18). Without expounding all these passages, and
others in this connection, let me adduce the apostolic benediction: " THE GRACE of the Lord Jesus Christ, and THE LOVE OF
GOD, AND THE COMMUNION [communication] OF THE HOLY
GHOST be with you all " (2 Cor. xiii. 14) ; words containing
an invocation to all the persons of the Godhead, and in point
of import tantamount to saying: " O Lord Jesus Christ, let
Thy grace ; O Father, let Thy love; O Holy Ghost, let the
communication of Thyself be with them all."

5. The name of GOD is indirectly given to the Spirit. In
the early centuries, the opponents of the doctrine of the Spirit
were wont to challenge the orthodox Church, asking, Where
is the Spirit designated God ? Dr. Samuel Clarke was in the
habit of affirming, according to his Arian bias, that the Holy
Ghost is never spoken of as God either in the Old or New
Testament. The language they desiderate may not be found
in the express form which they desire. But we find an
ample use of divine names applied to the Holy Spirit; and
when we compare one passage with another, and with the
connections of the context in which they stand, no possible
doubt can remain on an unbiassed mind that the Spirit is
supreme God, having a divine personality of the same kind

with that of the Father and the Son, with whom He is named as of equal rank. It is happily remarked by Lampe: " It is befitting that *He who speaks by all the prophets and apostles,* as His scribes and amanuenses, *should speak less of Himself,* when the work abundantly commends the author ; " a just and happy observation, by no means to be neglected. But there are express instances where He who is called THE HOLY GHOST in one clause is called GOD in another. The narrative of Ananias and Sapphira is of such a character (Acts v. 3, 4). If Ananias lied to the Holy Ghost, and his culpability lay in the fact that he lied not to man, but to God, it is very evident that in Peter's account the Holy Ghost is God. (Compare similiar interchangeable phraseology in Ps. xcv. 7 and Heb. iii. 7.)

6. The predicates of supreme Deity, such as eternity and the authority of a divine director, are ascribed to Him. He is called the Eternal Spirit (Heb. ix. 14) : " How much more shall the blood of Christ, who through THE ETERNAL SPIRIT offered Himself without spot to God, purge your conscience from dead works to serve the living God." The language intimates the absolute eternity of the Spirit of God ; that is, that Jehovah never was or could be without the Spirit of God. As to His authority and wisdom as a divine director, it is said (Isa. xl. 13) : " Who hath directed the Spirit of the Lord ? with whom took He counsel ? " The words emphatically set forth that all the treasures of wisdom and knowledge are His.

It would be superfluous to pursue the proof of the supreme Deity of the Spirit at greater length. For having established the Personality of the Spirit, and proved that the Holy Scriptures uniformly describe the Spirit as a person, His Deity at once becomes manifest from all the actions which He is said to perform. It is always HE, not IT—a person, not an influence, and a person obviously divine.

On this point, before I pass from it, I cannot but advert to the excellences and defects of the Anglican theology.   The Church of England has done more than any other Protestant Church to assert the great doctrine of the Trinity ; and every other Church in this land and in other lands has received an invigorating impulse from her unhesitating testimony to the truth of this essential article.   The literature produced by her great divines, and the peculiar form of her Church-services, have all acted in the most favourable manner to vindicate and uphold a trinitarian tone among the English-speaking race.

There the great writers of the English Church, such as Barrow, South, Burnet, Jackson, and others, stop short.   But there is another division of the subject, viz. the office and work of the Holy Spirit, on which the Church of England has, for two centuries, bestowed far less study and attention than were due to such a theme.   I cannot better describe the two parts of the subject than in the words of the Heidelberg Catechism (53rd question) :   " What dost thou believe concerning the Holy Spirit ?—A. " *First*, that He is true and co-eternal God with the Father and the Son ; *secondly*, that He is also given to me, to make me by a true faith partaker of Christ and all His benefits, that He may comfort me and abide with me for ever."   The Anglican writers are very full on the first branch, but not so on the other.   The reason of this one-sidedness in the Church of England, which I cannot but lament, must be traced to the Arminian theology, and to the ritualistic elements which found a large place within her pale, and turned away the mind from the Spirit's inward work.

LECTURE II.

A TRINITY of persons in the Godhead, and a covenant of grace according to which they act in all the plan and exercise of grace, are brought before us in the ANOINTING of our Lord by the Holy Spirit. The term MESSIAH, the Anointed One, carries with it the idea of the Trinity, inasmuch as it implies THE ANOINTER and THE ANOINTED, or THE CHRIST and THE HOLY SPIRIT, the oil or the unction with which He was anointed. The term implies, too, a covenant of grace in which the different persons act their part, according to a paction or agreement, for man's redemption. The Father and the Son come before us as two contracting parties, the sender and the sent ; while the Holy Spirit is a concurring party in the entire provisions of the covenant. The task assigned to the Spirit, and carried out by Him in all respects, was to anoint and equip the Mediator for all the duties of that servant's place which He was abased to fill ; then to be sent as the Spirit of the Father and of the Son on the errand of revealing the redemption to be purchased by the Son; of announcing its historical fulfilment ; and of actually applying the redemption to the souls of men. The Lord Jesus disclosed the nature of this covenant when He spoke of Himself as receiving the Father's command (John x. 18) ; and of the Spirit as not speaking of Himself, but speaking whatsoever He should hear (John xvi. 13) ; of glorifying Christ ; of taking of His and showing it to the disciples (John xvi. 14).

Parties indeed there are in our day, the representatives of modern thought, who take exception to every phase of federal theology.   But that is only to be expected from a class disposed to accept the wide-spread Sabellian opinion which admits no Trinity in any sense.   It is enough to remark that the supposition of a covenant, pact, or agreement among the persons of the Godhead involves no greater difficulty than the supposition of a Trinity.   There is beyond all question but one divine essence but three persons in the Godhead; and Owen happily remarks : " The distinct acting of the will of the Father and of the will of the Son with regard to each other is more than a decree, and hath the proper nature of a covenant or compact." [1]

Two great thoughts confront us in reference to Christ throughout the Old and New Testament—(1) that He is a DIVINE PERSON, and (2) that He is THE ANOINTED SERVANT OF THE LORD.   On the one hand, the child born is designated the Wonderful, Counsellor, THE MIGHTY GOD (Isa. ix. 6); and, on the other hand, our attention is turned to Him as THE SERVANT OF THE LORD upon whom the Spirit has been put (Isa. xlii. 1).   And these two thoughts are never disjoined in Biblical theology.

A twofold line of thought might here be pursued by us to show the constant agency of the Spirit on Christ's humanity. (1) The idea of man implies it (Gen. ii. 7) ; and (2) the great fact of the Incarnation takes for granted that Christ's manhood was immediately filled and led by the Spirit.   Many modern writers who deal with Christology, and venture to write Lives of Jesus, are wont to describe the Redeemer in glowing language as a man replenished with an absolute fulness of the Spirit,—whatever meaning they may attach to that term,— but maintain for the most part an ominous silence on His higher nature and on His divine pre-existence as the second Person of the Trinity.   But both thoughts must be combined.

[1] See Owen's *Works*, Edin. ed., vol. xii. 496.

The passages which refer to the Spirit as anointing Christ are chiefly given historically. The teaching of the Baptist on the anointing of the Messiah is full of significance. It gives conclusive evidence that the Baptist by no means taught, according to the views largely adopted by the uninspired writers of the Life of Jesus, that it was the absolute fulness and presence of the Spirit which constituted all the higher element that was in Christ, or that this was all that is involved in what is called His Incarnation.

It is worthy of notice that, prior to the mission of the Comforter to act with convincing power on the world, Scripture speaks of a mission of the Spirit conjoined with that of the Son. The Messiah is introduced by the prophet Isaiah saying : " And now the Lord God has sent me and His Spirit" (Isa. xlviii. 16) ; for, as Cocceius, Vitringa, and Lampe have conclusively proved, the words should be so translated. They bring before us a twofold or conjunct mission, which was appointed to take place together. They set forth that the Spirit of God had a part to act in and with the incarnation on the Person of the Messiah and in the whole performance of His mediatorial work.[1] We need not refer again to the remarkable testimony of Isaiah to the anointing of Messiah by the Spirit, already noticed by us in connection with that prophet.

With regard to the Incarnation, it was a conjunct act of the Trinity, in which the Spirit is represented as preparing the body which the Son assumed, by making it *His own* in a sense not to be affirmed of the other Persons of the Godhead. Here I would make one preliminary remark. The Incarnation was among the category of MEANS to a given result, and introduced by occasion of sin, which it was

---

[1] In the Symbolum fidei Concilii Toletani XI. a. 675, the Council adopts the wrong translation of Jerome or the Vulgate, and argues : " missus tamen Filius non solum a Patre sed ab Spiritu Sancto missus credendus est in eo quod ipse per Prophetam dicit : et nunc Dominus misit me et Spiritus Sanctus."

intended to put away. Several writers among the scholastics represented the ultimate design of the Incarnation as the self-manifestation of the Son of God, thus making it an object for Christ Himself, and something sought for its own sake. But it is to think unworthily of God to make it AN END.

Such a notion destroys the grace of the Incarnation, and too readily leads to the conclusion that it is of the nature of God to become incarnate. Not less active in the same direction is the modern theory of Dorner [1] and others, that the Incarnation was included in the eternal idea of the world, irrespective of a fall. We cannot affirm that either the creation or Incarnation was necessary, or that they were anything beyond a free result of God's will. No inner want was involved; it was only a self-moved act of divine love. That the Incarnation is but a MEANS to an end, not an ultimate object in itself, is a position which must be held, if we would not open the way for that style of speculation to which we have just adverted. Such a theory is subversive of the deep foundation on which the atonement rests. Nothing short of such means—for the Incarnation was but a *means*, costly as it was—could suffice to bring about the end designed. The problem was, How could a guilty creature appear not guilty, and the partition-wall erected by sin on the one side and justice on the other, be abolished, that unimpeded love might flow forth, and man again be the temple of the Holy Ghost? The end contemplated was, how every attribute of God could be magnified, all the persons of the Trinity equally honoured, and man's wants so fully met, that from the broken fragments of the first vessel another should be fashioned with still larger capacities of happiness and glory.

For all His office the Lord Jesus received THE UNCTION OF THE SPIRIT: and here a question has been raised: Are we to refer this unction to the humanity of Christ or to the Person? Theodoret, who too much betrays a Nestorian bias, limited

[1] Dorner's *Entwicklungsgeschichte der Lehre von der Person Christi*, 1845.

the unction to the humanity alone.[1]   On the other hand, Justin Martyr and Ambrose, not to mention others, refer the expression UNCTION to the Deity of our Lord.   Others, whom Petavius adduces, refer it to both natures.   Unquestionably, wherever allusion is made to this unction, it must be understood as referring to the Person.   The opinion that limits the unction to His humanity originated from the circumstance that the propounders of that view concluded—as was by no means unnatural—that the expression could have no further allusion than to the sanctification of our Lord's humanity at His nativity and baptism; and they did not duly attend to the wider acceptation of the phrase in Scripture.   The mode in which the Redeemer subsequently to His exaltation received the promise of the Holy Ghost, together with the power of dispensing such a gift to others, is of such a nature, however, as conclusively proves that the unction is competent to Him only as God-man [2]—that is, in both natures.   As the humanity was assumed into the hypostatic union, we may fitly say, on the one hand, that THE PERSON OF CHRIST was anointed, so far as THE CALL TO OFFICE was concerned; while we bear in mind, on the other hand, that it is the humanity that is anointed in as far as we contemplate the actual supplies of gifts and graces, aids and endowments, necessary for the execution of His office.

The unction to which we have referred did not preclude, but presuppose the knowledge of divine things involved in Christ's pre-existence, and His divine fellowship with the Father before the world was.   That was not an ideal, but a real pre-existence, and included an immediate intuitive knowledge of divine things.   The Lord Jesus affirmed of Himself such things as are not competent to any finite being when He said: "No

---

[1] ἐχρίσθη δὲ οὐχ ὡς Θεὸς ἀλλ᾽ ὡς ἄνθρωπος (*Epitom. div. Decret.* ch. 11).   See Petavius, *Theol. Dog. de Incarnat.* lib. xi. c. 8.

[2] Maestricht puts it happily thus: "Proinde unctus est quoad *utramque* naturam, quatenus unctio designat *vocationem;* sed quoad *humanam* tantum, quatenus notat *qualificationem*" (*Theor. Pract. Theol.* p. 426).

man hath ascended up to heaven but He that came down from heaven, the Son of man who is in heaven " (John iii. 13). As our Lord existed from eternity, and as an intimate relation obtained between Him and the Father before the foundation of the world, His knowledge of divine things was intuitive and absolutely perfect to such an extent that He could say : " We speak what we know, and testify what we have seen " (John iii. 11).   He refers to Himself as participant of the divine counsels, and as being in heaven before He came down to earth.   And the additional clause: " the Son of man who is in heaven,"—which is not only genuine,[1] but essential to the sense,—describes, in contrast with the clause : " no man ascended up to heaven," the sense in which He affirmed that He testified what He had seen.   With the omnipresence of the divine nature He was in heaven while He spoke these words on the earth ; for we must by no means translate the words (ὁ ὤν) " who WAS in heaven," but " who IS in heaven."

The remark of Owen is worthy of deep consideration. " The only singular immediate act," says he,[2] " of the Person of the Son on the human nature, was the assumption of it into subsistence with Himself."   That mode of contemplating the Person of Christ is Biblical.   But that we may not be ingulfed in one-sidedness, it must be also added that the Spirit, according to the order of the Trinity, interposes His power only to execute the will of the Son.[3]   And so far is this from interfering with the glory of the Son, that it rather reveals Him more conspicuously, that in the work of redemption the operations of the Spirit are next in order to those of the Son.

The two natures of our Lord ACTIVELY CONCURRED in every mediatorial act.   If He assumed human nature in the true and proper sense of the term into union with His divine person,

[1] See Dean Burgon's *Revision Revised*, p. 133.   Lond. 1883.

[2] Owen, vol. iii. p. 160, Edin. ed.

[3] *Vid.* Lampe's excellent Disputationes Philol. Theol. *de Spiritu Sancto*, vol. ii.

that position must be maintained. The Socinian objection, that there could be no further need for the Spirit's agency, and, in fact, no room for it,—if the divine nature of our Lord was itself active in the whole range of Christ's mediation,—is meant to perplex the question, because these men deny the existence of any divine nature in Christ's Person. That style of reasoning is futile ; for the question simply is, What do the Scriptures teach ? Do they affirm that *Christ was anointed by the Spirit ?* (Acts x. 38), that He was led out into the wilderness by the Spirit ? that He returned in the power of the Spirit to begin His public ministry ? that He performed His miracles by the Spirit ? and that, previously to His ascension, He gave commandments by the Spirit to the disciples whom He had chosen ? (Acts i. 2). No warrant exists for anything akin to that *Kenotic* or depotentiation-theory which denudes Him of essential attributes of the Godhead, and puts His humanity on a mere level with that of other men. And as little warrant exists for denying the Spirit's work on Christ's humanity in every mediatorial act which He performed on earth or performs in heaven.

The unction of the Spirit must be traced in all His personal and official gifts. In Christ the Person and office coincided. In His divine Person He was the substance of all the offices to which He was appointed ; and these He was fitted by the Holy Spirit to discharge. The offices would be nothing apart from Himself, and could have neither coherence nor validity without the underlying Person. But He was also anointed with the Spirit, nay, the absolute receiver of the Spirit, poured on Him in such a plenitude that it was not by measure (John iii. 34).

As to the UNCTION of the Lord Jesus by the Spirit, it was different according to the THREE GRADES successively imparted. The *first* grade was at the Incarnation ; the *second* coincided with His baptism ; the *third* and *highest* grade was at the ascension, when He sat down on His mediatorial throne and received from the Father the gift of the Holy Ghost to bestow upon His Church in abundant measure.[1]

I. The FIRST GRADE of this anointing with the Spirit took place at the Incarnation or nativity.   The words, as given by Luke, contain a brief description of the supernatural conception : " The Holy Ghost shall come upon thee, and the power of the Highest shall overshadow thee : wherefore that holy thing that shall be born of thee shall be called the Son of God " (Luke i. 35).   And they show that the Lord's humanity was sinless, and that it never was in Adam's covenant.   The second clause describes more fully what was said in the first clause, according to the exegetical rule, that in corresponding members of this sort the darker is to be explained by the clearer.   The import of both clauses is, that the Holy Spirit was the former of Christ's human nature ; and that the Son by assuming it into personal union, made it His own by a right peculiar to Himself—that is, by a union personal and incommunicable to the other Persons of the Godhead.[2] And these words are important as serving to refute the ancient and recent Errorists, who disliked the idea that our Lord's flesh was formed by the Spirit from Mary's substance, and fancied to themselves a certain heavenly flesh brought with Him from above.

Another point demanding notice is the statement that the holy thing born of Mary should be called the SON OF GOD. In construing this clause, we must make " the holy thing born

[1] Dr. M'Crie well remarks, in his sermon on the love of the Spirit : " In the glorious person of the Redeemer, next to the GRACE OF UNION, which is the effect of the assumption of human nature by the Son of God, THE GRACE OF UNCTION is the most wonderful object of contemplation " (vol. iv. p. 362).

[2] It was united to Him in such a sense that it also (καὶ) is the Son of God. That holy thing began to be at the conception by the Spirit.   The words *of thee* (ἐκ σοῦ), deleted by many in the phrase, should probably be retained in the text, for they are found in such a number of Fathers (Justin, Irenæus, Tertullian, Cyprian, Athanasius, Chrysostom, Epiphanius, Jerome) that the balance of authority from this source alone goes far to counterbalance the evidence of faulty manuscripts against them.

of thee " the nominative of the sentence, and " shall be called
Son of God " the predicate.   They[1] who put the adjective
HOLY as the predicate thus : " that which is to be born shall
be called holy," not only misapprehend the grammatical construction, but eliminate the truth which the clause was intended to convey.   The true meaning is : the holy thing
born of thee shall, in virtue of the hypostatic union, be also
called the Son of God, thus asserting the unity of the Person.
The words διὸ καί intimate that there is both an eternal
generation and a holy thing begotten, created when assumed,
and assumed when created, and that the result is not two
Persons, but one ; for the holy thing to which Mary gave
birth is ALSO called the Son of God.

This explanation meets the argument of the Unitarians,
whose plea, derived from this verse, is, that the future tense,
" shall be called," implies that Christ was not the Son of God
by eternal pre-existence, and that He only began to be the Son
of God when He took the flesh ; thus confounding the difference between His eternal Sonship and His being called so in
the knowledge and confession of the Church—that is, the difference between being and manifestation.   The nativity by the
Holy Spirit from the Virgin could not make humanity the Son
of God.   As the humanity, however, was assumed into personal
union by the Son, it also is called the Son of God.   Everything
included in the Spirit's work on Christ's humanity is of the last
importance.   Thus it is abundantly evident from Scripture—
unless we give an arbitrary meaning to the phrase : " The Holy
Ghost shall come upon thee, and the power of the Highest shall
overshadow thee " (Luke i. 35) — that the Lord's humanity
was produced by the Holy Ghost in a supernatural way, which
at once obviated *the possibility of contracting guilt from Adam*,
or of deriving any *transmitted corruption*, and which, by an
act of infinite wisdom and power, put Him within the human
family as a kinsman-Redeemer, and yet exempted Him from

[1] So Bornemann and the Revised Version incorrectly.

being in Adam's covenant; for He was the second Adam, the Son of man.

Nor did the mother need an immaculate nature. The question, How could pure humanity be derived from a defiled source which uniformly entails corruption on others? is a difficulty which has staggered many—the Valentinians, the Anabaptists, the Quakers, and some modern Plymouthists on the one side, and the entire Church of Rome on the other. The sects above named attempted to meet the difficulty by representing Mary as but a pipe or channel ($\sigma\omega\lambda\acute{\eta}\nu$) through which a heavenly body or flesh, immediately created by the Holy Ghost, but not formed from her substance, was introduced into the world. But on that principle the Lord Jesus would belong to another order of beings, and would not be our brother, born into our family (Heb. ii. 14). And redemption was only possible when effected by a GOEL or kinsman-Redeemer. As to the way in which the Romish Church met the difficulty in the Bull which affirmed the immaculate conception of the Virgin Mary and her exemption from all taint of original sin before she was born,[1] the presupposition (or, as theologians express it, the $\pi\rho\hat{\omega}\tau o\nu$ $\psi\epsilon\hat{\upsilon}\delta o s$) can be no other than the repetition of the exaggerated theory of Flacius on the subject of original sin, from which the entire Protestant Church, Lutheran and Reformed, recoiled with equal horror—viz. that sin had become the very essence of man. The divines who confuted Flacius at once saw that on such a supposition an incarnation would have been impossible, and replied that human nature, corrupted as it was by the sin of Adam, was still, as a work of God, good, and capable of redemption; that we can distinguish in idea between the good work of God and the vitiating taint superinduced upon it, though we cannot separate these elements; and that God can do both—redeem His creature, and separate the sin. On the ground of this distinction, which is presupposed in the

[1] See the definition of 10th Dec. 1854.

whole redeeming and regenerating grace of God, nature could
be made available as the substance out of which, by the
miraculous intervention of the Holy Ghost, the sinless
humanity of our Lord could be produced. The theory
of Rome makes a sinless mother indispensable ; and it is as
faulty as that of the above-named sects, which resorted in
their perplexity to the conclusion that Mary was but a medium
of transmission. If both these tendencies egregiously fail by
regarding original sin as an insuperable difficulty to the supposition that our Lord derived His flesh from a fallen mother,
Schleiermacher and his school, from antagonism to the supernatural in miracle, place themselves on a Pelagian view of
humanity, and concede that there was nothing more than the
ordinary generation. As to the theory of Menken and Irving,
that our Lord took fallen humanity, it wholly mistakes the
great end of the supernatural conception. According to the
first promise given in Genesis (iii. 15), and announced by
Isaiah a second time, the Saviour was to be born of a virgin
(Isa. vii. 14). The Holy Spirit was upon Him, accordingly,
from the moment of His conception, displaying His power in
supplying Him with the endowments, capacities, and gifts—
physical, intellectual, and spiritual—which were necessary for
His high work. As sanctification belongs to the Spirit's
operations, there can be no doubt that everything required
for the sanctification of the Lord's humanity was plentifully
supplied by the agency of the Holy Spirit, who warded off
every taint from whatever quarter it could possibly approach
Him. Not only so ; the soul of Christ, from the first moment
of conscious existence, was filled with actual communications
of the Spirit for such exercises of trust, and love, and holy
affections as were necessary in the experience of Him who
came as the second Adam, with the image of God restored in
all its fulness (Ps. xxii. 10). He who made man a temple of
God at first, and who was restoring it in the Incarnate Son,
was incessantly active in conferring every conceivable gift,

and in signally augmenting these gifts in ever-increasing measure at successive stages for the great work to be performed.   All this was for His private life.

"*And the child grew and waxed strong in Spirit* ($\pi\nu\epsilon\acute{\nu}\mu\alpha\tau\iota$ [1]), *filled with wisdom*" (Luke ii. 40).   This passage proves that we must ascribe to the Spirit all the progress in Christ's mental and spiritual development, and all His advancement in knowledge and holiness.   He went through the successive stages of acquirement in a manner absolutely unique, because His humanity had its existence in the personal union.   He was filled by the Spirit with a wisdom which replenished all the powers of His rational nature.   Though the increase, at first sight, seems incompatible with His being the Son of God, yet perfection is compatible with progress in a created nature, and He must needs be made like to His brethren.   He knew as a boy what He had not acquired as a child ; and as all the gifts were supplied to Him by the Spirit, we can trace the progress in the following stages which come to light in our Lord's history.   The Spirit was given to Him, in consequence of the personal union, in a measure which no mere man could possess, constituting THE LINK between the Deity and humanity, *perpetually imparting the full consciousness of His personality,* and making Him inwardly aware of His divine Sonship at all times (Luke ii. 49).

Thus the Spirit at the incarnation became the great guiding principle of all Christ's early history,[2] according to the order of operation that belongs to the Trinity.   It was the Holy Spirit that formed His human nature and directed the tenor of His earthly life.   His human nature had no distinct personality, nor any self-directing principle ($\tau\grave{o}$ $\dot{\eta}\gamma\epsilon\mu o\nu\iota\kappa\acute{o}\nu$), apart from the personal union ; and as He was not less perfect, but

---

[1] This reading has a preponderance of authority in its favour.

[2] On this point see the remarks of OWEN in his *Discourse on the Holy Spirit* (vol. iii. Edin. ed.) ; of HURRION *On the Divinity of the Holy Spirit ;* and of GUYSE *On the Holy Spirit, a Divine Person.*

more perfect than any other of the family of man on this
account, it must be carefully remembered that THE FULL CON-
SCIOUSNESS that He was the only Son of God, who came from
God and went to God (John xiii. 3), flowed perpetually from
the Spirit. *The communication*[1] *from the one nature to the
other was by the Spirit*, the EXECUTIVE of all the works of
God. Hence He never spoke or acted but at the proper time
(John vii. 6). He had His hour for everything that He performed, and a full consciousness derived from the Spirit that
He was the Son of God. The Godhead dwelling in Him
made all DUE COMMUNICATIONS TO HIS MANHOOD BY THE HOLY
GHOST. All the evangelists, but especially the Gospel of John,
show that the Spirit prompted all His actions, and gave

---

[1] The following quotation from Bishop Horsley's sermons will serve to
elucidate the position which we have here affirmed : "Neither of the two
natures was absorbed in the other, but both remained in themselves perfect,
notwithstanding the union of the two in one person. The Divine Word, to
which the humanity was united, was not, as some ancient heretics imagined,
instead of a soul to inform the body of the man ; for this could not have been
without a diminution of the divinity, which upon this supposition must have
become obnoxious to all the perturbations of the human soul,—to the passions
of grief, fear, anger, pity, joy, hope, and disappointment,—to all which our
Lord without sin was liable. The human nature in our Lord was complete in
both its parts, consisting of a body and a rational soul. The rational soul of our
Lord's human nature was a distinct thing from the principle of divinity to which
it was united ; and being so distinct, like the souls of other men, *it owed the
right use of its faculties, in the exercise of them upon religious subjects, and its
uncorrupted rectitude of will, to the influence of the Holy Spirit of God.* Jesus
indeed 'was anointed with this holy oil above His fellows,' inasmuch as the
intercourse was uninterrupted,—the illumination by infinite degrees more full,
and the consent and submission, on the part of the man, more perfect than in
any of the sons of Adam ; insomuch that He alone of all the human race, by
the strength and light imparted from above, was exempt from sin, and rendered
superior to temptation. To Him the Spirit was given not by measure. The
unmeasured infusion of the Spirit into the Redeemer's soul was NOT THE
MEANS, BUT THE EFFECT, of its union to the second person of the Godhead. A
union of which this had been the means had differed only in degree from that
which is, in some degree, the privilege of every believer,—which, in an
eminent degree, was the privilege of the apostles, who, by the visible descent of
the Holy Ghost upon them on the day of Pentecost, were, in some sort, like their
Lord, anointed with the unction from on high. But in Him the natures were
united, and the uninterrupted perfect commerce of His human soul with the
Divine Spirit was the effect and the privilege of that mysterious conjunction."
(Sermon IX.)

direction to all His words.   Nothing was undertaken but by the Spirit's direction ; nothing spoken but by His guidance ; nothing executed but by His power.   This anointing with the Spirit, foretold in prophecy and accomplished in fact, may be traced in all His official words and deeds.   The personal life of Christ as the God-man full of the Spirit, was the natural basis of all His official activity.

II. The SECOND GRADE of the donation or unction of the Holy Spirit was at His BAPTISM.   Before Jesus appeared invested with HIS PUBLIC OFFICE, the Holy Spirit had formed the human nature, and replenished it with perfect wisdom and faultless holiness ; and the baptism, AS THE PUBLIC IN-AUGURATION of the Lord Jesus INTO HIS OFFICE, was the occasion of conferring THE SUPERNATURAL GIFTS which had been promised in Old Testament prophecy.   The evidence of His inauguration was furnished by the Baptist, the voice cry-ing in the wilderness,—that is, the voice of the law and the prophets,—and by the visible descent of the Holy Spirit. The Baptist had a divine revelation that the Messiah should be pointed out to him by the visible descent of the Holy Spirit resting and abiding upon Him (John i. 33).   If he supposed that the Messiah should appear after the stern and vehement manner in which the Old Testament prophets pre-sented themselves, he was to learn that God had chosen another way.   The Messiah came among others to be bap-tized ; and when He was baptized, the Spirit, like a dove, the emblem of gentleness, purity, and love, descended upon Him from the open heaven, and rested or abode upon Him.

This descent of the Spirit was intended to confirm and encourage the Lord Jesus before entering on His arduous work ; and it took place in that public concourse of people which assembled to hear the Baptist, and became the occasion of His public introduction into office.   On this august occa-sion all the Persons of the Trinity were distinctly manifested

—the Father revealing Himself by an audible voice, the Son appearing in the flesh which He assumed, the Holy Spirit descending in a bodily shape like a dove. The anointer was the Father, the anointed was the Son, the unction, or anointing oil (Ps. xlv. 7), was the Holy Ghost, a divine Person of equal rank. It was not beneath the dignity of the Holy Spirit at the inauguration of the Messiah—whose office implies the reception of the Spirit not by measure (John iii. 34), and the dignity of receiving authority to dispense that Spirit to others —to make use of that visible emblem, that dove-like descent, to accredit the great fact, and to bear testimony to it. Enough for us that it occurred. We are not warranted in the case of every Biblical narrative to demand an answer to the question, Why was this? The abiding of the dove on Jesus, or the appearance of a dove, indicated that the Spirit of the Lord now RESTED upon Him (Isa. xi. 2). To the same purpose Peter said: "God anointed Jesus of Nazareth with the Holy Ghost and with power" (Acts x. 38).

Thus the unction for the office of MESSIAH or CHRIST is seen in the sinless nature and endowments of every kind that qualified Him for His task (Isa. xlii. 1–4, lxi. 1, 2). The full supply of the Spirit with which the Son was replenished from His nativity, was shadowed forth by many anointings instituted in the typical services of Israel, especially in the appointments to the three principal functions—prophet, priest, and king (Isa. lxi. 1 ; Ps. xlv. 8). There was, in the Lord's human life, a combination of all the graces that seem the most opposite,—meekness and boldness, the assertion of truth and deep humility, greatness and gentleness ;—nay, the scattered beauties of all the saints were jointly found in Him. The expression: " the Spirit of life in Christ Jesus," unfolds to us the source of all His actions, and demonstrates that more habitual grace dwelt in Him than in all created beings. The Baptist therefore declared: " God giveth not the Spirit by measure to Him " (John iii. 34) ; for though the words " to

Him " are not in the original Greek, they are undoubtedly implied, as will appear from the following reasons :—(1) The passage cannot be generalized into an allusion that shall take in the Church.   It is a very forced interpretation that would refer it to the general outpouring of the Spirit on the Church, —a comment for which the context supplies no warrant. Moreover, (2) the expression GIVETH THE SPIRIT, in the present tense, is there used in connection with the fact, and is the reason of the fact, that Jesus " speaketh the words of God," but is not to be construed in connection with the authority subsequently conferred of giving the Spirit to others.

If it is asked by the Unitarians : What need had He of the divine teaching of the Holy Spirit when He had known the heavenly Father from eternity ? the answer is : The Son of God, as such, needed no further teaching as to divine things. But as it behoved Him to be man, to be made like to His brethren, and to occupy the servant's place as the one Mediator between God and man, He NEEDED THAT UNCTION with which He was supplied.   The Socinians, who will have it that whatever higher knowledge of divine things is found in Jesus was obtained at His baptism, put the two statements in antagonism to each other.   But they are in perfect harmony.

That unction with the Spirit which preceded Christ's miraculous activity when He began to go about doing good, was bestowed on the occasion when He came to receive baptism and to be PUBLICLY INAUGURATED into His Messianic office. The Spirit descended upon Him and abode on Him in such fulness that He could communicate His miraculous power to His friends, which no mere prophet could ever perform (John i. 33 ; Matt. iii. 11).   He was anointed to be the supreme Prophet (Matt. xvi. 20) ; and as the prophets had immediate revelations when the Spirit of God came upon them, the same thing held true of Him, but with this marked peculiarity, that the Spirit did not occasionally reveal the will of God as in their case, but evermore permanently dwelt in Him to reveal the divine mind, and make Him conscious of His own Sonship.

The visible descent of the Holy Spirit, not only for the sake of the Jews and of the Baptist, but for a testimony to Christ Himself (Matt. iii. 16), took place while Jesus was praying to the Father, probably with a view to obtain the Spirit, which had long before been promised to the Messiah by the prophets (Luke iii. 21).

As to the object designed to be served by the descent of the Holy Spirit, it showed that Jesus of Nazareth was the Messiah promised to the Fathers, and that He was filled with the Spirit, who, on the one hand, would fit Him for the execution of *His high office ;* and, on the other hand, *enable Him, when His work was accomplished, to dispense the Spirit* to His people without let or hindrance ; for the Spirit is the efficient cause of all His divine operations outward to the Church and to the world.   The operations of the Son of God upon His human nature were effected by the Holy Spirit, as the immediate efficient cause of its existence, and the source of its fitness for the accomplishment of the great work for which the Son of God had assumed human nature.

The Spirit given at the baptism was intended to equip Him for the execution of His mediatorial office, as Prophet, Priest, and King.   That the Spirit qualified Him for His prophetic, priestly, and kingly offices is evident, because, with a full consciousness of His divine Sonship awakened and perpetually sustained by the Holy Spirit, He (1) not only spoke the words of God, but (2) offered Himself without spot to God ; and (3) draws all His people to Himself by the constant aid of the eternal Spirit.

Is it strange that He Himself should be under the guidance of the Spirit which He gives to others ?   This will not appear strange when we call to mind that He was man, and that

His human nature without a separate personality of its own had its activity only in personal union with the Son of God, who, though neither depotentiated, nor holding any of His divine perfections in abeyance, *acted on the human nature*, in every mediatorial act, *by the power of the Holy Spirit.* The divine nature did not absorb the human nature in any of its functions. Both natures were perfectly distinct, but united in the one Person. The light of Christ's understanding, the holy purity and the unswerving obedience of His will, the exercise of all His faculties and powers in religious things, were due to the immediate guidance of the Holy Spirit of God, giving Him the full consciousness that He was the eternal Son, and authority to act as such in all His words and works.

The next fact in Christ's life was THE TEMPTATION, of which it is said that He was *led up of the Spirit into the wilderness to be tempted* (Matt. iv. 1). The human nature was confirmed by the Spirit, and made victorious at every point of assault by the sustaining power of the Holy Spirit.

And when the temptation was ended, it is said: "Jesus returned *in the power of the Spirit* into Galilee" (Luke iv. 14), to begin a ministry of unprecedented authority and power. Coming from the scenes of the temptation with a victory over the Devil which gave Him the right of conquest, He, with an absolute plenitude of the Spirit, began to call disciples to Him, partly as trophies of His victory, partly as office-bearers in the kingdom which He was warranted to erect on the ruins of Satan's kingdom, which had already sustained a signal reverse. Every converted soul was a new prey taken from the adversary by the HOLY SPIRIT, on the ground of the meritorious obedience, which was accepted as perfect at every point, and which had its commencement at the point where the battle was lost by the first man. Jesus had now won authority to take the first steps for setting up His kingdom.

Another memorable fact was the sermon preached in the

synagogue of Nazareth, where He was well known (Luke
iv. 17). Having read the words of the prophet Isaiah, which
are expressly put into the mouth of the Messiah,—" The Spirit
of the Lord is upon me, because He hath anointed me to
preach " (Isa. lxi. 1),—-He expounded it, and added: " This
day is this Scripture fulfilled in your ears." The doctrines
which He uttered exhibited the unction to which the prophecy referred, and His townsmen wondered at the *gracious
words* (τοῖς λόγοις τῆς χάριτος) which proceeded out of His
mouth, as He spoke of divine grace by the Spirit which
anointed Him.

The next fact which discovers that He acted by the Spirit,
was the CASTING OUT OF SATAN. " If I cast out devils BY THE
SPIRIT OF GOD, then the kingdom of God is come to you "
(Matt. xii. 28). The Lord Jesus was then face to face with
Satan's kingdom, and was setting up the kingdom of God.
This was not the GENERAL DOMINION over the world. It was
that SPECIAL KINGDOM referred to in the first promise, where
it was said that the seed of the woman should bruise the
serpent's head. By the Spirit of God which rested on Him,
He was able to work miracles in general, and to cast out
Satan in particular from his fortress in the human heart;
thus showing an authority and a miraculous power which
sufficiently attested that the KING OF A NEW KINGDOM was on
the scene, and had begun His sway over those who are born
of the Spirit. The Holy Spirit was for a time largely shut
up and limited to Christ's own Person. But when the
atonement was consummated, the life-principle of His own
Person was also to be the life-principle of His kingdom.

I next refer to the Spirit's work in connection with Christ's
priestly oblation: " *Who, through the eternal Spirit, offered
Himself without spot to God* " (Heb. ix. 14). The expression:
" the eternal Spirit," can only mean the Holy Spirit according
to the usual acceptation of the term,—not the divine nature
of Christ, as too many expositors have unhappily understood

it. The meaning is, that the Son of God, moved and animated by the Holy Ghost, offered Himself without spot as an atoning sacrifice. An infinite merit attached to His work in virtue of His Incarnation as the only-begotten Son of God. And the Spirit is further said to have rendered Him an unspotted sacrifice. The Spirit discovered to Him the inflexible claims of God as well as inflamed Him with such a love to man and such a zeal for God as prompted Him to go forward in spite of every hindrance, pain, and difficulty, to effect the world's redemption. Thus the Spirit fitted Him as man for His work. The Holy Spirit, in a word, filled His mind with the unflagging ardour, zeal, and love which led Him to complete the sacrifice.

To explain the text as if it described the divine nature as priest and the human nature as the sacrifice, is inadmissible. The WHOLE PERSON is priest and victim; for all done by either nature belongs to the Person: HE offered Himself, says the apostle, and what could be meant on the other interpretation by the additional words, "through the eternal Spirit"? In that view of the matter, it would be a mere tautology. If the eternal Spirit is interpreted of the divine nature, it would be a flat and superfluous repetition of the same thing to say that He offered Himself through the divine nature. It would on that principle be only an expression of the same thing. If we take it, however, as intimating the action of the Holy Spirit, it will vividly represent the holy fire by which the sacrifices were consumed. One does not find, except on this interpretation, anything in the sacrifice of Christ that could be adduced as the antitype of the holy fire employed in the sacrifice. Nor are the objections to the view which we have propounded of any weight. When it is objected that the Holy Spirit was not the Priest who offered the sacrifice, the obvious answer is that Christ as Priest offered Himself a sacrifice possessed of infinite value and excellence in consideration of His divine Person, and then we have the additional fact that it was unspotted and offered through the Holy Spirit. Because the Spirit was in Him as a Spirit of faith and zeal and love, the Redeemer took upon Him with the utmost alacrity all that was to be performed and endured for man's redemption.

The Holy Spirit, that framed the Redeemer's mind as well as body, perpetually rested on Him during all His earthly sojourn, imparting to Him the full consciousness of His Sonship in the highest sense, and prompting Him to execute the mediatorial work imposed on Him (Isa. xlii. 1–4). That our Saviour was also raised from the dead by the Holy Ghost, is clearly taught by Peter, when he affirms that He was put to death in the flesh, but quickened by the Spirit (1 Pet. iii. 18).

III. The THIRD DEGREE of Christ's unction, reserved for His exaltation, is thus described: "Therefore being by the right hand of God exalted, and *having received of the Father the promise of the Holy Ghost*, He hath shed forth this which ye now see and hear" (Acts ii. 33). This third degree of unction to which reference is made in the Psalms (Ps. ii. 6, xlv. 7), and which became apparent at Pentecost, was an ascension-gift, the description of which by Peter is but a paraphrase of the words: "Thou hast ascended on high; Thou hast led captivity captive; Thou hast received gifts for men" (Ps. lxviii. 18). That supply of the Spirit was meant for the Church to be erected and organized; and it was fitly bestowed after the ascension on those for whom the Spirit was purchased as well as destined.

When we follow the sequence of events on the day of Pentecost, we see the Spirit acting in a twofold way—as the Spirit of conviction, and as the Spirit of adoption. He *convinced* the multitude *of their sin* and guilt, that they might seek repentance and forgiveness. To minds penitent and receiving baptism for the remission of sins, He was further promised as the Spirit of adoption : " Ye shall receive the gift of the Holy Ghost " (Acts ii. 38).   The order of salvation is repentance, forgiveness, and then the inhabitation of the Holy Ghost as the Spirit of adoption.

We are now brought to the ACTUAL MISSION of the Comforter.   Previous to His resurrection Christ had been the Receiver of the Spirit, and the Spirit was mainly limited to Christ's own Person.   With His resurrection the day came when He was to be the GIVER of the Spirit, when He was to show that the great result of His atoning death was the power of bestowing the Spirit upon others ;—a blessing so momentous that it may be described as that in which all other blessings are included.   This is the grandest display of Christ's exaltation—the culminating point—arguing at once His reward and His divine dignity.   For no mere servant could occupy the position of conferring upon others the gift of the Spirit, who is a divine Person.   He only who had put away sin by the sacrifice of Himself, and who Himself had the Spirit to bestow, could exercise the authority of sending Him.   The Spirit was given by the risen Christ to equip His ministers, and to be the all-directing as well as sanctifying power in the kingdom of heaven which was now set up, as had been expressly promised by the Old Testament prophets, and by the Lord Himself (Ps. lxviii. 19 ; John xiv. 16).

As Mediator, the Lord Jesus was anointed with the Holy Spirit for the execution of all His offices, and for the performance of all His meritorious work.   The RIGHT TO SEND THE SPIRIT into the hearts of fallen men was acquired by His atonement.   Many, indeed, had been saved in virtue of His covenant engagement from the day of the first promise.   The operations of the Spirit in every epoch presuppose the vicarious sacrifice or the meritorious work on which depended the right of giving the Holy Spirit in any case : " He redeemed us that (ἵνα) we might receive the promise of the Spirit by faith "

(Gal. iii. 14). The promised Spirit followed the great work of cancelling the curse as the effect follows the cause. Countless multitudes had been saved on the ground of the coming sacrifice. But the precision of the language which connects the gift of the Spirit with the finished work of Christ is never forgotten, and the Holy Spirit was never spoken of as actually SENT while the old economy stood.

The Holy Ghost, supplying Christ's humanity with light and strength for His mediatorial work, was, according to the divine order, only carrying out the will of the Son, and interposing His power to execute the intimations of the Son. The Spirit's operations revealed the will and purpose of the Son.

The power of WORKING MIRACLES was also derived from the Holy Spirit, though the authority flowed from Christ Himself. The Holy Spirit is described as acting in Christ's prophetical office in the same way as in the apostles and prophets. He performed miracles : He showed that the kingdom of God was come; and I may add that the distinction which Peter employs when he uses the expression, " anointed with the Holy Ghost and with power," may refer to both gifts—to the sanctifying as well as to the miraculous works (Acts x. 38).

From the statements already adduced in reference to Christ's unction for all His offices, it sometimes appears as if He were in the subordinate position of needing direction, aid, and miraculous power for the purposes of His mission ; at other times He is said to GIVE THE SPIRIT and to SEND THE SPIRIT, as if the Spirit's operations were subordinated to the Son. It is, however, evident from the whole tenor of Scripture, that there was a conjoined mission in which the Son and Spirit acted together for man's restoration, according to the well-known order of operation in the Trinity.

Every one who has been taught the meaning of that anointing from which Christ derives His name, will cordially concur in the beautiful remark of Dr. M'Crie when he says that "next to THE GRACE OF UNION, THE GRACE OF UNCTION is the most wonderful object of contemplation." Nor are the remarks of Bishop Horsley less worthy of notice when he says that "THE UNINTERRUPTED PERFECT COMMERCE of His human soul with the Divine Spirit was THE EFFECT and privilege of that mysterious conjunction."

LECTURE III.

THE WORK OF THE SPIRIT IN THE INSPIRATION OF PROPHETS AND APOSTLES.

ONE of the great and far-reaching questions raised among us is : Are we to take Scripture as a supernatural production of the Holy Spirit ? and are we to believe on the AUTHORITY of Scripture as a Revelation ? What was once deemed axiomatic is turned into a question for debate. It is openly avowed by many, that Christianity must either be placed on another basis than that of AUTHORITY or pass away; that science now looks down upon it in the old position, and that, unless it gain for itself a legitimate place in the sphere of reason and conscience, or in the speculative field, the minds of men, who are represented as unsettled and slipping away from it, will soon come to open revolt. The claim for the autonomy of the human mind in the field of theology, and an opposition to all authority, are marked features in the current opinions of the day. This is what is called modern thought; and I wish to survey it at the point where the unsettling current has been rushing in. The assumption of our day is that Revelation is to be restricted to the divine facts and words of the personal Redeemer, apart from any inspiration on the mind of those who composed the records ; in other words, that the Historical Revelation is to be wholly isolated from the Biblical Revelation. This disjunction of the one from the other is, in fact, the centre-point of the new Theology, and it is at the widest remove from all Patristic and Protestant theology which leant on Theopneustic authority. It is of paramount importance to form a correct estimate of its character.

The attempt made during this generation to sunder the Revelation of Historic fact from the Biblical Revelation, and to treat the Bible as a literary work alone, apart from every other consideration, is the most marked feature of modern thought, and the ground on which the so-called autonomy of the human mind claims to be emancipated from outward control. That is the source of all the great conflicts of our time, and the breach in the embankment through which the tide of error is sweeping in. To the Protestant Church, holding Scripture as HER FORMAL PRINCIPLE, as Justification by faith alone is HER MATERIAL PRINCIPLE, a compromise or concession on the authority of Scripture, or, which amounts to the same thing, an admission that it is but the human document of a revelation, and that the Bible is nothing more than the literary work of men, carries with it consequences the most disastrous. To make the Bible merely a literary work, however historically accurate, forfeits all appeal to it as the court of last resort, and only opens the floodgates of uncertainty and error. A surrender of Biblical Revelation is fatal.

We purpose to treat the question of Inspiration in a concrete way, which we think is the only way fitted to produce conviction and ensure assent—that is, in connection with the supernaturally gifted Prophets and Apostles.

In the Old and New Testament we find two kinds of gifts, dividing the community into two classes. We find (1) the ORDINARY SAVING GIFTS in the religious body, or people of God : (2) the EXTRAORDINARY GIFTS for official service. The latter created duties rather than dignities ; and the authority conferred on their possessors was only a further obligation. They were the necessary endowments for qualifying office-bearers called to administer the covenant, and in whom God spoke (Heb. i. 1).

It may be proper to show that the extraordinary gifts were

intended to fit men for office ; that they were but temporary ;
and that they were conspicuously displayed, now here and
now there.

Extraordinary gifts were given from the earliest times to
the recipients of the divine oracles, first to Moses, through
whom the law was given, and then to the cycle of prophets
who spoke the word of God to their own generation, or wrote
it, by divine command, for all coming times.   These gifts
were intended to show men generally, that in receiving their
word as a divine message, they were not misled by cunningly
devised fables.   The Spirit is referred to as the author of
these supernatural gifts (Heb. ii. 4) ; and they ceased when
no longer needed for the great end which they were intended
to subserve.

1. As to prophecy, it was not, as some will have it, mere
religious enthusiasm, or the exaltation of the religious sentiment.   Though Abraham is called a prophet (Gen. xx. 7), and
so were all by whom the Spirit uttered a divine communication, we find it was specially from the time of Samuel that a
series of PROPHETS, with a commission supernaturally accredited, appeared in succession, down to the time of Malachi, to
recall Israel to their law,—to reprove the nation's vices, to
declare the divine judgments,—and to proclaim the greatest
events in the world's history — the incarnation, atonement,
and gracious reign of the Messiah.   This gift of prophecy was
the chief gift of Old Testament times ; and an act of divine
immediate intervention conveyed that gift to those who were
invested with it.

The Holy Spirit is referred to as THE SPIRIT OF PROPHECY
in that very variously expounded passage of the Apocalypse :
ἡ γὰρ μαρτυρία τοῦ Ἰησοῦ ἐστι τὸ πνεῦμα τῆς προφητείας :
" the testimony of Jesus is the Spirit of prophecy " (Rev. xix.
10) ; the meaning of which appears not so much in the order
of the words given in the Authorized Version, as in their trans-
position, which the Greek warrants and the sense demands,

thus: "the Spirit of prophecy is the testimony of Jesus."[1] The expression: "the Spirit of prophecy," according to the uniform usage where a genitive follows the term Spirit, intimates that the Spirit spoke in all the prophets; and the import of the clause is, that the scope or aim of all prophecy was to testify of Jesus (John xv. 26, v. 39).

The nature of the Spirit's operation on the prophet's mind is further explained by Peter when he thus declares, in full harmony with all that the historic outline of the Old Testament narrative contains: "No prophecy of the Scripture was of any private excitation ($\epsilon\pi\iota\lambda\upsilon\sigma\epsilon\omega\varsigma$); but holy men of God spoke as they were moved by the Holy Ghost" (2 Pet. i. 21). The antithesis intended to be conveyed by the two clauses is, —no private impulse, but a moving influence of the Spirit. The allusion of the words, though variously interpreted, seems to be to the mission of the prophets, to the removal of the barriers, or to the opening of the lists when they started on their race; for they ran only when the Spirit sent them (Jer. xxiii. 21). They remained silent till they received the Spirit's communication, or the unmistakable impulse of the Spirit (Jer. xx. 17); in other words, they did not start till the lists were opened, and they were told to run. The Spirit did not give them this gift as a permanent habit, or as so much reserved wealth from which they could draw at their discretion. He gave them light and divine communications for the official purpose which all inspiration subserved only at certain times; and He so moved them that they could not but speak or write what the Spirit enjoined them to declare. The prophetic Spirit imparted a supernatural illumination in virtue of which they understood fully what they were commissioned to announce,—whether things past, present, or to come,—beyond the range of the unaided human faculties.

---

[1] See to this effect a dissertation by Stade, published under the auspices of Mosheim, *de Spiritu Propheticæ de Christo testante*, 1734. The purport of the verse is thus put: "ita ego quoque jussus sum testem Christi agere."

As to the mode of communication to the human mind, whether given by dream, vision, or ecstasy, we should not attempt to scrutinize it; partly because we have had no experience of the thing, partly because our faculties are not commensurate to the task.

2. The supernatural gifts in the New Testament Church were very abundant, but all culminated in THE APOSTLES, who were the organs of Christ's revelation to the Church, and who were invested with an ecumenical commission which extended to all lands, and which endures through all time. The Church is built on the apostles, and will continue to stand on that foundation till the second advent. As to those supernatural gifts which the Spirit thus dispensed in the apostolic Churches in the most ample fulness, according to His will, even beyond the circle of the apostles, we find that to one He gave the gift of knowledge, to another the gift of healing, to another the working of miracles, to another prophecy, and the like. These gifts were limited to individuals, and not universal; they were temporary, so that one might possess them to-day and want them to-morrow; and they were by no means co-extensive with the possession of divine grace. That rich supply of supernatural or miraculous gifts with which the apostolic Churches were adorned, was a standing pledge and sign that the inward miracle of inspiration continued. The cessation of these gifts, after they had served their purpose, was a significant fact. But during the whole time of their continuance, these miraculous gifts, and especially THE GIFT OF TONGUES,—that is, the gift of speaking in languages which had never been learned,—were a conclusive proof and illustration that the miracle of inspiration was still present in the Church.

These extraordinary gifts of the Spirit were no longer needed when the canon of Scripture was closed. Up to that time they were an absolute necessity. They are now no longer so. Nor is the Church warranted to expect their restoration, or to desire prophetic visions, immediate revelations, or miraculous gifts, either in public or in private, beyond, or besides, the all-perfect canon of Scripture.   The Church of Rome, which still claims these extraordinary gifts, is to that extent injurious to the Spirit as the author of Scripture.   And enthusiastic sects[1] that cherish the belief of their restoration, or an expectation to that effect, have not learned or duly pondered how great a work of the Spirit has been completed and provided for the Church of all times in the gift of the Holy Scriptures.

When they began to be abused for purposes of display on the one side, or of envy on the other, they were put in a secondary place ; and a more excellent way was presented to men's attention.   Then the saving graces—faith, hope, love— were so commended and preferred as to eclipse the most imposing extraordinary gifts (1 Cor. xii. 31 ff.).   The inestimable blessings of regenerating grace, and of true spiritual life, were set forth as of paramount value far beyond all the transitory gifts.

The presence of miraculous gifts in both dispensations served a twofold purpose.   They were (1) an indubitable proof of a supernatural revelation from God to man in general (Heb. ii. 4) ; (2) they were a reliable pledge as well as elucidation of the inward miracle of inspiration.   The man who possessed them, that is, who was invested with what was in its own nature miraculous, and who gave evidence that he could at proper seasons reveal the future, was entitled with authority to say : " Thus saith the Lord."

When it is alleged that the restoration of these gifts is not an unwarrantable expectation, the answer is, they are no longer required.   The closing of the canon has superseded their necessity and value, inasmuch as the Church possesses in the Scriptures all that they were intended to accredit and

---

[1] *E.g.* the Montanists of the second century and the Irvingites of the nineteenth century.

commend.   Beyond the written word which was completed before the apostles passed away, the Spirit has no further revelations or immediate communications of the divine will to impart.   The extraordinary gifts, limited as they were to the primitive Church, wholly passed away, because they were no longer necessary.

When it is argued by Irving and his followers that they have been lost by the Church's fault, and that they would be restored to the believing expectation of the Church,—if she had faith to wait for them in prayer,—the answer is, that the prophecy of Joel was fulfilled at Pentecost and during the entire apostolic age.   To the allegation that these gifts ought still to be possessed, we reply by denying the supposition that the miraculous gifts were to continue.   What would they accredit if the canon is closed ?   Had they been intended as a part of the Church's chartered rights, they would not have been withheld for nearly two thousand years.   The link with a miraculous past would have been kept up.   But they had served their purpose.

The proposition which I shall here endeavour to set forth and vindicate is the following : *The Holy Spirit supplied prophets and apostles, as chosen organs, with gifts which must be distinguished from ordinary grace, to give forth in human forms of speech a revelation which must be accepted as the word of God in its whole contents, and as the authoritative guide for doctrine and duty.*

This proposition I will now assert and elucidate.   But let me at the outset obviate a difficulty as to the order in which we take up the question.   It has been objected by certain writers that we reason in a circle here, first proving the truth of Scripture by its unerring inspiration, and then establishing inspiration by Scripture.   It is not so.   We proceed by a strictly inductive method.   In the whole argument, which goes to establish the fact of a divine revelation as well as the genuineness, authenticity, and canonical authority of Scripture, nothing is assumed. We neither forestall historic proof nor dispense with rational evidence. All this is completed before the question of inspiration is even taken into consideration. It is only when these points have been conclusively proved and established, that we interrogate the books committed to the Church as the oracles of God on the question of their higher origin. The evidence from MIRACLES and PROPHECY, which accredits a divine commission, accredits also the inspiration to which the apostles laid claim.

As to the credentials supplied by MIRACLES, wrought as they were by the same Spirit, who is the Spirit of revelation and the Spirit of prophecy, it must be held that the miracles performed by Moses, by the prophets, and by the apostles, furnish undeniable evidence that they spoke and wrote by divine inspiration. It is a first principle to which no valid exception can be taken, that the Holy Spirit, the divine author of all miracles, will by no means give countenance to an impostor, or give a divine sanction to falsehood. The Deists and sceptics generally are so well aware of this, that they have left no means untried to invalidate this proof. As it would carry us away from our subject to enter into this topic at large, I shall only touch its salient points. Whether miracles prove a commission to reveal a divine message and the truth of the doctrine IMMEDIATELY or MEDIATELY, has been debated with much acuteness. I unhesitatingly attach myself to the view which asserts that miracles immediately prove the truth of the doctrine and the inspiration of the messenger.

If, therefore, any one declared,—as Moses and the prophets declared in the Old Testament, and as Christ and His apostles declared in the New Testament,—that he was divinely commissioned to perform miracles in attestation of his doctrine, the acceptance of their testimony with unhesitating confidence was only a compliance with divine authority. They were organs of a heaven-attested revelation, speaking and writing with divine inspiration; for God evidently spoke in them

(Heb. i. 1). They who attempt, as many now attempt in a more open or more modified way, to expel the miracles from Scripture, are virtually endeavouring — whether they consciously mean it or not—to make the writers false witnesses, and to undermine all certainty.

Another test of not less validity than the former is the evidence derived from PROPHECY, which is A MIRACLE OF KNOWLEDGE as the other is A MIRACLE OF POWER. The great test of a true prophet was that the prediction came to pass (Deut. xviii. 22). As this test, however, could not be applied by his contemporaries, if the matter were remote, we find that those credentials which established him as a prophet of the Lord were based on the fulfilment of things which could be known by experience. In proof of this we have only to recall the predictions of Moses, Samuel, Elijah, and Elisha, in reference to things near at hand, and verified before the eyes of their contemporaries. We have only to recall such near predictions as Micaiah's (1 Kings xxii. 28) or Isaiah's (Isa. vii. 4, xxxvii. 34); and when they were summoned to write, so vividly had all been presented to their minds, and so accurately had all been retained in their memory, that we find a Jeremiah, at the end of twenty years, making the selection of the matter and digesting it into form by the Spirit's guidance in a manner succinct enough to prevent the book from exceeding reasonable bounds; and we must clearly hold that thoughts and words were, as it were, fused and molten together, or formed and shaped together (Jer. xxxvi. 32).

As for the apostles in the New Testament, it is only necessary to recall their opportunities and the terms of their commission, to see that they were armed with historic information obtained in the Lord's immediate presence, and subsequently brought back, as occasion required, to their remembrance by the Holy Spirit, who also furnished the communication of new truths, which were supernaturally

imparted as the necessities of the Church required.   Their
authority, accordingly, was the same with that of Christ,
because He took all the responsibility of their official
teaching upon Himself, when He said: " He that heareth
you heareth me " (Matt. x. 40).

It is important to keep in mind, that while the Holy Spirit
is the author of supernatural revelation with all its accompaniments, adjuncts, and evidences, there are two aspects of
the question—one IN FACT and one IN WORD.[1]   The former is
the objective manifestation of the Son of God; the latter is
the written word prepared by men whom the Spirit specially
called and endowed.   THE PERSONAL SELF - MANIFESTATION
preceded ; the WRITTEN WORD followed.   The former conveyed
the revelation to the minds of prophets and apostles ; the
latter conveyed it in appropriate terms from their minds to
the Church at large, securing for it such a safe communication as became the oracles of God.

Both operations were from the Holy Spirit.   Revelation
always existed in GREAT FACTS, with an appended explanation
in spoken or written words.   In these facts we find the
various attributes of God and the aspects of His moral
government exhibited to the faith of the Church and for
the enlargement of her knowledge.   And THE REVELATION
OF WORD showed how the facts answered this purpose.
Revelation of fact and revelation of word, emanating from
one and the same Spirit of God, were conjoined from the
beginning.   From the time of the fall, the types and prophecies—foreshadowing and predicting the great sacrifice—
opened up a revelation of fact in due time to be accomplished, of which also a thousand deliverances in the history
of the Church were the pledges.   To this revelation of fact
the patriarchs looked forward, just as we look back to the
accomplished reality.   In the New Testament the revelation
is embodied in THE HISTORIC FACTS of the incarnation, atone-

[1] See *Studien und Kritiken* for 1861, H. 1.

ment, and resurrection of Christ, and in THE PERFECT NARRA-
TIVE or record of these facts in the written word.

Of this written revelation the Holy Spirit is the author.
The fact that the personal Spirit not only conveyed the
truth to the writer's mind, but found adequate expression
for it, involved a certain limitation or abasement in condescending to speak in human forms of speech. We may
not unfitly say that, as God is said to humble Himself to
behold the things that are in the earth (Ps. cxiii. 6), and as
the Son humbled Himself when He became obedient to
death (Phil. ii. 8), so the Holy Spirit abases Himself in
giving His message, however lofty the matter, in a form of
speech which often resembles a mother's accommodation to
the capacity of an infant. And this was necessary in order
that the written word might, without constraint or difficulty,
pass into the articulate speech and the written language of
every nation on the surface of the globe.

I have referred to divine fact as underlying the inspired
word, because the principal argument at present urged against
inspiration—as is well known to those who know German
theology—is, that the revelation is not in the documents or
in the written word at all. It is argued that the latter are
mere literary productions, composed under the same conditions
with ordinary writings, or differing from them only in the
circumstance that the writers were holier men; and hence
they have no reserve or fear in permitting any liberty to be
taken with the Scriptures. They fall back on the fact.
They say the revelation of fact is secure. This mediating
theology, which took its rise from Schleiermacher, and has
been represented on this point by Tholuck, Rothe, and the
great body of German divines, allows a revelation in historic
facts, but denies the Biblical revelation in any true acceptation of the term. In a word, the historic revelation of fact
is isolated from the book-Revelation. The books, according
to them, are no more than any other narrative digested by

pious men——mere literary productions having no supernatural origin whatever. The revelation, according to this theory, is not in the records at all, which, in fact, are correct and trust-worthy just in proportion as the writers had access or had not access to reliable information, and who are by no means supposed to be exempt from the infirmities, mistakes, and even moral obliquities into which men, acting from ordinary motives, are betrayed.

The Biblical revelation, if capable of proof at all, can be established only as a historically guaranteed fact. All other modes of proof which have been made use of have already been found unserviceable. Thus the arguments drawn from the necessity of inspiration are of no weight, because the *a priori* style of reasoning is carried into a sphere to which it cannot fitly be applied. Arguments of this sort, which can be set aside as nothing more than assumptions, are of little value. As nothing but DIVINE TESTIMONY can assure us of A DIVINE FACT, we must, after being satisfied with the validity of the credentials, interrogate revelation itself. The authority of the Old Testament, confirmed by a vast array of miracles and by the evidence of accomplished prophecy, was accepted not only by the Old Testament Church, but by our Lord and His apostles; and all this passed over into the Christian Church with a divine sanction before the New Testament literature, properly so called, was prepared for the Church's use.

As to the New Testament books, to which we shall now more specially refer, we may affirm that it is only on the authority and credibility of a divine teacher——the Messiah Himself——that the proof of the theopneustic character of the New Testament Scriptures rests. The Lord Jesus said it, and His guarantee or promise secured its historic certainty. He promised to the apostles, that for the delivery of the communi-cations made to them by His oral teaching or subsequent revelations, they should be supernaturally guided by the Holy

Ghost the Comforter.   We conclude, accordingly, that they
were so guided.   The cogency of this deduction needs no confirmation.   The theopneustic character of the apostles' instruction, whether historical or doctrinal, whether oral or written,
belongs to a class of extraordinary or miraculous operations of
the Holy Spirit.   They belong to the invisible miracle, and
Luthardt well observes: " He who says revelation says
miracle, and miracles cannot be explained."

From this it follows that we need make no attempt to
prove the inspiration of apostles to a theological disputant
who sees in Jesus only an ordinary human teacher, or one,
like the old prophets, only under the general influence of the
Holy Spirit.   With such an opponent it is vain to debate on
this subject; and this is the case with a considerable number
of those who are opposed to supernatural or plenary inspiration.
They recognise in Jesus only a man of like passions with ourselves, on whom the Deity wrought, and in whom the Deity
dwelt, in a peculiar way, by providences and influences of an
exceptional character, but not the only-begotten Son.   But,
on the contrary, he who acknowledges the Lord Jesus as the
Messiah, and as the Only-begotten of the Father, cannot for
a moment entertain a doubt as to the truth of any of His
promises or declarations.   Hence the only point of which it is
possible to make a question is—Whether the promise of the
Spirit's inspiration was actually made, and whether He
promised it in the sense which we have put upon His words.

It is conceded that the proof of the promise as to the
mission of the Comforter for imparting this theopneustic gift
must be drawn from the recorded sayings of Christ in a few
passages which we can analyse and examine (viz. Matt. x. 19
and Luke xii. 14 ; John xiv. 16, xv. 26, xvi. 7, 14).   These
passages — spoken by our Lord in immediate view of the
commission which the apostles were to discharge, first within
the cities of Israel, and next on a far more extended scale—
contain express assurances that they should receive the Holy

Ghost, and be qualified by the Holy Ghost in the exercise of a specially conferred gift, to discharge the duties of their mission in propagating or spreading the gospel among the nations; that they should receive from the Spirit of God a mouth and wisdom for the purpose of directing them when summoned before governors and kings [1] HOW and WHAT they should speak on every occasion; that the Spirit should recall the words of Christ as they were originally spoken to their remembrance; that the Spirit should further instruct them on points which could not for the present be comprehended; and that the Comforter, as a peculiar teacher, should descend upon them, and equip them in such a way that they would be endued with power from on high.

An objection has been made, indeed, to the employment of those passages as a proof of the theopneustic character of their writings, on the allegation that *the men* might have the Spirit, but that the tenor of the promise does not in so many words extend to *their writings*, which might be prepared like any other literary productions. The objection has been frequently repeated by one theological school after another. The passages, it is said, do not contain a word to prove that in the composition of their writings the apostles were favoured with any higher guidance of the Spirit. It is contended that the Lord merely names occasions when they might be summoned unprepared, or under embarrassing circumstances, to give an oral statement of their beliefs and Messianic convictions; and hence it is alleged that this animating promise of the immediate operation of His Spirit and of His special guidance in arduous times might not extend to their written statements. Nay, it is argued by way of challenge: How can it be warrantable to hold that the promise extended to a wholly different case, of which at the time when the words were uttered the apostles could have no anticipation?

---

[1] μὴ μεριμνήσητε πῶς ἢ τί λαλήσητε (Matt. x. 19).

The objection now stated might have some appearance of plausibility if that was the only passage, and if there were no other passages descriptive of the extraordinary gift of inspiration conferred on the apostles, except where the promise was in some sort limited. But that is not the case with the passages preserved to us by John, where Christ speaks with a certain indefinite generality. He promised that after His departure to the Father they should enjoy the peculiar teaching and guidance of the Comforter, who should permanently abide with them, at once to teach them all things and lead them into all truth. We do not need to prove again, that by the Holy Ghost the Comforter we are to understand a divine instructor, helper, or patron who should not only qualify them for their commission, but impart a full insight into Christ's religion. He was to come as a divine Person to impart a permanent theopneustic gift, which was to be exercised in every department of apostolic activity. They were to be under the constant influence and higher guidance of the Spirit for all official duty. We are fully warranted to conclude that if Christ promised the immediate guidance of the Comforter as often as they were called, in their capacity of apostles, to give instruction in the facts and doctrines of His religion, He unquestionably comprehended within the scope of that promise the case of giving religious instruction through the medium of written documents addressed to the various Churches of the apostolic age and to the Church of all succeeding times. And *the apostles, in prefixing their name and office to their various Epistles*, intimated this fact to them and to us. As the theopneustic gift was permanent, while they continued to discharge their functions, we must suppose them to have been as much under divine guidance in the composition of their writings as in their oral instruction. The validity of this inference cannot be denied or disputed.

The opponents of Biblical revelation, accordingly, have

recourse to another mode of assault. Some expressly deny that in the passages to which we appeal anything is promised even remotely approaching to the theopneustic gift. This is the favourite modern theory. It is maintained that nothing more is meant than the ordinary influence of grace, and that our Lord and His apostles never thought of a special higher power, or of IMMEDIATE divine inspiration imparted by the Comforter the Holy Ghost. The recent exegesis holds that Christ promised no more than the common supply of divine grace and the ordinary concurrence of divine Providence ; and that it is unwarrantable to explain the words of any extra-ordinary immediate assistance in the way of plenary inspiration, or in the exercise of a theopneustic gift. In reply to this, it may suffice to say that we have only to reflect on the circumstances and condition of the apostles at the time when the Lord uttered the words, to be convinced that, according to the usage and scope of language, it is unwarrantable to refer those memorable promises as to the Holy Spirit's operations on their minds either to ordinary grace, or to the enlargement of their minds in the natural leadings of Providence. The Lord Jesus was preparing the disciples in these later promises for the approaching separation, when they should be left without the visible guidance and immediate direction they had heretofore enjoyed. They had up to that moment turned to Him in every difficulty, distrusting their own wisdom, and willing to be led. And as they would be troubled and paralyzed at His death, He promised another guide, the Comforter, who should be to them what He had been, and who was permanently to abide with them.

In the proposition laid down, it was affirmed that prophets and apostles were supplied by the Spirit with gifts which must be distinguished from ordinary grace. The modern doctrine maintains the opposite of this ; and the advocates of the mediating theology agree in the denial of it. Dr. Rothe, who is usually represented as the author of a conclusive discussion on the subject, labours to make out that the inspiration of the Biblical writers is identical with the spiritual illumination imparted to every Christian.   He limits the aid of the Spirit to the work of enlightening their minds to apprehend the objective revelation, but does not place it in the immediate production of a divine message, or of religious knowledge for officially guiding and directing others.   But inspiration, whether found in the Old Testament prophets or in the New Testament apostles, must be distinguished from common spiritual illumination, if we are not minded, in the indulgence of mere prepossessions and theories, to confound what Scripture has plainly separated.   The modern identification of the two must be denied if we take into account either the distinction of natural and supernatural, ordinary and extraordinary gifts, or the purpose for which the latter were expressly given.   The object of the Spirit in conferring the purely personal illumination was to enable men involved in corruption and darkness to appropriate the offered grace of the gospel.   The object of the Holy Spirit in conferring inspiration, on the other hand, was OFFICIAL, to qualify prophets and apostles to deliver a divine communication unmingled with foreign elements.   It is only necessary to appeal, in proof of this, to the terms of the commission with which they were invested.

As to the Old Testament prophets, their commission, as well as their official messages, is sufficiently apparent from the preface commonly prefixed to their communications : " Thus saith the Lord."   And we cannot examine their lofty, and frequently awful, announcements without perceiving that they had received their intimations as to the future in so many words.   Often they did not themselves comprehend them, and had to inquire and search what the Spirit, which was in them, did signify (1 Pet. i. 11).   And they were held bound, under the penalty of death, to fulfil to the letter what the Spirit enjoined, as appears from the sad end of the unnamed prophet, who had been sent to cry against the altar in Bethel (1 Kings xiii. 21 ff.).

In their oral communications to the people, to kings and princes, they seem to have had a copious flow of discourse, or a brief and condensed message according to the peculiarity of the times and occasions.

When we inquire whether divine action was suspended or withdrawn from the apostles in the execution of their office, we find—(1) that the promises given to them went far beyond the idea of their being left to the exercise of their own wisdom; (2) that miracles and supernatural gifts in all their rich variety abode with them to the end of their career. And these miraculous gifts were signs and pledges of the unseen miracle of plenary inspiration upon their minds. The following considerations will suffice to prove that the theopneustic gift is not to be reduced to the level of ordinary grace :—

1. The theory which merges the distinction between ordinary and extraordinary gifts of the Spirit, loses sight of the divine sovereignty which the entire Scripture presupposes as to God's speaking by chosen organs to His Church (Heb. i. 1). All believers, it is true, receive in the same way the renewing of the Holy Ghost and the salvation of the gospel. But it was not so with the communication of the supernatural gifts. Let me illustrate this by an example. When Peter said to the impotent man: "In the name of Jesus Christ of Nazareth, rise up and walk," we trace the clearest evidence of a divine communication (Acts iii. 6). When he said again: "Æneas, Jesus Christ maketh thee whole: arise, and make thy bed" (ix. 34), we see such an intimation conveyed by the Spirit to the apostle's mind, that he was left in no doubt as to the issue. He fully believed and expected that the words, which were divinely inspired and prophetic, would no sooner be uttered than they would be accompanied with the miraculous result which followed.

There we see the invisible inspiration and the visible sign, the latter the pledge of the former. We can trace a divine communication or invisible miracle on Peter's mind, as well as the visible miracle in the immediate cure,—a miracle of knowledge and a miracle of power conjoined, a prophecy and an accomplishment united. Without adducing other instances of the same thing scattered over the whole page of revelation, let it suffice to say that in all such miracles the theopneustic gift was announced and attested by the supernatural fact. The cessation of those miraculous gifts at the close of the apostolic age — when they had served the important function to which we have referred in the infancy of the Church — was a noteworthy and significant fact. But, during the whole period of their continuance, they were a sign and pledge, as well as an explanation, of the presence and reality of the theopneustic gift. The theory which identifies the composition of Scripture with the exercise of ordinary grace, is burdened with insuperable difficulties. The design of referring all to a general law, is to make the matter more acceptable to the understanding. It is not by general rationalistic reasonings, however, that historic facts are to be determined; and this point must be decided as a matter of fact.

The conclusion to which we come, therefore, is, that the gift of inspiration *differs in kind*, and not merely in measure, from the operation of ordinary grace. We have ample evidence to prove that the apostles, as the organs of Christ's revelation to the Church, were the subjects of a supernatural intervention absolutely unique, and essentially distinct in kind, from the general experience of Christian disciples. The gift of plenary inspiration was limited to individuals selected by divine sovereignty, and temporary in duration. It terminated with the closing of the canon, that is, when the revelation was completed. The other is common to all true Christians.

2. It must be further remarked, that the theory which makes inspiration identical with ordinary grace, fails to account for the AUTHORITY which Scripture uniformly claims and asserts for itself as the word of God, and which the Church, Jewish and Christian, has always with one consent ascribed to it. If the prophets of the Old Testament, or the apostles in the New Testament, had nothing of direct and divine communication essentially distinguishing their words and writings from those of ordinary disciples, it is not possible to give any explanation of the divine authority always ascribed to their announcements as distinct from those of ordinary men. The declaration on the part of the prophets when they said: " Thus saith the Lord," or on the part of apostles when they introduced their Epistles with the words : " Paul, an apostle," " Peter, an apostle of Jesus Christ," not only implies that they derived their commission from above, but intimates : " He that despiseth, despiseth not man, but God, who hath also given to us His Holy Spirit " (1 Thess. iv. 8).

3. And what would necessarily follow if, according to the current German theory, inspiration were identical with ordinary illumination ? A simple *reductio ad absurdum* will here suffice. If the difference between the two was merely in degree, and not in kind, the theopneustic gift must be regarded as universal and coincident with true discipleship. But every one perceives that this is not the case. More than that, revelation on such a supposition would have no finality, but be an ever increasing quantity with new developments without limit. Nor do we see how, on the theory which we impugn, extravagant or enthusiastic developments could be either reduced to a standard or stopped. If Scripture were not viewed as a completed revelation, with an absolute finality, we should be compelled to canvass in every age the claims of such growths as Montanism, or Irvingism, or modern Romanism, whose ecclesiastical organs, as is

proved by the Vatican decrees, lay claim to a self-developing advance in doctrine, which asserts itself as equivalent to a sort of inspiration. By the finality of apostolic doctrine, we can nip all this in the bud. We conclude, therefore, that it is a vain attempt to identify illumination common to all believers, with inspiration peculiar to prophets and apostles. The latter are said to speak with the same authority as Christ Himself (Luke x. 16), which they could do only on the ground of official commission, not on the ground of personal illumination.

I said, moreover, in the proposition laid down, that supernatural revelation was given *in human forms of speech.* This is one significant proof of the divine condescension of the Holy Spirit, that instead of speaking in an elevated style of diction, and in the communication only of ideas above the capacity or range of the bulk of mankind, or merely for cultured and philosophic minds, He speaks from one mind to another in easy, clear, and perspicuous language, level to the apprehension of all tribes and nations. This is the glory of the Spirit's work of revelation, however profound the things themselves may be to which the revelation refers. It is not necessary to define the MODE OF INSPIRATION, but only to assert the divine fact. We take the historic fact; but we decline every attempt to explain the inscrutable mode. That the theopneustic gift was imparted, is evident from the explicit statement that all Scripture is God-inspired (2 Tim. iii. 16), and that holy men of God spoke as they were moved by the Holy Ghost (2 Pet. i. 21). But no finite mind can venture, without presumption, to say how the human faculties concurred and acted with the Spirit's activity in the expression of a divine oracle. So various, in fact, was the mode of His divine communications, that it is impossible to frame a theory which either takes in all the facts or exhibits the manifold variety of ways in which the Almighty Spirit, who alone has the key to the human heart and to all its powers, was pleased to communicate His will.   We repudiate all attempts to explain THE MODE in which revelation was conveyed to the human mind, or by inspired men to the mind of others.   We conserve the miracle and the mystery.   All such theories as that of the suggestion, elevation, and guidance or superintendence, propounded by Doddridge and others, only darken counsel by words without knowledge.   With Dr. Chalmers we fully agree when he says : " The important question with us is not the process of the manufacture, but the qualities of the resulting commodity.   The former we hold not to be a relevant, and we are not sure that it is a legitimate inquiry." [1] Our system is to have no system.   We maintain the fact, and leave the mode untouched, because beyond our ken.   The French writers, such as Gaussen, M. d'Aubigné, Monod, Jalaquier, and Remond, write with more reserve and caution than any other class of theologians in modern times.   Thus Gaussen, in the same spirit with Chalmers, said, when taken to task for his admirable book : " My theory," said he, " is to have no theory."   While repudiating the notion that the human element absorbed the divine, and the theory that every word was given by direct dictation, we hold that the only safe and judicious ground to occupy is to maintain the fact, and to regard the mode as inexplicable.   The Scripture, with that reticence which is one of its marked peculiarities, gives no disclosure of the mode which the Holy Ghost adopted.   And on this whole subject, enveloped as it is in inscrutable mystery, we may affirm with confidence that the facts are so various as to be incapable of classification by any investigator ; that the message came in the Old Testament in audible words, in dreams, in visions, in ecstasies or raptures ; and that it came in the New Testament by the Spirit's recalling to memory the things spoken by Christ, and by showing the apostles many things which they could not bear while Christ was with them.   But our ignorance of the method

[1] See his admirable chapter on Inspiration in his *Evidences.*

not only disqualifies us from forming a consistent theory, but actually supplies a source of security and satisfaction.

The Scripture is the word of God, inspired throughout by the Spirit of God in every part, and given in human forms of expression.   We must by no means maintain that the sacred writers were nothing but machines—nay, must be upon our guard against the attempt to define the undefinable.   That a supernatural and miraculous operation prompted holy men to speak as they were moved by the Holy Ghost, and that the mental peculiarity of the writers was not suppressed by the theopneustic gift, as appears from their peculiar style and expression, must be accepted as the two sides of a great truth, which some have attempted to explain by immediate suggestion or dictation.   But it is better not to attempt to explain the inexplicable.   We define not the nature or mode of the miracle or divine intervention; for miracle it was; and Scripture omits all more particular definition beyond the fact that holy men were wrought upon and moved by the Holy Ghost (2 Pet. i. 21).   And we accept its silences as well as its disclosures.   When Scripture stops, we stop.

That there was infallible supernatural guidance, and that this extends to all the canonical books in the Old and New Testament, is undoubted.   But how it acted it would be at once perilous and audacious to define; and a contented nescience is better than a presumptuous knowledge.   The analogy between Christ's Person and the Scriptures has often been adduced, and truly serves as an illustration.   The two-fold nature in the one Person of our Lord is there, and concurring to one result.   But it is not possible to say where the one nature begins and the other ends in the production of the great redemption-work.   His utterances and actions, divine yet human, were the utterances and actions of the God-man.   I repeat, I retain the miracle and the mystery.

Another point laid down by us was, that the *theopneustic gift and Scripture are co - extensive.*   The current theory of the day is the reverse of this. It asserts that a line is to be drawn between Scripture and the word of God; that God's word must be held to mean, not Scripture as we find it, but a certain spiritual kernel or religious substance which is to be extracted by a critical process; that, in a word, the Scripture is but the husk or shell in which the word of God is found, as the quartz is separated from the gold embedded in it.

Though many theologians of this century make this the foundation of their system, there is absolutely nothing to countenance or support it from Genesis to Revelation. And to establish the opposite, it is enough to adduce what Jesus said: "Is it not written in your law, I said, Ye are gods? If He called them gods, to whom *the word of God* came, and *the Scripture* cannot be broken," etc. (John x. 34). That saying of Jesus, containing two conclusive proofs, represents the word of God and the Scripture as identical, and affirms that what is written in the law was spoken by the mouth of God. That twofold testimony to the fact that the theopneustic element and Scripture are co-extensive, is conclusive, and cannot be evaded.

To adduce another out of many passages to the same effect, let me notice that the Apostle Paul uses interchangeably these two expressions: "Scripture has concluded all under sin" (Gal. iii. 22), and "God hath concluded them all in unbelief" (Rom. xi. 12). There, beyond all doubt, we find God and Scripture so identified, that they cannot, on any fair interpretation of the word, be disjoined. Scripture is represented as identical with the mouth of God Himself.

But it may be asked: Does not the Apostle Paul in some of his utterances imply that the theopneustic gift was intermittent? Does he not give countenance to the idea that while some directions given by him were inspired, others were not? Did not Paul give some instructions relating to conjugal duties without having received full supernatural

guidance ? To this I answer, No. The only passage supposed
by some writers to lend countenance to that idea contains
directions relating to marriage, which those who hold a false
notion of inspiration have quite misapprehended and distorted
to suit their theory. When Paul says (1 Cor. vii. 6) : " But
I speak this by permission, not of commandment," some
have supposed that he was merely acting according to the
best of his judgment, but without supernatural guidance. It
is by no means so. The apostle does not speak of a permission or discretion committed to himself, but of a
permission, allowance, or indulgence given to the parties at
Corinth who asked or needed his advice and direction. The
true rendering of the words, as given in the original, is :
" I speak this by allowance or indulgence to you, not of
commandment to you, that is, not as an obligation demanding
compliance on your part" (κατὰ συγγνώμην, οὐ κατ᾿ ἐπιταγήν).

Another passage, not less misapprehended than the former,
is this (1 Cor. vii. 10–12) : " And unto the married I
command, yet not I, but the Lord, Let not the wife depart
from her husband : but if she depart, let her remain
unmarried, or be reconciled to her husband : and let not the
husband put away his wife. *But to the rest speak I, not the
Lord :* If any brother hath a wife that believeth not, and she
be pleased to dwell with him, let him not put her away," etc.
The antithesis is not between commands which were given
by plenary inspiration and commands given according to the
best of the apostle's own judgment. No such contrast is
either referred to or recognised in any part of Scripture.
When the apostle says in the one verse (ver. 10) : " Not I, but
the Lord," the allusion is plainly to be referred to the Lord's
own teaching in the days of His flesh, when the Incarnate
One revealed the Father's mind and will to all who came to
Him or sought direction from Him. When he says in the
other verse (ver. 12) : " But to the rest speak I, not the
Lord," he refers to the fact that he imparts an inspired

communication of the divine will made to the apostle
himself.   There is no difference as to the source of the
announcement, nor any difference of authority as to the
reception which it was to receive in the Church.   Both
utterances were from the Spirit of God, and both of them
were equally divine.

We have thus seen that the composition of Scripture,
though written by a human penman, was in reality carried
into effect by the immediate operation of the Holy Spirit,
who moved the writers to prepare what is left on record for
the Church of all time,—who not only inspired the thoughts,
but sustained and guided the writers till they gave fitting,
full, and adequate expression to the thought in the words [1]
which they were commissioned to put on record,—and who
guarded them from error in the statements which were
actually made.   The truth on this matter is as follows : The
Canonical Books were in substance and form inspired by the
Holy Spirit.   On this fact duly understood and maintained
depends the divine authority of the Scriptures.   It is their
divine origin that grounds their claim to speak with divine
authority.   The peculiar properties of the sacred Scriptures,
such as their SUFFICIENCY, PERSPICUITY, CERTAINTY, PERFEC-
TION, and DIVINE AUTHORITY, are all derived from the fact
that they were given by inspiration of God (2 Tim. iii. 16).
Theologians may distinguish between the word of God

---

[1] We cannot have accurate ideas without precise words, nay, we cannot think
without words. I may add, there was a great outcry made and repeated against
the admirable men who drew up the *formula Consensus Helvetica*, because,
while laying down the position that the divine word was inspired both in THE
MATTER and IN THE WORDS, they referred to the consonants and vowels of the
Hebrew text as within the theopneustic element. They only wished to state
in the most explicit way what we have here said. But those who superficialize
this matter have a far more difficult question for them to solve. The apostles
constantly used the gift of tongues, and in using that gift communicated
intelligibly with men of all nations by speaking languages which they had
never learned (Acts ii. 11). How the Spirit framed their organs to convey their
message to other nations in their own language, is an unfathomable mystery to
our minds, and a marvellous display of omnipotent power. But it was done
during the whole apostolic age (1 Cor. xiv. 18).

spoken and written, but the same divine authority belonged to both.

We do not contend for any system of dictation, direct and immediate, such as the writing of the decalogue at Mount Sinai by the finger of God, or the giving of the words of the Lord's Prayer dictated for the perpetual use of the Church, as the system applicable to all the parts of Scripture alike; for such a theory would be out of keeping with the mental peculiarity easily traceable in the case of all who had a part in the composition of the sacred Scriptures. We do not attempt to delineate either the nature or the manner of the divine intervention; for Scripture omits all explanation of it.

Let me only, in a few sentences, notice the two conflicting schools of the present day, separated as they are by the unspeakably important question which we have been discussing—the one based ON DIVINE AUTHORITY, the other asserting the unbridled AUTONOMY of the human mind.

The theory advocated by the Schleiermacher school, with a zeal worthy of a better cause, simply explodes the revelation of word, and appeals to the revelation of fact. It disjoins what cannot be disjoined. It declares, with an audacity approaching to bravado, that Christianity can dispense with any doctrine of inspiration. On the contrary, the plenary inspiration of the Scriptures may be called a question of existence for the Protestant Church, which is not supported by that reserve power of tradition and of authority which gives coherence and strength to the Romish system. It is obvious that the Protestant Church cannot forego the authority of Scripture, or, which amounts to the same thing, permit it to be regarded as the word of man, without inevitable defeat and ruin. The theological conflicts of the time may be said to hinge for the most part on the view which has been accepted on the doctrine of inspiration, or may be traced back to the opinions which have found currency on this point. In fact, we may affirm that no doctrine has assumed more varying aspects in the Protestant Church,—every change of theological opinion finding its echo or making its vibrations felt in the question of inspiration, on which all other truths ultimately depend.

In conclusion, I will subjoin a brief allusion to some points of moment connected with this topic.

1. The testimony of the Holy Spirit to the Scriptures. This is an operation of the Spirit in the exercise of His applicatory grace, by and through the Scriptures themselves. Whatever enthusiasts may have held, no judicious divine ever asserted that the Spirit gives this internal criterion, or testifies without the word or apart from the word itself. On the contrary, they always, in express terms, declared that we owe this testimony to the efficacy of the Spirit and word conjointly not separately. They ascribed the effect to the Spirit not without the word, but by the word (not *extra aut citra verbum*). The testimony of Scripture about itself, and the efficacious testimony of the Spirit, concur to one result. The enthusiasts who have been wont to call the written word a dead letter, commonly speak of the Spirit as illuminating and regenerating the mind without the word ; and Calvinistic divines have often had occasion to complain of a wrong done them by the Lutherans, in representing them as maintaining an immediate testimony of the Spirit. None of their best divines did so. They held that as the sun is seen by his own light, Scripture is known by its own efficacy and the power of the Holy Spirit.

2. The reception of the Spirit's supernatural inspiration lays the foundation for ALL THE AUTHORITY of revelation. Revelation is accepted and obeyed, not on the ground of its adaptation to my reason or conscience,—though it is in harmony with both,—but on the ground of its supernatural and theopneustic character. Its " Thus saith the Lord " carries with it the demand for prompt unquestioning submission. And though it accredits itself experimentally, it starts from

a heavenly attestation which constrains consent. All true faith, in a word, is from authority, and rests primarily on the evidence of miracles and prophecy. It is this faith of authority that has given rise to all the achievements, devotional ardour, and martyr zeal of the Christian Church.

The other school, known as that of CHRISTIAN CONSCIOUSNESS, advocates the autonomy of the Christian mind and the Church's emancipation from the outward letter of the Scripture. It maintains bold and perilous positions. It maintains (1) that the New Testament is rather the expression of the Christian consciousness and of the Church's life than authoritative revelation; (2) that the Church is rather to be governed by the living progressive Spirit of the Church than by the letter of Scripture; (3) that evangelical doctrine receives new forms and phases from the Christian consciousness and the ever-developing influence of the Spirit.

Schleiermacher, to whom the school owes its origin, broke away from a faith of authority, and assumed the Christian consciousness or pious feeling as the source of knowledge and the matter of his science. He wished to secure for theology an independent territory against philosophy and the higher criticism. And, with a boldness amounting to bravado, the leaders of that school propound the most negative opinions. To affirm that the Christian consciousness is the source of spiritual knowledge is, in fact, a Quaker principle—defective and one-sided. It puts in the place of authority the Spirit within instead of the word without, the only full expression of the Spirit's mind. It furnishes nothing but guesses at truth. The Christian consciousness is not the NORMA NORMANS, but NORMA NORMATA.

LECTURE IV.

THE Spirit's work in the application of the redemption purchased by Christ to the individual will next engage our attention. The work of atonement was finished when Christ expired. The everlasting Righteousness was brought in, and no addition to our title can afterwards be made. But the Spirit must apply what the Lord Jesus completed and purchased. And we must carry with us the thought that the whole interposition of the Spirit of God rests on the ground of the Mediator's finished work. Obstacles stood in the way of the Spirit's return to the human heart of such a kind, that they were insurmountable by any finite resources. But they are put out of the way by Christ's vicarious sacrifice and royal priesthood—that is, by merit and efficacy, or purchase and power.

The efficacious operation of the Spirit presupposes God's sovereign love to individuals, or a personal election. Considered from the true point of view, the electing purpose of God implies that the Spirit's saving efficacy has a special destination, and that it will reach its proper objects. They who interpret the divine word by the primary axiom that all men must share alike, and who impugn the absolute right of God to bestow salvation as men bestow their alms on whom He will by a purely free donation, forget, in their anxiety to be on a friendly footing with the spirit of the age, that the advantage which their theory seems to gain by enlarging the extent of God's love is more than counterbalanced at another point—by lack of efficacy. God's love finds out its objects. It is something far other than a mere benevolent but inefficacious desire in the divine mind which wishes, but does not potentially *will*, the salvation of men.

The presuppositions or postulates of the doctrine of the Spirit, so far as man's necessities are concerned, are the following:—Their impotence for good takes for granted— *first*, their want of the Spirit and of all spiritual life; *secondly*, a subjection to the kingdom of sin and Satan; and *thirdly*, a voluntary aversion to God and rebellion against Him. This suggests a threefold corresponding inquiry: *first*, how is the forfeited presence of the Spirit restored to the human heart, and what effects accompany His return? *secondly*, how are the effectually called translated from the family of Satan into the state of adopted sons? and *thirdly*, how is corrupted nature fully changed and made meet here and hereafter for the love and service of God? The first two points will be considered by us in the present lecture.

I. The forfeited presence of the Spirit is restored by Christ's mediatorship and obedience to God's law in precept and penalty. They who fail to apprehend the atonement, or reduce it to an empty pageant or governmental expedient, in effect remove this mission of the Comforter from its dependence on the finished work of Christ as the basis or meritorious ground of the Spirit's return to the human heart. They connect the atonement, not with the requirements of the divine nature and the inflexible law of God, but with a supposed public justice, which amounts only to a rectoral display or a deterring motive, but secures nothing. They forget, in the zealous advocacy of their universalism, that the Lord God is the only august public worthy of regard, and that there is no other to which the Most High will adapt His administration. But the question is not as to the extent of the atonement, which rests with the divine good pleasure, but as to its validity as a procuring cause or price, which many, in their anxiety to represent it as meant for all, totally denude of its efficacy.   They thus undermine the suretyship, substitution, and imputation on which the gift of the Spirit proceeds.   They explode the deep federal oneness which lies at the foundation of the whole transaction, and secures the inalienable supply of the Spirit to all for whom the atonement was offered.

The nature of man's ruin, as implying the forfeiture of the Spirit, furnishes the *rationale* of the entire doctrine of the Spirit.   Man is no longer a SPIRITUAL BEING, and they who speak in that way of his capacities and powers, and of the condition of human nature as it now is, introduce a form of speech which has no true application to the subject.   Viewed in his unfallen state, of which the renewed man has some faint conception, and of which the Spirit-filled humanity of Jesus was the true image, man might be described as a spiritual being.   But with no propriety of language can the expression SPIRITUAL be applied to man in his fallen state. So far as the expression is intended to obviate the objection that the operations of the Spirit violate the integrity of man's moral nature, the language may be capable of some vindication, because it brings us back to the true idea of anthropology, and because original sin was never understood, except by Flacius, to have become the substance of the man.   But the term "spiritual" has so precise a sense, and is so connected in our language with Biblical usage, that every other acceptation is to be avoided as liable to misconception.

If we delineate men's actual relation to God, they are described as having not the Spirit (Jude 19), and, as the necessary consequence of this, as sensual or natural (1 Cor. ii. 14); in other words, so sunk into animal life that their wisdom is earthly (Jas. iv. 15), and they themselves without God (Eph. ii. 12).

God gave the Spirit to Adam, the earthly and spiritual elements of his constitution being so fully balanced that he was neither preponderantly animal nor absolutely pneumatic, but a living soul occupied in all his faculties by the indwelling Spirit. And had he continued stedfast, or taken the true way, which corresponded with the idea of man, he would have passed in a straight course into the pneumatic or spiritual without tasting of death. But by his apostasy the Spirit departed, and he was left in possession of a mere natural or animal being, having not the Spirit (Jude 19). That the soul is deprived of the Spirit and of all divine light, and that he is not disposed to those objects which the law of God enjoins, is too evident to be questioned. Only conscience is left to act in him along with the dim outline of the moral law, of which the lingering remains may still be traced on every human heart. And it may be said of conscience, that its voice is heard more in accusing than in excusing. It is noteworthy that in the entire earthly life of Jesus there is no mention of conscience, for the obvious reason that He had the full image of God, and received the Spirit not by measure.

Thus detached from his primeval ties by the forfeiture of the Spirit, man follows the natural rather than the spiritual, the human rather than the divine. The religious sentiment gives way in all his course before the prevailing influence of the worldly mind. The wrong choice, which in fact is uniformly adopted, must be traced to a wrong bias; and till the nature is renewed by the restoration of the Spirit, no motive brought to bear on men's minds avails to turn them toward God. Acting from a bias which draws the mind away, they prefer the shadowy to the real, the speculative to the practical, the superficial and sensuous to those profoundly spiritual and humbling discoveries which are called forth by the divine word. On this point it is necessary to adjust the balance with the utmost delicacy to preserve the due equipoise. Full emphasis must be given, in all the discussion of this question, to the original state of that fair structure, of which Howe remarks with novel beauty: " The stately ruins are visible to every eye that bear in their front yet extant this doleful inscription: HERE GOD ONCE DWELT." [1]

The absence of the Spirit, which man, as originally formed, possessed as the Spirit of illumination in his understanding, and of power in all his faculties, has left the mind in moral and spiritual impotence. If regard be had to the understanding, the unconverted cannot know the things of the Spirit of God (1 Cor. ii. 14); to the will, he cannot[2] be subject to the law of God (Rom. viii. 7); to worship, he cannot call Jesus Lord (1 Cor. xii. 3); to practice, he cannot please God (Rom. viii. 8); to fruit, he cannot bear fruit (John xv. 4); to faith, he cannot receive the Spirit of truth (John xiv. 17). His familiarity with sacred truths, which he does not love, only leaves him seared in conscience and twice dead. For this impotence the regenerating power of the Holy Ghost is absolutely indispensable.

The fact of man's inability, which Scripture everywhere asserts or implies, is to be explained by the withdrawal of the Spirit, which left him in SPIRITUAL DEATH. Scripture, therefore, in terms the most express, denies to man the power or ability to think a good thought (2 Cor. iii. 5), or to receive the things of the Spirit of God (1 Cor. ii. 14); and declares that human nature is wholly turned away from God, and enmity against Him (Rom. viii. 7); and this state of the heart has a determining influence on the will in all religious and moral judgments.

That decisive fact is not apprehended in the same way in Christian and philosophic thought, even where the latter makes the nearest approximation to the truth. The uniform language of Christianity is that it is the state of the will, in

---

[1] See Howe's *Living Temple*.
[2] No true exegete will allow that the οὐ δύναται is simply equivalent to οὐ θέλει.

other words, of the heart, that either illuminates or darkens
the understanding in its spiritual or moral views, and that
the relation between the two is not like ordinary knowledge,
according to which we must first know a thing before we love
it ; for, on the contrary, the secularized mind must first love
divine things with a spiritual relish before it fully knows
them.   Hence there is an important sense in which we may
affirm that it is not the intellectual knowledge which determines the conclusions of the will, but, conversely, the
tendency of the will or heart which determines the judgment
of the understanding.   That is, beyond question, the mode of
statement given in the Scriptures, which put spiritual life
before true knowledge, the renewal of the heart before the
possibility of a spiritual judgment.   Coleridge, in his *Literary
Remains*, beautifully remarks : " I believe and hold it as the
fundamental article of Christianity, that I am a fallen
creature ; that I am of myself capable of moral evil, but not
of myself capable of moral good, and that *an evil ground
existed in my will* previously to any given act, or assignable
moment of time, in my consciousness : I am born a child of
wrath.   This fearful mystery I pretend not to understand.   I
cannot even conceive the possibility of it, but I know that it
is so.   My conscience, the sole fountain of certainty, commands
me to believe it, and would itself be a contradiction, were it
not so——and what is real must be possible."

Into the discussion of the relation of free-will and divine
grace we are not required, by the topic which we are treating,
to enter in all its bearings.   As it is often handled, it is
frequently more a metaphysical debate on the laws of mind
than a question in exegetical or Biblical theology.   On the
subject of free-will and the Spirit's agency, the following
remarks may suffice : Man's *free agency is postulated* by every
one who apprehends the subject with any measure of precision,
as a point which may be described as necessary to his
personality and responsibility as a rational creature.. But

along with the admission of spontaneity and freedom, we must not less strongly hold that man in his natural state, under the forfeiture of the Spirit, uniformly chooses the evil in preference to the good. On the one hand, he is free from co-action or constraint, even when the will is carried headlong in a career of sin. On the other hand, THE WILL ITSELF IS DISEASED and vitiated. These are the two sides of the question; and when we put them together, we say with Augustine : " The will is always free, but not always good." The will cannot cease to be free, without ceasing to exist. Man could not be deprived of that freedom without the entire destruction of his mental being, as a rational and responsible creature. The liberty of the will consists in this, that he is not carried headlong by blind fatalistic impulse or by natural necessity or constraint. Whatever he does, he freely does. But the will may be free, and not liberated. He may be a free agent, and yet the servant of sin. The will may be free, and only exercise its freedom against the will of God. I strongly hold the duty of asserting the freedom of the will and the necessity of divine grace as two sides of an inexplicable mystery in the same way as holds true of many other theological points. My duty is to conserve the mystery which the Rationalistic understanding is only too prone to invade—to assert it, not to explain, far less to explode it.

THE SAYINGS OF JESUS ON THE SPIRIT'S WORK IN REGENERATION.

1. " *Verily, verily, I say unto thee, Except a man be born again, he cannot see the kingdom of God. . . . Except a man be born of water and of the Spirit, he cannot enter into the kingdom of God. That which is born of the flesh is flesh ; and that which is born of the Spirit is spirit* " (John iii. 3–6). Nicodemus came to question the Lord about His mission, and the kingdom of God which he plainly saw was about to be set up. But he was at once met by the practical question

bearing on his personal salvation. By this it at once appeared that Jesus came not to be catechised and to answer curious questions, but to teach what bore upon the salvation of His hearers. He made answer rather to the state of mind than to the words of Nicodemus. He showed that a change upon the whole man was indispensably necessary, if he should ever have a right of citizenship in the kingdom of God, which does not here mean the eternal felicity, but the Messianic kingdom in all its amplitude of meaning,

As to the phrase " born again," it is expounded by one class of interpreters as meaning *a second time*, by another as meaning *from above*, and the decision based on the general parallelism of Scripture falls very commonly in favour of rendering it *again, a second time*. But it must be admitted that neither the import of the term (ἄνωθεν) nor the style of expression used by John in speaking of regeneration lends it any countenance.[1] For my own part, I am more disposed to accept it as a peculiarity of John's style of language borrowed from his Master, and as denoting FROM ABOVE. The Lord repeats His statement as to the necessity of regeneration, and adds the twofold principle or cause by which it is produced :

[1] Most of the versions, the Lutheran, French, English, Dutch, translate *again*, and have been mainly influenced by the reply of Nicodemus, who, in asking whether a man could enter his mother's womb again, uses the term rendered *a second time* (δεύτερον) (ver. 4). On the other hand, the Greek exegetes, Origen, Chrysostom, Theophylact, and of the moderns Storr, Noesselt, Schleusner, Lücke, and others, render the word *from above ;* and their arguments are these : (1) The general, though not uniform, New Testament usage (John iii. 13, xix. 11, 23 ; Jas. i. 17, iii. 15 ; Mark xv. 38 ; Matt. xxvii. 51). (2) Jesus alternates the expression with another which is equivalent to *from above*, when He says that which is *born of the Spirit*. (3) The Evangelist John, when referring to regeneration, always describes it as a birth from God (John i. 13 ; 1 John ii. 29, iii. 9, iv. 7, v. 1, 4, 18). (4) Nicodemus' word, which has done more to sway expositors than anything else, is not construed with being born, but with entering again into his mother's womb. All these reasons incline the balance toward the rendering *from above*. But, on the other hand, the general New Testament parallelism seems to incline it in favour of the rendering "a second time " (Tit. iii. 5 ; 1 Pet. i. 3 ; 2 Cor. v. 17). If we decide in favour of the translation *born again*,—with most of the Protestant versions,—it can only be upon the ground of the general parallelism of the apostles' language.

born of water and of the Spirit.   These terms intimate the meritorious and efficient cause.

The term WATER has been variously interpreted.   (1) Some refer it to baptism,—an opinion current in Patristic theology from the earliest times, and asserted in the Greek and Latin Church and in some of the Protestant formularies.   But it is untenable, as will be evident to every mind that weighs the matter in the light of common observation.   The water to which the Lord refers CERTAINLY REGENERATES, and entitles those who receive it to enter the kingdom of God, from which no true member can ever be cast out again,—which cannot be affirmed of baptism in every case.   (2) Some take it as a hendiadys,—a view in which most of the Reformed divines concur,—implying that the Spirit acts with a cleansing efficacy like that of water.   (3) Some of the ablest Dutch divines, for example Cocceius, Vitringa, Lampe, interpret the water here named in the light of Ezekiel's words : " Then will I sprinkle clean water upon you, and ye shall be clean" (chap. xxxvi. 25).   With these last interpreters I fully concur. The *sprinklings, ablutions, lustrations*, common in the Mosaic ritual, primarily referred to the removal of the guilt which rendered the person of the worshipper unclean, and removed him from all approach to God in sanctuary service.   The purification of the leper, and of those who were unclean by contact with the dead, was effected by sprinkling them with water in which a portion of blood, or of the ashes of the red heifer, according to the law, was mingled (Lev. xiv. 1 ; Num. xix. 1 ff.).   It is not to be forgotten that Nicodemus was an accomplished teacher, and was profoundly conversant with all the Mosaic rites.   He knew well that on the occasion of taking Israel into covenant Moses took the blood of calves and of goats, with water and scarlet wool and hyssop, and sprinkled both the book and all the people (Heb. ix. 19) ; and that a laver, deriving all its value from the altar, or the victims slain on it, was prepared between the altar and the entrance of the tabernacle, that they who approached the Holy One might be made clean. The water referred to by our Lord in this connection was but the ceremonial expression for the cleansing of our person by His own obedience or atoning sacrifice, proving the complete removal of guilt and of everything that could exclude us on the ground of law from the kingdom of God.

The second term, SPIRIT, is the personal Holy Spirit, who gives the inward capacity or fitness for the kingdom of God, who breaks the power of sin, and makes all things new. The water and the Spirit are not to be confounded. They are THE TWO CONJOINED ELEMENTS ; in other words, the MERITORIOUS CAUSE and the EFFICIENT CAUSE, which introduce the sinner into the kingdom of God. The WATER and the SPIRIT are not to be explained as a mere hendiadys, or the use of two words for one. The terms are plainly adapted to the tenor of Ezekiel's prophecy (chap. xxxvi. 25 ff.) (comp. Zech. xiii.), and are both intended to be significant.

A third time, with a view to make the statement as to the necessity of regeneration more urgent and emphatic, our Lord substantially repeats His declaration : " Marvel not that I said to you, You must be born again." And then, to anticipate all cavil or exception to the mode in which that omnipotent act of God displays itself, He adds : " The wind bloweth where it listeth, and thou hearest the sound thereof, but canst not tell whence it cometh, or whither it goeth : so is every one that is born of the Spirit " (ver. 8). That this analogy is taken from nature, and is much like one of the parables, is not doubtful. They who have attempted, with Origen and Augustin, to dismiss the comparison and take the term translated *wind* for the personal Spirit, have nothing to say in answer to the argument that all these expressions : " bloweth," " the sound thereof," " the hearing of the sound," and the implied analogy in the words " *so is every one*," must be accepted as an illustrative description or comparison. The wind, as a natural phenomenon at that moment,—as in the case of many of our Lord's illustrations,—might arrest their attention.   The points of comparison are obviously these: (1) The Spirit's agency is sovereign, like the wind blowing where it will;[1] (2) The mode of His activity is inscrutable; it is like the wind, in regard to which we can neither say where it begins to blow nor where it is hushed to rest; (3) The efficacy is irresistible, and the effects indubitable; we hear the sound thereof.

2. A passage of similar import is the following: "*It is the Spirit that quickeneth; the flesh profiteth nothing*" (John vi. 63). Christ does not say *my flesh*, as in the previous context, where He carries on a discussion with the men of Capernaum; and the change of expression is significant.   Interpreters, not perceiving this, have been carried away with the misleading impression that the design was merely to remove an offence in the Jewish mind caused by the declaration that Jesus was the bread of life.   They think that He still continues to declare that the true life of redeemed men is meritoriously connected with His atoning death.   But Luther, when pressed by this text in the sacramentarian controversy, saw the change of expression, and accurately referred the words to the carnal sense of unrenewed men.   It is no longer " my flesh," as in all the previous context; the expression "the flesh" has no reference to the flesh of Christ.   It is the same antithesis that we find in the interview with Nicodemus: "That which is born of the flesh is flesh."   The five thousand who would have made Him king were so deeply offended by His teaching, that they had in a body forsaken Him; and the reason of their conduct is here traced to the unspirituality and enmity of the carnal mind.   Our Lord declares: it is the

---

[1] Bishop Andrews says: "There shall be an hundred or more in an auditory; one *sound* is heard, one *breath* doth blow.   At that instant one or two and no more—one here, another there, shall feel the spirit, shall be affected and touched with it sensibly; twenty on this side of them and forty on that side shall not feel it, but sit all becalmed and go their way no more moved than when they came: *ubi vult spirat* is most true" (p. 602).

Spirit that quickeneth, or imparts the life of God—a boon requiring omnipotent power. To one acquainted with the antithesis between flesh and spirit, or with Scripture language generally, it is plain that the allusion is not to the human spirit nor to Christ's divine nature, but to the Holy Spirit.

THE CONVINCING WORK OF THE SPIRIT.

3. We come now to what may be called, perhaps, the most conclusive passage on the Spirit's work in connection with conversion in the whole compass of Scripture. *"And when He is come He will reprove* (better : *convince) the world of sin, and of righteousness, and of judgment : of sin, because* (better : *in regard to the fact that) they believe not on me ; of righteousness, because* (better : *in regard to the fact that) I go to my Father, and ye see me no more ; of judgment, because* (better : *in regard to the fact that) the prince of this world is judged "* (John xvi. 8–11). The passage contains a full and exhaustive description of the Spirit's work in the application of redemption, as well as of the mission of the Comforter by the Son from the Father (John xv. 26). This memorable passage was meant to show the order of salvation, and how freely salvation is bestowed by the effectual working of the Spirit. It is summarized in the Apostle Paul's words (1 Cor. ii. 12) : " Now we have received not the spirit of the world, but the Spirit which is of God ; that we might know the things that are FREELY GIVEN TO US of God." The verb setting forth the Spirit's function (ἐλέγξει) may bear one of two senses—TO REPROVE or TO CONVINCE. The grounds for the decision, in every special instance, are supplied by the context. The signification TO REPROVE, which the term sometimes bears, implies that a person is reproved for some error which he has previously held. The other meaning, TO CONVINCE, implies that a person is convinced of some truth previously unknown or unrealized. The term may either mean to reprove and

refute a false opinion, or to convince one by cogent arguments and ample evidence as to truth hitherto unknown. Both senses are closely linked together. The notion of reproving, for which some contend, is wholly to be removed from the use of the term in this passage. Though they can both be made to have a show of probability, it is every way preferable, for various reasons, to accept the meaning TO CONVINCE.

To take one conclusive argument. All the objects are not reprehensible, and therefore the idea of reproof is not applicable to them all. Not only so ; the verb is introduced but once, and not three times, in connection with the three nouns SIN, RIGHTEOUSNESS, and JUDGMENT ; and therefore no possible ground exists for admitting any other than a uniform sense, which is equally applicable to them all.

Another point is the signification of the particle, which is three times expressed in connection with the several members (viz. ὅτι). It cannot be rendered, as in the English version, *because*, but *in respect to the fact that*. It is here an exegetical or specifying particle, setting forth that specific kind of sin, of righteousness, and of judgment, to which allusion shall be made. In all the members it must certainly be so taken, because the grammatical structure is uniform, and the maintenance of the same signification yields throughout an appropriate sense. This conclusion militates decidedly against giving to the verb the signification " to reprove," because things are mentioned which, so far from being censurable, are infinitely to be desired in the last two clauses.

We are told, indeed, by the celebrated Gerhard that some exegetes did give in this way the specific meaning to the particle (ὅτι), and yet contrived to interpret the verb as meaning *to reprove*, by the addition of certain words which it was thought might competently be supplied though they were not expressed. They filled up a supposed ellipsis as follows : He shall reprove the world of sin committed, of righteousness despised, of judgment neglected.

But when we examine that exposition, which found favour with not a few, many objections present themselves. It is a harsh ellipsis on the most indulgent consideration. Reproof always strikes on what is reprehensible—that is, either upon evil done, or upon persons favoured with privileges and chargeable with neglect. But the special neglect must always be expressed. Not only so; on such a construction of the words, not one expression, but various supplementary words, must be supplied to bring out the import. It renders the whole unnatural and obscure to introduce a different verb to every noun, and it is somewhat presumptuous; for who is warranted to supplement the language of our Lord by additions which are not in the text? Nor are such additions at all in harmony with the plain and obvious tenor of Christ's words. We are not then—under the impression that the verb means "to reprove"—to resort to any supplement so harsh, unnecessary, and unsuitable. The words are natural and perspicuous as they stand, if we adopt the other rendering —TO CONVINCE. The meaning is then plain. The proper idea is that of convincing one of anything not truly or fully known. And the objects, as they stand, are of such a nature that one may be convinced of them all, but not reproved for them all. And if we carry with us the thought that the Spirit is occupied about the sin of unbelief, which is the greatest of sins,—about imputed righteousness, the only valid plea with God, acquired by Christ's obedience unto death,— about the judgment of the prince of this world,—the language is easy and the sentence natural.

To come to the import of the term "shall convince." When it is said that the Spirit shall convince the world,— that is, men generally without the partition-wall between Jew and Gentile,—it means much more than mere instruction in revealed truth. Rather it implies that the Spirit, in spite of the ignorance and resistance of the carnal mind, will bring men to such a perception of the reality and importance of saving truth that they will no longer resist its evidence. The meaning is, that He shall convince men of something hitherto unknown; and all the three members of the sentence are linked together as follows: He shall convince men in respect to the fact that they believe not on me; in other words, He will demonstrate to the mind that unbelief is a sin—yea, the greatest sin; He shall convince the world of righteousness in respect to the fact that a true and proper righteousness has been wrought out for men by Christ's suffering and death; He shall convince the world of judgment in respect to the fact that Satan has at the great tribunal lost his cause, and is denuded of the right which he previously possessed. The efficient cause of all these effects is the personal Holy Ghost, the Comforter, and the Spirit of truth.

Christ's own words, as here recorded on the convincing work of the Comforter, is the *locus classicus* to which all fitly turn, whenever discussion is raised or inquiry awakened, as to the way in which the Spirit applies redemption: "*and when He is come, He will convince the world of sin, and of righteousness, and of judgment*" (John xvi. 8). As to the nature of that convincing influence which the Spirit brings to bear upon the mind, several things come under our consideration. He sets forth truth to the mind, and maintains it against every prepossession or contrary opinion. The Holy Spirit, by the word alone, or through the ministry of those who preach it, convinces the unbelieving world by the prophecies of the Old Testament,—by the testimonies of the New Testament,—by law and by gospel,—so fitly and seasonably, that the unwilling are made willing, and are compelled to feel and to admit in their conscience the truth of the gospel— an impression which is followed by faith in the heart and confession with the mouth. They are pressed by the force of truth, and yield. More particularly, He convinces the mind in A THREEFOLD WAY, viz. that unbelief is the greatest sin; that the righteousness procured by Christ is the only righteousness which avails before God; and that all the right or claim which Satan had to the possession of man, once his captive but now redeemed, is so invalidated—because the process has been decided against him—that he cannot tyrannize over any but by their own will.

Let me briefly notice the several objects in reference to which the Spirit yields His convincing influence.

1. The first object is UNBELIEF, the sin of contravening and rejecting the proposals of the gospel. The Redeemer, the true interpreter of His own words, subjoined what sin He meant when He added: "In respect to the fact that they believe not on me." This explanation by the Lord Himself refutes the opinion of Piscator and others, that the allusion is to His crucifixion by the Jews, as well as another opinion, that the expression must be generally understood of every sin committed. These interpreters are all of the class who hold that the verb which we render " convince " must have the meaning of " reprove," and will not admit the specifying force of the particle (ὅτι), which we have rendered " in respect to the fact that." But the Lord's meaning is express: the words point to the sin of unbelief, which, abstractly considered, is a violation of a divine command, and, concretely considered, is a refusal to accept the merits of a divine Redeemer.

To understand the criminality of unbelief, it may be remarked that it contracts guilt from the law, as the latter pronounces condemnation generally on all disobedience to the expressed will of God. The law may be taken in a twofold way—that is, as having a general and a special use. The first table of the law condemns generally all unbelief toward the word of God, and charges it as sin.

To be more explicit, let me add that the gospel has its own rule in reference to its *credenda*, or things to be believed. There an object of faith is presented to our view, with a special rule or mode divinely prescribed for apprehending it; and, according to this rule, the man must act who wishes to

be saved.   To that rule or mode many of the names applied
to faith are found to have respect.   Thus it is called God's
commandment (1 John iii. 23); the way of righteousness
(2 Pet. ii. 21); the law of faith (Rom. iii. 27); the work of
God (John vi. 29); and compliance with it is called obedience
to the faith (Rom. i. 5).   In all these passages allusion is
clearly made to that rule, way, or method by which the
blessings of redemption are applied and conferred.   But, on
the contrary, he who contravenes that rule, and refuses to
walk in that way, incurs the guilt of disobedience.   Not only
so : when unbelief, which is just an act in opposition to the
tenor of the gospel, is persistently and resolutely carried out,
the law comes forth to fulminate against it.

The sin of unbelief is here described, with all the enormous
guilt attaching to it, as a rejection of the proposals of reconciliation, as the chief and supreme sin, because a sin against
the remedy,—sinful in itself, and preventing the remission of
all other sins.   As unbelief is the sin by eminence, it is upon
this that the convincing influence of the Spirit is mainly
brought to bear.

Considered in its consequences, this sin of unbelief has its
immediate ground of condemnation in the fact that all other
sins, original and actual, with all their guilt, are remissible
through faith in Christ.   But this sin involves the rejection
of the graciously provided remedy ; and final unbelief has
nothing to interpose between the sinner and righteous condemnation.   Hence Luther was wont to affirm that unbelief
alone condemns, since it makes the person evil and the works
evil.

The sin of unbelief is here described as if it were the only
sin, because, according to the happy remark of Augustin,
while it continues, all other sins are retained, and when it
departs all other sins are remitted.   Not only so: it constantly produces new sins.   For, as faith may be considered
either as it apprehends Christ or as it works by love, unbelief

in like manner may be considered either as refusing Christ's redeeming work, or as it works by sin against the conscience. Unbelief may be called the mother-sin, because it not only leaves all guilt remaining, but gives force to reigning sins, and origin to a polluted conscience. But however great and perilous this sin may be, such is the ignorance in which men naturally are involved, that *its criminality is totally unknown* till it is brought home by the CONVINCING INFLUENCE OF THE HOLY GHOST the Comforter. Conscience may convince men of ordinary sins, but never of the sin of unbelief. Of the enormity of this sin no man was ever convinced but by the Holy Ghost Himself.

2. The second object of which they are convinced is RIGHTEOUSNESS, which is immediately after the former brought before the mind in order to prevent despair. This expression must not be understood as meaning that He who was crucified on the charge of sedition and blasphemy is proved to be innocent and righteous. That interpretation is supported by ingenious arguments, and specially by this, that God vindicated His innocence by raising Him from the dead; but it is by no means suited to the context. For, when Christ promises the Comforter to convince them of the sin of unbelief, He must be understood as meaning unbelief as to His Messiahship and saving work, and not merely as to His being a righteous man. The first clause presupposes that He is a Saviour, and so must the second. To convince the world of righteousness, must mean that the Spirit gives convincing evidence, not merely that His cause is good, and that He is innocent, but that in Him is found the righteousness which the world needs, the imputed righteousness which was graciously provided for us and becomes ours by faith.

When it is added: *He shall convince the world of righteousness, in respect to the fact that I go to the Father, and ye see me no more*, we see that the righteousness is equivalent to an obedience which culminated in suffering and death, and not an infused righteousness, as the Romanists allege; nor God's essential righteousness, as was alleged by Osiander, and as is re-echoed by the modern Plymouthists.

According to Carpzovius on this passage, and the great divines of the Lutheran Church, the meaning is : " By my departure—that is, by my death and sufferings—a valid righteousness has been procured for all true believers ; " for all the actions of Him who is by eminence the Servant of the Lord are at once mediatorial and redeeming. The figure is taken from a returning exile or traveller who has been from home; and in this case from the end of that work of abasement, or atonement and expiation, for the completion of which He had come forth from the Father (John xvi. 28). The same language had been several times used before, not only to the disciples (John xiii. 33), but on previous occasions to the Jews (John vii. 34, viii. 21). This whole style of language presupposes a commission or office to be discharged, a coming forth from the Father to perform it, and a return with all the demonstrations of acceptance to Him who sent Him. The language implies all Christ's offices, but especially His meritorious work as the Servant of the Lord and the High Priest of our profession (Heb. iii. 1). The additional words : " and ye shall see me no more," are a mere supplement to the previous thought, conveying little more than a filling up of the description by a reference to the mental state of the disciples, who must needs prepare themselves for losing that visible intercourse and that exchange of thought and speech in which they had found their satisfaction. But the appended phrase is a mere adjunct, and no constituent of the righteousness such as the previous clause involves, the allusion being merely to the apostles.

This language intimates that the righteousness which avails with God consists not, as the Romanist will have it, in that which is infused, or in the mere act of faith regarded as our obedience, as the Arminian will have it,—but in His going to the Father by His meritorious and atoning death. It implies that He who was sent on such an errand, and who returned with all the tokens of cordial welcome and great reward, must have brought in the everlasting righteousness and sealed up the vision and prophecy (Dan. ix. 24). But of that righteousness the world must be CONVINCED, if it is to be of any value to the sons of men. It must be duly announced or testified by apostles orally and in writing, and by the Holy Ghost the Comforter inwardly (John xv. 26, 27). Hence it is said that the Holy Ghost is sent to convince the world of this everlasting or imputed righteousness—that is, to show men that they who are denuded of any proper righteousness should, without delay, avail themselves of that which has magnified the law and made it honourable.

3. The third object of which the world is convinced by the Comforter is JUDGMENT. This benefit stands very closely related to the former. The righteousness which Christ acquired by His going to the Father, as already explained, and which is applied by imputation to all them that believe, puts them in a friendly relation to God, and God in a friendly relation to them, because they are righteous in Christ's righteousness; and this is the reason why our Lord immediately subjoins the mention of judgment. In due order, and based upon the former, comes deliverance from Satan.

As to the JUDGMENT here mentioned, it is not to be interpreted as meaning the authority which Christ, as victor over Satan, and as the accepted Surety, wields as supreme Lord of heaven and earth. That view, embodying a precious truth, is too general here, and misses the point of the clause, though held by Chrysostom, Cyrill, Piscator, and many recent commentators. Obviously, the import of the words does not refer to what is deposited in Christ as a potentate, able to disarm the strong man armed, but to what was inflicted on Satan, when the cause which was before the supreme tribunal for final adjudication was decided against him. The work of the second Adam, satisfying every claim of law and justice, terminated Satan's right, and reversed his authority acquired by conquest. We are led to this conclusion, as in the two previous classes, by the specifying particle (ὅτι), which must still have the same meaning, and only declare what had been yet but obscurely expressed. It is but one thing, only more fully declared. It is not statement and reason of the statement, as given in the English Authorized Version. The meaning is as follows : He shall convince the world of judgment *in respect to the fact that the prince of the world has been judged*. The use of the perfect passive (κέκριται) intimates that it was within a few hours—that it was as good as done,—a mode of speech by no means uncommon in our Lord's style (see John xii. 31). The meaning is, that Satan has been judged in the sense that the great cause has gone against him, and that he has no more right to retain the world, which he previously held by right of conquest.

What is THIS WORLD, and who is its prince ? It is not the fabric of the universe, which God created, upholds, and rules ; but the world of men seduced by the tempter, and held by a certain claim of right ; his subjects and his sons doing the lusts of their father (Eph. ii. 2 ; John viii. 44). The phraseology is borrowed from a legal proceeding carried on by two contending parties—Satan, on the one side, contending that he had a right of property in men who had become his subjects ; that a rebel cannot be restored to favour, but must be left in his hands ; that the highly extolled rectitude of the supreme Judge must carry out the same sentence on men that had been carried out, and was for ever to be carried out, on himself ;—and the Mediator, on the other side, appealing to the fact that, as He took man's place under the broken law to fulfil its obligations and bear its penalty in their room, justice as well as mercy required that Satan's right of conquest should be reversed, and that the world should be given to Him who was its second Adam and

Lord of all. Such was the cause to be finally and irrevocably decided, and, on the ground of Christ's satisfaction and sufficient ransom, the adjudication was rightfully decided against the prince of this world, who was to be cast out of his dominions and compelled to surrender the world—that is, the human family — into other hands. He can no longer keep his goods in peace when the stronger than he appears upon the scene (Luke xi. 21 ; Isa. xlix. 24 ; 1 Cor. xv. 54). Of all this, THE HOLY GHOST THE COMFORTER COMES TO CONVINCE THE HEARERS OF THE GOSPEL, to whom the apostles testified (John xv. 26, 27). Men are thus convinced that they may be free indeed (John viii. 36), no more subjects of the tempter, no more bound to obey him, but loyal subjects of Christ, and made willing in a day of His power (Ps. cx. 3).

As to the issue of this convincing process, exegetes are by no means at one. Many who are correct in expounding the term " convince " assume unwarrantably a twofold result, and assert that it may sometimes end in the obdurate mind and sometimes in saving faith. Even Calvin arrives at the conclusion, that under the term WORLD may be comprehended an allusion to hypocrites and reprobates as well as to those who are truly to be converted. Tholuck, after putting together a variety of opinions, comes to no firm decision. On the other hand, practical writers and preachers, weighing the passage in its bearings upon religious experience, come, for the most part, to the conclusion that the result of this convincing process ends in true conversion. I cannot but regard that as the only true and legitimate interpretation.

As so much uncertainty prevails, I have gone into a full consideration of this passage, with all the light reflected from the history of interpretation, believing that this was by no means unnecessary. My full persuasion is, that THE CONVINCING PROCESS OF THE SPIRIT, thus described by Christ in the last evening of His intercourse with the disciples, is so put as to bring out the successive steps, or the order of salvation, through which the Spirit leads the awakened mind; and that we can only view it as issuing in a sound conversion. I hold that it means to convince by clear and cogent arguments. It brings the ruin and the remedy together. It is a thunderbolt against all the views of Legalists.

These sayings of Christ, when put together, show, in the most conclusive manner, the necessity of the Spirit's regenerating work. They prove that this is the peculiarly Christian element, and that there is no doctrine which, in the evangelical system, more imperatively requires to be placed in the forefront. If justification by faith alone is one pole on which all evangelical theology moves, the renewing work of the Spirit is the second; and unless these two pivots are in their proper place, everything is deranged and put out of order.

The necessity of the regenerating work of the Spirit is enforced in Scripture with the greatest urgency. Thus, when our Lord unfolded to Nicodemus the nature of His kingdom, He did not begin by telling him that he must do this or that, but that HE MUST BECOME SOMEWHAT. He tells him that man's nature must be changed; that the tree must first be made good. Life is presupposed if any spiritual act is to be performed. Education cannot avail; for it may refine, but cannot give life. For the same cause, the influence of fear and the offers of reward, as well as the effect of solemn vows and earnest endeavours, are only dead works, till the man himself is made alive. Nor can the influence of the highest examples breathe life into the dead soul, or make the amendments or changes to which they may give rise anything beyond a lifeless resemblance. The necessity of regeneration appears (1) from the fact of man's fall, which has ushered in an incapacity for all good, and a dislike of the divine presence and of the divine service. The necessity of regeneration appears (2) from the fact that without it we have no enjoyment of God, and could find no happiness even

if translated to heaven itself, because we are by nature
destitute of the eye, the taste, the relish, and the necessary
organs for enjoying God in any of those ways and means by
which we could participate in the blessedness of the celestial
state, or take part in its exercises of holy love and endless
praise.

We may set forth the truth connected with regeneration,
if we advert to THE NATURE OF THE CHANGE, to ITS CON-
COMITANTS, and to ITS EFFECTS.

As to THE NATURE of regeneration, it is one in kind, and in
every case uniformly the same, while it is instantaneously
effected.   Though some writers have described the successive
steps of the Spirit's operations, these descriptions are rather
taken from the human consciousness and experience than
from the Spirit's action, which is performed at once.   Not
only so: the Spirit's action is PERFECT IN KIND, as an infant
may be regarded as perfect in its nature, though its powers
have still to be developed through a long-continued process
till it reach the maturity of its powers.   Regeneration is,
moreover, an action WHOLLY SUPERNATURAL, not less so than
Creation or Resurrection, which are described as the incommunicable acts of that same Spirit by whom we are renewed.
It is not effected by moral suasion on the one hand, nor by
the natural man on the other, making so good a use of the
light of nature as to win or procure the greater grace of this
renovation.   For all the subsequent movements are still
effected by that same Spirit who works in us both to will and
to do (Phil. ii. 13).

As to the CONCOMITANTS of regeneration, the reigning
power of sin ceases in the regenerate, and their seed that
remaineth in them becomes fruitful of results, which evince
a constant increase till the renewed man reaches the full
development to which he is destined.

As to THE EFFECTS of regeneration, they are known by such
terms as the new creature (2 Cor. v. 17); the new man

(Eph. iv. 24); the divine nature (2 Pet. i. 4); as wisdom in the understanding, holiness in the will; as faith, love, and hope, and all those fruits of the Spirit which are expressly enumerated by the apostle (Gal. v. 22). When we inquire who are regenerated, they are the elect (Rom. viii. 30). When we ask what is regenerated in the man, the answer is, the whole soul in all its powers : for though no new faculties are created, they are all renovated. The author of the change is the Holy Spirit; the pattern after which we are pre-destinated is Christ; and the means of this regeneration is the word of truth (Jas. i. 18).

The essential feature of Christianity, according to our Lord's own delineation, is the new birth; and so indispensable is it, that without the new nature there can be no evangelical health or progress, nor any interest in Christ and in the blessings of His purchase.

To go back to the Lutheran type of doctrine,—the eldest daughter of the Reformation,—we find that this Church was well-nigh stranded when THE SYNERGISTIC CONTROVERSY took its rise within her pale. Whoever has bestowed any attention on that discussion, is aware that nothing but the profound views already lodged in the mind of the Christian community on the vast ruin of the fall, and on the indispensable necessity of the efficacious grace of the Holy Spirit, at that time saved the life of the Church. The majority maintained, agreeably to Scripture, that the natural man, apart from the supernatural work that the Holy Spirit does in him, CAN DO ABSOLUTELY NOTHING, and that he needs to be replenished by the Spirit of life. The Church righted again by adopting the position that *the subject of conversion cannot also be a co-operating factor*, and that the sole cause of conversion and faith is the Holy Spirit working through the word—that is, as giving a full proclamation of law and gospel. No Protestant Confession has assigned any agency for the human will as a THIRD CAUSE; for to do so were to fall into the logical absurdity of confounding the subject of conversion with its cause. To show the dangers of Synergism, we quote a sentence from a German writer : " This article," says he,[1] " did not fail to exercise a leavening influence both in a forward and backward direction,—backward, on the doctrine of original sin ; forward, on that of justification." We believe that this is the inevitable consequence, as a few words will show.

With regard to the first, the doctrine of ORIGINAL SIN, it is obvious that a theory which asserts A SYNERGISM, and by this means qualifies the sole operation of the Holy Spirit, does not presuppose a human nature which is subjected to such a moral change as is seen in the issue of the fall. The *rationale* of every gospel doctrine, and, in a particular manner, of the Spirit's operations, is furnished by clear discoveries as to the extent of inherent depravity. And to assume a doctrine of original sin less than coextensive with the essential powers of the soul,—though it has left that essence undestroyed, and still capable of extrication from the ruin,—is to neutralize the provisions of the Holy Spirit's work.

Not only so ; the effect of synergistic views on man's JUSTIFICATION by imputed righteousness is not less disastrous. It is an attempt, as futile as foolish, to accept a surety-righteousness and repudiate a surety-strength, exercised upon man by the omnipotent efficacy of the Holy Spirit, when not an argument can be adduced against the one but may equally be directed against the other. And hence Luther said, with his usual vehemence : " What need of God, what need of Christ, what need of the Spirit, if free-will can accomplish all ? " The entire success in the last resort is made to hinge on the individual himself.

With others in this age, and they are a very numerous class, all the application of redemption is resolved into the exercise of natural power as the effect of mere moral suasion. The man is thrown back on himself. It seems to exalt

---

[1] Schubring in Rudelbach's *Zeitschrift für Lutherische Theologie*, 1848, p. 316.

and flatter man's nature, but it paves the way for its deeper degradation.   Here I may notice that Amyraldus has been followed by not a few in the unhappy distinction which he drew between the PHYSICAL AND MORAL ABILITY to believe in Christ.   He asserted that man had the former, though he had not the latter.   That notion of ability, copiously imported into America, gave rise to many ill-considered state- ments which can only be received with caution.   Whatever system leaves human nature as it is, to make the best of its resources, or to be wrought upon merely by a class of motives, though the most sublime, but which introduces no new supernatural element into fallen humanity, is as little Christian in its essence as it is stale and flat in its conception. If man's soul is not to be elevated from its degradation by the regenerating grace of the Spirit, which alone can raise it, but to be flattered with its ability and power,—if nothing but a class of motives, higher indeed than Plato's, but yet mere motives, is brought to bear upon it, no high conception is formed of the transforming influence of Christianity.   That system of moral suasion often imposes on its own advocates : it seems to avoid the outward appearance of Pelagianism, because it limits the view merely to the matter of accepting salvation as a gift.   But it is only in appearance that it evades the grosser form of Pelagianism, by limiting the language to the reception of a gift.   Thus, while there are schools of theology, such as the Puritans and Jansenists, which have endeavoured to vindicate the spiritual life as a reality, the views in question contribute directly, and not in their remote effect, to obliterate all the distinction between spirit and flesh, grace and nature.   Of the fruits of Naturalism, whether it be Pelagianism, Arminianism, Socinianism, Rational- ism, we have seen enough in the history of the Church to be convinced that it does not tend, with all its praise of man's ability and dignity, to elevate our race.   If all good flows from the Spirit of God, *down to the very first desire*, then dependence and prayer constitute the only fitting attitude for the Church in general and for every individual soul.

The leading principle which helps us to find our way through all the difficulties of these questions is, that THE SPIRIT, in returning to the human heart, ANTICIPATES THE WILL—that is, WORKS IN US TO WILL, at the first moment of conversion and at every subsequent step. The first desire, wish, or resolution to return to God, as well as the first prayer offered with this end in view, is from the Holy Spirit. That all spiritual good emanates from the Spirit of God, is a simple formula, which keeps every inquirer in this department right. That the Spirit's power and grace precede the will is a maxim to be carried with us, *unless we are prepared to ascribe a merit to the first step*, or to view the first step as originated on the man's own side.

And from the moment that the soul begins to act in spiritual things, it acts with its NEWLY ACQUIRED SPIRITUAL POWERS, imparted by the Spirit of God. The Spirit's operation, *always spoken of in the present tense*, and as prevenient grace, prompts the soul to co-operate with its newly acquired powers of life. But the expression SPIRITUAL POWERS does not imply a change on man's essential nature, or the donation of faculties which were never found in the human mind before, but simply a NEW APTITUDE AND POWER to comply with what is truly good, as derived from the Holy Spirit. With a new will, that is, a will renovated and endowed with a spiritual capacity, the soul becomes active, and co-operates with God.

We have thus seen that the application of redemption is from first to last by the Holy Spirit; that the faith by which we receive the adoption of sons is THE FIRST POINT; and that this faith in man's heart is only from the Spirit of God, which is the SECOND POINT. If there be admitted any natural power or capacity in man for the exercise of faith, this necessarily overthrows in the second instance the great doctrine of divine grace that was announced in the first. This doctrine of the

Spirit, therefore, really maintains, more than anything else, a Church's connection with evangelical religion; and where this is wanting, nothing can intercept or arrest a Church's descent to the lowest depths of naturalism. The Wesleyan system diverged from the path and imbibed most of the Arminian tenets; but it was rescued from the irreparable ruin that otherwise would have awaited it by the fact that it unequivocally recognised the Holy Spirit as the sole author of a supernatural regeneration and of spiritual life; for Wesley said with unhesitating decision: " There is no more of *power* than of merit in man; but as all merit is in the Son of God, so all power is in the Spirit of God; and therefore every man, in order to believe unto salvation, must receive the Holy Ghost." They conceded too much as to the extent of divine grace and of the Spirit's operations, but they retained what was essential to the spiritual life. But the theology that contemplates nothing higher than moral suasion and free-will, and which repudiates the supernatural, is soon divested of all evangelical power as well as of all permanence and strength. The current objection to the Spirit's work, that man must have inherent strength to believe, because divine wrath rests on those who do not believe, is but a plausible sophism. If it had any meaning, it would be as applicable to the law as to faith, as applicable to the work of Christ as to the work of the Spirit. If a man must have power in the one case, he must have power in the other case. He who vindicates the Mediator's meritorious work against the sceptic or Deist, cannot without the most flagrant inconsistency take Pelagian ground against the Spirit's work. There is not an argument against the one that is not equally capable of being directed against the other; and he who rejects the one is bound in consistency to reject the other. There is as little interference with human liberty in receiving the work of the Spirit to regenerate us, as in receiving the work of the Son to redeem and justify us.

THE INHABITATION OF THE HOLY SPIRIT.

The Spirit inhabits and replenishes all the mental powers, and supplies them with the help which makes them fit for active service. Discussions have long been carried on as to the relation and priority of the understanding and will, and as to the influence which the one may be regarded as exercising on the other. Without complicating our inquiry, as is too frequently done, both on the Calvinistic and Arminian side, with discussions which yield no satisfactory result as to the priority of the understanding and its necessary influence on the will, we may better describe the change which is effected by REGENERATION as taking effect ON ALL THE POWERS OF THE SOUL, and as underlying the exercise of them all. The change appears in new modes of activity or in new phenomena over the whole compass of the mental faculties, and in the whole sphere of the Christian life. But we would rather speak of the entire soul as one, and as displaying its activity in different STATES OF MIND, than separate the mental powers into so many divisions or compartments, each acting on the other, and opening the gateway to the other. If the entire soul is a unity, and acts only in certain states of mind, as Dr. Thomas Brown was wont to represent the matter in philosophy, and as Witsius was wont to represent the exercise of faith in theology, we may more fitly describe the Spirit's operations *as taking effect on the whole soul*, than limit ourselves to one faculty acting on another.

The restoration of the Spirit takes for granted that He comes in TO INHABIT THE WHOLE MAN, according to the idea of anthropology, with which all Scripture is replete ; and the Spirit's presence becomes anew for us the indefectible source of light and life and fruitfulness, as well as of perseverance and progressive holiness. The allusions to the inhabitation of the Spirit are manifold and various. As a new impelling power, He occupies the human faculties, and so pervades them

that He is said to dwell in us and walk in us (2 Cor. vi. 16);
and the regenerate man is said to HAVE the Spirit of Christ as
the consequence of that gracious inhabitation (Rom. viii. 9).
The Spirit condescends to occupy all the chambers of our
hearts, and to dwell in them.

We may trace the Spirit's work on THE MENTAL POWERS,
and show that there is a divine influence decisive as to the
action of them all.   A single glance at the Spirit's operation
on the understanding, will, and conscience, will suffice to
show that, in the case of the regenerate, the Holy Spirit is
the efficient cause of all their spiritual activity.

With regard to the UNDERSTANDING, all spiritual light is
derived from the Spirit of wisdom and revelation in the knowledge of the Lord Jesus enlightening the eyes of their understanding (Eph. i. 17).   When the question is raised, Does the
illumination belong solely to prevenient grace ? it is necessary
to distinguish.   In the first act of illumination, the Spirit
acts much in the same way as when He commanded it to
shine out of darkness (2 Cor. iv. 6).   But WHEN THE MAN HAS
RECEIVED the power of vision, HE USES IT for the further
increase of his knowledge in the way of co-operating grace.
The truths which he believed to the saving of the soul had
reference to God, to himself, and to the adaptation of the
atonement.   By the illumination of the Spirit, he acquires
wholly different views of all these points and of God, who is
no longer regarded as an indulgent being, nor as a tyrant, but
as a gracious Father, all whose perfections are glorified by
the atonement.   And as to ourselves, the Spirit shows us the
ruin and the remedy.

The Spirit's operation is not less conspicuous on the WILL.
The principal effect of the Spirit's activity is seen in a new
principle of spiritual life diffused through all the mental
powers, and inclining the soul to yield itself to Christ in the
exercise of faith and subjection, as now enabled or made fit
both to will and to do.

And as to the CONSCIENCE, the sanctification of the Spirit contributes to a good conscience. In other words, the conscience purged with the sprinkling of the blood of Christ by the effectual application of the Spirit, is then committed to the Spirit, who corrects and teaches it, who purifies and comforts it, from day to day.

II. The effectually called become ADOPTED SONS, and are translated by the power of the Spirit into the family of God. According to the canon, that whatever is imparted in the exercise of Christ's grace implies the opposite in our state by nature, they who were born into God's family were in the opposite family—in the family of Satan —before.

It is the more necessary to set this in its proper light, because many do not hesitate to say, under the bias of a false system, that God is universal Father, and that all men are His children. They hold by what they call THE FATHERHOOD OF GOD in virtue of an alleged unbroken relation formed by creation, and assert that all men, without exception or distinction, belong to the family of God, much in the same way as Pope describes Him as Father of all in his universal prayer. Children, forsooth, who only disobey and dishonour their Father! No: all men by nature belong to a family antagonistic to the family of God, and they do the lusts of a father who is described as a liar and murderer from the beginning. That position is in harmony with the doctrine of Christ and His apostles. Men cannot, at one and the same moment, be of their father the devil, as Cain was (1 John iv 10–12), and as the Jews were, when our Lord announced to them their family (John viii. 44), and yet be recognised or called the sons of God. The doctrine of our Lord and His apostles sets forth that sinners and all unregenerate men are children of the evil one.

Though the doctrine of depravity was not represented by

the early Christian writers, especially by those of the Greek Church, with the accuracy with which they were delineated in after times, it must be admitted that these early writers speak of men as subjected to the evil power with a Biblical fulness and accuracy to which modern theology can make no pretensions. They lay emphasis on THE POWER OF SATAN. The representations given in the early Christian literature as to the sinful power under which the human race has fallen, may be described as greatly more full and suggestive than in the literature of the present day. With regard to the doctrine of Satan that is emphatically true. With the Christian Church in post-apostolic times Satan was a reality, and his kingdom a fact, with which they daily felt themselves encompassed. The Fathers cannot find terms sufficiently strong to delineate the power of Satan, the seductive influence which he wields, and the subjection to his dominion under which men have fallen. In a word, the Patristic literature gives the utmost prominence to the terrible power and tyranny of Satan, though by no means greater than the subject warrants; and this subjection is always traced to sin. There is no disposition with them to shrink from representing men AS CHILDREN OF THE WICKED ONE.

THE TRANSLATION INTO THE FAMILY OF GOD.

In the translation of the individual from the one family to the other, it must be borne in mind that the Spirit is represented in Scripture as the great agent. He makes Christ and His people one, for the acceptance of their persons and the renovation of their natures. I refer to this the rather because there are schools of theology which make *the work of the Spirit and the commencement of His operations subsequent to the believing reception of Christ;* and many, under the spell of a theory from which they never escape, make the participation of the Redeemer's work turn in the last resort on the self-application of the individual. And setting out from the universal call of the gospel, they look with suspicion on any express allusion either to human inability on the one hand, or to the effectual application of the Spirit on the other. But the language of Scripture in reference to this application is so express as to leave no room for a moment's hesitation. Thus, if we consider any aspect of the question, the Spirit is said to shed abroad the love of God upon the heart, which must be taken *as the decisive turning-point* in that application (Rom. v. 5). The Holy Spirit is designated "the Spirit of adoption,"—a phrase which, according to the analogy supplied by every similar expression, means that He is THE AUTHOR of the adoption (Rom. viii. 15). The Holy Spirit is the efficient cause in communicating the blessings of redemption ; for the merits of Christ and the efficacy of the Spirit are placed together in the inseparable connection which follows : " But ye are washed, but ye are sanctified, but ye are justified in the name of the Lord Jesus, and by the Spirit of our God " (1 Cor. vi. 11). When the gospel produces saving effects, it is said to come not in word only, but in power, and in the Holy Ghost (1 Thess. i. 5). The sanctification of the Spirit is inserted by Paul and Peter as the intermediate link between election on the part of God and faith on the part of man (2 Thess. ii. 13). The Apostle Peter declares that men are chosen by the sanctification or separation which the Spirit produces to obedience, and sprinkling of the blood of Christ (1 Pet. i. 2). But there is one title of the Spirit which is peculiarly significant and suggestive in this light— THE SPIRIT OF FAITH ; that is, the Spirit is the author of faith (2 Cor. iv. 13), by whom we call Jesus Lord, and confide in Him. The conclusion to which we come, from all these testimonies, is, that in the application of redemption there is but one great agent, viz. the Holy Spirit—not the force of human will, according to the semi-Pelagian opinion, —not a double factor, according to the Synergistic theory.

The sole cause is the Holy Spirit operating through the word
—that is, by the proclamation of law and gospel—by means
of which He enlightens the understanding, and inclines the
will to receive Christ's finished work.

THE ADOPTION OF SONS.

The ADOPTION OF SONS, into which Christians are ushered
by the Spirit (Rom. viii. 15), differs from the privilege of
justification in this respect, that it brings the Christian before
God in the new relation of a child to a father. Whether we
regard this state of sonship, with many divines, as one of the
sides of justification, or as a further privilege into which the
believer passes without any interval of time, THE ADOPTION OF
SONS (υἱοθεσία) is, in a doctrinal point of view, of the utmost
moment in the system of divine truth, because it preserves
the equipoise, and prevents the juridical idea from being
exclusive. As it is set forth by the apostles, we find adoption
in THREE several delineations : (1) Paul describes the privilege
of sons as contrasted with the position of a servant (Gal. iv. 7);
(2) John describes adoption in connection with regeneration,
and with the underlying truth that we are made sons by grace
because Christ is the Son by Nature (John i. 13 ; 1 John
iii. 1); (3) the Synoptists, preserving our Lord's words,
describe adoption in connection with the restoration of the
divine image (Matt. v. 45). We have only to put together
THAT THREEFOLD DESCRIPTION of the apostles as the complement of each other, to give an exhaustive outline of the whole
doctrine of adoption.

The justified person, passing into the relation of a son,
enters into a relation of love, which we shall delineate in a
few particulars. (1) The foundation of sonship is based in the
incarnation of the eternal Son, who became the Son of man,
partaker of flesh and blood, that His people might become
the sons of God. It is not some mere inward change

produced by the operations of the Spirit that the Father loves ; *He loves them in His Son,* and extends to them the complacency and favour which rest on Him.   This is the great objective ground of their adoption and of their joint participation of that love wherewith He loves the Son, as far as a created being, in virtue of the federal and vital union, can share in it.   (2) The receptive hand by which Christians are made partakers of sonship and joint participants of the Holy Ghost, according to their measure, is FAITH, and the accompanying union which true faith involves.   (3) The adoption common to believers, and essentially the same in all, has NO VARYING DEGREES, but one equal degree wherever it is found ; and it is perfect at once : " Now are we the sons of God " (1 John iii. 2).   Hence no warrant exists for the opinion that there are distinctions or varying degrees in the love of God to His adopted children so far as this objective privilege is concerned ; for on each of them rests that divine complacency which rests on the only-begotten Son.   This adoption carries with it demonstrations of divine love, pledges of paternal care and salutary discipline, as well as foretastes of glory, honour, and immortality ; and also conformity to the image of Him who is the first-born among many brethren. (4) It is a privilege about which the Christian, replenished by the Holy Spirit, is to be left in no uncertainty and doubt, for the Spirit makes intercession with groanings that cannot be uttered, and bears witness with our spirit that we are the children of God (Rom. viii. 16).   On this central point of Biblical doctrine many divines expatiate, some in one interest, some in another, in order, if possible, to find a remedy for those controversies and debates that have long been carried on as to the matter of a sinner's acceptance.   Thiersch, in those erudite lectures in which he discusses the principles of Catholicism and Protestantism, speaks of this doctrine as furnishing a sort of meeting-point, and proposes an *irenicum* on this basis of agreement.   He goes so far as to say that the

Romish doctrine, antagonistic as it is to the position that all believers are equally accepted on the ground of the Redeemer's merits, is really met by this doctrine of adoption as a common basis of agreement.

THE WITNESS OF THE SPIRIT.

The doctrine of ASSURANCE, or the witness of the Spirit, connected with the adoption of sons, demands a few words of exposition (Rom. viii. 16). The witness is spoken of as the well-known accompaniment of adoption. And as the result of the Holy Spirit's operations, we cannot suppose that the testimony of the Spirit, of which the Apostle Paul speaks, was AN EXTRAORDINARY INWARD REVELATION, imparted only to apostles and to a few specially selected individuals of the apostolic age, as Romish divines are in the habit of affirming; for it is a common Christian experience. It is not an exceptional gift, but the ordinary criterion and accompaniment of adoption.[1] The notion, however, that he is no true Christian who does not perpetually enjoy an ever-shining assurance, as an unclouded sun in the firmament, has as little to say in its defence. The possibility of attaining assurance, and the duty of possessing it (*potest et debet*), must be inculcated. But beyond that we are not warranted to go; and we may not presume to go.

The subject of assurance was so identified with faith in the theology of the Reformation as to be well-nigh inseparable and indistinguishable from faith; and the Puritan doctrine may be called an advance to a clearer view. While these divines carefully distinguished it from faith, they contended that, in

---

[1] Bishop Andrews says beautifully: "As Christ is our Witness in heaven, so is the Spirit here on earth, witnessing with our spirits, that we belong to the adoption, and are the children of God; evermore in the midst of the sorrows that are in our hearts, with His comforts refreshing our souls; yet not filling them with false comforts, but as Christ's advocate here on earth, soliciting us daily" (p. 625).

God's design, and according to the constitution of things, assurance could neither be retained in an unholy walk, nor emerge
upon the consciousness apart from the Spirit's testimony and
the renovated will.   They directed the eye of faith to the all-
sufficiency of the Redeemer in a way not differing from the
Reformers ; but they suspended assurance neither upon joyous
emotions of acceptance alone, nor on the immediate revelation
of the Spirit alone, irrespective of the graces of the new creation.
And in one of the most precious chapters of the Confession of
Faith they have set forth their conclusion.   In their day they
furnished a corrective to an *excess*.   An equally great *defect*
required to be supplied in the following century, of the theology of which Warburton was a representative divine, when it
was necessary to exhibit assurance as AN INCUMBENT DUTY,
and as a benefit productive of higher holiness and deeper
love, as well as of a consecrated life.   Venn represents
it as one great cause of Wesley's success, that he urged
Christians not to rest without joy in God from receiving the
atonement.

DEPENDENCE ON THE SPIRIT THE ESSENCE OF EVANGELICAL RELIGION.

I cannot omit to notice, in this connection, the fact that,
according to the uniform testimony of history, all success in
extending religion, and in promoting its revival, has been
always connected with dependence on the Spirit of life, and
that the refusal to regard the Spirit as the author of conversion and the source of spiritual life, puts a Church or an
individual beyond THE PALE OF THE TRULY CHRISTIAN. Such a
religion has no claim to be classed among EVANGELICAL com-
munions.   A religion not acting in the Spirit as the supernatural principle of action, can only be the religion of nature.

The loss of the Spirit and the restoration of the Spirit—
the former the result of the fall, and the latter the result of

the atonement—have thus passed before us in review.   They are the two most momentous facts in the history of man. They are associated with the first man's sin and the second man's restoration of what was lost.   The fall left the human heart, once the temple of God, an utter ruin ; the Great Inhabitant who dwelt in it was under the necessity of leaving the polluted spot.   With the Spirit's return to the human heart, on the ground of that everlasting righteousness which Christ ushered in, a NEW CREATION began to dawn, and a new kingdom entered which will be dissolved no more. It is of little use—except for the analogy—to recall what might have been had the first Adam fulfilled the conditions imposed on him by his Creator.   The human race would have enjoyed without forfeiture the irrevocable aids and presence of the Holy Spirit beyond the hazards of falling.   And the same constant presence of the Spirit, with all the efficacy of His omnipotent grace, which the redeemed will for ever enjoy, would have been transmitted to his descendants of the human family upon a tenure liable to no disastrous forfeiture.

The Lord Jesus, the second man, having fulfilled all the conditions which devolved on Him as the Surety of those whom the Father had given Him, conveys to each of them a supply of the Holy Spirit irrevocably sure and indefectible. The ground of that supply is that THE SECOND ADAM STOOD ; and in consequence of His finished work, they who are effectually united to Him shall never finally forfeit the Spirit's communications.   While many grounds and reasons may be mentioned why Christ's disciples never fall away, the principal ground, based at once on divine law and justice, is that the second Adam, by fulfilling the conditions, and comply- ing with all the requirements of the law, received as His reward AN INEXHAUSTIBLE SUPPLY OF THE SPIRIT, which should be imparted to all His people, and dwell in them for ever.   The Spirit, accordingly, never permits them finally to depart. This is the grand security for the perseverance of the saints.

The Spirit will not abandon the souls which He has regenerated, and which He will use effectual means to reclaim when
they are prone, from inward feebleness or listless indifference,
to vacillate or waver.   He will not suffer them to depart for
ever, but will renew the exercises of repentance and faith so
that they will return to their allegiance (Isa. lix. 21), and
continue to have the place of sons in the family of God.   The
great work of the Spirit, with a view to adoption, IS OUR
SPIRITUAL OR MYSTICAL UNION TO CHRIST, which, in an objective
point of view, constitutes them the sons of God.

According to semi-Pelagian theories, the first good begins
with the man, and the Spirit of God is only a benevolent
well-wisher, but no Spirit of life in Christ Jesus.   The real
deed, according to that theory, begins on man's side, though
he is described as " *dead in sin*."   The grand evil of all these
systems is, that they insert a legal condition which men have
to perform, and all ends at last in the law of works, leaving
men to apply to themselves, as they best may, the benefits
which the Redeemer purchased.   Humanity is thrown back,
under a goodly guise, upon the principle—DO AND LIVE.   And
whether it be the influence of hope or fear, whatever imposes
on man an obligation *to act from himself as the principle of
action*, is legal in its inmost germ, and enmity to God—however concealed under an ostentatious attachment to grace in a
one-sided way.   In these systems the gift of salvation is *not
given to the man*, but to his strenuous self-application.   But if
the application in the last instance rests ON MAN'S INHERENT
POWER, he inevitably relies on his reliance, or believes in his
belief ; and no exercise of ingenuity can extricate him from
the vortex of legalism.   So much was Luther persuaded of
the legalism of all this, that in his treatise on the Bondage of
the Will, in answer to Erasmus, his whole reasoning assumes
that it is a mockery to present the finished work of Christ
to men who are taught that they possess INHERENT POWER,
as this undermines the whole.

The full development of all these systems appears in the fact that they preach A DEAD FAITH.   Their naturalistic tendency expresses itself in the assertion that they do not know a wrong faith, and that there are *not two ways of believing*.   On the contrary, the Bible speaks of a dead faith. The confessions of the Reformation, drawn from Scripture, delineate faith as a new religious principle of life, awakened by the Holy Spirit without man's active aid.   It is an instructive fact that some of the old Lutheran divines, in their apprehension lest an element of works should be introduced into our title, objected at one time to the designation " living faith ; " but it is said that not one now exists that does not solemnly abjure the error.   And no reflecting mind can fail to see that living faith must be given as the Spirit's gift when we apprehend the Saviour as our righteousness ; and *it never does or can exist without thus apprehending Christ.*   Hence in all the systems above delineated, in harmony with the dead faith which is propounded, there is the offer of a salvation, but a painful want of reference to the personal Redeemer.   They allude to an object in the past in formal contrast with a present object ; they preach a salvation in abstract separation from His Person, and as little connected with Him as if He had never risen.   Calvin says : Such a separation of Christ from His Spirit makes Him like a dead image or corpse.[1]

That man owes his renovation to the effectual supernatural operation of the Holy Spirit, is evident enough from what has been already said.   Any synergism or co-operation on man's side in the first instance would necessarily presuppose the existence of powers and faculties in order to that co-operation. But in the explicit statements of Scripture man is represented as impotent, nay, dead in trespasses and sins (Eph. ii. 1); thus rendering co-operative action toward his own resuscitation

[1] On Rom. viii. 10, Calvin says : " *Christum a spiritu suo qui divellunt, eum faciunt mortuo simulacro vel cadaueri similem.*"

impossible, and only an absurd idea.   On the contrary, the
Scripture emphatically describes the divine action of the
Spirit as working in us to will and to do (Phil. ii. 13).   But
whether He *works in us to will*, or subsequently works *with
us* when we are enabled to will, the entire glory of regeneration and of conversion belongs to the Spirit of God.   There
is no middle ground, no intermediate stage between death and
life, between conversion and non-conversion; for the origin
of spiritual life must be instantaneous.   It is compared to
creation (Ps. li. 10 ; Eph. ii. 10); it is compared to resurrection (Eph. i. 19); it is a making alive which God works in
us without our aid ; without the regenerating grace of the
Holy Spirit, man is "neither able nor willing[1] to return to God"
or to receive the Lord Jesus as his Saviour.   But it must by
no means be inferred that after the Spirit of God has done his
part, it still remains in the power of man to be regenerated or
not, to believe or not believe : for the Spirit works a supernatural operation, and compares it to creation or resurrection.
All who share in it are effectually converted and actually
believe.   The Spirit does not merely bestow the power or
ability to believe, and *then waits till man* in the exercise of
his own free will accepts the terms and actually believes ; for
the Spirit's efficacious grace produces both the will to believe
and also the act of believing.   The man who is the subject
of the change is the party on whom creative omnipotence
acts, to the exclusion of all mental preparations on man's
side,—for he is only receptive,—and all merits of congruity
of every description.

THE SIN OR BLASPHEMY AGAINST THE HOLY GHOST.

Having considered the Spirit's convincing work, which is in
reality equivalent to what is known as EFFECTUAL CALLING,
we shall next consider Christ's testimony to the blasphemy

[1] See Articles of Dort and Art. X. of English Church.

or sin against the Holy Ghost. " *Whosoever speaketh against the Holy Ghost, it shall not be forgiven him, neither in this world, nor in the world to come*" (Matt. xii. 32). On the occasion of healing a demoniac, the Pharisees wished to invalidate the proof of Christ's divine mission by the allegation that the miracle was not performed by the finger of God, but by Beelzebul, the prince of the devils. Without explicitly stating that they had committed, or were committing, the sin against the Holy Ghost, He gives them a solemn warning that there is a sin against the Holy Ghost which is unpardonable. He speaks absolutely of an irremissible sin ; for all other sin can be remitted on the ground of Christ's satisfaction through faith and repentance. But with the solemnity of an oath by Himself, as the " verily verily " indicates, He declares that this sin has no forgiveness.

As to the nature of this sin against the Holy Ghost, it is shrouded in a certain mystery, but it is neither calculated nor intended to give perplexity to any Christian mind. It may be difficult to define it ; and the most conflicting opinions were entertained among the ancient Fathers, and downwards from the Reformation times. Thus Tertullian, Hilary, and other Fathers maintained that the sin against the Spirit meant blasphemy, not against the human nature of Christ, which is pardonable, but against His divine nature, which is unpardonable. Cyprian explained it of apostasy, or the denial of Christ, and consequently held that the lapsed could scarcely, if at all, be forgiven. Origen expounded the passage of those sins which are committed subsequent to baptism. But these essentially Novatian comments, when fully carried out, come into collision with the Creed, which declares : " I believe in the forgiveness of sins." Athanasius is not consistent with himself. We may perhaps distribute the vast variety of interpretations scattered over the works of expositors, and over the theological systems of divines, into the three following classes :—

1. Those which virtually make it a sin possible only when Christ was among men in the exercise of His personal ministry. Chrysostom and Jerome explain it as if our Lord meant to say : he that speaks against the Son of man, regarding Him as nothing more than man, may obtain forgiveness ; but he who ascribes these miracles to Satan, while discerning in them the indications of divine power, shall never be forgiven ; for this is the unpardonable sin against the Holy Ghost, by whom Christ performed His mighty deeds. Pfaff and Klinkenberg, in last century, strongly asserted that interpretation.

2. Another view propounded by Augustin makes the sin against the Holy Ghost equivalent to final impenitence. A very large class of writers in all ages have held this view as the simplest and least complicated. The followers of Melanchthon in the Lutheran Church, many of our Scots divines,—such as Guthrie in his *Trial of a Saving Interest*, Chalmers, and others,—as well as writers in all countries who have followed Augustin, have accepted this comment as the best.

3. Calvin, dissenting from Augustin's view because it seemed not to do justice to the peculiar expression, that this sin shall not be forgiven *either in this world or in that which is to come*, held that it is resistance to the truth conjoined with malice, though the evidence in behalf of the truth of the Christian faith was such as rendered it impossible to plead ignorance. The thought is supposed to be, that this sin is committed before the close of life, and while the person has still a period to live in this world. And it is alleged that the distinguishing mark of this sin is conscious resistance or deliberate opposition to conclusive evidence supplied by the Spirit of God. The men who commit this sin are thought to be convinced of the truth of the Christian religion, and yet oppose and blaspheme it, not so much from sudden passion and the force of temptation, as from wilful malice. It is

argued that while God gives pardon to all manner of sin through the exercise of faith and repentance, the sin against the Holy Ghost is unique and irremissible, because conscious resistance is present to the mind, and because the voluntary denial of divine truth is combined with hatred and malice. This opinion of Calvin was adopted with a very general consent by the subsequent divines of the Reformed Church. If I were to adduce a *catena* of Reformed divines, they would be found almost uniformly to follow Calvin's opinion, and frequently with an exaggerated statement both of the extent of a gracious work of the Spirit on such minds, and of the almost Satanic character of their conscious resistance. This comes out in such writers as Maresius, Maestricht, Cocceius, Hoornbeck, and others.

One guiding principle, however, against excess of statement is supplied by the fact that the evidence furnished by the Spirit, and resisted by those who so sin against Him, is ONLY HIS TESTIMONY, not HIS WORK ON THE HEART ; for (1) the latter is irresistible ; and (2) he that hath begun a good work will perform it. Whatever evidence is brought to bear on the mind, it is but rational conviction derived from testimony, not the efficacious change of heart. And this enables us to draw a line between the Lutheran and Reformed exposition of this topic. The Lutheran exposition holds that the regenerate can fall from grace, and that only the regenerate are guilty of the sin against the Holy Ghost. So Gerhard, Balduin, Hülsemann, Quenstedt, and all their eminent divines speak. On the contrary, the canons of the Synod of Dort, giving as they do the most admirably correct expression of all the doctrines of special grace, include among the errors which are to be rejected, the opinion that the regenerate may be guilty of this sin.

It is commonly held that this is the same sin that is referred to by the sacred writers in those other passages of Scripture (Heb. vi. 4–6, x. 29 ; 1 John v. 16). It is true

Athanasius, Basil, Jerome do not regard these passages in the Epistle to the Hebrews and in John as referring to the sin against the Holy Ghost. Calvin says : " The apostle agrees with the Master."

I have given the principal opinions on this unpardonable sin, and endeavoured to distribute them into three classes. For my own part, I incline to Augustin's opinion ; at all events, I am convinced that the notion of FINAL IMPENITENCE must be taken along with us as a main element in any opinion which may be adopted or maintained on this subject.

LECTURE V.

ON THE SPIRIT OF HOLINESS, OR SANCTIFICATION OF THE SPIRIT.

IN our last lecture we discussed the Spirit's work on the individual, with special reference to the way and mode of His return to the human heart, and to the application of redemption. The heart resembles a dwelling - house. It belongs to some one, and it never is without an occupant. If the Holy Spirit does not inhabit it according to the original idea of making man for this end, it follows from the necessity of things that Satan occupies it. If the Spirit is there, He is master of the dwelling, and is attended by a great retinue of holy and spiritual faculties all used and replenished by Him.

By way of transition to the topic which will now occupy attention, let me recall the inseparable connection between the work of Christ FOR US and the work of the Spirit IN US — a connection which it is of the utmost moment for sound theology as well as practical religion habitually to apprehend. It is a connection of cause and effect, or of merit and reward. It is in express terms set forth in such passages as the sixth, seventh, and eighth chapters of the Epistle to the Romans, where, in every variety of form, the apostle declares that the link between the justification of the man and the sanctification of his nature is as close and inseparable as that by which God connected Christ's atoning death and His resurrection to a premial life. The link between the two is secured, not by the mere force of gratitude or by the influence of truth, but

by something immeasurably more powerful, and which touches
the deepest foundations of the divine government—viz. by
the righteous restoration of the Spirit of life in Christ
Jesus (Rom. viii. 2). There cannot be the application of
redemption in the way of pardon and acceptance without the
accompanying Spirit of holiness.

Here we must advert to THE PART WHICH CHRIST ACTS IN
GIVING THE SPIRIT. In all Protestant theology, Lutheran and
Reformed, there is a general consent that Christ is our acting
life-communicating head BY His Spirit. It is not Christ
without the Spirit, nor the Spirit without Christ. His
mediatorial function was not limited to His earthly life.
Nor is it something outward, which every man is left to
appropriate to himself. The whole application of redemption
is not to be regarded merely as man dealing with God, but
rather as the action of the God-man, in His capacity as His
people's representative dealing with the Father, and the
Father dealing with the Son, according to the counsel of
peace between them both, for man's acceptance. And the
participation of saving blessings is through the power of the
Spirit. The exalted Saviour has this in view in the entire
exercise of His priestly functions towards God, and of His
kingly office towards men. It is not man's will, which is
weak and changeful, but the effectual will of the God-man,
which is to be regarded as the turning-point or hinge. And
though He employs His Holy Spirit according to the economic
order in the Godhead, it is by His direct act as Head that He
attaches to Himself His members, and calls them into fellowship or joint participation with Himself. They are apprehended by Christ Jesus (Phil. iii. 12).

The FAITH by which the application of His merits is
instrumentally conveyed IS ITSELF THE GIFT OF CHRIST, exalted
as a Prince and Saviour, to give the blessings of His purchase, to incorporate the living members into vital union with
Himself, and to work effectually in His people by the efficacy

of His Spirit through the word, and in the whole ministerial commission.

It seems proper to notice in this connection some titles of the Spirit, and some operations carried on, according to these titles, in the heart of Christian men as they advance in holiness. Thus He is called THE SPIRIT OF WISDOM AND REVELATION (Eph. i. 17), THE SPIRIT THAT DWELLS IN US (2 Tim. i. 14), and the SPIRIT BY WHOM THOSE ARE LED OR MOVED, who are evinced to be the sons of God (Rom. viii. 14). As to the discharge of these several offices which He fulfils in our behalf, it is necessary to carry with us the thought that He measures Himself against all the opposite tendencies or corruptions in man's fallen nature.

THE SPIRIT OF WISDOM AND REVELATION. This title of the Spirit is by no means limited to the inspiration of the Scriptures. One of the errors advocated by Bishop Warburton and his school during last century was the position that the Spirit's work was limited to the supernatural aid imparted to the penmen of the sacred Scriptures, and that every internal work, by which the eyes of our understanding are said to be opened or enlightened, is something to be challenged as replete with perilous enthusiasm. But the Scriptures themselves assert in the most emphatic way that in the whole work by which men are turned to God and sanctified, there is a further work of the Spirit by which the understanding is enlightened and the will inclined to obey the divine will, and the affections are effectually drawn to love, serve, and enjoy God.

We see this Spirit of wisdom and revelation (1) in the Christian's personal salvation, and (2) in all the efforts of the Christian divine in seeking to expound the holy oracles to others.

1. When the Holy Spirit comes as the Spirit of revelation in the knowledge of Christ, He specially enables men to know sin, to discern the ruin and the remedy, to know the

righteous and holy nature of God, the authority, the depth
and spirituality of the divine law, as well as the antagonism
and enmity of the carnal mind, which is not subject to the
law, nor can be.   The same Spirit having begun the good
work on the mind, continues to carry it on by revealing in
and through the word the excellency of Christ's person, His
offices and merits, and the sufficiency of the atonement, as
the only way by which sinners can be put in a right relation
to God.   All this is carried home to the mind by what is
called "the demonstration of the Spirit" (1 Cor. ii. 4).
Their minds are enlightened to take in many great truths
of which they were wholly ignorant, or to which they gave
no attention.   A heavenly light, new and different from anything ever known before, shines into their minds, not indeed
without the word, but IN, BY, and UNDER THE WORD, as it
testifies of the grace of the Gospel and of a personal Saviour,
the one Mediator between God and man.   The scales fall
from their eyes: the clouds of ignorance are scattered; they
clearly apprehend the way of a sinner's acceptance with God,
through the obedience and death of Christ as their Substitute
and Surety.   By the operation of this Spirit of Revelation
they make surprising progress in the knowledge of Christ and
of heavenly things.   The revelation directly imparted by God
through the channel of the word, brings with it a relish or a
new sense for divine things, and is a wholly new and supernatural principle of life and action.

The difference between the natural man and the man born
of the Spirit is unfolded by the apostle in the most striking
and arresting manner (1 Cor. ii. 10–16).   The natural man,
it is said, receives not the things of the Spirit of God—an
expression which certain divines, such as Spener, regard as
derived from the friendly welcome of a guest to whom the
door is opened, and who is hailed with a cordial reception.
The natural man, who views the way of salvation by a
crucified Saviour as foolishness, is all the while yielding to a

groundless and false imagination in regard to it, supposing that he sees its nature and takes in the divine plan propounded to him; while, on the contrary, he is under the power of deep prejudice, averse to its very nature, and ignorant of its adaptation to man's wants. Notwithstanding his rationalistic self-complacency, he does not really know it; for it is spiritually discerned. On the other hand, the apostle shows that in the case of the mind enlightened by the Spirit, the understanding grasps it, the will chooses it, and the affections embrace it.

We do not suppose, indeed, that the Spirit reveals any new truths not found in the holy oracles; for the objective revelation was closed with the completion of the canon, and the Spirit cannot be supposed to teach what is not in harmony with the Scriptures, which are His own work. Nor are we to conclude that the light of the Spirit, which is different in its nature from anything that emanates from flesh and blood (Matt. xvi. 17), is a mere opinion, fancy, or impression on the feelings. It is a new sense given directly from the Divine Spirit, and is essential to all true religion.

If it is asked what more is needed besides the Scriptures, the answer is: Men need ability to understand them and to apply them. The Scriptures are always used in connection with the revelation of the Spirit. But without the Spirit acting as the interpreter of the revelation which He deposited in the Scriptures, and which are His own work, there would be no enjoyment of the light of life, no sense of divine love, no fellowship with God. He disposes the mind, under the power of deeply-rooted prejudices, to accept the truth, and to know what the Scriptures contain. He removes the veil and opens men's understandings to understand the Scriptures. They who previously saw no beauty in the Saviour to desire Him, are no sooner imbued with this spirit of wisdom and revelation than they regard Him in a wholly new light, as fairer than the sons of men, and as the adorable object of their daily contemplations. The Spirit shows Him in a new light to the understanding, which thus becomes an avenue to all the powers of the soul. They are transported with His excellency, and, seeing as in a glass His glory, are changed into the same image, from glory to glory, as by the Lord the Spirit (2 Cor. iii. 18).

2. I said, moreover, that the Spirit is necessary to aid the Christian divine to expound the Scripture. The Scripture can be understood and interpreted only by the aid of the Holy Spirit. This principle, that the Holy Scriptures can be understood only by the aid of the Spirit, is strongly expressed in all the Protestant confessions. And the reason of this position may be easily explained. The Scriptures, containing a revelation by the Holy Spirit, can be understood only by the aid of the same Spirit who is the author of the Book, and who must needs be its interpreter, if it is to be understood to any good purpose. The appeal is here made again to 1 Cor. ii. 14. Only he who has the Spirit, or is in a state of grace, can understand the Holy Scriptures. The true interpretation is the theological, as contrasted with a philological interpretation—the believing exposition as contrasted with an unbelieving—the Christian as contrasted with a heathen mode of expounding the divine word. In confirmation of this, the appeal is always made to the exegesis of the Reformers, who were in a remarkable manner led to the right sense, because, along with great learning, they were full of the Spirit, and had such a deep Christian experience, and such a sympathy with the tone and spirit of the sacred writers.

We wish, for the sake of non-theological readers, to refer to this point—viz. the reproduction of Christ's spiritual life in His people. As Adam's life is reproduced in the entire human family with all its alienation from the life of God, and with the organic ruin of their whole nature, so the new life of the God-man flows over to all His people. The natural birth connects us with the first man, and renews his life. The new birth connects us with the second man, who, by the Holy Spirit, gathers His people under Him by a self-communicating act. I am the more desirous to give a due place to this great truth, because it has been less developed within the last century than in the previous periods. The last Adam is a quickening Spirit (1 Cor. xv. 45). That life is in the Son, who, by the Spirit, apprehends the whole man in all his faculties; and the renewing process will be completed even on his body at the resurrection-day. Every believer, though not directly conscious of connection with the first man, is, or ought to be, permanently conscious of his union to the second Adam, who is our life.

The Spirit's work was specially intended to form a MYSTIC UNION with Christ for the application of redemption, and for the INHABITATION of the Spirit of life in Christ Jesus (Rom. viii. 2). I need not refer in detail to the several figures or similitudes under which that union is exhibited in Scripture as a potential reality (2 Cor. xi. 2 ; Eph. iv. 16 ; John xv. 1–6 ; Eph. ii. 20). These various figures taken from marriage, from the union of the human body with the head, from the vine and branches, from the temple and the corner-stone, are intended to set forth a real and intimate connection, and to show that the inmost soul of the redeemed is reserved for Christ's inhabitation by the Spirit, who thus becomes the life of their life, the soul of their soul, in a sense to which any other known union makes no approximation. The Spirit is the bond of union on Christ's side, and faith, produced by the Spirit of faith, is the bond on our side ; and when that union is effected, the soul, like the fruitful branch of the vine, brings forth abundant fruit.

As to the union, it is said by the apostle : " He that is joined to the Lord is one Spirit " (1 Cor. vi. 17); and the results that immediately flow from it are so extensive and so

powerful, for the supply of the covenant blessings, that
Christ's Spirit becomes theirs, His holiness their holiness, His
joy their joy.   Such is the Spirit's efficacy, that there is not
one thought, feeling, or emotion pervading the human bosom
of the man Christ Jesus amid the glories of the upper
sanctuary, but may be said to be renewed and reproduced in
the experience of His people,—perfectly in the bliss above,
incipiently in their present dwelling-place below.   So real
is the union through the Spirit, and so deep the sympathy
reciprocally exercised between the ever-living Head in heaven
and the spiritual body which He has united to Himself, that,
on the one hand, every want, necessity, and sorrow under
which His people groan vibrates to Him like the touching of
a chord, of which He is instantly aware ; while, on the other
hand, an injury offered to His cause awakens in them such a
sense of oneness and of conscious identification with His
interests and honour, that it constrains them to say : " Rivers
of water run down my eyes, because they keep not Thy
law " (Ps. cxix. 136).   By the Spirit our whole person is
united to His whole Person.   And the bond of union depends
not, as Romanists and Ritualists allege, on bodily contact or
local nearness, but on faith, by means of which we are one
with Him ; for Christ does not come down corporeally from
heaven for the accomplishment of any of the objects contemplated by that union in this our earthly pilgrimage.

Whether the elect of God were already united to Christ
before the actual exercise of faith, was a point keenly
debated in England two centuries ago between the followers
of Crisp, who affirmed it, and their opponents, led by Dr. D.
Williams, who denied it.   As the exaggerated terms in which
the former spoke of eternal justification caused suspicion and
alarm, Witsius, the celebrated Dutch divine, prepared his
admirable *irenicum* to bring the parties together.[1]   The

[1] *Vid.* Witsius, *Animadversiones Irenicæ ad Controversias quasdam Angli-
canas*, Leyden 1700.

solution which he gave of the controverted point was contained in the distinction that the saints were in Christ by
a federal and legal union before the foundation of the world,
but that the actual union—called the mystical or vital union
—takes place only WHEN THE HOLY SPIRIT UNITES THEM to
the Son of God.   From that moment, they who are united to
the Lord Jesus by one Spirit obtain a true and actual participation in all that He procured by His obedience unto death.
If Christ satisfied divine justice, they who are united to Him
by faith have also satisfied it.   When Christ overcame, they
overcame ; when Christ received perfect acceptance as the
Surety, they received the same acceptance in and with Him.
And, on the other hand, as Christ obtained a resurrection-life,
a life of holiness and joy at God's right hand for ever, they,
too, who are found in Him, have an incipient life of the same
nature, a life hid with Christ in God (Col. iii. 3).

THE INHABITATION OF THE SPIRIT.

This brings us to the great truth, frequently affirmed and
repeated in Scripture—THE INHABITATION OF THE SPIRIT in
all true believers.   The passages are very numerous which
teach this great doctrine.   Thus Christ, in promising the
Comforter, who should abide with His disciples for ever,
added, by way of contrasting the world and them : " I will
pray the Father, and He shall give you another Comforter,
that He may *abide with you* for ever—the Spirit of truth,
whom the world cannot receive, because it seeth Him not,
neither knoweth Him : but ye know Him ; *for He dwelleth
with you and shall be in you* " (John xiv. 16).   The Apostle
Paul, in writing to Timothy, says : " That good thing which
was committed to thee, keep *by the Holy Ghost which dwelleth in
us* " (2 Tim. i. 14).   I shall notice, further, the passages where
the Christian is called the temple of the Holy Ghost : " Know
ye not that ye are the temple of God, and that *the Spirit of*

God dwelleth in you?" (1 Cor. iii. 16). " Know ye not that your body is *the temple of the Holy Ghost which is in you, which we have of God?*" (1 Cor. vi. 19). We may compare other similar passages (2 Cor. vi. 16 ; Eph. ii. 22). In all these passages the Holy Spirit who dwells in Christ, and who is given to inhabit His people, is said to occupy the Christian's heart as His temple, not by a mere inactive presence, but by an efficacious inhabitation which must be regarded as animating and pervading all the faculties and powers of the human mind.

The regenerate man, accordingly, is said to HAVE THE SPIRIT OF CHRIST. The expression is used by the apostle in the Epistle to the Romans in two connected clauses in such a way as implies that there is an inhabitation on the part of the Holy Spirit, and a consequent possession of Him on our side as a graciously imparted privilege : " But ye are not in the flesh, but in the Spirit, if so be that the Spirit of God *dwell in you.* Now, if any man HAVE NOT THE SPIRIT of Christ, he is none of His " (Rom. viii. 9). TO HAVE THE SPIRIT, then, is inseparably connected with the inhabitation of the Spirit. We are thus said to " have " the Spirit as the consequence of His effectual inhabitation, which evinces itself by a renewing and transforming principle of life, which constantly operates in the most active manner. And we are conscious of having so great a guest, because He condescends to occupy the soul in all its faculties.

It may be proper at this stage to obviate a common misinterpretation, which tends to evacuate the phrases in the passages to which we have referred of their full significance. From a speculative reluctance to accept the idea of the Spirit's personal inhabitation, sometimes in one interest, and at other times in another, many interpreters, scholastic as well as Protestant, have superficially expounded the allusions to the indwelling of the Spirit as referring only to the gifts which He confers.

That is an arbitrary exposition on the part of the interpreter for which no good ground can be assigned. When the
allusion is to gifts conferred,—except in the case of temporary
disciples like Judas,—we must rather say that the personal
Holy Spirit was given along with the gifts which were
bestowed. He did not produce them as an absent regulator
of their distribution, but as a present inhabitant. Nay, we
may affirm that A PERSON WORKS ONLY WHERE HE IS; and
it was only as inhabiting the hearts of believers that He
imparted either the sanctifying gifts or the ministerial gifts.

Here let me elucidate a point of no small moment in
reference to the personal inhabitation of the Spirit in the
Christian heart. And in doing so I shall endeavour, with
due caution, to avoid excess of statement on the one hand,
and defect of statement on the other. To suppose, as some
enthusiasts have done, that the Spirit communicates any
portion of His own divine essence to the new creature, can
only be called an extravagant excess of statement for which
there is no warrant and no excuse. On the other hand, it
can only be regarded as an error by defect when we pause at
the notion of a bare influence or operation, as if the phrase
" who dwelleth in us " (2 Tim. i. 14) carried with it nothing
more than a merely figurative or metaphorical allusion, and
could not be regarded as meaning anything more than an
influence.

The latter superficial view is maintained by not a few in
various Churches. They understand nothing more than a
power or influence from God, which produces an impression
or brings home divine things with a certain clearness and
comfort to the mind. It amounts to a true renewing influence in some writers and to moral suasion in others. Divines
sometimes hesitate to accept the idea of inhabitation in the
full sense of the term, lest they should seem to fall into
excess or to adopt the language of the enthusiasts. We are
as fully alive as they can be to the duty of speaking with

sobriety and caution, when we recall the language of the mystics of mediæval times and the extravagances of the heady, high-minded sects of the time of Cromwell, which produced a recoil from the Scripture doctrine of the Spirit, from which many have not recovered to this day. But we ought equally to be on our guard against the opposite extreme of erring by defect, lest we obscure or misrepresent the supernatural work of the Holy Spirit. We must hold on the sure ground of Scripture, that not only are the gifts of the Spirit poured into the heart of believers, but the personal Holy Ghost, who had left man's heart in ruins, and no longer His temple, returns to take up his abode in the redeemed, and occupies them with a personal hidden indwelling presence which our limited faculties in this transitory state do not permit us to measure or comprehend. Enough that the fact is plainly taught us in the Holy Scriptures, however incapable we may be to grasp or explain it to ourselves or to other minds.

The personal indwelling of the Spirit in the Christian is put beyond doubt by a few passages which we shall adduce :—

1. " Because ye are sons, God hath sent forth the Spirit of His Son into your hearts, crying, Abba, Father " (Gal. iv. 6). Here we must take notice of the person sent, the same that rests on the Son of God—the heart of the believer where He abides—and the petitions, cries, or prayers which are awakened by Him. It is clear that there is not only a certain influence working on the heart of the believer and giving rise to prayers and intercession (comp. Rom. viii. 26), but that the Spirit enters into the exercise of supplication, so as to awaken and inflame it, and to mingle with it, that it may rise up as incense to heaven.

2. " The fruit of the Spirit is love, joy, peace, long-suffer-ing, gentleness, goodness, faith, meekness, temperance " (Gal. v. 22). The effect is distinct from the cause or workman. The fruits of the Spirit are spoken of as distinct from the

Spirit Himself. But of one thing there can be no doubt when we consider the whole passage in its connection : these Christians are said to carry the workman and His gifts in their bosom; for He is sent into their hearts (Gal. iv. 6); and they walk in the Spirit (v. 16); and are led by the Spirit (v. 18); and live in the Spirit (v. 25).

3. " Ye are not in the flesh, but in the Spirit, if so be that the Spirit of God dwell in you. Now, if any man have not the Spirit of Christ, he is none of His " (Rom. viii. 9). This passage plainly shows that the personal Holy Ghost is referred to. In Christ Jesus reside not only all the gifts of the Spirit, but the Spirit Himself; and in like manner the members of Christ are not only supplied and adorned by every variety of gifts, but made partakers of the Spirit Himself.

4. " Know ye not that ye are the temple of God, and that the Spirit of God dwelleth in you ? " (1 Cor. iii. 16). From that passage divines are wont to prove the supreme deity of the Spirit, because He is there said to occupy His temple, and so receives divine honour, service, and worship. We go through with the proof, and maintain that the Divine Spirit dwells in His people by an ineffable inhabitation, in much the same way as the Shechinah of old dwelt in the temple of Jerusalem.

5. " If ye are reproached for the name of Christ, happy are ye; for the Spirit of glory and of God resteth upon you " (1 Pet. iv. 14). This language cannot refer to mere gifts, but to the person of the Spirit, inhabiting the reviled and persecuted Christian, who is said to have resting on him and in him, as in a holy and permanent resting-place (ἀναπαύεται), the Spirit of glory and of God.

6. " Hereby we know that we dwell in Him, and He in us, because He hath given us of His Spirit " (1 John iv. 13). The hidden union of which the apostle speaks in the previous verse is there more fully defined. The Christian dwells perpetually in God, and God in Him, by the bond of the

Spirit personally occupying the renewed heart and filling all
its powers and faculties, that thus we may be carried beyond
ourselves to a sanctifying union with God.

7. " After that ye believed [better, *having believed*], ye
were sealed with that holy spirit of promise " (Eph. i. 13).
The seal of the Holy Spirit is a phrase of great significance, and
is frequently referred to by Paul as attesting that we are God's
property (comp. Eph. iv. 30).   There are many comments on
this expression, but by far the most natural is that which refers
it to a right of property on God's side, that is, to the general
notion of a seal-attesting that the property to which the
seal is attached belongs to Him whose seal is attached.   It
carries with it also the idea that the IMAGE and LIKENESS of
God is again impressed on believers.   There are two purposes
for which men use a seal, viz. to secure a property from
hazard, and to impress the owner's image on it.   None can
ever share in eternal life, unless the broad seal of heaven is
imprinted on them, and the image of God is legible on their
heart; and it is thus that God makes them meet to be
partakers of the inheritance of the saints in light.   This seal
is the Holy Ghost impressing every feature of the divine
image on them; and the perseverance of believers is thus
secured amid all the trials and temptations encountered in
their way to heaven.   Sealed by the Spirit of God to the day
of redemption, they are kept safe as the property of God.
The safety which believers derive from the sealing of the
Holy Spirit is traced to His inhabitation and to His influence; for the Spirit of God is at once an EARNEST and a SEAL
—an earnest as He is part of that inheritance in store for
them, or the first-fruits of heaven—-and a SEAL to secure their
salvation.   This INHABITATION is therefore their real security.

As this inhabitation is associated with the active exercise
of divine power, it may be further noticed that it underlies
all the Christian's holiness and growth, all his conformity to
the divine image and his final perseverance.   It is the peculiar

feature of every system that takes this truth in earnest, that it prompts its advocates to bring out the essential difference between grace and nature,—to vindicate the spiritual life as a new creation,—to assert its actual reality, its peculiar organs, its habitual graces implanted, — with the several actings, experiences, wants, and appetences which belong to it as a distinct existence, but never separated from the living Head. To the neglect of this inhabitation of the Spirit must be ascribed much of the naturalism of the modern theology which ascribes the graces of the Spirit only to the ordinary exercises of the mind as it unfolds itself in joy or sorrow, in faith or love, on a spiritual object; and they lose sight of the fact that the indwelling Spirit, filling and animating the renewed mental faculties, calls these graces into action over the ruins of the opposite corruption. On the contrary, the schools of theology which do justice to the great fact of the Spirit's inhabitation, such as the true followers of Augustin and of the Puritans, were happily exempt from that evacuating theology. They contended not only for Christ's abiding PRESENCE IN EVERY SPIRITUAL ACT (John xv. 5), but for the real implantation of the graces of the Spirit as well as for THE IMPOSSIBILITY OF PUTTING THEM IN MOTION without His heavenly help.

The most eminent Lutheran divines, in the brightest period of their theology,—Luther, Chemnitzius, and the like, —were wont to teach that the inhabitation of the Spirit consisted in two things: IN THE SPIRIT'S PRESENCE AND OPERATION, or, in a single phrase, in gracious presence. They were accustomed also to distinguish the modes of the divine presence in this fourfold way: *first*, a universal presence over all the wide realms of creation for the conservation of all things; *secondly*, a special sanctifying presence, whereby the Spirit abides in true Christians, and inhabits them continually through life and in death, till they fully enjoy the beatific vision; *thirdly*, the personal union of the Son of God, whereby He assumed humanity with all that the assumption carried with it, and replenished that humanity with His indwelling presence; *fourthly*, the presence of the Spirit in glorified saints, whereby He not only fills the heart with all the communications of His grace, but leads them to behold God's face in righteousness, and to be satisfied when they awake with His likeness.

LED BY THE SPIRIT.

The expression, LED BY THE SPIRIT, means in both the passages where it is found (Gal. v. 18; Rom. viii. 14), that they who are the sons of God are actuated by a motive power on the part of the Spirit of God that will never be withdrawn. They are first passive and then active. They are not mechanically moved, like a block or stone; but by the Spirit occupying all their faculties and moving in them, they are carried onward in the exercise of new powers supplied to them by the quickening Spirit (*ita a Spiritu sancto agimur ut ipsi quoque agamus*). In a word, we may fitly say, with Edwards and other eminent divines, that God PRODUCES ALL, and that man ACTS ALL. This leading of the Spirit is by no means to be limited to mere moral suasion, or to such impressions as an orator produces by just expressions, by the wisdom of words, or the presentation of arresting objects to the imagination. He moves the Christian to the reception of doctrine, to the discharge of duty, to the exercise of worship, and to the enjoyments of religion, by the exceeding greatness of His power to usward who believe, according to the working of His mighty power, which He wrought in Christ when He raised Him from the dead (Eph. i. 10).

This appears when we take into account the Biblical description of the beginning, progress, and end of that activity which is prompted and carried out by the Holy Spirit. Thus, when God promises (Ezek. xxxvi. 27): " I will put my

Spirit within you, and cause you to walk in my statutes; and
ye shall keep my judgments and do them," we are taught
that the Spirit so far anticipates the first tendency or inclination of man as to make him act according to the divine
precepts. God's free grace, and not man's free will, originates
the action and makes all effectual. In like manner Paul
describes the concurrence of man's activity and God's effectual
operation, when He gives absolute priority to the divine power
(Phil. ii. 13): "It is God that worketh in you both to will
and to do of His good pleasure." The language there used
proves, beyond doubt or cavil, that before man either wills or
acts in the ways of God, there is in the recesses of the heart
a divine operation anticipating our will, and giving effect to
our action. That language has nothing in common with
the naturalism of the modern theology, which ascribes all
Christian action to free will more than to free grace, and
attributes what is in reality a fruit of the Spirit to the ordinary
exercises of the mind, as it unfolds itself, in faith and love, in
joy or sorrow, on a spiritual object.

The grand security for the FINAL PERSEVERANCE of the
saints is this leading of the Spirit. The Spirit ever leads and
never departs from the soul that He has once occupied; and
the ground to which we must trace the irrevocable aid and
presence of the Spirit is the fact that the Lord Jesus, as the
second Adam, having stood and fulfilled all the conditions of
the first covenant, obtained the Spirit, and gives Him to us
as His gift. When the soul is weak, the Spirit helps us;
and when the soul grows languid or indifferent, the Spirit
animates, keeps, and quickens us, and restores to us the joy
of God's salvation (Ps. li. 12). With a marked harmony,
both in the Old and New Testament, Scripture sets forth that
the believer in every truly spiritual act is moved and guided
by the efficacious work of the Holy Spirit; that as the mind
cannot dispense with the Spirit, he evermore receives the
Spirit's aid; and that as the graces of the new creature cannot

put themselves in motion without the Spirit's help, this is ever-
more imparted, even after the divine image is renewed; for
Christ says, " without me ye can do nothing " (John xv. 5).
That Spirit is given to abide for ever, and to lead us for ever.

This statement, it may be added, has nothing in common
with the language of the enthusiasts who have asserted, in
various epochs of the Church's history, that they were
mechanically moved by the Holy Spirit, and who, while so
speaking, have lived in an antinomian way, and disavowed
every spiritual change.   On the contrary, the mind LED BY
THE SPIRIT discovers that it has all the graces of the new
creature,—ears to hear the Shepherd's voice, eyes to see the
King in His beauty, a true Christian life animated by the
spirit of prayer, and an enlargement of heart to run in the
way of God's commandments.   But along with all this they
cry, in the language of the Psalmist, " Teach me to do Thy
will; for Thou art my God: let Thy good Spirit LEAD ME to
the land of uprightness " (Ps. cxliii. 10).

The Spirit's work, as the great inhabitant of the regenerate
heart, appears in continually sanctifying all the mental
powers; and a marked line of distinction must be drawn
between THE PREVENIENT GRACE OF THE SPIRIT and His
CO-OPERATING GRACE.   The former belongs to effectual calling,
regeneration, conversion, and faith, in which the man with all
his powers is the object in whom the Spirit operates by the
word; the latter belongs to His progressive sanctification, in
which the Spirit calls into exercise the new powers of the
renewed mind, and where there are NO IMMEDIATE ACTINGS OF
THE SPIRIT superseding that co-operation: for who can see
without an eye, or hear without an ear ?   The Holy Spirit
does not move the hearts of regenerate men by mere power, but
on another principle.   He moves them by THOSE SPIRITUAL
POWERS or graces with which they are now provided.   The
Spirit which is in Christ without measure, is in them by
measure as a Spirit of life ; not moving the mind as a stone,

or as a wheel, by mere power, but according to the new nature which has been created and formed in it. To lose sight of this is to ignore the fact that Christ is the source of the Spirit of life, and that the Christian has to add to his faith virtue, and to virtue knowledge, and all the various excellences which are perfect in Christ Jesus (2 Pet. i. 5). Hence, they who are renewed after their Lord's image have, according to their measure, a certain spiritual power, a certain law of their mind, the law of the Spirit of life in Christ Jesus, which enables them to overcome and triumph in their Lord (Rom. viii. 2).

The practical neglect of this distinction may sometimes be traced in Church history and on whole generations of men. The Lutherans, for example, though they spoke much and admirably of grace and liberty, were too easily satisfied that the good tree, by the inevitable law of its existence, would bring forth its fruit. They neglected the due cultivation of the graces of the Spirit in the new creature. On the contrary, the Puritans pruned and cultivated the good tree with unwearied diligence, and made every Christian grace and duty, after scriptural example, the subject of wholesome exhortation.

Before I leave this point, let me add that the indwelling Spirit is EVER ACTIVE IN THE HEART which He condescends to inhabit. His is no mere otiose, but an ever operative presence in all the ways according to which the Spirit acts IN and UPON the Christian mind. He enters by casting out Satan (Matt. xii. 28); He quenches the deep thirst of the longing soul (John vii. 38); He sheds abroad the love of God in the heart (Rom. v. 5); He is the Spirit of faith (2 Cor. iv. 13), the Spirit of power, and of love, and of a sound mind (2 Tim. i. 7); He is the Spirit of grace and of supplication (Zech. xii. 10), the Spirit of wisdom and revelation in the knowledge of Christ (Eph. i. 17). The Spirit thus occupying the Christian heart, must be regarded as perpetually engaged in stirring up

all its activities and powers, sometimes as imparting joy
(Rom. xiv. 17), sometimes as glorifying Christ in the understanding and heart of the disciple (John xvi. 14). And if the
Christian is cold, uncollected, prayerless, or inactive in the
prosecution of good works, the Spirit by manifold reminders
carried home from every quarter evinces that the very
opposite is an incumbent duty.

Here I would adduce a brief notice of the BAPTISM OF THE
SPIRIT as the great promise of the Lord to the New Testament
Church (Acts i. 5). It was contrasted with John's baptism
with water; for John could not give the Spirit,—and we are
expressly told that the Lord Jesus never personally baptized
with water (John iv. 2). When the Baptist announced that
the Lord Jesus should baptize with the Holy Ghost and fire
(Matt. iii. 11), we must bear in mind that it is of the nature
of fire to send forth LIGHT; and when the Lord came to
baptize the Church with the Holy Ghost and fire, truth was in
a new way shed abroad upon the heart, and Christ was in a
new way set before the disciples' eye in all His meritorious
obedience and atoning sacrifice. This sacred fire purified
their hearts from unholy desires. It is of the nature of fire
to send forth WARMTH; and when the Lord came to baptize
the Church with the Holy Ghost and fire, He kindled cold
hearts into a flame of love to God and man. It is the nature
of fire to SPREAD ABROAD or extend a conflagration—as Jesus
said: " I am come to send fire upon the earth; and what will
I if it be already kindled ? " And when the Lord came
to baptize the Church with the Holy Ghost and fire, the
word spread like a conflagration from mouth to mouth, from
land to land. The results were marvellous. They who a few
days before were reproved as slow of understanding and of
little faith, now penetrated into the inmost nature of the
revelation of God. They who had previously discovered a
proud heart and a thirst for honour, now envied each other no
more, but displayed a single eye to the Redeemer's glory.

They who had been easily diverted from prayer and from the work of Christ, now came under the Spirit's guidance to give themselves to the Lord, with an entire consecration of time and talents to the things of Christ.

THE SPIRIT AND CHRISTIAN ETHICS.

I have been led, by various considerations, to attempt a very brief discussion, in connection with the inhabitation of the Spirit, of the whole subject of CHRISTIAN ETHICS. It is never safe to leave this department a blank in theological study, or to hand it over, as is commonly done, to the cold region of moral philosophy, as if it were unworthy of special cultivation. The Church is never safe without an independent study of Christian ethics based on union to Christ, and deduced from the renewing grace and inhabitation of the Spirit. The position I lay down is, that Christian ethics, while occupying a well-understood relation to philosophic morals, are vitally connected with the inhabitation and renovation of the Holy Spirit, and that they have THEIR OWN PECULIAR PRINCIPLE, and produce their own independent results.

I said CHRISTIAN ETHICS have a well-understood relation to PHILOSOPHIC MORALS. When it is asked, What is that relation? we answer, one point may safely be postulated. They cannot contradict each other in their ultimate decisions. If they could be supposed to contradict each other, this would involve the startling result that there are two moralities, one of nature, and another from the Spirit of life; in other words, that natural religion in its ethical rules held that to be duty which revealed religion condemned as sinful or unwarrantable. Such a collision cannot be supposed. It is true they start from totally different principles, and move in totally different spheres. But in their ultimate results they can involve no mutual contradiction.

But it may be asked, Is not one of them superfluous?
May we not take from some of the systems the whole frame-
work and nomenclature, and content ourselves with the
simple task of replenishing these with a new spirit or higher
life?   Letting the mould remain, may we not pour into it a
new life?   In some such way those must have argued who
adopted with satisfaction the maxim that philosophy is the
handmaid of theology, forgetting that this is the certain way
for her becoming mistress.   We may take an illustration from
Aquinas.   Aware that there is a point of contact between the
Christian ethics and the systems of antiquity, and unwilling
to regard as fruitless the imposing outline which Aristotle
bequeathed, he would superinduce the Christian on the
classical, or put the new wine into the old bottles.   He
would take the FOUR CARDINAL VIRTUES as comprehending all
that is purely human, and only supplement them by the
so-called theological virtues,—faith, hope, and love,—along
with the seven graces of the Spirit.   Had he put the two
systems—the philosophical and the Christian—in juxtaposition as shadow and reality, as law and grace, as nature's deep
sigh after an unrealized ideal, and the realization which the
Holy Spirit confers, it might have been an interesting as well
as useful outline.   But, as it was, the result was to the injury
of both.   Similar illustrations may be drawn from any period
of the Protestant Church, where we find Christian ethics
poured into the mould supplied by the systems of benevolence
or of the moral sense.

Are they never to run into one, even in the last problem
awaiting the earth, when reason and revelation shall sweetly
coalesce?   I answer, philosophic morals belong to us as
reasonable beings: Christian ethics belong to us as redeemed
men.   Melanchthon, who may be named along with Butler as
one of the greatest ethical writers of the Protestant Church,
happily said: " Moral philosophy is that part of the divine
law which treats of external actions."   If we accept this

definition, which may be frankly done, philosophic morals differ from Christian ethics as law from grace, demand from obedience, shadow from substance. We cannot speak of TWO MORALITIES. Christianity is not, according to the Unitarian interpretation of the Sermon on the Mount, a new and stricter law. It has not come to usher in a different ethics, but to make the preceptive " thou shalt " an attained reality by renewing man's nature, and by shedding on him a transforming power, which shall ennoble and elevate all his faculties and all his relations.

Christian ethics have their own peculiar source, and produce their own independent results. The entire subject must be placed in immediate connection with the Spirit of Christ. It is THIS CONNECTION WITH THE SPIRIT which ensures to Christian morals their proper independence, and their cultivation as a department of theology. When we reach this point of view, it is no more with abstract ethical laws that we have to deal, nor is it a mere ideal that we have to contemplate. A realized ideal of ethics stands before us in the human life of Christ—into which we are engrafted by the Holy Spirit in the nearest conceivable way.

From this view of Christian ethics we can look down on the faulty and ineffectual systems that have been presented to the minds of men. It has been customary, in some quarters, to consider Christian ethics as produced by THE MERE FORCE OF MOTIVES operating on those who are the subjects of redemption. Nor is that influence to be repudiated : for it is a half truth. It has been common among others to restrict the matter to a CATALOGUE OF RULES, or to a doctrine of duties. Nor is that to be forgotten or despised. But Christian ethics occupy a much more close connection with the Spirit as uniting us to Christ. We come to a point, whenever we touch the resurrection-life, where PRECEPT AND FULFILMENT may be viewed AS ONE. If the subject presupposed in all the exercises and precepts comprehended in Christian ethics is the risen Christian,—if nothing is enjoined but what may be developed from his spiritual life,—and it is thus that the apostolic Epistles always put the matter,—then it is not mere self-acting motives, not a mere doctrine of duties, but something more intimately connected with the divine Redeemer, that is the principle of Christian ethics. That principle is the risen life through the Spirit of life.

To place the relation of Christian ethics to the personal Christ in its true light, I shall notice the modifications which the entire subject undergoes, according to the conception which men entertain of Christ's Person. A brief survey of this point will show in what close connection they stand to His Person. Greatly should we err were we to suppose that any view of Christ's Person would equally avail for the production of Christian ethics. It is the more important to notice this point, because it has often been said that it is well-nigh indifferent for this department whether the mind is attached to evangelical sentiments or the reverse. A cursory glance will immediately show the modifications of the whole subject, according to the opinions entertained of Christ's Person.

On the UNITARIAN VIEW of Christ's Person, the inquirer comes at once to the conclusion that we have nothing in Christian ethics beyond what reason can give—a code of rules, a book of duties. It has been found that, among the Unitarians, there is an ethical system irrespective of Christ's Person ; and that there is nothing to prevent men from hoping to surpass Him in the use of means and aids furnished by the course of centuries.

On the PELAGIAN THEORY, which has no renewing work of the Holy Spirit, the effect on ethics is disastrous. Ethical laxity at once ensues. They who dispense with the Spirit's aid to restore man to a position higher than his present imperfection, and who include in their view of grace nothing more than exhortations and moral suasion to faculties neither hurt by the fall nor incapable of good, have no high theory above their practice. And when the distinction between theory and practice is merged, the consequence is a lax and defective system of ethics.

On the ROMISH THEORY, which transmutes the gospel into a new law, the system of ethics never escapes from legal bondage, and is never ushered into liberty; for it discourages all assurance of salvation. So long as men are exhorted to merit salvation, pride—the inmost sin of the human heart—never can be destroyed. While attention is limited to single sins, to the neglect of the sinful nature, men have no humbling discovery of sin; and thus their whole ethical system oscillates between bondage and spiritual pride.

The Biblical principle of justification by faith alone affects, to its utmost limits, the whole domain of Christian ethics. One broad position characterizes scriptural Protestantism. Ethical action is not pursued TO MERIT SALVATION, but because the man is saved by grace; or, to adopt the Biblical representation, it is the good tree that yields the good fruits; while the fruits cannot prevail to change the tree. The notion that ethical action goes before acceptance, and with a view to secure it, vitiates the entire character of the action. Christian ethics, on the contrary, are the fruits, results, and evidences of the salvation. In this all the Protestant Churches are at one, having the liberty of grace, and dependence on the Holy Spirit.

I have adduced these illustrations from various systems to show that Christian ethics lean on the Person of Christ, and are an emanation from the law of the Spirit of life in Christ Jesus (Rom. viii. 2). They are the effect or issue of living in communion with Christ through the power of the Holy Spirit, or they are the mode of acting to which that communion gives rise. When the Christian dwells in communion, the practice of the virtues is in consequence of the Spirit's operations not so much an arduous effort as the natural expression of his life. It is his nature, his life to practise them. All those single graces and virtues given with the Spirit of life in Christ Jesus (Rom. viii. 2) only wait to be called into action; and that communion with Him who is the life lends the motive power in most cases without an effort. The passive effortless facility with which the Christian practises many of the virtues is often strikingly expressed by Luther.

But this does not supersede exhortation in any case. The possibility of practising the Christian graces, while presupposed and assumed in the whole domain of the Christian life as a life in the Spirit, does not preclude earnest admonition (Gal. v. 25). It is taken for granted that they are possible, nay easy, and that the living Christian, risen with his Lord, is in a position to exhibit them; and Scripture, accordingly, when inculcating the practice of the graces, only touches some secret spring that has power to evoke them. Whether we look at the Sermon on the Mount, where various graces are enforced, from the deepest relations of the kingdom of God, of which Christ is the centre,—or at the grace of humility, enforced by the consideration that He who was in the form of God humbled Himself (Phil. ii. 3–7), or at the grace of liberality, commended by the motive that He who was rich became poor,—we find the same peculiarity. Christian ethics are never isolated from Christ and the deep relations of His kingdom.

There are only two other points, in speaking of Christian ethics, called into action by the Holy Spirit, viz.: that every thing is viewed in relation to God, and that love is made the principle of ethical unity.

1. The grand peculiarity of Christian ethics is, that in the entire range of this department nothing is to be isolated from God. As we know Him who is Light, and Love, and Spirit, —as all is *from God* in the power of the Spirit, and *to God* under the influence of the same Spirit, nothing is to be done

but in connection with the divine. In the Person of Jesus we see the divine replenishing the human. And His followers, in like manner, in proportion as they drink into the same Spirit with Him, ennoble and glorify the scenes of earthly life by the divine Spirit derived from Him. While the sphere of Christian ethics is so closely connected with the divine,—that is, from God and to God,—it must be added that every earthly relationship, and every scene in these relationships, must be made a vessel to contain and diffuse the heavenly treasure. Hence the lives of the early Christians shone with an unearthly beauty which attracted all eyes. The moral glory of their life, their purity and happy love, their self-denial and benevolence, as reflected from the surrounding vice and moral lassitude of heathenism, shone like a vision from another sphere. By the renewing Spirit the divine was brought within the circle of the human.

2. In the Christian ethics LOVE is the principle of unity. The philosophic morals, however much they might struggle toward general principles, could not advance to the ethical unity of love; and no system, uninfluenced by Christianity, ever dreamt of it. This draws the line between Christianity and all other ethics in ancient or modern times. That the unity of ethical life is love, may be proved from the nature of love, which unites the mind to the object, which is the very result to which all the operations of the Spirit conspire. The Lord and His apostles teach that the various virtues and graces of the Spirit are not so much separate qualities, as diversified forms, modifications, and applications of the same thing which the Spirit produces as the principle of ethical unity. Paul, in his exhaustive delineation of the one diffusive principle of love, describes the fundamental Christian virtues as all reducible to love (1 Cor. xiii.). He who has love, accordingly, has all the virtues. The four cardinal virtues, the distribution of which was well and happily given in the ethics of antiquity,—wisdom, temperance, forti-

tude, and justice,——are only love as directive, as self-controlling, as militant, as attentive to the rights of others; and as love gradually advances, one of these may be at one time in greater prominence and another at another. But they are only diversified forms of ethical unity——of love.

We have now to notice the GROWING SANCTIFICATION produced by the Spirit, or the increasing CONFORMITY TO THE DIVINE ÎMAGE. That which enables Christianity to achieve what human speculation fails to accomplish, is the fact that it is a life derived from the Spirit of life,——not an idea, truth, or opinion,——and that as such it cannot but grow. In all systems that are of the earth, we have mere ideas which are as jejune and impotent as their propounders; whereas the last Adam is A QUICKENING SPIRIT. Whenever Christ is considered as a present fountain of life, and Christianity is considered as opening the way for the Spirit of life, it is essentially distinct from the mere influence of philosophical speculation. For where a new supernatural element of life is introduced into fallen humanity, and nature is not left to be wrought upon by a mere idea or a system of thought, but animated from within by the Spirit of Him who says : " I am the life,"——humanity is in connection with the great archetype to whose image we are predestinated to be conformed. This life is in the Son, who apprehends the whole man in all His faculties : all His people are included in Him as one man; and though their individual personality is not destroyed, they are included in the second Adam as they were in the first. In the figure of the vine (John xv. 1–6), employed to explain this mystery, we are taught that as the vine diffuses life through numberless branches distinct from one another but not separate from the stem, so none of His people can for a moment be independent or isolated from the Spirit of life. On the contrary, they are conscious of a union to Him who is our life, and who awakens every spiritual desire in His people to such a degree that He says : " Without me ye can do nothing."

Nor does the Spirit's subjective operations in any measure destroy man's freedom, though many theological systems urge the PLEA OF FREEDOM to exclude the Spirit of God from the heart. But if the taint of the fall has not destroyed the essence of the soul, though infecting all its powers, it is capable of separation without prejudice to its freedom. No more does this put man's freedom in jeopardy, than the cures which Christ of old performed on men's bodies—the analogy being precisely similar. But those objections which are based on the plea of freedom proceed on an entire oblivion of the disturbing element of the fall. There is, in reality, no interference with man's freedom when the renewing and sanctifying work of the Spirit commences and advances, though it involves all that is implied in a birth to which the man himself does not at all contribute,—in a new creation which argues almighty power, — and in a rising from the dead, which involves an energy wholly from without. The subjective operations of the Spirit no more interfere with man's freedom than the objective work of the Son.

Two MISLEADING INFLUENCES run counter to the active prosecution of progressive sanctification in the Spirit. Some regard sanctification as occupying the subordinate place of furnishing but an evidence of our salvation. They consider that Scripture, in enforcing sanctification of the Spirit, means little more than to supply an evidence that we are justified by faith. It is thus made A MERE MEANS to an end, whereas it is everywhere inculcated in Scripture as the express command of God (1 Pet. i. 16 ; 1 Thess. iv. 3). Another tendency, in a different quarter, is to regard sanctification in the Spirit as SOMETHING NECESSARILY DEVELOPED of its own accord, without any exercise of the will. But Scripture allows no quarter for Quietism in any of its forms.

While the actual possession of the Spirit of life is always presupposed, and the Christian in the pursuit of sanctification is always reminded to reckon himself as dead indeed to sin, and alive unto God through Jesus Christ our Lord (Rom. vi. 11),—in other words, as distinctly appreciating the specially MERITORIOUS GROUND OF ACCEPTANCE with the Moral Governor as well as the Person of THE RISEN CHRIST, the source of all spiritual life and influence,—the Scriptures do not refrain from adducing motives. They touch many motives. Thus they adduce all the motives drawn from the threefold department of liberty, love, and spirituality (Gal. v. 13–26), from the fear of God (Phil. ii. 12), and from the doctrine of gracious reward (Matt. x. 42).

The obvious distinction between PHILOSOPHIC MORALS and CHRISTIAN SANCTIFICATION is, that the former commonly endeavour to produce their results by a single dominating principle, whereas the latter wields many various motives. We have only to recall any of the systems of antiquity or of modern times to perceive this marked distinction. The enumeration of the distinctive principle which the several systems avowed will suffice to show this. The principle of Plato—conformity to the divine image by idea—was a sort of unconscious anticipation of what was to come, but which there were no powers to effect in the classical world, apart from that life in the Spirit which was to revolutionize the human heart FROM WITHIN over all its bounds. That system, which may be called nature's dumb unuttered sigh for something higher, which the grace of the Holy Spirit alone could usher in, found in Christianity a realization—a spiritual and ethical conformity to the divine image in all the relations of earthly life—which was never dreamed of by its first propounder. The principle of another philosophic system, that of HAPPINESS AS THE CHIEF GOOD, mental repose, was a sort of sigh for that peace of mind and positive enjoyment of God which Christianity alone affords. The principle of another system, that of A LIFE AGREEABLE TO NATURE, or the Stoical principle, which assumed that man continued in a nature pure and undisturbed, found its realization in Him who showed the full harmony of man with His nature, and who renews us after His image. The principle of another system, THE ROYAL MEAN between two extremes, which Aristotle applied to civil virtue in the relations of state - life, are realized in Christian ethics when we rise to the higher relations of the kingdom of God. The modern systems in like manner, whether we call up to view those which are known as the systems of BENEVOLENCE or of THE MORAL SENSE, correctly enough make the moral problem, or the chief end of man, the starting-point of their philosophy, and propose a single principle as a lever to move this human life. But they only evince a partiality in favour of a single element or influence, if it could be set in motion. And when it is asked in certain places, What can Christianity do more?— the answer is, it is the REALIZATION of all that these systems, as the deep helpless sigh of nature, longed to realize, but failed to call into play. Christianity was the counterpart of that which nature sighed for, but could not produce. The truth anticipated in a mere vague expectation here found its truth, completeness, and reality. But what the gospel furnishes is not ONE principle, but many. The new life of the Spirit, indeed, IS ONE, and a principle unknown to philosophic morals. But the motives which are touched and evoked are MANIFOLD and numerous.

Closely connected with this line of thought, the whole subject of the Redeemer's character, as the perfect exhibition of a divine ideal, comes under our consideration. And we are changed into the same image as by the Spirit of the Lord when we behold it (2 Cor. iii. 18). The character of Christ as the loftiest ideal, the realized standard of human excellence, and the only exhibition of that image of God in which man was made, and to which he is predestinated to be conformed, is meant to be in the constant view of the Church as sketched by the pen of inspiration. All that can be done is to touch those springs which recall the reality, and which is to be surveyed and pondered with the earnest prayer that the Spirit of wisdom and revelation in the knowledge of the Lord Jesus may open the eyes of our understanding (Eph. i. 17). Owen, in his great work on the Person of Christ, well remarks: "Some men speak much of the imitation of Christ, and following of His example; and it were well if we could see more of it really in effect. But no man shall ever become like unto Him by bare imitation of His actions, without that view or intuition of His glory, which alone is accompanied with a transforming power to change them into the same image."

The character of Christ, thus seen through the word and by the illumination of the Spirit, impresses every mind that gazes on it with a sense of full-orbed completeness and perfection. But it is of a kind so new and unprecedented, that minds devoid of the Spirit are insensible to the glory of it. Let me here bring out more particularly one or two of the distinguishing features of Christ's moral perfection.

The foundation of all lay in HIS HUMILITY. He laboured not to rise aloft; He was the meek and lowly One. His public was not what men thought, or mere public opinion, but the eye of an omnipresent Father, before whom all human distinctions are of no account. This humility, which has been made THE TRUE FOUNDATION of all Christian ethics, found vent in the Lord's history in a renunciation of His own will, in a retreat from worldly honour, and in the words: "I am among you as one that serveth." As President Edwards has well remarked: "Christ, though He was the most excellent and honourable, yet was the most humble; yea, He was the most humble of all creatures."

Christ's moral eminence was there before any of His works were done. The latter only revealed Him and discovered what He was. But these manifestations of spiritual excellence bring us before One who, in the possession of the full supply of the Spirit, shows a full completeness and perfect equipoise of all the graces. Unlike every other human life, where the excellences and defects are nearly balanced, all graces were found, and all perfect. One grace did not displace another, nor overshadow another. There was such a harmony of all the gifts and graces of the Spirit, that the exercise of one did not limit or interfere with the full energy of all the rest. He discharged the various duties of the family, and evinced to the last hour the most tender love and filial regard.

And the simple principle which regulated that whole marvellous life was obedience to His Father's will: "My meat is to do the will of Him that sent me, and to finish His work" (John iv. 34). It was an unvarying obedience at every moment to the living Lawgiver pervading all the steps of life; and without an unconditional subjection to His Father's will, He never spent a moment. His whole life was A LIFE OF LOVE. His whole obedience was one of faith and love.

The superiority of a living example to mere precept is proverbial. And duly to affect the minds of men, the moral code required to be embodied in a life which should engage all eyes and win all hearts. What was said by Plato, that if perfect Virtue appeared among men, as a stranger from another sphere, all men would fall down and worship her, was not realized in the sense in which he expressed the anticipation,— for perfect virtue did appear, only to be despised and rejected, —but IT IS VERIFIED in the case of all whose minds have, by THE REGENERATING GRACE OF THE SPIRIT, become susceptible of impressions from that high and ennobling standard. The Holy Spirit that dwells in Christ fashions believers after His image as the perfect archetype. This is the image of God which appeared in the Redeemer on earth, and we know Him in the Gospel in His words and deeds and sufferings. It is He who imparts His Spirit that we may have the same mind that was in Him, and that in character we may be like Him. This is effected by His Spirit dwelling in us. The Holy

Spirit glorifies Christ in us and by us: in us as He reveals Him to us, and then by us (2 Cor. iii. 18). The human life of the God-man stands before us as a pure emanation of humility, obedience, and love: as an imperishable treasure, and an ideal to be reproduced in us. And, unlike all [merely human histories, that example has the peculiarity attaching to it, that in proportion as it is beheld and contemplated in the light of the Holy Spirit, and by the opening of the eyes of our understanding, it exercises a sanctifying power beyond all other influences. It forms in us by the Spirit and through faith the very image of God which we behold in Him (2 Cor. iv. 6). This is a creative example, INFINITELY MERITORIOUS as a procuring cause, and DIVINELY EFFICACIOUS in producing transforming results on the believing and adoring mind. It is an ideal which reproduces itself in the experience of the enlightened saint. His example becomes, in the Spirit's hand, when duly used, a plastic power, whereby we are changed into the same image. It is not a cold, distant example to which we stand in no living relation, and frowning upon us from an unapproachable elevation: it is the achievement of a forerunner whom we follow, the attainment of the first-born among many brethren to whom we are predestinated to be conformed. It embraces all life; it is an example in solitude and society, in joy and sorrow, in poverty and the loss of friends, in suffering and death. And there it is to shine on our path, to elevate and transform us to what He was.

The spiritual perception of divine things is invariably accompanied with a sanctifying influence; and knowledge is no further genuine or spiritual than as it leads to this result. When it is a mere natural and intellectual perception of divine things, the mind is only elated (1 Cor. viii. 2), not imbued with the humility which is the effect of all true spiritual knowledge. When it is a perception which takes its rise from the Holy Spirit, and is kindled by the contemplation of the divine perfections, excellence, and glory, the taste is so changed that it is separated from the pleasures of sin. They who have a spiritual perception of the divine beauty of God our Saviour are drawn by a high attraction, and induced to forego, not only the sins, but the pleasures, emoluments, and distinctions which absorb men's present thoughts. The knowledge of God, taught by the Spirit, is invariably connected with a new spiritual relish, or a new sense, which inclines the mind to rest in God as better than the creature,—to regard sin as repulsive, and holiness as the element in which the mind delights to dwell. The heart is weaned by the revelation of the surpassing excellence of God, and so drawn by the cords of a man, by bands of love, that the supreme God is not only accepted as its portion, but enthroned as its Lord, to whom every power must be subjected, and who is nearer and dearer than self.

THE MEASURE OF HOLINESS ATTAINED.

Thus far we have followed the operations of the Spirit of Holiness, and traced His work of sanctification, which is, on the one hand, A BLESSING UNCONDITIONALLY PROMISED in the covenant of grace (Ezek. xxxvi. 27); and, on the other hand, a COMMANDED DUTY according to the will of God (1 Thess. iv. 3). When we inquire what attainment is possible, or what progress is actually made, it appears at once how far men are, for the most part, from attaining the highest degree of sanctification. Except in the cases where YOUNG DISCIPLES, in the warmth of first love, are PRONE TO EXAGGERATE their own measure of attainment, and the powers with which they think themselves invested, or to misconceive the strength and ramifications of the sin which lurks within them, Christians are commonly ready to acknowledge how far they are from having apprehended the great end or object for which they have been apprehended by Christ Jesus. Legal perfection there is not; and none will claim it. The evangelical attainment which the Scriptures hold up before the mind, and sometimes term PERFECTION, consists only in the fact that they who have the perfect righteousness of Christ imputed to them are so largely occupied by Christ's Spirit, and so powerfully wrought upon by the Spirit's grace, that they have the first beginnings of a perfect obedience which will reach its full measure and degree in the celestial state. At present, it is more in aim and purpose and unfeigned sincerity than in performance. Even Paul had not attained, however much he forgot the things which were behind, and reached forth to those things which were before (Phil. iii. 13).

A peculiar phase of Christian experience has, in recent times, been presented to men's attention by those who are commonly known as the advocates of THE HIGHER LIFE, or of the life of faith. They are in principle and sentiment very much allied to the mysticism of Madame Guion and the mediæval mystics. Professor Upham, of America, is the representative of the class. They have given it to be understood, as their sort of watchword, that the Christian can in this life do the will of God without inward opposition, WITHOUT THE INNER CONFLICT, or at least without the consciousness of it. They, moreover, connect the entering into rest with certain subjective frames or phases of inward experience, instead of representing rest as connected with the acceptance of the Person, offices, and work of the one Mediator between God and man.

As much loose thinking and unsound doctrine are always disseminated when THE SPIRIT'S WORK WITHIN is made to eclipse or overshadow THE REDEEMER'S FINISHED WORK WITHOUT, it may be useful to notice the points at which such a theory diverges from sound doctrine. These are two : (1) defective views of Christ's imputed righteousness ; and (2) a misapprehension of a Christian's double being. Instead of extolling the surety - righteousness of the Lord Jesus, all Perfectionists speak only of what is infused. They call in an exaggerated, overweening estimate of their own sanctification, and depreciate imputed righteousness, that is, the law-magnifying obedience of Christ as the Lord our righteousness. As to THE DOUBLE BEING of a Christian, consisting, as he does, during this mortal life, of flesh and spirit, they do not make the necessary distinction, and involve themselves in painful confusion of thought.

That there is an inner conflict in the bosom of every Christian man, is put beyond all doubt by the testimony of all the saints in every age. That there is a carnal mind (φρόνημα σαρκός) even in the regenerate, is emphatically brought out by the Apostle Paul in describing his own experience in the latter part of the seventh chapter of the Epistle to the Romans (vii. 14–25). Though Pelagians, Arminians, Plymouthists, and Romanists oppose that interpretation, there can be no doubt, as Augustine and all the Reformers have conclusively proved, that the apostle in that passage refers to a conflict carried on in his own soul at the time when he penned the Epistle. And this plainly argues that he laid claim to no perfection of holiness within. There was an internal conflict between flesh and spirit—between an old and new nature. And the strange thing is, that in this conflict the powers and faculties of the Christian seem to be occupied at one time by the one, and at another time by the other. The same intellect, will, and affections come under different influences, like two conflicting armies occupying the ground, and frequently in turn driven from the field. To the astonishment of the Christian himself, the mind and affections engaged in the exercise of holy love by the power of the Holy Spirit, may all of a sudden be turned away by some old root of sin or strange law of association in our mental economy to the very opposite ; and thus the conflict continues to the end. We may compare it—though no analogy can exactly portray it—to one in a state of convalescence, where disease and health are struggling for the mastery, sometimes the one predominating, sometimes the other, till the disease is fully and for ever expelled from the veins.

The apostle draws a distinction, indeed, between his true and PROPER SELF and THE SIN that dwelt in him (Rom. vii. 17 and 20). But that was not intended to divest himself of responsibility, or to escape from repentance and confession. Rather it was to rise above THE DEJECTION of such a constant, unintermitting conflict. He describes a law of sin warring against the law of his mind, constraining the cry for help, as a captive cries, and a divine interposition which sets him free. This is a vivid picture of conflict, of defeat, and then of the Spirit's help given in answer to his cry for deliverance. The delineation is given in such a way as proves that the flesh resists the Spirit. The resistance is felt whenever we put forth any spiritual activity, like the effort to move a palsied member or a wounded arm ; for when it is passive there is no resistance. In like manner, any holy activity is met by opposition from the opposite corruption.

This exposition will suffice to prove that while the Spirit of holiness is ever active, the measure of attainment is always IMPERFECT and defective. While the Christian presses toward the mark, he is never perfect ; nor does he ever reach a stage when there is no more conflict, and when he attains performance of God's will without the consciousness of inward opposition.

LECTURE VI.

THE WORK OF THE HOLY SPIRIT IN THE CHURCH.

I SHALL direct attention in this lecture to the Spirit's work in the Church, first in founding it, and then in making its ordinances available to their true design.

The Church of Christ, in the days of His flesh, did not, properly speaking, exist, though His word had found entrance into individual souls. It was at Pentecost that the Lord, by the power of His Spirit, welded into a Church the souls on whom the word had exercised a saving efficacy. The Holy Spirit, at the commencement of what is called His " mission," collected the disciples into a living unity ; and this great work of the Spirit is called the Church, the kingdom of God, the body of Christ, the temple of the Spirit, the habitation of God in the Spirit (Eph. ii. 22) ; a conquest from the kingdom of darkness and death. It rises, as a fabric, in all the majesty of its proportions, on the ruins of that empire of rebellion and sin which previously occupied the world. It forms a true city of refuge to all who desire to escape from the tyranny of the destroyer.

In the apostolic age, the idea of THE KINGDOM OF GOD, to which ample allusion is made in the prophets and in our Lord's parables, is less presented to our notice than the idea of THE CHURCH. Let me advert to the relation which Christ occupies to the Church as King and Head, and to the place which the Spirit fills in this living organism.

Here the mediatorial acts of Christ are not to be omitted from our consideration. Thus, in two sayings which may easily be harmonized, the Lord said : " It is expedient for you *that I go away ;* for if I go not away, the Comforter will not come unto you " (John xvi. 17) ; and again : " I will not leave you comfortless [better: orphans] ; I *will come to you* " (John xiv. 18). The two things—the departure and coming —are there conjoined without disharmony or contradiction. The Lord departs, and yet comes ; and the solution of that variety of statement is by no means difficult ; for He comes in the power of His Spirit.

The influences of the Spirit on the Church are considered by many as emanating rather from the Spirit's own proper motion than as communicated by Christ, whose deputy He is, according to their economical relations. To obviate this one-sided representation, we have only to recall the Baptist's statement, taken up and repeated by the Lord Himself : " *He shall baptize* you with the Holy Ghost and with fire " (Matt. iii. 11 ; Acts i. 5). This momentous truth, that Christ baptizes with the Holy Ghost,—in other words, has authority to dispense the Spirit,—is not to be obscured for the sake of another truth which may, if unduly urged, be made the occasion of introducing the notion of isolated action in the Godhead, than which it is hardly possible to imagine any opinion more replete with disastrous consequences. All the Persons act indivisibly in every divine act, but according to their order in the Trinity.

An analogy may be traced between the baptism of Christ, by which He was inaugurated into office, and the effusion of the Spirit on the day of Pentecost, after He received the plenary unction of the Spirit (Acts ii. 33). In a word, these two events indicated two grades of unction, or two stages in the communication of the Spirit to Him. The former, accompanied with the descent of the Spirit, was meant to equip the Redeemer for entering on His office. The latter was intended to found the Christian Church and supply it with the living organs and various gifts, by which it efficiently exercises the

spiritual life for the advancement of Christ's cause.   The
Lord Jesus personally abstained from any step of His ministry
till the Spirit descended upon Him, and John's baptism
introduced Him to His work.   The apostles, in like manner,
tarried in Jerusalem, as the Lord directed them, till they were
endued with power from on high.   As a historic fact, the
Christian Church came into existence only when the Spirit,
by a miraculous effusion, was shed on the assembled multitude
of disciples, and constituted them the Church of the Lord.
The Twelve were honoured with a peculiar calling, for the
execution of which the Spirit furnished them with capacities
and endowments.   The Church came into being with the office-
bearers, and was never without the offices and spiritual gifts.

The Church, in seeking to further the cause of Christianity,
uniformly realizes the indispensable necessity of the Spirit, and
responds to the call : " be filled with the Spirit " (Eph. v. 18).
Had the first disciples omitted to continue with one accord
in prayer and supplication till the Spirit came, or had they
begun at their own caprice without waiting till they were
endued with power from on high, their labour would have
been of no avail.   Only such as are baptized with the Holy
Ghost produce in Christian effort any good results ; for God
does not pour out His Spirit, to any large extent, without
fitting for the work those special instruments whom it shall
please Him mainly to employ.   But, on the other hand, it
may be affirmed with confidence that such as already enjoy
the baptism of repentance for the remission of sins, are
warranted to expect supplies of the Spirit very much greater
than any they have ever known ; for to him that hath shall
be given, and he shall have abundantly (Matt. xiii. 12).

That heavenly baptism of the Spirit, according to the tenor
of the divine procedure, is not withheld when the disciples
discover a humble compliance with Christ's will.   Thus the
hundred and twenty disciples who were enjoined by their
Lord to tarry in Jerusalem till the Spirit came, neither

returned to their homes nor suffered their minds to be distracted from the great work assigned to them, but continued to wait as they were told, engaged in the unceasing prayer of faith, and the Spirit came upon them with power.

They who have the Spirit of Christ filling them and continuously animating them with new supplies of knowledge, humility, courage, and decision, such as can be traced in the first disciples, succeed in bringing men into living contact with God. The disciples were first visited with a new unction before the blessing spread to the impenitent; and to look for a great awakening among masses of men before the labourers or preachers of the truth are themselves recipients of the baptism of the Spirit, is to expect the end without the means. It was so at Pentecost. Nothing is so calculated to strike the heart of a callous age as the arresting spectacle of men filled with the Spirit—the awe-inspiring spectacle of men whose hearts the Lord has won, openly separating themselves from the world, that they may invite and persuade men to accept the great salvation. Unless this fresh baptism is maintained in its intensity, or repeatedly renewed, declension will certainly ensue; for to be content, like many declining Churches, merely to hold a form of sound words, when the Spirit is forfeited or sinned away, is in the last degree delusive, and only like a removed landmark, ready to be swept away, or carried down a swollen river.

With the rise of the Christian Church a new epoch dawned; new transforming influences entered into history. They who were called out of the mass of mankind by the sanctification of the Spirit (1 Pet. i. 2) were constituted THE CHURCH, a society of believers with a common interest in Christ's redemption and a common hope of glory. As a corporate society, they have communion with the Lord Jesus Christ in His saving blessings, and with all believers in the living Head. The Church, animated by His Holy Spirit, came into existence in virtue of the election of the Father, the redemp-

tion of the Son, and the regenerating grace of the Holy Spirit.
How closely the Spirit is connected with that living organism
—its functions, office-bearers, sacraments, gifts, and ordinances—will appear when we call to mind that He creates it
by His life-giving agency, sustains and supports it in its
functions, infuses life, unction, and ability for the exercises
by which the members edify and comfort one another, and
without whom it could neither exist nor cohere. By the
Holy Spirit every true member of the Church is consciously
joined to the Head; and the several members are held together
rather by inward than by outward bonds.

The Lord Jesus in the days of His flesh, without fully
dilating on all the aspects of the Christian Church which
was in due time to arise, was content to prepare its chief
functionaries, the apostles, and to institute the two sacraments which would draw a line between His disciples and
the world.   When the Church was duly instituted, the
apostles referred to one or other of its essential constituents.
It is called an holy temple in the Lord, in whom believers
are built together for an habitation of God IN THE SPIRIT
(Eph. ii. 21, 22).   It is described as "one body and one
Spirit;" that is, as occupied by ONE SPIRIT animating and
directing it (Eph. iv. 4).   The Apostle Paul delineates the
Church as one family in heaven and earth, in reference to
which the earnest prayer is offered up by him to God that
they may be strengthened with all might BY HIS SPIRIT in
the inner man (Eph. iii. 16).

But to show what the Church is as the habitation or city
of God, perhaps no more appropriate passage could be
adduced than the striking description in Heb. xii. 22–24:
" Ye are come to Mount Zion, and to the city of the living
God, the heavenly Jerusalem, and to an innumerable
company of angels, to the general assembly and Church of
the first-born, which are written in heaven, and to God the
Judge of all, and to the spirits of just men made perfect,

and to Jesus the mediator of the new covenant, and to the blood of sprinkling that speaketh better things than that of Abel." When we direct due attention to this memorable passage, which may be called AN ANTICLIMAX, we find that the blood of Christ is represented as calling, not for vengeance like the blood of Abel, but for the forgiveness of sins, and for the acquittal of sinners on the basis of a new covenant, of which the Lord Jesus is the mediator. We find the members of the Church brought to the city of the living God, to the communion of saints, and to a certain union to the spirits of just men made perfect, who have finished their course and kept the faith, and now, in the bliss above, long with deep spiritual desires that their brethren still fighting the good fight on earth, may be perfected and brought to the possession of that immortality in which they rest from their labours, and God is glorified in them. The Church, partly militant on earth, and partly triumphant in heaven, thus forms one society, one Church of the first-born so called, with special allusion to those who were protected by the blood of the Lamb from the sword of the destroying angel, and were thus made a holy nation, a peculiar people. The statement that they are written in heaven, adds the further thought, that according to the eternal decree their names are written in the book of life, that they are the enrolled citizens of the new Jerusalem,—and, in a word, washed, sanctified, and justified in the name of the Lord Jesus, and by the Spirit of our God. This is the city of God. The indwelling of God in this city constitutes its glory, which the natural eye cannot discern. Mention is also made of an innumerable company of angels, who are at once their fellow-citizens in the city of God, and ministering spirits sent forth to minister to the heirs of salvation. These lofty terms belong not merely to the Church triumphant, but to the Church militant on the earth : for it is expressly said that true believers are COME TO THE CITY OF GOD. From all this it is evident that the true Church is invisible, that God is a wall of fire about it, and the glory in the midst of it (Zech. ii. 5) ; and that all true Christians are a spiritual priesthood, carrying on a true spiritual worship, and having access to a throne of grace.

When we examine the description of the Church in Scripture, we find the emphatic announcement that it is one body, and that one Spirit inhabits and animates it (Eph. iv. 4). The Church has a twofold function, neither side of which can be neglected. It is (1) a HOLY SOCIETY in the world, maintaining a state of separation from the world, meeting together for the worship of God, and walking according to His will for mutual edification as well as for God's declarative glory; it is (2) A MISSIONARY INSTITUTE, with a view to propagate or extend the gospel to them that are without. Let us briefly look at both.

I. With regard to the Church as a HOLY SOCIETY meeting for worship and edification, the Epistles are replete with allusions to this feature. Thus THE UNITY of the Church is expressly named when it is said: "There is one body and one Spirit" (Eph. iv. 4). Whether we regard it as living through a succession of economies or existing contemporaneously in the world in many lands, it is ONE, a society holding the Head and knit together by the same Spirit ; though, at some parts of its history, rather believed than capable of being distinctly traced. All true members of the Church, because joined to the Lord, are one Spirit (1 Cor. vi. 17), however differing in language, country, or condition ; while they who are without the Spirit cannot be regarded as true members of the Church, because not animated by its vital principle. The Church is ONE not in consequence of its efforts after union,—nor in virtue of the mutual harmony which pervades its different parts, for these are but fruits and pledges of a previous unity in the Lord,—but in virtue of the one indwelling Spirit.

From the essential relation in which it stands to Christ, the Church, moreover, is described under figures, which will more appropriately aid our conceptions of its nature than all other definitions put together. Besides the striking figure already named, that of *one body and one Spirit*, it is called *the bride of Christ*, showing a mutual relation, a perpetual union, and a preparation for the final perfection (Rev. xix. 7 ; 2 Cor. xi. 2), a *temple* or habitation compacted together,—of which Christ is the foundation and chief corner-stone, and each member is a living stone (1 Pet. ii. 5) ; *the vine* and branches,—one vital principle sustaining the whole (John xv. 1–6).

These illustrations suffice to prove that Christians are a corporate society, a habitation of God in the Spirit, and that He as truly dwells in the Church by His Spirit, as He dwelt in the temple of Jerusalem, by clear pledges of His presence. The assemblies of Christians, replenished by His Spirit, are His temple, where He dwells in a more glorious manner than in Israel (2 Cor. iii. 7). That this is the import of the allusion is obvious from the elucidation which the apostle subjoins from the Old Testament Scriptures (2 Cor. vi. 16–18). For He warns them against such as preached the wisdom of men instead of the revelation of divine grace ; and declares the culpable character of their proceedings by allusion to the inhabitation of the Holy Spirit, who condescends to dwell among His people and to walk in them, and to make them the sons and daughters of the Lord Almighty.

The four epithets applied to the Church in the Nicæno-Constantinopolitan Creed may be accepted without hesitation as furnishing the marks of the Church, viz. ONE, HOLY, CATHOLIC, and APOSTOLIC CHURCH. But, without expatiating on these predicates of the Church in detail, let me notice that the Church, as a living organism, enjoys the inhabitation of the Holy Ghost, and makes itself felt in society in a great variety of ways. It is INVISIBLE, so far as it rests on the gracious operations of the Spirit.   But that distinction between the visible and invisible Church, proper enough,—nay, necessary in connection with the points involved in the Romish controversy,—was never meant to paralyse the hands of those who labour, within due bounds, to conform the Church to the standard and ideal presented to us in apostolic Christianity. The Church, animated by the Spirit, evinces its vitality and influence in every sphere.

The connection of THE INDIVIDUAL with the Church rests *on the possession of true faith,* or effectual calling by the Holy Spirit.   According to the Protestant distinction, as it has been happily formulated, it is THE BELIEVER'S RELATION TO CHRIST that puts him in connection with the Church; not HIS CONNECTION WITH THE CHURCH that puts him into a saving relation to Christ.   And to this universal Church belong all of every age and country who have been engrafted into Christ by the Spirit, whether they are of the Church militant or of the Church triumphant.   The four constituents or essential qualities which come to light in connection with the Church as an organized body, may be briefly noticed before we proceed to describe the Spirit's agency.

1. The *constitution* of the Church was the form according to which the apostles, as the organs of a plenary inspiration, moulded the Christian society.   And the whole discussion on the true organization of the Church has always turned on the one question, Which form is the most close resemblance to the apostolic model ?   A constitution of some kind has always been deemed necessary ; and apostolic sanction, at least in its great outlines, has never been denied to it.

2. The *element of worship,* another constituent of the Church, is that exercise of the assembled congregation by which the holy priesthood, in a befitting way, by the aid of the Spirit, approaches God through the intercession of the

High Priest of our profession, and offers not external sacrifices, which have all been abolished by the one valid and
accepted sacrifice, but themselves as living sacrifices (Rom.
xii. 1). And their praises, thanksgivings, and prayers,—the
fruit of their lips, — are represented as spiritual sacrifices
acceptable to God by Jesus Christ (1 Pet. ii. 5 ; Heb. xiii. 15).

3. *Confession with the mouth* is another constituent of the
Church. The Christian body replenished with the Holy
Ghost, expresses a common testimony, or the consciousness
of holding a sum of knowledge or of truth based upon the
apostles' doctrine (Acts ii. 42). And this is so connected
with the exercise of faith that the two are as inseparable in
the Christian society, as in the case of the individual who
believes with the heart and makes confession with the mouth
(Rom. x. 10). Faith assimilates to itself the objective word
of God in such a way that it reproduces that word in the
form of a COMMON CONFESSION through the influence of the
Holy Spirit. It is the Spirit of life that enables the Church
to find the adequate expression. On this topic let me add,
that only extensive advances in the doctrine and life of the
Church render a new Confession warrantable. And as the
enlarged experience which sheds increased light on the
various truths of revelation not seldom runs parallel with
the rise of new errors, the Church has generally to do two
things—present a negative side to error, and fill the forground
with positive truth. Theology is made subservient only so
far as to furnish the due expression for the truth held by all
in common.

4. *Discipline,* a fourth constituent of the Church, is an
important addition or appendix to the other three, for the
removal of scandals and for the correction of those who incur
censure. The Reformed Church warrantably made this a
constituent of the Church as well as the other points already
named. Writers in foreign Churches, like Guericke and
others, do not scruple to condemn the Churches of the

Reformed as receding from the sound idea of a Church, and in so far approaching to that of Rome, when they include the elements of discipline and constitution as well as word and sacrament among the conditions or constituents of the Church. These views are a forgetfulness of the fact that the laws of Christ are to be administered under the solemn charge of responsibility to Him ; and His approving salutation at last will be based only on faithfulness to Him. To neglect this constituent element, as has been proved by all history, is only to forfeit purity and spiritual influence. Of this the Greek Church is a striking monument. Her downfall to the lowest degradation is traced by Sozomen —one of her own historians — to the dilapidation of her discipline.

How are we to explain Christ's presence in the Church along with the Spirit's agency ? Many of the theories on the mode of Christ's presence—in Patristic, Romish, Lutheran, and Anglican theology—would never have been agitated, or would even now be immediately exploded, if these relations were duly considered and understood by the controversialists on both sides.

Christ's activity as Lord and Head of the Church seems at first sight to militate against the action of the Holy Ghost the Comforter, and conversely. That these aspects of truth may not have the appearance of coming into collision, let me refer to their relation. The regulation of the Church's life —sometimes spoken of as if it were retained in Christ's own hand, sometimes described as if it were committed to the Holy Spirit—must be regarded as two announcements of the same great truth, without any difference,—as but two sides of one and the same thing. The Lord Jesus, the Mediator, does all by the Holy Spirit in fostering, quickening, guiding the Church ; and so intimately are these two things conjoined,— the Melchizedek-priesthood on the one hand, and the dispensation of the Spirit on the other, — that they must constantly be seen together (Acts ii. 33). The exalted Christ —as may be seen in the Book of the Acts of the Apostles,— continuously acts for the Church's good by His Spirit through the word.

Where these two doctrines are sundered, as they sometimes are, in the theological conceptions of individuals or bodies of men, it is to the prejudice of right views of Christ's Person, and to the deterioration of sound views of the sacraments. Thus the Lutheran Church, to maintain her peculiar views of the Lord's Supper, is compelled to lay emphasis on the alleged ubiquity of Christ's humanity. But by so doing they evacuate the Spirit's work in that proportion. The Lord's own teaching is that He acts by the Spirit on His Church, and that *He is present* not by the ubiquity of His human nature, but *by His omnipresent Spirit, who is at once in Him and in us*, as a perpetual bond or link. The presence of the Holy Spirit in the Church — that is, of Christ by the Spirit whom He obtained by His obedience, and whom He confers from His throne—constitutes the Church's glory.

To put Christ's own OMNIPRESENCE in its proper light, it is necessary to remark that it is one of the perfections of His immutable divine nature — a fact belonging to Him as a divine Person, and that cannot be more or less. It is not a matter of promise, but A FACT, an inalienable fact. But HIS GRACIOUS PRESENCE, as the Incarnate One, is MATTER OF PROMISE, and may or may not be according to His relations with His people; and when Christ promised to be with His Church subsequently to the ascension, He intimated not His divine omnipresence, but a presence by the Spirit— as must be evident to every mind that duly considers the above-mentioned statement. His presence with His people involved gracious privilege, which might be imparted or with-held according to His good pleasure or the emergencies of His Church. And He gave His disciples to understand in

His last discourses, that, without the agency of the Holy Spirit, the New Testament Church could neither come into existence nor be perpetuated in the world.   Nor was the promise of the Spirit's presence limited to public occasions or to external institutions.   Christ is there undoubtedly by His Spirit.   But His presence, while felt there by His living disciples, is neither bound to more public occasions, nor to ecclesiastical institutions, as its exclusive sphere.

According to the mediatorial economy, based on the order of the Trinity, Christ sends the Holy Ghost, the Comforter, as His deputy.   There is no isolated action among the Persons of the Godhead, and cannot be, because they all equally participate in the same divine essence, and act, according to their order of subsistence, in all divine acts.   Where the one is, there the others are.   This fundamental axiom, in which every intelligent Trinitarian must concur, enables us to obviate those half-truths which are incautiously admitted in many of the Churches.

The action of Christ and of His Spirit, conjoined, comes vividly before us in all the services and worship of the Church.   When the Lord uttered the memorable words: "Where two or three are gathered together in my name, there am I in the midst of them" (Matt. xviii. 20), He intimated that by the Spirit He would inhabit ordinances, and make His presence consciously felt.   According to the scriptural view of worship, the company of the disciples, depending on Christ's merits, and conscious that by one Spirit they are all baptized into one body and made to drink into one Spirit (1 Cor. xii. 13), has to continue, as in the first days of the Christian Church, stedfast in the apostles' doctrine and fellowship, and in breaking of bread and in prayers (Acts ii. 42).

According to this economy, CHRIST IS PRESENT BY HIS SPIRIT, conducting the communications OF GOD TO MAN, and the WORSHIP OF MAN TO GOD, the channel of divine supplies to us, and the medium by which the returns of praise, prayer, service, and obedience are acceptably offered.   The Holy Spirit acts in both respects as the Comforter or Deputy in Christ's name, filling His mystic body and presenting their spiritual sacrifices (1 Pet. ii. 5).   This view of worship to which the action of the High Priest and the aid of the Spirit are absolutely essential, is brought out in a memorable psalm : " I will declare Thy name to my brethren ; in the midst of the Church will I praise Thee " (Ps. xxii. 22 ; Heb. ii. 12).   The Lord Jesus acts from God to us and from us to God, in both instances by the power of the Holy Spirit.

This view of Church worship is vitiated in two opposite ways, to the manifest injury of the doctrine of the Spirit— (1) by a blighting Ritualism, and (2) by an evacuating theory not less blighting.   Ritualism, Romish or Anglican, agrees in making the Church's action a substitute for the action of Christ and His Spirit.   On whatever ground it is placed, whether it represents the Church's action as a perpetual continuation of Christ's life on earth, and therefore a sort of perpetual incarnation, which was Möhler's theory, or describes the Church's action as, in some measure, meritorious and propitiatory, — which is the common theory, — it entirely ignores the operation of the Spirit of God, and binds the results to a mere array of forms.   It makes the ever-acting High Priest a mere inactive spectator, and is irrespective of the SPIRIT'S GRACE and of the RECEIVER'S FAITH.   The whole transaction is lodged in other hands.   Ritualism conjoins the sacraments and the Spirit in such a sense that the dispensation of the one is simultaneous with and equivalent to the communication of the other.

An opposite extreme is the FALSE SPIRITUALISM which makes the sacraments but empty signs (*nuda signa*).   Too many in the Reformed Churches, under the spell of an evacuating system which the Germans call Zwinglianism, have gone far to denude sacraments of the Spirit's presence, as if there were no sacramental union between the sign and the thing signified.   That there is no virtue in the mere emblems, or in the administrator, is true on the one side ; but it is true on the other side that there is always the blessing of Christ and the working of His Spirit *to them that by faith receive them*.   Mr. Stowel, for example, in his work on the Spirit, assails a theory applicable to every Church in Christendom, and one which he owns was not abandoned by the Puritans of England nor by the Nonconformist clergy, in the following terms : " If by means of grace," says he, " no more be meant than states of mind in which the Spirit gives us grace, and the connection of such states of mind with the instructions of teachers, and with offices of devotion believingly attended to, we should be only fastidious in taking exception to such language ; but if it be the old Church-doctrine of *media gratiæ*, the notion that *through* these means as channels and instruments the Holy Ghost works invisibly within men—against that notion, by whatever words conveyed, we must gravely and conscientiously protest.   Neither the Scriptures nor the Christian's experience permits us to doubt that prayer for what God has promised, offered with faith in His promise, is followed by the blessing prayed for ; and the history of Christianity abounds with proofs of some established connection between the preaching of the word and the salvation of men's souls.   But who that ponders the meaning of words can believe that either prayers or preaching is the means through which the actual gift of salvation is conveyed ?   It can be no disparagement of so vital an exercise as prayer, to conceive of it as being what it really is, the address of the devout heart to God, but not the channel of God's grace to man.   Neither can it be any disparagement of the preaching of the gospel to regard it as being what it really is, the truth of God addressed to men, *but not the vehicle of the Spirit* by which man is prepared to receive the message with the faith whereby we are saved " (p. 223).

These are unhappy views, and too widely diffused, repudiating the theory that the Spirit of God imparts the grace of regeneration through the Church, and the notion of spiritual power belonging to an outward institution. But the gospel is the ministration of the Spirit, and we maintain that the word and sacraments are made the vehicle or channel of conveying what they announce. These evacuating principles were unknown to the theology of the Reformation and of the Puritanic age as well as to Patristic literature. A false spiritualism separating itself from sacraments and ordinances which God instituted as the channels through which His Spirit is conferred, would, if carried out to its legitimate consequences, lead to a treatment of the sacraments as if they were a superfluous form. The view which Calvin propounded as a safe middle ground was: That sacraments do not impart grace (*ex opere operato*) by their mere administration, but that they are not mere barren signs (*nuda signa*); that they are channels of blessing TO EVERY BELIEVING RECIPIENT; the blessing being given by Christ's own hand, and through the working of the Spirit to them that by faith receive them.

ONE CHURCH AND ONE SPIRIT BOTH IN THE OLD AND NEW TESTAMENT.

Here it may be proper to show that it is ONE CHURCH OF GOD under a different guise in the Old Testament and in the New. The same Spirit of faith filled the heart of believers, whether they lived before or after the advent of Christ (2 Cor. iv. 13). The Trinitarian relations were the same; and the divine perfections in the matter of our salvation were exhibited in the same way. The sacraments, it is true, were changed more than once to be adapted to different epochs in the history of redemption. Their efficacy, however, was the same through the power of the Spirit in every economy to all those that by faith received them. On this point the Churches

of the Reformation were for a time at one in opposition to the
Romish doctrine in its erroneous position that the sacraments
of the Old Testament were but types of those of the New
Testament; that the former communicated nothing, and that
the latter conveyed blessings in the mere order of operation.
The Reformers maintained without exception, that in both
economies the sacraments were identical in import and efficacy.
With the Romanists it had long been a dogma that the sacraments of the Israelitish dispensation were only shadows of
those instituted for the Christian Church.   All the Protestant
Churches with one consent maintained the opposite till a
different view began to be propounded among the Lutherans.
But down to the time of Chemnitzius we find it held as an
accepted opinion in opposition to the Romanists, that there
was no essential difference in the sacraments of the two
economies.   That eminent Lutheran theologian maintained
that there was NO OTHER GRACE AND NO OTHER FAITH by which
men were saved in the Old Testament than that grace and
faith by which men are saved in the New, and no real difference between THE SPIRITUAL EFFICACY of the sacraments in the
two economies.   A general assent was given in the Lutheran
and Reformed Churches to the doctrine laid down by
Augustin, that the only difference between the sacraments
of the two economies was, that those in the Old Testament
announced a Saviour about to come, while those of the New
Testament announced a Saviour already come.   In process
of time, however, Lutheran divines began to modify the common Protestant doctrine; and step by step, by one concession
after another, they found themselves constrained, by the
necessities of their new position, to drop their confession to the
essential identity, and to the equal spiritual efficacy, of the
sacraments of both economies.   They began to assert, with
the Romanists, that the sacraments of the Old Testament
were but a type or shadow of the sacraments of the New
Testament.   In the same way Anglican Ritualists are wont

to expound their sentiments. The Reformed Churches never wavered. With Calvin, they have all continued to assert that the covenant of grace was substantially one and the same, though economically different in form. They never conceded that in the Old Testament there was only type or shadow and nothing of reality. They maintained that under the Old Testament believers not less really apprehended Christ's atoning sacrifice than is done by believers now, though it was exhibited to them in another way than it is exhibited to us in the New Testament sacraments.

II. Let me now advert to the Church as a MISSIONARY INSTITUTE, and to the work which the Holy Spirit condescends to discharge in connection with the ingathering of new disciples, with the propagation of the gospel, and the revival of religion. It may be noticed that there are three titles— ministers of Christ, ministers of the gospel, ministers of the Church—which are an exhaustive exhibition of the office (Col. i.) ; and that there is an exercise of the Spirit's power through them analogous to that which was exercised on the day of Pentecost. The union of disciples in prayer and supplication, and in waiting for the promise of the Father, is also analogous, and never to be interrupted. The instruments by whom the Spirit works are also prepared for service in a similar way, only without the miraculous accompaniments. They are Christians first, and then called to official labour.

The rich supply of EXTRAORDINARY GIFTS bestowed at Pentecost was not intended to continue when they had served their purpose in founding the Christian Church. The other GIFTS OF AN ORDINARY CHARACTER were given for the permanent advantage of the Church, and are so essential to her edification, that, without them, she would collapse or disappear. Their continuance is a constant proof that Christ lives as the dispenser of the Holy Spirit. Some of them are

gifts of office—and of every conceivable variety—for acting
on the mind of others; while the general body of Christians
are supplied with gifts and endowments, wealth and influence,
which the Spirit induces them to wield for the common
benefit. The permanence of the Church does not depend on
OFFICES ALONE, as Irving and Löhe represented the matter,
NOR ON GIFTS ALONE, as the Plymouth Brethren will have it,
but on both conjoined.

Every minister truly called to office by the Spirit of God
has a gift which may be described as innate, but brought to
light and activity by the regenerating work of the Holy Spirit.
Fundamentally, it is a natural or concreated endowment, but
called into exercise by the Spirit for the good of the Church,
and fitting the possessors of it to do a work which no other
can do so well; and the conscious possession of which should
have a twofold effect,—should disengage their mind from all
tendency to envy the gifts of others, and all disposition to be
discontented with their own.

The first disciples were called to wait in the attitude of
humble supplicants for the power with which they were to be
endued by the Holy Spirit coming upon them (Acts i. 8);
and we have there an example of what is ever to be reproduced. Before this time they evinced ignorance and prejudice,
timidity and shrinking from the cross, ambition and pride.
After the descent of the Spirit there was no more debate who
should be the greatest; they forgot self, and rose to an elevation previously unknown. They imbibed new ideas of the
spirituality of Christ's kingdom. The Spirit brought all
things back to their remembrance. The instruments that the
Spirit formed felt that they were rather passive than active in
the whole work—tools in another's hand.

Here we must refer to THE MINISTRY OF THE SPIRIT (2 Cor.
iii. 8). With regard to this remarkable expression, it may
denote one of two things. It may mean—(1) that the Holy
Spirit, as the author of the ministry in its manifold varieties,

constitutes the offices, raises up the men, and endows them with their rich variety of gifts; or (2) it may mean, as I rather think it does, that the gospel ministry, whether in the hands of the apostles—the chief functionaries—or of ordinary office-bearers, is exercised with the accompanying power of the Holy Spirit sent down from heaven. The expression will thus convey the thought that the Spirit gives the spiritual and edifying effect along with the gifts and ordinances which have been appointed in the Church. In speaking of the union between these ordinances and the Spirit's accompanying power, precision is necessary in order to avoid excess of statement on the one hand, and defect of statement on the other. An examination of the Acts of the Apostles discovers to us the Spirit's present operation everywhere along with the preaching of the gospel. And whenever the veil is lifted up, the reader gets a glimpse into the movements of the kingdom of God, and into the unseen agency of the Spirit, which is everywhere disclosed. And from this we infer His ever present activity in all centuries and localities alike. The Church has not been left to herself.

We find united in the history of the apostles the greatest apparent opposites: weakness and power, emptiness and sufficiency, limitation and the boundless resources of omnipotence, the earthen vessel ready to go to pieces at the slightest pressure, and the excellency of power, an unimposing agency with the mightiest force that stirs humanity; in a word, what Milton calls "the unresistible might of weakness," or what the prophet calls the worm Jacob thrashing the mountains and beating them small. The ministry is so connected with the Spirit that the human speaker is but the instrument, and the Spirit is the hand that moves them; and nothing remains to man but the labour.

An inscrutable sovereignty appears in dispensing the divine blessing, and in founding the Church in any locality (Acts

ii. 1, xi. 20). This appears even in connection with an apostle. It may be proper to say that success did not lie within his resources or appliances in such a sense that it could be made the subject of human calculation; that the increase was of God (1 Cor. i. 6); and that men cannot dispense blessings at their discretion. While that is one side of a great truth, it is not to be denied that the preacher must have an organic aptitude for his office, or be a fit instrument. And, among other things comprehended in this, —such as personal consecration, dependence on God's Spirit, incessant prayer, and the like,—it is commonly the man imbued with the greatest desire for fruit who most plentifully reaps it.

Here the question may be raised : Has any connection been divinely established between the Spirit's exercise of saving power and the proclamation of reconciliation or redemption by the cross ? It is a momentous question, but capable of a distinct answer. We must distinguish. On the one hand, God never puts the blessings of salvation out of His own hand into the hand of others, nor diffuses the operations of His Spirit by any other channel than in the line of His electing purpose. On the other hand, *a connection is established between the preaching of reconciliation by the cross and the exercise of the Spirit's power, to an extent that cannot be affirmed of any other type of doctrine.* In making this statement, we are neither treading on the region of mystery, nor treading insecurely—for we have the guidance of the divine word. The apostle says : "This only would I learn of you, received ye the Spirit by the works of the law, or by the hearing of faith, that is, the preaching of faith " (ἀκοὴ πίστεως) ; a statement intimating that the Spirit had been received by the Galatians, not in connection with a doctrine which laid stress ON RITUAL OBSERVANCES or a mere MORAL CODE legally enforced, but in connection with the proclamation of redemption by the blood of Christ, and received by faith. To human view no obvious link of connection can be perceived between that style of preaching and the transforming power of the Holy Spirit. But a divine connection does exist, as is there explicitly declared. When the apostle calls the gospel " the power of God " (Rom. i. 16), and the preaching of Christ crucified " the power of God " (1 Cor. i. 24), we have a statement which explicitly affirms that the DIVINE POWER of the Spirit goes associated with the proclamation of THE ATONEMENT, but will not be associated with a style of teaching which substitutes any other theme.

The first and most momentous question is : On what footing does the preacher take men up in reference to the Judge of all the earth, and what is the specific which he brings home to them as adequate to meet their case ? Where an uncertain sound is given on RUIN, REDEMPTION, and REGENERATION, the sinner fails to recognise himself in the mirror held up to him. There is nothing to bring him into the divine presence, or to bring home the pointed address, " Thou art the man." Nothing can be named as more important than the precision with which the line is drawn between law and gospel, which was the distinctive feature of the Pauline theology, and the restoration of which was the great achievement of the Reformation, which, after the long torpor of ages, brought back preaching to the place it occupied in apostolic times. Without that distinction preaching loses its edge. The law is enforced on the impenitent, and the gospel commended to the contrite. The Reformation made this distinction familiar to all men as a household word, and gave it the prominence that belongs to it.

The Church is gathered in any given locality only where Christ crucified is preached. This held true in the founding of the Church at first, and holds true in the planting of it in any heathen land. And the same doctrine which formed it is necessary to sustain it from age to age ; for, as Luther happily expressed it, the article of Justification is the article of a standing or falling Church. The only security of the Church is to give no uncertain sound on the great doctrines of Christianity; the deep-seated ruin of mankind and their vast guilt; the Deity, the mission, and atonement of the Lord Jesus Christ; the necessity of Regeneration by the Holy Ghost; the need of forgiving grace; the assurance of salvation; the tenor of the covenant of grace. "I am not sensible," said Dr. Chalmers, when referring to the actual though undesigned experiment which he prosecuted for upwards of twelve years in Kilmany, "that all the vehemence with which I urged the virtues and the proprieties of social life had the weight of a feather on the moral habits of my parishioners. And it was not till I got impressed by the utter alienation of the heart in all its desires and affections from God; it was not till reconciliation to Him became the distinct and the prominent object of my ministerial exertions; it was not till I took the scriptural way of laying the method of reconciliation before them; it was not till the free offer of forgiveness through the blood of Christ was urged upon their acceptance, and the Holy Spirit given, through the channel of Christ's Mediatorship, to all who ask Him, was set before them as the unceasing object of their dependence and their prayers; it was not, in one word, till the contemplations of my people were turned to these great and essential elements in the business of a soul providing for its interest with God and the concerns of its eternity, that I ever heard of any of those subordinate reformations which I aforetime made the earnest and the zealous, but I am afraid at the same time the ultimate object of my earlier ministrations." [1]   My object in adducing this remarkable experience is to show an instance how the preacher who withholds the doctrine of the cross and the immediate reconciliation with God, which must always go along with it,—whether the silence is due to the fact that the

[1] See Dr. Chalmers' memorable address to the people of Kilmany.

preacher's own mind has never adequately been awakened to
discern its value, or whether he acts upon a system of reserve
without making the central doctrine of Christianity bear on
man's relation to the Judge of all,—fails to wield any power.
The opposite doctrine awakens souls, is associated with the
Holy Spirit, and plants or propagates the Church.

THE SPIRIT IN A RELIGIOUS AWAKENING.

I shall briefly advert to THE SPIRIT'S WORK IN A RELIGIOUS
AWAKENING. Though this cannot be made the subject of
human calculation, we find it occurring sometimes in a continuous ingathering of individuals, sometimes in a multitude
of simultaneous conversions, or in great movements which
carry with them the marks of a genuine work of the Holy
Spirit. Many things may occur of a mixed character in an
exciting period of religious effervescence. The opinion of a
large class, who betray a lack of spiritual discernment and an
incapacity to form a judgment as to its nature and tendency,
will always be opposed to such an awakening, and ought to be
received with little deference. They also who are wedded to
a theory of development, are in danger of denying any interposition of the Spirit from on high. Others, embarrassed by
a system of sacramental grace by which they allow their minds
to be swayed, mistake a movement which overleaps these
barriers and marches forward in a path of its own. And
having adopted a principle with which a religious awakening
on a large scale will not coincide, they run the risk of denying
it as a legitimate religious phenomenon. Any system which
has no place for the universal priesthood of believers is prone
to look askance on an outpouring of the Spirit connected with
the immediate action of the Church's living Head on His
disciples. An awakening of this more general kind constitutes for the most part a new epoch with a well-defined
peculiarity, and is replete with great results. The gleaner in

Church history, at a subsequent stage, estimates its influence on thought, on action, and on ecclesiastical life as at the Reformation, when the effusion of the Holy Spirit was more marked than at any previous period from the apostolic age. The effusion of the Spirit in the Puritanic age, followed as it was by the cognate movement of Spener and Francke in the German Churches, exercised an influence, the force of which continued long, nay, continues to this day. The great awakening of last century, pervading England, Scotland, and America, under Whitefield, Wesley, and Edwards, gave rise to those Bible, missionary, and tract societies which still continue in the Churches. Only under such influences can a solvent be found powerful enough for producing such results.

The work of the Spirit, wherever it occurs, requires to be discriminated from its accompaniments and from the counterfeits that may be expected. It is asked, Can these be genuine cases of conversion where the whole is effected in an hour, and where the mind passes with astonishing rapidity from deep conviction to triumphant faith? We reply, it is not a question of time, but of thoroughness and intensity. That a man, and a multitude of men, may under the overwhelming pressure of conviction consequent on a manifestation of God's holiness and inviolable law, and of that utter ruin and boundless guilt in which men are involved, be shut up by the Spirit to Christ within the space of an hour or two, while not a characteristic of a sound conversion and not a single fruit of the Spirit are found to be awanting, is proved by the evidence of facts. But the sudden deliverance of the converts from the dangerous errors in which they previously lived, receives an explanation in the same way. At such a moment, when men come under deep convictions, the previous cavils against the doctrines of the gospel are found to pass away like a cloud; the Arminian accepts election; the Arian, the Deity of Christ and the atonement; the Romanist, the sole mediatorship of Christ, without hesitation.

But it is further asked, How can cases of conversion be admitted, when they receive impressions, amid their common avocations, suddenly and without any special application of the word ?   I answer, There is no need for asserting that the word is not employed : as the sword of the Spirit, the word is used in every case.   The word, deposited in the heart from childhood, and quickened by the addresses, conversations, or providences which lead to the decisive issue, may have occupied the mind before the convictions reached their climax.

Many things occur which all too plainly prove that it is necessary not only to pray for an awakening, but for wisdom equal to the occasion when it is imparted.   Mere religious excitement is no unchallengeable evidence of the genuineness of a spiritual awakening, nor any passport to the confidence of the Christian community, unless it be conclusively proved that divine truth—that is, the word of God in what may be called the true outline of that word—was the means of producing it.   If not called forth by the instrumentality of divine truth, it may be little better than a spurious medley, or a spasmodic movement by mere human appliances.

It is not to be expected, indeed, that no tares will be mingled with the wheat, or that there will be no over-hasty admissions or over-confident assertions as to numbers, no exhibition of converts prematurely thrust into public notice, no censorious judgments, no noisy profession followed by a fall.   It would not be a work of God if there were no imitations; for where the Spirit builds a church, Satan builds a chapel.   The tests which Shepard adduces in his treatise on the parable of the ten virgins, or which Edwards employs in his work on the religious affections,—though they cannot be applied in the early stages of a religious awakening, when the two classes cannot be distinguished from each other,—ought never to be absent from the mind of those who are called to guide a religious movement.

These memorable seasons are to be hailed as interpositions of the Spirit's power.   "It may be observed," says Edwards,[1] "that from the fall of man to our day, the work of redemption in its effect has mainly been carried on by remarkable communications of the Spirit of God.   Though there be a more constant influence of God's Spirit always in some degree attending His ordinances, yet the way in which the greatest things have been done towards carrying on this work always has been by remarkable effusions at special seasons of mercy." The Church's ever-living Head knows how to usher in creative epochs, to rally His people to some converging point through the lapse of centuries, and to gather up under this powerful influence isolated opinions into one consistent whole.   When a former awakening has spent its force, when the elements of thought or action previously supplied threaten to become *effete*, a new impulse is commonly communicated by Him who interposes at various stages to make all things new.   The previous condition of things is commonly such as renders a new sect or a new organization well-nigh inevitable.   In a dead or stagnant period, such as prevailed at the time of the formation of not a few of the existing Churches, the spiritual life found no welcome within the pale of the denomination from which the separation was made.   But when existing Churches take up the new life by a process of assimilation, they are recruited by numbers and refreshed by a new stream of divine life.

In a devotional publication of Neander, on our Lord's entrance into Jerusalem, he points out that the kingdom of God comes at first as the leaven or as the grain of mustard seed ; but that when it has continued to work for a season in this hidden way, the effect next becomes perceptible in great facts, which force themselves on men's notice and form the great moving powers in the world's history.   He adds, to suppose that the kingdom of God must always be as the

[1] *History of Redemption*, Period I. part 1.

leaven, would be as great an error as to conclude that the visible results come first. Men look on with awe and wonder when some supply of the Spirit, of which they can neither tell the laws nor estimate the momentum, breaks forth from the kingdom of God and sweeps over the community.

Without entering into other things involved in this theme, let me close with a few words on two points which, more than any other, give tone and colour to a time of general awakening.

1. As to the peculiar mode of preaching, to which the instruments employed are usually led, it largely partakes of the inculcation of immediate conversion. Forgiveness and repentance, the one leading up to the other, and ever viewed in their inseparable connection, are always the earnestly enforced themes. While the other truths connected with law and grace, the ruin and the remedy, are duly brought out, the occasion naturally leads the preacher—(1) to exhibit the freeness and magnitude of saving grace and the atonement of Christ as the sufficient means of meeting all the demands of God and all the wants of man; and to OFFER SINNERS, AS THEY ARE, a free and present forgiveness, in the exercise of that grace which triumphs over man's guilt, and the oppressive sense of sin. The occasion (2) leads him also to urge THE NECESSITY OF THE GREAT CHANGE, and the duty of immediate compliance with all those awakening motives that go to determine the choice. The criminality of every hour's delay is enforced by the thought that it is another hour's rebellion. This must be accompanied with the further statement, that *without the Holy Ghost they cannot turn ;* that they must, and yet cannot ; that they are under obligation, and yet helplessly unable ;—a double motive brought to bear upon the mind together, which has been remarkably owned in the preaching of America, and fitted to drive from every refuge those who choose for themselves some middle ground or debateable land where in the meantime they may rest. At

this point this preaching comes in with overwhelming force. It shuts up the sinner under a twofold motive—of obligation and inability. It compels action and dependence. It brings a twofold force to bear on the secure. These two truths must go together; for the one without the other deprives the enforcement of conversion in a large measure of its power. Withhold a sense of man's dependence, or tell him that whenever he pleases God is ready to second his efforts, and the entire force of every motive is removed. But tell him that all his actions are at the best but the efforts of an enemy till his nature is changed, and that God is, notwithstanding all these efforts, under no obligation to any unconverted man; let him feel the force of both motives,—the present duty, the awful issues that enter into his choice, the utter inability to turn, the absolute freedom and sovereignty of God to give or to withhold His renewing Spirit,—and there is nothing more calculated to shut up the mind to immediate submission. He must, yet cannot turn. He must, yet cannot convert himself. Whitefield, referring to the effects of this style of American preaching, says: "It is for preaching in this manner that I like the Messrs. Tennent. They wound deeply before they heal. They know that there is no promise but to him that believeth." Such is Whitefield's testimony, than which we could not have a higher. Dr. Griffin accounts for the numerous revivals in America from the belief of an instantaneous regeneration, and the sinfulness of every moral effort up to that moment, and the duty of immediate submission.

2. As to the peculiar mode of praying, we may say that in every season of general awakening the Christian community waits just as they waited for the effusion of the Spirit, with one accord in prayer and supplication, in the interval between the Ascension and Pentecost. No other course has been prescribed; and the Church of the present has all the warrant she ever had to wait, expect, and pray. The first disciples waited in the youthfulness of simple hope, not for a spirit

which they had not, but for more of the Spirit which they had ; and Christianity has not outlived itself. Ten days they waited with one accord in prayer, when of a sudden the Spirit came to give them spiritual eyes to apprehend divine things as they never knew them before, and to impart a joy which no man could take from them. It was prayer IN THE SPIRIT (Eph. vi. 18), and prayer FOR THE SPIRIT, the great promise of the Father. But the prayer which brought down the Holy Ghost was not that style of petition which ceases if it is not heard at once, or if the heart is out of tune. The prayer which prevails with Him who gives the Spirit is that which will not let him go without the blessing. When the spirit of extraordinary supplication is poured out from on high,—when an ardent desire is cherished for the Holy Ghost,—when the Church asks according to God's riches in glory, and expects such great things as God's promises warrant and Christ's merits can procure,—the time to favour Zion, the set time, is come (Ps. cii. 16–18). When we look at the prayers in Scripture, we find that God's glory, the Church's growth and welfare, her holiness and progress, were ever higher in the thoughts and breathings of the saints than personal considerations (Ps. lxvii. 1–7). And if we are animated with any other frame of mind, it is not prayer taught by the Spirit, nor offered up in the name of Christ (Isa. lxii. 1–7).

The praying attitude of the Church in the first days after the Ascension, when the disciples waited for the Spirit, should be the Church's attitude still. I need not refer to the copious references of the apostles to the urgent duty of praying *in the Spirit* and praying *for the Spirit*, nor shall I refer at large to the habits of all true labourers, such as Luther, Welsh, White-field, and others, in proof of the great truth that prayer is the main work of a ministry. And no more mischievous and misleading theory could be propounded, nor any one more dishonouring to the Holy Spirit, than the principle adopted by the Plymouth Brethren, that because the Spirit was poured out at Pentecost, the Church has no need, and no warrant, to pray any more for the effusion of the Spirit of God. On the contrary, the more the Church asks the Spirit[1] and waits for His communication, the more she receives.[2]   The prayer of faith in one incessant cry comes up from the earth in support of the efforts put forth for the conversion of a people ready to perish.   This prayer goes before and follows after all the calls to repentance.   The company of labourers associated together in such work, come to feel as they proceed that they are encircled with a mighty power, and have an authority not their own.   The interest taken in the work of advancing the Redeemer's Kingdom thus has much of a personal concern, and is far elevated above the vague and pointless efforts of mere official routine.

The apostles, in their various Epistles, when referring to their own unceasing exercise of prayer, hold up the mirror to others; and never do men more realize than in a time of revival that in all their previous career they have been scarcely half-awake.   In such a time the conviction is borne home

---

[1] As I do not deem it proper to exceed the limits of the required six lectures, I would take occasion to direct attention to the great work of OWEN, *The Work of the Holy Ghost in Prayer*, and also to GURNALL'S discussion of the same theme in *The Christian in Complete Armour*.

[2] A remarkable passage on prayer, and on working by the power of prayer, occurs in Foster's essay on the application of the epithet "Romantic:" "I am convinced," says he, "that every man who, amidst his serious projects, is apprised of his dependence on God, as completely as that dependence is a fact, will be impelled to pray, and anxious to induce his serious friends to pray, almost every hour.   He will as little without it promise himself any noble success, as a mariner would expect to reach a distant coast by having his sails spread in a stagnation of air.   I have intimated my fear that it is visionary to expect any unusual success in the human administration of religion unless there are unusual omens; now a most emphatical spirit of prayer would be such an omen; and the individual who should solemnly determine to try its last possible efficacy, might probably find himself becoming a much more prevailing agent in his little sphere.   And if the whole, or the greater number of the disciples of Christianity were, with an earnest, unalterable determination of each to combine that heaven should not withhold one single influence, which the very utmost of conspiring and persevering supplication would obtain, it would be the sign that a revolution of the world was at hand."

upon them that no fitful exercise of prayer will avail to obtain the blessing. And their purpose, as they seek to take the kingdom by force, is to do violence to the lethargy and disinclination of nature, and to act as the Lord's remembrancers, who keep not silence and give Him no rest, till He establish Jerusalem and make her a praise in the earth.

THIRD DIVISION.

HISTORICAL SURVEY OF THE DOCTRINE OF THE HOLY SPIRIT.

IT only remains for me, in this last division, to subjoin as briefly as possible, a historic outline of the development of the doctrine of the Holy Spirit, and a sketch of the discussions which it has undergone in the course of centuries. The history of this doctrine touches theology at so many points, sometimes in connection with the Trinity, sometimes with inspiration, sometimes with the doctrines of grace, at other times with the Person and mediation of Christ, that were we to attempt a survey of all these debates, there is scarcely a point in the whole field of polemical theology or Church history which we should not be compelled to traverse. We must fix our eye on the salient points, therefore, and on the marked epochs in the history of the doctrine, that we may not be engulfed in details personal, dogmatic, or ecclesiastical. History, with its parallel testimony to Scripture, has a great importance which is not to be ignored; and it must be borne in mind that certain points of the doctrine at one time come more prominently into view, and others at another; that this topic at one time acquires interest, and that it falls again comparatively into abeyance.

In the very earliest Christian literature—that is, in the Apostolic Fathers,—and in the Epistle of Clemens especially, we find that the allusions to the Holy Spirit are all in the interest of spiritual religion, and by no means polemical (Clem. chap. xlvi.). The circular letter issued by the Church of Smyrna after Polycarp's death is of the same nature. The

whole doctrine of the Spirit was at that time practical.   The
doctrine of the Spirit was accepted from the earliest age as an
elementary truth in connection with the baptismal formula
by young and old, by learned and unlearned.   This formula
was a rudimentary truth to every baptized man : for there
never was a time when a Christian disciple did not confess
the Deity and saving work of all the three Persons of the
Godhead—that is, when he was not thoroughly instructed as
a catechumen in the doctrine of the Trinity, and accepted it
as a primary truth with the first profession of Christianity.
In the Creed, which was only an echo of the baptismal formula, the Christian Church, from the first, over all her
borders, never hesitated to declare : " I believe in the Holy
Ghost," and Christians were guided by this rule in the course
of ages to find their way through all the Trinitarian controversies — the Church simply appealing to that baptismal
formula, and applying it for the refutation of every single
error on the subject of the Trinity.

The doctrine of the Spirit was for a considerable time
unassailed.   The early Fathers, having no occasion to define
the topic, as was done at a later time, simply speak of the
Spirit as a divine Person.   As regards the article of the
Spirit, the doctrine of the Marcionites formed a marked
antithesis to what the Church had always maintained ; and
this led to a style of language which the Nicæno-Constantinopolitan Creed retains to this day.   Marcion, the erratic
leader of the sect, in his violent polemic against the Old
Testament and the God of the Old Testament, made use of
language disavowed by all Christian men.   He represented
the Old Testament as the production of the subordinate God
of the Jews, and endeavoured to overthrow the entire Old
Testament revelation on the plea that it did not proceed from
THE SAME SPIRIT that animated the founders of the Christian
Church.

As Marcion and his followers took up such an antagonistic

attitude to the whole Old Testament, the entire body of Church teachers testified to the prophetic Spirit, and confessed that one and the same Spirit spoke in both economies, —THE PROPHETS by the Spirit foretelling the Messiah's advent, and THE APOSTLES by the same Spirit announcing the historic fact. The words which they put into the Church's mouth, and which we find repeated in the Constantinopolitan Creed, were: " The Spirit who spoke by the prophets." It is clear from the Patristic literature that has come down to us, that from the earliest times the Church had the doctrine of the Spirit in its substance and practical bearing, though the points were not fully thought out, and the terms of the later nomenclature were not as yet employed. The defects which we shall have occasion to trace came in afterwards, and were mainly due to the Greek philosophy and to the false adjustments which were attempted in regard to it.

We come next in order to the Christian apologists. Justin Martyr is an emphatic witness to the distinct personality of the Holy Spirit. Semisch, who devoted a life-long study to this writer, states that the title " prophetic Spirit " occurs twenty-seven times ; the title " Holy Spirit," thirty-two times ; " the holy prophetic Spirit," four times ; " the Spirit of God," four times ; " the divine Spirit," three times ; the " prophetic Spirit of God," once ; " the divine holy prophetic Spirit," once. There is not so much said, nor so clearly said, of the third Person of the Trinity as of the second. But the Spirit's personality is clearly and emphatically stated. Thus he speaks of the explicit confession of the Trinity in connection with baptism, when he says that it was performed in the name of the Father of the universe and Lord God, and of our Saviour Jesus Christ, and of the Holy Ghost (1 *Apol.* lxi.). The same Trinitarian formula was used in the celebration of the Supper, the officiating minister offering up praise and glory to the Father of the universe, through the name of the Son and Holy Ghost (chap. lxv.). In the same first *Apology*

(A.D. 139) there are passages where Justin once and again
denies the charge of Atheism, and names as the objects of
Christian adoration, the Father, Son, and Holy Ghost.   I shall
adduce two of these passages, because they are conclusive as
to Justin's Trinitarianism : " What man of sound mind will
not acknowledge that we are not Atheists, since we worship
the Maker of this universe . . . and Him who was our teacher
(τὸν διδάσκαλόν τε) in these things, Jesus Christ, Son of this
true God—holding Him in the second place ; and the prophetic Spirit (πνεῦμά τε προφητικόν) we with reason honour "
(chap. xiii.) ?   The one God and the three objects of Christian worship cannot be more explicitly exhibited, connected
together as they are by a Greek particle (τε) which, as Hand [1]
has proved, links together objects of co-ordinate rank with a
certain dissimilarity peculiar to themselves.

The same thing may be traced in the well-known passage
which has received so much discussion from Romanists on
the one hand, and Unitarians on the other.   But if we take
along with us the passage which we have just adduced, little
difficulty will be found either in its structure or its import.
The passage is as follows : " Whence also we are called
Atheists.   And we confess that with regard to such reputed
gods we are Atheists ; but not with regard to the true God,
the Father of justice, temperance, and the other virtues, without any mixture of evil.   But Him, and the Son (who came
from Him and gave us instruction in these things and concerning the host of the other good angels following Him and
made like to Him), and the prophetic Spirit (πνεῦμά τε τὸ
προφητικόν), we worship and adore, honouring them with
reason and truth " (chap. vi.).   That we have (1) the three
Persons of the Godhead linked together by the Greek par-
ticles (ἐκεῖνόν τε καὶ τὸν υἱὸν πνεῦμά τε τὸ προφητικόν), is
evident at a glance to any true philologist.   That we have
(2) the well-known Greek expression of two accusatives after

[1] See Hand's dissertation on τι.

the verb " to teach," the one denoting the person taught, and the other the art and science in which he is instructed, can admit of little doubt (διδάξαντα ἡμᾶς ταῦτα καὶ τὸν στρατόν). Scultetus, followed by Bishop Bull, was led by the true instinct of sound philology to see that this sense alone satisfies the import of the words and the demands of the connection ; and they both pour out well-merited scorn on the Romanists who wrested them, and still wrest them, from their scope to countenance the worship of angels, with a different degree of honour. This is to make a fourth object of worship, and to thrust it in between the Son and the Spirit. As I have already assigned the only admissible translation, I need not refer to the rendering which construes the words so as to intimate that Christ came teaching us and the host of other good angels. That is the rendering of Dr. Samuel Clarke, who puts it thus : " Who came forth from Him and taught these things to us, and to the whole host of good angels." It will in that case be a declaration that the angels as well as we are instructed by our Lord. But that statement was by no means in Justin's scope or design.

It has often been said that Justin confounds the Logos and the Holy Spirit. But a more critical inquiry into his words serves to prove only that these two divine Persons are in office closely connected, but not confounded. Justin certainly held that the Father, Son, and Spirit are from eternity, though he might not put his thoughts in the same definite form that was used in subsequent times, either to define the generation of the Son or the procession of the Spirit. But he was beyond all doubt a Trinitarian, though he might not clearly bring out that the economic Trinity presupposes the ontological Trinity.

We are precluded, both by our limits and by the scope of this historical survey, from taking up the Fathers in succession, or adducing their testimony in detail; we shall merely glance at those who wrote before the personality of the Spirit

was disputed. All those Fathers, acting on the great truth
enunciated in the formula of Baptism, breathe a Trinitarian
spirit in a highly practical way. Thus Theophilus of Antioch,
about A.D. 175, speaks of a Triad in the Godhead. His gifted
and profound contemporary, Irenæus, the scholar of Polycarp,
a few years later, speaks of all the persons of the Godhead in
a very fresh and glowing manner. It has been incorrectly
alleged, by no less an authority than the Magdeburg Centu-
riators, that Irenæus speaks more rarely (*rarius*) of the Holy
Spirit. But unless that is said by comparison with his copiousness in speaking of the Logos, it is a great mistake, as is
well known to every one who has carefully read his work
against heresies, where we find the most explicit allusions to
the work of the Spirit in the primeval formation of man after
the divine image and likeness,—in the supernatural production of Christ's humanity,—in the anointing of Christ for His
high office,—and in His coming down to reunite man to God,
after the great atonement had been offered. Though his object
in refuting the Valentinian errors led him to say more of the
Logos as identified with Christ, he does not withhold a fresh
and vivid outline of the doctrine of the Spirit, whom he calls
the Holy Spirit, the Spirit of God and Wisdom, the latter
name being taken from the allusion to Wisdom in Proverbs
(Prov. viii. 22).

It is in Tertullian, however, that we first find the precise
dogmatic expression of the truth in regard to the divine persons in the use of the term TRINITY, which has ever since been
accepted in the Church.

1. The doxologies to the Father, Son, and Holy Ghost,
which were everywhere in use in the early Greek Church,
furnish a conclusive proof of the acceptance of the doctrine
of the Spirit, and of the prevalence of Trinitarian views.
Thus, in the narrative of Polycarp's martyrdom, the truth of
which, as given in the encyclical of the Church of Smyrna,
and in nearly the same terms by Eusebius, is above suspicion,

the martyr declares in his closing act of worship : " For this, and for all things, I praise Thee, I bless Thee, I glorify Thee, with the eternal and heavenly Jesus Christ, Thy beloved Son, with whom, to Thee and to the Holy Ghost, be glory both now and through all ages to come." Basil, in his treatise on the Holy Spirit, states that " the glory to the Father *with the Holy Ghost*" was a familiar usage older than human memory, and that it was practised in the Church ever since the gospel was preached (chap. xxix.). That a doxology to the Holy Ghost implies a belief in His personality is self-evident, because worship is never given to mere names or personifications. And we may regard these doxologies as taking their rise in the most natural way,—as, in truth, nothing else but the inward and devout response of the worshipper to the baptismal formula. The Creed was the response in the confession of the mouth, and the doxology was a similar response in the devotion of the heart. Basil adduces another doxology of Africanus from the fifth book of his *Chronicon :* " We render thanks to Him who gave our Lord Jesus Christ to be a Saviour, to whom, *with the Holy Ghost*, be glory and majesty for ever." Basil also quotes to the same purpose from others—for example, a passage from Clemens which ascribes life to the distinct Persons of the Godhead ($\zeta\hat{\eta}$ $\dot{o}$ $\Theta\epsilon\dot{o}\varsigma$ $\kappa\alpha\grave{\iota}$ $\dot{o}$ $\kappa\acute{\upsilon}\rho\iota\sigma\varsigma$ $\mathrm{'}I\eta\sigma\sigma\hat{\upsilon}\varsigma$ $X\rho\iota\sigma\tau\acute{o}\varsigma$, $\kappa\alpha\grave{\iota}$ $\tau\grave{o}$ $\pi\nu\epsilon\hat{\upsilon}\mu\alpha$ $\tau\grave{o}$ $\mathrm{\ddot{\alpha}}\gamma\iota\sigma\nu$) ; and another passage from the doxology introduced into the Church of Neo-Cæsarea by Gregory Thaumaturgus : " Glory to God the Father and Son, *with the Holy Ghost*," the import of which, as Gregory was careful to set forth in the Confession of Faith preserved in the Church which he formed, was to confess a perfect Trinity in glory, eternity, and power, without separation or diversity of nature. And in answer to Aetius, who would argue for a disparity in the Persons, Basil is at pains to prove that an equality of honour was intended by the terms, and a full belief that the Spirit possessed the same divine nature. By the use of these doxologies two things were intimated. The Persons were held to be distinct because they were distinctly worshipped, and all the three Persons to whom the glory is ascribed must have been regarded as participating in the same numerical divine essence.

2. The supernatural work of the Spirit in the inspiration of the Scriptures of the Old and New Testament was never exhibited with greater clearness and force than by the early Fathers of the Greek Church. The impieties of Marcion and the Gnostics induced them to mature and formulate their views. They vindicated the apostles' authority and the plenary inspiration of the Spirit with a fulness of conviction and energy such as has rarely ever been evinced, and certainly never surpassed in any other quarter. The ordinary operations of the Spirit, as we shall see, have been much more correctly and fully displayed in other schools which were less under the spell of philosophic systems and sacramental grace. But nowhere has the miraculous gift of the Spirit in inspiring prophets and apostles been more amply displayed. Thus Justin Martyr, in speaking of the sacred writers as a stringed instrument, says: "Their task was but to surrender themselves wholly to the working of the Spirit of God, that the divine plectrum descending from heaven might make use of holy men as of a harp or lyre, in order to reveal to us the knowledge of divine and heavenly things." With not less point Irenæus says of the Scriptures: "They are spoken by the Word of God and His Spirit; while we in the degree in which we are inferior, and stand at the greatest distance from the Word of God and His Spirit, are in need of the knowledge of His mysteries." And again: "The Logos has given us a fourfold gospel which is held together by one Spirit."

The quotations which have been collected from the Greek Fathers on the subject of inspiration by Lardner, Töllner, Rudelbach, and Westcott show how the early Church regarded the Scriptures as the Spirit's wonderful work. Thus Origen, speaking of the perfection of Scripture in connection with inspiration, says: "The sacred books are pervaded by the fulness of the Spirit. There is nothing, either in the prophets, or in the law, or in the Gospels, or in the Epistles, which does not spring from the fulness of the divine majesty." The mode in which the Greek Fathers often introduce a quotation by omitting the human writer and naming the Holy Spirit as the real author, is one of their most marked peculiarities: "As the Holy Ghost saith." The importance and value of all parts of the Scriptures, as the productions or words of the Holy Spirit, are constantly asserted. Thus, to mention Origen, we find him saying: "We can by no means say of the writings of the Holy Ghost that there is anything superfluous or idle in them, although many a thing may appear dark to many."

3. But the Greek writers, it must be admitted, labour under great defects. Of the ordinary operations of the Holy Spirit they have little to say. The remarks of Semisch embody a criticism which, however depreciatory it may seem to the literature of the Greek Church, cannot be regarded by any one who is largely conversant with that literature on the subject of the Spirit's inward operations as either prejudiced or unjust. "When treating of this subject," says Semisch, "they seem embarrassed and perplexed. They felt themselves obliged by the Biblical writings, and especially by the baptismal formula, to place the Spirit as a third object of devotion ; but, in truth, they knew not how to bring this object into a living connection with their existing theology ; they were kept in constant vacillation on the question, *What position ought to be assigned to the Spirit* in His relations to the Father and Son—to the world—and especially to the work of redemption ?" A little farther on, Semisch says of Justin Martyr, to whom his remarks were meant more expressly to apply : "Of a continued operation of the Spirit

on Christians he has nothing to say ; he also regards the heathen world as hermetically sealed against it."

Some may regard that estimate as prejudiced and one-sided. But it is the testimony of a man whose judgment, from long and sustained inquiries, is entitled to great respect ; and every one who knows the Greek Fathers will, to a large extent, agree with him. A difference obtained between the Eastern and Western Church, as will afterwards more fully appear. The Greek apologists, with somewhat superficial views of sin, and spellbound by the Greek philosophy, from which they never fully emancipated themselves, extolled Christianity as the absolute reason, rather than God's remedy for guilt and sin. Thus Justin, who went from one philosophical school to another in order to ease a restless mind and pacify an aching heart, found what he sought in Christianity. But by him it was largely viewed as the adequate relief and resting-place of the soul, because it met his previous inquiries, and shed light upon problems which were previously inscrutable.

To the Greek mind SIN was always too much an outward fact or a moral infirmity rather than an all-pervading reign of corruption and guilt for which an adequate remedy was to be provided. The Greek mind was satisfied with a too superficial discovery of the doctrine of sin. And this goes far to explain why it is that they have so little to say upon the Spirit's continued operations on the individual Christian. The Greek literature, considered as an edifying and spiritual literature, is of immensely less value as to everything bearing on the Spirit's work than the writings of the school of Augustin, or of Anselm, or of Bernard, or of Luther, or of Calvin, or of the Puritans.

The rise of MONTANISM in Mysia between A.D. 157 and 171 forms the next fact in the history of opinion in reference to the Holy Spirit, and its refutation served a most important purpose in the Church. As the supernatural gifts conferred by apostles had but recently ceased, it was only what was to be expected in the course of things that some enthusiastic Christian of weak mind but fervent piety and zeal should appear to claim their restoration in his own person. Montanus was just such an one, a man of extravagant opinions and ascetic rigour, who lamented the prevalent laxity, and was carried headlong by Chiliastic sentiments. His way was prepared for him by the common belief based on what was deemed apostolic statements, that the Spirit of prophecy should not be withdrawn from the Church till the Lord should come. Hence many were ready to listen to an enthusiast who should arrogate the function of a prophet. And the crude utterances, ecstasies, and prophecies to which Montanus and his female associates Maximilla and Priscilla gave expression,—however offensive to sober minds,—found credit with many, and even with Tertullian. As to the Montanist views, I shall touch only those which bear on the work of the Spirit.

While they held the Catholic doctrine of the Trinity, their error consisted in maintaining that the Paraclete who animated the apostles was restored to Montanus; that it was necessary to recognise the spiritual gifts in Him; and that *the Christian rule which imposed a full restraint on the flesh,* and which could not be received even from the apostles, was now announced by Him as the instrument which the Comforter used for that purpose. He declared that for Christians we must hold that mature manhood was now attained, as it had not been attained either under the law and prophets or under the gospel. These men held that all true Christians have the Holy Ghost; that the rights of such as possessed the spiritual gifts were paramount; and that all office in the Church must make way for their exercise.

The discussions to which these views gave origin were important, and the refutation of their extravagant first principles lodged important truth in men's minds both as to the mode of divine revelation and as to the finality of Scripture.

As to the mode of a divine communication, we have fragments preserved by Eusebius of a work written by Miltiades which aimed to prove, against the Montanists, that a prophet could not speak in ecstasy, that is, without the calm possession of his mental powers. This fact implies that the Montanist effusions must have been like similar effusions of later times—turbid, fanatical, and confused. Tertullian threw his shield over that excited mood of mind as not only necessary, but befitting in one who was overshadowed by the divine power. But in saying so he spoke as the apologist of the system which he had embraced. The Church of whom Epiphanius may be taken as the representative expressed a wholly different view : " Let us," says he, " compare what is asserted by these parties with that which is undeniably contained alike in the Old and New Testaments, which is also seen and predicted in truth, and thereby test what is true prophecy and what is false. The true prophet spoke with the complete tranquillity of the mental powers, so that one thing followed another in a certain order ; he spoke by the Holy Ghost, and therefore uttered everything with great confidence." We find similar sentiments expressed by Basil. " Some suppose," says he, " that the prophets prophesied in ecstasy, so that the human spirit was as it were overshadowed by the divine. But this is against the premiss of the divine inhabitation ; for how can the Spirit of wisdom and knowledge deprive any one of his senses ? "

Another question was : Is the Church—since the canon of Scripture was closed—warranted to expect any further immediate revelations or prophetic visions ? The ancient Church, as against the Montanists, answered in the negative. It was a question, not what God can do, but whether He will, besides the written word, communicate any further revelations of the counsel of His will. And the discussion of this question with the Montanists anchored the Church in the conviction that it is rash and unwarrantable to expect any further disclosures from the Spirit of God, and that immediate revelations are rather to be viewed as emanating from the adversary changed into an angel of light. To the allegation that the Church ought to enjoy extraordinary miraculous gifts, and that she has lost them by her own fault and through her own unbelief, the answer then given was that extraordinary gifts were never promised to the Church as a permanent inheritance, subsequently to the closing of the canon. And that style of argument has been confirmed by the unbroken experience of nearly two millenniums, attesting that they were withdrawn, and that they are not to be regarded as forfeited by her own fault.

We turn to the discussions which assailed THE DIVINE PERSONALITY of the Holy Spirit. The truth on this point required to be vindicated against two phases of error, known as SABELLIANISM on the one hand, and ARIANISM or Macedonianism on the other, which were in a certain respect antagonistical to each other, and yet at one in their ultimate ground. There was a certain collision of mind between the two, but they occupied the attitude of producing or stimulating each other. And they agreed in regarding the divine Being as unipersonal, not Trinitarian.

As to Sabellianism, the theory of modalism, or the Trinity of mere manifestation, it found its first utterance (A.D. 200) in Praxeas of Asia Minor, who succeeded about the end of the second century in forming a party, and even in gaining over to his views Victor, Bishop of Rome. This theory was accepted by Noetus of Smyrna, against whom we have the valuable homily of Hippolytus. It was accepted by Beryllus of Bostra, whom Origen reclaimed at a council held in A.D. 244. Above all, it was resolutely maintained by Sabellius, presbyter of Ptolemais in the Libyan Pentapolis, who from the year 218 became the head of the party, and who is described as the subtilest of the anti-Trinitarians.

A certain obscurity envelopes the origin of Sabellianism, but it long troubled the peace of the Church. It propounded the opinion that the terms Father, Son, and Holy Ghost were but different names of a unipersonal God. It was the first, or one of the first, errors on the Trinity *that got a footing within the Church*,[1] and it is the error to which modern thought discovers a decided inclination to return. It was borrowed in a large measure from the Gnostics or Cerinthians, who not only denied a proper Trinity, but resolved all into appearance or manifestation. These forms of error were outside the Church. Sabellianism was the first anti-Trinitarian tendency that found access within the pale of the Church, and became the occasion of introducing a form of thought opposed to the most elementary truths of Christianity. Within the Church's pale, Sabellianism sprung from the desire to solve the mystery of the Trinity in unity by propounding the notion of a unipersonal God variously manifested, or a mere modal distinction in the Godhead. During THE THIRD CENTURY it acquired a wide diffusion; and in many quarters it was boldly asserted. On this principle, of course, the Son and Spirit could have no part *in creation*, for they were not yet. There could be no *atonement* on this principle, for there was no other person of the Trinity to whom it could be offered; and the Holy Spirit's *power* was nothing but a vague, baseless influence that did not lean on a Mediator.

When Praxeas introduced the opinion that Father, Son, and Holy Ghost were but different names for one and the same Person, Tertullian, in a treatise that has come down to us, assailed it with the utmost vehemence, and so far influenced the person who originally taught the theory at Carthage, that for a time at least he was brought to a recantation. The error soon broke out anew, and spread over the whole Libyan Pentapolis, the territory adjacent to Tripoli, to such an extent that, according to the statement

[1] See Stillingfleet on the Trinity.

of Athanasius, the Son of God was scarcely preached in the churches of that district. Dionysius, bishop of Alexandria, warned the leaders of that speculation to desist from propagating such opinions, answered inquiries, and wrote letters to reclaim the Libyan bishops. And when they persisted in propagating their Unitarian opinions, he prepared a dogmatic treatise in which he brought out the personal distinctions of the Godhead, and the necessity of asserting them, though with such a want of due caution as laid him open to assault. Nor can all the vindication with which Basil and Athanasius have too generously shielded and defended him from those charges of Arianizing, which were made against his statements, exempt him from merited blame. He prepared an explanation in consequence of the remonstrances sent to him by Dionysius of Rome, which restored him to the confidence of the Church, and to the reputation of orthodoxy. Sabellius was excommunicated in A.D. 261 ; an act of discipline that went far to check his opinions, and to bring back the Church to the two ideas of Trinity and unity.

One fact presents itself to our notice in all these discussions. Whenever an error arose on the subject of the Trinity in the Ante-Nicene Church, we find that the Fathers uniformly appeal to the baptismal formula. That was regarded as the secret of their strength ; and it carried weight with ordinary Christians as well as theologians. Thus Tertullian, in his address against Praxeas, proves that Christ required His disciples to baptize into the Trinity and not into one of them (*ad singula nomina in personas singulas tingimur*). There was no possibility of resisting the emphatic language of that sacramental formula, of which the express purport was that it must run distinctly in the name of the Father, and of the Son, and of the Holy Ghost. Tertullian adduced, with not less force, an argument from the passages which refer to the mission of the Comforter, as affording the clearest proof of a Trinity in unity. It was against the Sabellians that the

Church introduced the term PERSON in the ecclesiastical
acceptation which it has ever since retained. Athanasius
emphatically declared that he abhorred Sabellianism equally
with Arianism.[1]

The special controversy, however, on the DIVINE PERSON-
ALITY of the Holy Spirit began with Arianism in the fourth
century. SABELLIANISM and ARIANISM were more closely
connected than at first sight appears. With an apparent
antagonism, but an inner bond of connection, they acted on
each other with a reciprocal influence, producing and being

[1] Nothing strikes the inquirer more than the eager desire evinced by the
modern Unitarians to appeal to the early Fathers negatively or positively. Fond
as they are of declaring that they stand on the shoulders of the Fathers and
Reformers, they find it necessary to consider this early testimony, however little
it serves their cause. The attempt of Sand, the Arian, to make the early
Fathers speak his sentiments, was exposed by Wittichius in his *causa Spiritus
sancti*, 1678, and by Bishop Bull. The groundless statements of Curcellæus
received merited chastisement from the hand of Stillingfleet. The more
cautious appeal to the Fathers by Dr. Samuel Clarke was sufficiently met by
Waterland, Hurrion, Abraham Taylor, and others. The bold statements of
Priestley, on a subject where his information was far from extensive or correct,
received the most overwhelming refutation from Velingius, Segaar, and Gavel
in Holland, and from Bishop Horsley in this country. One of the effective
treatises on the subject is Burton's testimonies of the Ante-Nicene Fathers to
the doctrine of the Trinity *and of the divinity of the Holy Ghost*, 1831. In the
face of all this evidence, Dr. Lamson, a Unitarian writer of some reputation, in
a work entitled, *The Church of the First Three Centuries* (Boston 1860),
announces this as the conclusion to which he has come : " The modern doctrine
of the Trinity is not found in any document or relic belonging to the Church of
the first three centuries. Letters, art, usage, theology, worship, creed, hymn,
chant, doxology, ascription, commemorative rite, and festive observance, so far
as any remains, or any record of them is preserved coming down from early
times, are, as regards this doctrine, an absolute blank." Whether that representation is ignorance or reckless misstatement I shall not take it upon me to
decide. Baur's elaborate work, in three elaborate volumes, *Die Christliche
Lehre von der Dreieinigkeit und Menschwerdung Gottes in ihrer geschichtlichen
Entwicklung*, is very far from being a reliable history of the doctrine, not
because he intends to be unfair, but because he makes for the various writers
a system which never had any existence except in his own brain. The three
erudite volumes always remind me of what Schiller said playfully of himself,
but which may be gravely said of Baur : " Ich werde immer eine Schlechte
Quelle für den Geschichtsforscher seyn, der Unglück hat sich an mich zu
wenden. Die Geschichte ist überhaupt ein Magazin für meine Phantasie und
die Gegenstände müssen sich gefallen lassen was sie unter meinen Händen
Werden."

produced. Arius, teaching presbyter of Alexandria, would solve the mystery in an opposite way from that which Praxeas and Sabellius had adopted. Living in the heart of the Sabellian district at Alexandria, Arius saw that the Sabellian theory was untenable; that it gave no explanation of the pre-existence and creative agency of the other Persons of the Godhead, and of their connection with the Old Testament generally (A.D. 318).

The Rationalistic bias of Arius' mind appeared in this, that he would not allow distinct personality and co-ordinate rank to the three Persons named in the baptismal formula. He would destroy the Trinity in unity *by laying stress on the subordination* of the second and third Persons,—which, so far as a certain order of action is concerned, the Church teachers never scruple to admit,—*and by denying their consubstantiality.* He held the relation of the Son 'and Spirit to be nothing more than a created relation, and he thus showed that his mind was swayed and dominated, as Sabellius' was, by the theory of a unipersonal God. He vehemently contended that Deity and derivation from another person involved contradictory ideas. The numerous arguments propounded by Arius, and especially by Eunomius,—who was by far the ablest of the Arians,—as these are stated and referred to by Athanasius, Basil, and Gregory Nazianzen, may all be reduced to two—that the same ETERNITY and the same INDEPENDENCE cannot possibly be possessed by a person who is OF or FROM another. There Arius paused, and resolutely adhered to the mere dictates of his own reason. He maintained as the only warrantable explanation, that the Father originated the Son by the *fiat* of creation, and that the Holy Spirit was but the creature of a creature. He dismissed in the most abrupt way the whole array of Biblical evidence, which goes to prove that the divine essence, numerically one, is possessed in common by Father, Son, and Spirit.

It is stated, both by Epiphanius and Augustin, on evidence

that seems liable to no suspicion, that Arius regarded the Holy Ghost as a creature of the Son, that is, as the creature of a creature; because, according to his beliefs, the Son of God occupied no higher position than that of a creature. It does not appear, however, that Arius at first openly assailed the Deity of the Spirit. At least Alexander of Alexandria, in the letter which he sent to the bishops of the Christian Church expressly recording the erroneous views of Arius and of his followers, makes no mention of this point. And the Nicene Creed, directly intended to refute his opinions, contains nothing more on the Holy Spirit than the simple statement which had been confessed in the Church from the beginning: "I believe in the Holy Ghost." If we compare the several statements that have come down to us, we may warrantably conclude that, at the commencement of his career, Arius having no direct occasion to express his sentiments on the Holy Spirit, and being challenged ecclesiastically only for his avowed opinions on Christ's Deity, was content for a time to let the controversy be carried on in connection with the topics which gave rise to it; and that it was only at a later date, when pressed by arguments and demands that summoned him to declare himself explicitly and without evasion, that his error on the Holy Spirit, at least in its full extent, was at length brought to light. This is confirmed by what is recorded in connection with Athanasius' disputation with him. During the sitting of the Council of Nice, Athanasius held a disputation with Arius, and in the course of that discussion Arius declared without concealment or evasion his belief that the Holy Spirit was but a creature. We are further told that the proof which he adduced was the weakest that can be conceived, viz. that the Father sent the Paraclete from heaven, and that all things were made by Christ (John i. 3), leaving the inference to be deduced that He was among the creatures that Christ created.

We come to the remarkable period between the First and

Second General Council (A.D. 325–381), a period memorable for the great men who appeared in it, but equally memorable for the fundamental errors that agitated and distracted men's minds, and for the indecision, uncertainty, and unsettled opinion on the work and agency of the several Persons of the Godhead. After the divine Sonship of Christ had been asserted, the next fifty years may be described as a chaotic period, when men's minds were in many quarters perplexed and bewildered on the subject of the Holy Spirit's divine personality. It was only by slow and measured steps that the opinion of the Church on the doctrine of the Holy Spirit — under the guidance of her living Head — came to acquire consistency and calm rest. But she had to pass through a fiery trial.

The principal assailants of the Deity of the Spirit were the Macedonians (πνευματόμαχοι), called also Semi-Arians, because they denied the Deity of the Holy Ghost, even while they admitted the divine dignity of the Son. The founder of this sect was Macedonius, a man in no way venerable, who obtained the episcopal dignity by bloodshed, and who, after an unworthy occupancy of the post for a year, was ejected from it amid sedition and turmoil. It was after his deposition that he propounded his heresy, which consisted in denying the Spirit's Deity, and in proclaiming Him to be a mere creature, though it does not appear that he and his followers had arrived at any firm opinion as to the created nature, angelic or super-angelic, which ought to be ascribed to Him. The grounds on which the Macedonians assailed the Deity of the Holy Spirit were much the same with those which the Unitarians have urged in more recent times, but scarcely with the amount of ingenuity and plausibility which the latter have displayed.

Before the Second General Council was assembled, the arguments of the Macedonians (πνευματόμαχοι) were fully confuted by Athanasius, Basil, Gregory Nazianzen, Gregory

Nyssen. They drew out the proof for the Deity of the Holy Spirit, much in the same way as they had used in establishing the supreme Deity of the Son, by texts ascribing DIVINE DIGNITY, OMNIPOTENCE, OMNIPRESENCE, and OMNISCIENCE to the Spirit, and especially from THE BAPTISMAL FORMULA, because a creature could not be put into the formula as of co-ordinate rank with the Father and the Son. And Athanasius brings out that the Father works all BY the Son IN the Holy Spirit.

In the strangely agitated period which preceded the calling of the Second General Council, the part which Basil acted was that of concession and of moderate demands. He was content if, in the eager efforts which were put forth to reclaim the Semi-Arians, they could be brought to declare that the Holy Spirit was not a creature, even though they did not take the positive ground of asserting His supreme Deity. To some, Basil's action has always, down from his own time to this day, seemed to argue the character of a trimmer; to others, it seems the part of a wise Church leader. His maxim was as follows : " Union will take place if we adapt ourselves to the weak, and do not provoke the minds of men. As many speak against the Holy Ghost, I request that you will reduce them as far as lies in your power to a small number. *Those who confess that the Holy Ghost is not a creature,* receive into your society, in order that the blasphemers alone may be left ; and either reduce them to the truth by shame, or, if they remain in their sin, attach no more weight to the insignificant number. Let us require nothing further; let us lay before them the Nicene Confession, and if they assent to it, let us ask them to call the Holy Ghost not a creature. He who confesses this, let him be received into the Church. I think we should require no more " (*Epist.* cxiii.).

Some ecclesiastics to whom Basil's conduct was an enigma and a cause of anxiety made representations to Athanasius

regarding it; and the letters in reply which have come down
to us sufficiently attest that Athanasius entirely approved of
the measures which Basil had taken. "I wonder," said
Athanasius, "at the audacity of those who presume to
reproach our beloved Bishop Basil, the true servant of
God." "They may be assured," says he again, in writing
to Palladius, "that he is the glory of the Church, a combatant
for the truth, and a teacher of the needy; they must not
fight against such a man." "He is, I am fully convinced,
weak to the weak, that he may gain the weak."

To show the state of that agitated transition-period, a few
facts may be added. Basil tells us that some held the Holy
Spirit to be neither lord nor servant, but free (ἐλεύθερος).
Basil himself distinguishes the Spirit from the creature as
follows: "The creature serves; but the Spirit makes free.
The creature needs life; but the Spirit is the quickener. The
creature needs instruction; but the Spirit is the teacher.
The creature is sanctified; but the Spirit is the sanctifier.
Though you name angels, archangels, and all the super-
mundane powers, they have their holiness by the Spirit."
Basil says: "The Holy Spirit is of God, not as all things
are, but as *proceeding out of God* (προελθών)." And yet this
eminent man, with not a few of the orthodox of that period,
while fully believing in his own mind the supreme Deity of
the Spirit, abstained for the sake of peace, and to avoid giving
offence, from insisting on calling Him God.

Athanasius also, in his epistle to Serapion, writing against
the Semi-Arians or Pneumatomachi, says in reference to those
who make the Holy Spirit a creature: "Is it not madness,
then, to say that the Spirit is a creature? For if He were a
creature, He would not have been ranked in the Trinity, the
whole of which is our God." He, in the same epistle, strongly
urges that the Holy Spirit is in God (ἐν Θεῷ), and that a
creature is outside the divine essence (ἔξωθεν τῆς τοῦ Θεοῦ
οὐσίας). He lays out the whole strength and energy of his

powerful mind to demonstrate how much the Spirit transcends every predicate of creaturehood, calling Him " the sanctifying and illuminating life."

During the continuance of that Semi-Arian or Macedonian controversy, which was as long as it was saddening and paralyzing, many were completely unsettled and at a loss what to hold.   Thus Gregory Nazianzen states (*Or.* 37): " Some say that the Holy Spirit is a mere energy ; others that He is a creature ; and others that He is God.   And some will not affirm that He is any of these, out of reverence for the Scriptures, which, according to them, do not clearly indicate which of these He is.   And they neither do Him honour nor dishonour, but are very much in the position of men who are indifferently affected toward Him.   Some," he proceeds, " acknowledged that a ternary must be understood in our religion, but they so widely distinguished the Persons from each other as to make one of them infinite in substance and in power ; the other infinite in power, not in substance ; and the third circumscribed in both."

For such a condition of things the definitions of the Council of Constantinople in A.D. 381 offered a mental relief and satisfaction that could not be expressed.   The weary and agitated mind of Christendom — on which such distracting controversies had been let loose—welcomed the repose.   The decision given by that Council—and which at once entered into the universal creed of Christendom—was singularly calm and measured.   It was appended as a mere addition to the Nicene Creed, neither inserting the term HOMOOUSIAN nor the words VERY GOD OF VERY GOD, which had been already applied to the Son, and leaving it to be inferred that they were equally applicable to the Holy Spirit.   The addition made to the Nicene Creed on the Holy Ghost was simply the words : " THE LORD AND GIVER OF LIFE, WHO PROCEEDETH FROM THE FATHER, WHO, WITH THE FATHER AND SON TOGETHER, IS WORSHIPPED AND GLORIFIED, WHO SPAKE BY THE PROPHETS."

The whole tenor of that invaluable addition to the Nicene Creed furnishes a clear though indirect proof that the Macedonian error, against which it was meant to be directed, denied the supreme Deity of the Holy Spirit. It does not appear what sort of created nature was ascribed to the Spirit by that heresiarch. But the refutation, which is contained in the simple enumeration of these positive predicates, is the most complete that could have been devised. Some, indeed, from an inadequate apprehension of its scope and aim, have expressed surprise that in a creed expressly prepared against a heresy that represented the Holy Spirit as a creature, the framers of the article did not in so many words designate Him God. Others, putting a construction upon the tenor of the article from what they know of Basil's mode of action, have conjectured that the assembled Fathers abstained from the use of the term GOD as applied to the Spirit, in order to avoid offence, because the heretics could not endure the application of the term God to the Spirit. Petavius appeals to Gregory Nazianzen's confession as regards his friend Basil. There is no foundation for such a sinister view. Basil had died two years before ; and the bishops assembled at Constantinople exercised—as the transactions of the council prove—an independent judgment in this matter. They prepared the Confession on the article of the Holy Spirit in terms directly antagonistic to Macedonius' error and completely subversive of his opinions. A few words will suffice to show this.

1. Macedonius held that the Holy Spirit as a creature derived His life from Christ; and he based his argument on a false interpretation of the words in the preface of John's Gospel (John i. 3). We are told by Chrysostom, Epiphanius, Theophylact, and others, that Macedonius, in order to prove that the Holy Spirit received His life, like any other creature, from Christ, punctuated the two verses in an incorrect way, thus : " All things were made by Him, and without Him was

not anything made. That which was made in Him was life."
To obviate that misinterpretation, the framers of the Creed
inserted the terms: " the Lord and Giver of life " (τὸ κύριον
τὸ ζωοποιόν), intimating that He is Himself the source of life,
and that it is He who imparts it in all its forms to others
who stand related to Him as His creatures.

2. The Macedonians argued that if the Holy Spirit were
true God, He must either be begotten or unbegotten ; and as
neither predicate is given to Him in Scripture, He must be
held to be a creature. Against this argument the framers of
the article inserted from Scripture the words: *who proceedeth
from the Father* (τὸ ἐκ τοῦ πατρὸς ἐκπορευόμενον). Their
intention was to show that the Holy Spirit might be true God
without being either begotten or unbegotten, and that this
was the peculiar style, according to Christ's own delineation,
by which we are to mould our language in speaking of the
personal subsistence of the Spirit, and through which we are
to think our thoughts regarding Him.

3. The Macedonians, the assailants of the Spirit's Deity,
commonly appealed, moreover, to an alleged fact, but which
in reality had no foundation, viz. that the Scripture nowhere
commands us to adore and worship the Holy Spirit. This
was one of their chief arguments, as it has been the main
argument of the Unitarians of subsequent times. And the
Fathers of Constantinople expressly avowed the opposite in the
words which they inserted : " Who, with the Father and the
Son together, is worshipped and glorified " (τὸ συμπροσκυνού-
μενον καὶ συνδοξαζόμενον).

4. The last thing inserted was a point which, from the
earliest times, the Christian Church had always adduced as a
proof of the supreme Deity of the Spirit, and which was
confessed in the first creeds, viz. that He spoke by the
Old Testament prophets (τὸ λαλῆσαν διὰ τῶν προφητῶν).
This was the last clause of the article inserted in the Constantinopolitan Creed.

Before proceeding with our historical sketch, two questions presented by the critical inquirer demand an answer.

It is asked: Why did not the First Council, THE NICENE COUNCIL, anticipate or preclude much of the painful dubiety which agitated men's minds during the interval between the two councils, by pronouncing in terms much more definite and express on the supreme Deity of the Holy Spirit? The reason was, that they could not fitly condemn an undeveloped error, which Arius, indeed, cherished in his heart at the time of the Council of Nice (for he regarded Him as a creature), but which had not been so publicly avowed as to become the subject of ecclesiastical action. Though the subsequent attack on the Spirit was but the natural and necessary consequence of the opinions which he entertained, the Fathers at Nice could neither speak of it as an actually existing error, nor act against it when it was but a possible heresy. As to their own belief in the Deity of the Spirit, that is evident enough from the three clauses of the Nicene Creed which relate to the Trinity.

A second question which has a plausible appearance, when taken in connection with the subsequent history, is: why did the Fathers of the Second Council, the CONSTANTINOPOLITAN COUNCIL, declare the doctrine of the Spirit's procession in so defective a manner, merely saying: "who proceedeth from the Father"? The reason was, that the Semi-Arians or Macedonians, against whom the Council pronounced, maintained an error which rendered it necessary to use language which should neutralize and obviate that error, and which was of a nature entirely different from those subsequent debates on the procession of the Spirit which were carried on between the Oriental and Western Churches several centuries afterwards. With the Fathers at Constantinople the one question was, whether the Holy Spirit was supreme God or a creature. It was not the later question, whether the Holy Spirit, CONFESSEDLY A DIVINE PERSON, proceeded from the Father, or from the Father and the Son (*filioque*). If the Fathers at Constantinople would set forth sound orthodox doctrine in contrast with the new heresy, and so far only as the new heresy assailed it, it was necessary for them to affirm that HE WAS GOD BECAUSE HE PROCEEDED FROM GOD, and received His essence from the Father by procession. This was what the Creed declared, viz. that He proceeded from the Father, and was therefore true God, because by procession partaker of the Father's essence. On the contrary, the Macedonians or Semi-Arians had changed their ground. They had, as Arians, in the first step denied that the Son was consubstantial with the Father. Afterwards they held that all beyond the circle of the Father and the Son WAS A CREATURE OF THE SON, and consequently that the Holy Ghost was created by the Son.   The Semi-Arians were thus obliged, according to their principles, to deny that the Holy Spirit proceeds immediately from the Father. That would involve His Deity and participation in the divine essence ; and hence the Fathers of the Constantinopolitan Council felt it necessary to assert, and accordingly did assert, the opposite in the simple use of Christ's own words, which were held to be conclusive of the whole question : *who proceedeth from the Father* (John xv. 26).

But none of the great men who at that age adorned the Greek Church entertained any doubt that the Spirit proceeds not only from the Father, but from the Son. I do not anticipate the history of this discussion which agitated the Eastern and Western Church at a later day. But in connection with the peculiar expression of the Constantinopolitan Creed, "who proceedeth from the Father," it is only fitting and appropriate to remark—what all students of this remarkable period will admit—that the peculiar phrase employed in the Constantinopolitan Creed, enlarged at a later day by the addition of the *filioque* to meet the views of the West, and resolutely retained in its original form in the East,—when viewed in its true significance before that angry controversy began,—was so expressed in order to meet the Semi-Arians, who wished to reduce the Spirit to the rank of a mere creature.

HISTORIC SURVEY OF THE DOCTRINE OF THE PROCESSION OF THE SPIRIT.

This expression means, according to the opinion of the Greek and Latin Fathers who employ it, that the Spirit receives His essence and personality from Him from whom He proceeds (John xv. 26), just as the Son is said to receive His personality from the Father by whom He is begotten. The Son is from the Father alone, and on this account is called the Only-begotten of the Father; whereas the Holy Spirit, the Spirit of the Father and the Spirit of His Son (Gal. iv. 6), is warrantably held to have His essence and personality from both. Though it is nowhere expressly said in the Scripture that the Spirit proceeds from the Son, yet no one who submits his mind to the evidence supplied by many passages can doubt that the thought is diffused through the entire Biblical testimony on the subject. But as to THE HISTORY of the doctrine, we may affirm that there are three epochs, which may be identified with the three names of ATHANASIUS, THEODORET, and PHOTIUS, in Greek Theology on the question before us.

In the FIRST EPOCH, that is, from the rise of Greek theology till the time of Epiphanius († 403), the received opinion, shared equally by the writers of the East and West, was that the Spirit proceeds from the Father and the Son.

Didymus, a monk of Alexandria, blind, but a man of extraordinary learning, composed a work in three books on the Holy Spirit, a work translated into Latin by Jerome, in which he writes: "Christ said of the Comforter, 'He will not speak of Himself, but shall receive of mine'—that is, because

He is not of Himself, but of the Father and me,—for *His personality* (hoc enim quod subsistit) *He has from the Father and me*" (Book II.). Epiphanius explicitly says: "If Christ is believed to be from the Father, God of God, so the Spirit is believed to be from Christ, or from them both" (τὸ δὲ πνεῦμα ἅγιον παρὰ ἀμφοτέρων) (*Anc.* § 70, 71). Gregory Nyssen and Basil in like manner use the same language in various passages, as has been repeatedly proved by those who know their works, and who have always been profoundly struck by the fact that *the Greek Church never had any scruple in her best days*, and when she had her greatest divines in the fourth century, *in speaking of the procession of the Spirit from the Son* as well as from the Father. Athanasius says that "the Holy Spirit has the same order and nature in relation to the Son that the Son has to the Father" (*ad Serap.* § 21); "along with the Father the Son is the fountain of the Holy Ghost" (*Ari.* § 9). These quotations, which might be indefinitely multiplied, leave no room to question the theological opinion of that first epoch in the Greek Church. Before we pass from this epoch we may adduce the words of Augustin as a witness in the Western Church to the same effect in those remarkable elucidations of the Gospel of John, which he has supplied in a series of 124 *tractatus*. In the 99th Exposition, taking up the procession of the Spirit with his usual profoundness, he declares again and again that it is both from the Father and Son; and he lays down a position which Anselm several centuries afterwards handled with consummate power, both in his oral discussion with the Greeks and in his treatise on the procession. Augustin asks: "If, then, the Holy Spirit proceeds from the Father and the Son, why did the Son say: He proceedeth from the Father?" To that question he replies: "A quo autem habet Filius ut sit Deus (est enim de Deo Deus) *ab illo habet utique* ut etiam de illo procedat Spiritus Sanctus: ac per hoc Spiritus Sanctus ut etiam de Filio procedat sicut

procedit de Patre, ab ipso habet Patre." Not only so : when
Christ says, " who proceedeth from the Father," it must be
borne in mind that, according to the uniform tenor of Christ's
teaching, He refers all to the Father because He Himself,
as the only-begotten Son, is of the Father, and thus He
has it from the Father that the Spirit proceeds from Him,
the Son.

The SECOND EPOCH in Greek Theology, in which we find
voices raised for the procession FROM THE FATHER ONLY, begins
with the Council of Ephesus in A.D. 431. Theodore, in the
creed drawn up by him, to which attention was directed by
that Council, declared that the Holy Spirit did not receive
His subsistence through the Son (οὐδὲ δι᾽ υἱοῦ ὑπάρξιν
εἰληφός). Theodore qualified many things, and was permitted to close his career in the Church, notwithstanding all
the crude and divergent views to which he had given utterance. Not long afterwards, when Cyrill launched his anathe-
matisms against Nestorius, he revived the subject by saying :
" If any one shall not confess that the Spirit by whom He
wrought miracles was His own, let him be anathema." To
that anathema Theodoret, the attached friend of Nestorius,
replied in a defiant attitude : " That the Spirit is the Son's own
Spirit we shall confess and accept as a pious utterance, if he
meant of the same nature and proceeding from the Father ; but
if he meant that He has His subsistence from the Son or by
the Son (ὡς ἐξ υἱοῦ, ἢ δι᾽ υἱοῦ τὴν ὑπάρξιν ἔχον), we repudiate
it as blasphemous and impious " (Theod. on Cyrill's Anathe-
matisms). Though it is confessedly difficult to trace or conjecture the purpose which prompted that resolute attitude of
THEODORET, he was the first who openly avowed that the
Holy Spirit is not of the Son, nor by the Son, but from the
Father only. The opinion was not at that time generally
accepted or approved in Greek theology. Men were for a
long time left to a free judgment upon the question. Opinion
was in process of being decidedly formed in the West, under

the influence of Augustin, in favour of the procession from the Son as well as from the Father.

We come to the controversy on the *filioque,* that is, the addition from the Father *and the Son,* which after centuries of polemical discussion ended in the permanent disruption of the Greek and Latin Churches. The Western Church, in accordance with the views of Augustin, laid emphasis on the procession from the Father and the Son, and naturally wished to elevate the doctrine to confessional authority in the Creed. But how was that to be done? Instead of effecting it by a Council of the whole Church, the only competent way, and by a common understanding, it was introduced into the Nicæno-Constantinopolitan Creed by the arbitrary and un-authorized addition of the *filioque* at the Council of Toledo, A.D. 589, under King Reccaredus, who had abandoned Arianism from an enlightened preference for the orthodox faith. From that time the third article of the Creed was always read and chanted in Spain, France, and Germany with this addition. When the Greeks became acquainted with this fact, they not unnaturally charged the Latins with the falsification of the Creed, and with an unwarrantable addition without the concurrence of the entire Christian Church. The Western Church had the truth, but their mode of action was unwarrantable. Instead of interpolating the Creed,—which was the less warrantable from the fact that the clause so altered was expressed in the very words of Scripture,—their proper course was to have taken another part of Scripture which ascribes the procession to the Son as well as to the Father. Had they, for example, inserted such a clause as this: "Who is the Spirit of the Son as well as of the Father," and had an Ecumenical Council inserted it, they might possibly have forestalled the schism, or at least have removed the occasion. As it was, the action of the Latins cannot be vindicated. For, though the doctrine that the Holy Ghost proceedeth from the Son as well as from

the Father is undoubtedly well-founded, the Latins, instead
of presuming to interpolate the Creed of the entire Church,
should have recollected that the Nicæno-Constantinopolitan
Creed was everywhere accepted; that not a word could
warrantably be altered without the general concurrence of the
entire Church; and that such an arbitrary enlargement must
be offensive to their Oriental brethren. The addition first
made in Spain was generally received in the West, in France,
Italy, and England. Leo III., however, who was raised to
the Papal dignity A.D. 795-816, when appealed to for permission to insert the *filioque* in the repetition of the Creed,
firmly refused, from the earnest desire which he always entertained to be in friendly relations with the Greek Church. To
show how firm his purpose was,—a purpose from which he
was not to be moved even by Charlemagne, who defended the
filioque,—Leo caused the unaltered Creed to be engraved on a
silver plate for the Church of St. Peter in Rome. But the
addition had been made, and was not to be undone. The
Churches in Spain, France, and elsewhere sung the Creed
with this addition. What Pontiff was prevailed upon to
permit the addition is not certain; for different writers have
given different names. Petavius says correctly that it is
not known by whom the concession was made. Nor did
the preparation of the Athanasian Creed, as it was unwarrantably called, improve the matter. The opposite sentiment
was diffused by it throughout all the East.

The controversy soon became A DOGMATIC ONE. The
Greeks now actually began, as a body, to deny the procession
of the Holy Spirit from the Son. And the acrimony as well
as disingenuous artifices which speedily ensued from heated
minds, the assumptions on the one side, and the violent
antagonism on the other, form a sad chapter of ecclesiastical
history. Not a few of the Greek writers, though they constantly rejected the phrase "procession from the Father AND
the Son," yet acknowledged a "procession from the Father

THROUGH the Son;" and they explained it sometimes in one
way and sometimes in another way. But for the most part
they would not admit that anything more was indicated than
AN ECONOMICAL RELATION or THE IDEA OF MISSION.[1] Thus
John Damascen puts the matter in the following way : "We
believe in one Holy Spirit in all things like the Father and
the Son—proceeding from the Father and *dispensed by* the
Son " (*Orth. F.* c. 10).

What may be called THE THIRD EPOCH in Greek theology,
took its rise with PHOTIUS, who wrote on the procession
according to the current view of the Greek Church, and condemned as blasphemous the opinion entertained in the West
(A.D. 867). He brought together all the arguments which
could be adduced for his side of the question. But they are
inferential, presumptuous, and little better than vain logic
applied to a theme beyond the scope and application of mere
logical deduction. This so offended the Latin Church, that
the addition to the Creed, hitherto used only in Spain, France,
and Germany, was now openly accepted everywhere. The
division inevitably assumed the form of a schism about the
year 1054. But a new necessity arose, of a national kind.
Though there had always been individuals among the Greeks
who had concurred in sentiment with the Western theology
on the doctrine of the procession, a new element came into
operation. The Greeks were harassed by the Turks on every
side ; and as it began to be apparent that the Eastern Empire
could not for a long time support itself against these powerful
and constantly advancing enemies without help from the West,
they made eager and repeated requests for help. They sent
ambassadors to the Council of Constance (1414–1418), and
also to the Council of Basel (1431–1449), but they effected

---

[1] Kyriakos, in his singularly clear and comprehensive Church History
in the modern Greek language (Athens, 1881), says : ὅτε δὲ ὁ πάπας Μαρτῖνος
εἶχεν ἐκφράσει ἐν Κωνσταντινουπόλει τῷ 650 γνώμην ὑπὲρ τῆς καὶ ἐκ τοῦ υἱοῦ
ἐκπορεύσεως, ἀπεκρούσθη ἡ διδασκαλία ὑπὸ τῶν ἀνατολικῶν διαρρήδην.

nothing.   Only on one condition could help be accorded—
that the Greeks should be reunited to the Western Church.
To bring this about, every effort was used—from the effect of
fear on the one side, and ambition on the other.   At length
Eugenius IV. called a council at a time when the Turks
threatened to accomplish the overthrow of the Eastern Empire.
To this council, known as the Council of Florence, which first
met at Ferrara at the end of 1438, and was transferred to
Florence in 1439, the Greek Emperor and the Patriarch of
Constantinople anxiously repaired, in the vain hope of receiving help from the West.   But they were required to accept
the Western view of the procession, together with some points
of Romish doctrine to which it is not necessary here more
particularly to refer.   These conditions were accepted under
the pressure of necessity, when it was too late.   But it may
be useful to refer to the formula or article of union, as it
serves to show the true position of the whole question which
was disputed between the Churches.   This formula, drawn up
by Scholarius, afterwards called Gennadius, was as follows :
" Since we Greeks hitherto supposed that the Latins affirmed
that the Holy Ghost proceeds from the Father and the Son
as from two principles or by two spirations, and did not affirm
that *the Father is the fountain of Deity, viz. of the Son and
Holy Spirit*, we with much aversion withdrew both from the
addition made by the Latins to the Creed, and from their
communion.   But now, being by the singular grace of God
assembled in this sacred and ecumenic synod in order to
cement a sacred union between us, after many questions
ventilated on both sides, after keen discussions and the adducing of many testimonies both from sacred Scripture and from
the Church-teachers, *we Latins* declare and profess that in our
affirmation respecting the Spirit's procession from the Father
and the Son, we *do not express it in the sense of excluding the
Father from being the fountain and origin of the whole Deity—
that is, of the Son and Holy Spirit*, or as if we believed that

the Son received not from the Father that procession of the
Spirit from the Son, or as if we held two principles or two
spirations of the Holy Spirit ; but we firmly believe and profess that the Holy Spirit from eternity proceeded from the
Father and the Son as from one principle, and by one single
spiration.

"And we Greeks in like manner assert and profess *that the
Holy Spirit proceeds from the Father*, but we also believe and
affirm that it is the property of the Son *that the procession
should also be from Him*, and that the spiration be from both,
viz. by the Father through the Son according to essence.   And
now in this unanimous profession we unite in a mutual union
and join hands."

This formula, drawn up in such circumstances, neither
pleased all the Greeks nor all the Latins.   The emperor
subscribed, and the majority reluctantly followed, though
some of the Greeks withdrew in disgust.   And on returning
to Constantinople the Greeks were ill received, more especially
as the assistance promised by the Latins against the Turks
was never sent.   The whole proved a failure, and nothing
was actually effected by all the negotiations of the council.
Shortly afterwards Constantinople was taken by the Turks
(A.D. 1453), the Greeks describing this as a divine judgment upon them for the Florentine Council.   On the other
hand, Bellarmine says that they were delivered to the Turks
because of this error.

The Greek Church, notwithstanding the reluctant concession which was made by those who represented it at the
Florentine Council, continued, after the fall of Constantinople,
to assert, with not less vehemence than before, the position
that the Holy Spirit proceeds from the Father only.   No
probability exists that any change will be made by the Greek
Church, or that any proposal of this sort will ever be calmly
considered.   The correspondence into which the Tübingen
divines entered subsequently to the Reformation with the

Greek patriarch, is of importance only as bringing out this fact. The sad fate of the Patriarch CYRILLUS LUCARIS, who had cordially accepted the distinctive doctrines of the Protestant Church, proves the same thing. The formula which would have been accepted by him, that the Holy Spirit proceedeth from the Father through the Son (δι' υἱοῦ), was at once branded with the stigma of heresy by the Council of Constantinople in 1642. Any attempt like that recently made at the Bonn Conference by Dr. Döllinger and some Anglican divines, in the line of the same formula, is only time and effort thrown away in vain negotiation.

We hold strongly the view of the Western Church, which was asserted and maintained by all the Churches of the Reformation ; and it might be important, did space permit, to examine the various grounds by which the Greek Church seeks to confirm her opinion, and the replies which the Greek theologians have produced to the arguments of the Western theologians.[1] They mainly appeal to the fact that the Ecumenical Council of Ephesus prohibited (A.D. 431) as unlawful any further addition to the Nicæno-Constantinopolitan Creed. They give no heed to the allegation of the Western Church, that the addition was only with a view to give a more precise explanation, and not to establish a new dogma. The constantly reiterated Greek reply is, Who gave the Latin Church the authority to alter the accepted Creed of universal Christendom ?

The keen feeling entertained in the Greek Church since the days of Photius still continues. We find that, so late as the Encyclical issued in 1863 at Constantinople, the doctrine

---

[1] The arguments of the Greeks for their side of the question are given with great erudition and ingenuity by the Archbishop of Novogorod, Procopovicz, in his *Tractatus de Processione Spiritus Sancti*, 1772. Ernesti's erudite review of the book is replete with interest.

On the Latin side of the question, the most interesting historical work is Walch's *Historia de Processione*, 1751 ; Pfaffius' tractate on the same topic ; and Sweet's *History of the Doctrine to the Death of Charlemagne*, 1876.

involved in the *filioque* is denounced as heresy. There is no doubt that the Greeks as a body abide in this opinion, and speak and write upon it as a point of capital importance, and as essential to their system of theology.

As to the importance of the doctrine from the Biblical point of view, this cannot be questioned. It will not accomplish anything to say, with Grotius, from the Indifferent point of view, that the dispute is a mere logomachy. Its importance is such that it can neither be dropped nor ignored, though Protestant theologians, such as Pfaffius, Walchius, and others, who have fully traced the historic course of the controversy, admit that the dogma belongs to the less fundamental articles, and that it should not have disturbed the peace of the Greek and Latin Churches. At the same time, these writers assert that he who denies that the Holy Spirit is the Spirit of the Son, denies a truth, though the error may not exclude him from the hope of salvation. It is a delicate question: Was the error of the Greek Church of such a nature as to destroy the foundations of the faith?

Without entering into a sphere which, in truth, does not belong to man, we prefer to advert to the disastrous consequences of its ecclesiastical denial. Every one who has fully traced the course of this controversy historically, and perused the solid and massive literature on the subject from such men as ANSELM, ZANCHIUS, and others, or read LE QUIEN, or the collection of treatises compiled by LEO ALLATIUS, or still more recently the publications of PUSEY and others, called forth by the recent Bonn Conference, must feel how deeply the Greek Church has placed herself in the wrong by the attitude which she has taken up. She has acted under a one-sided and passionate feeling, which has operated to her detriment and loss as an ecclesiastical body. The unction and spirituality of the Church have been sadly affected to her disadvantage.

While calm inquirers must concede that unwise steps were taken by the Western Church, and that her course of action was marked all too evidently by precipitance and mistakes, we must declare with equal emphasis that the Latin Church brought out and gave due weight to a momentous truth which lies at the foundation of the whole mission of the Comforter : How could the Son send the Spirit if the Spirit were not His ?

We might concede that the separation of the Eastern from the Western Church can scarcely be vindicated, if the separation hinged on this question alone. But there is another inquiry : Has not the denial of the *filioque*, which withdrew the Greek Church from the ground occupied in Athanasius' time by the whole Church in the East and West, operated to the deep injury of vital religion in the East ? Has it not tended to subvert, in the general sentiment of the Greek mind, the deep ground on which the Lord Jesus, as Mediator, acts as the Dispenser of the Spirit, and as the Baptizer with the Holy Ghost and with fire ? Has it not operated in an unsalutary way, in raising a barrier between the living Head of the Church and His people, considered as the habitation of God in the Spirit, and on the whole spiritual life of the Greek Church ? Our conviction is, that it has done so. So calamitous, indeed, have been the practical results of denying the essential relation of the Spirit as the Spirit of the Son, that we cannot fail to perceive them. The Spirit, economically considered, is largely dispensed from the Son. And the Greek Church has become much of a fossil, untouched by any of the reformations or revivals that renovated the Western Church.

THE WORK OF THE SPIRIT.

Having sketched the course of opinion as to the Holy Spirit considered as A PERSON OF THE GODHEAD, we come in due course to consider the history of THE SPIRIT'S WORK as it was discussed and canvassed in Church history in connection with the doctrine of grace. There are various marked epochs to which we shall more particularly refer, such

as the testimony given forth in the time of the Pelagian Controversy, and at the Reformation, and also in the Puritan
period—of all which it may be affirmed that the clear and
emphatic doctrine then declared on the Spirit's work was
accompanied with a memorable revival of the spiritual life
of the Church.   As it is by no means the aim of this survey
to compile a *catena patrum*, or to discuss minutely the point
raised by Arminian writers, such as Whitby and Bishop
Tomline, how far the Christian writers, prior to Augustin,
can be regarded as giving an explicit testimony to efficacious
grace, but rather to notice the great turning-points in the
history of opinion, we shall only touch the prominent questions as they arose.

There is a marked difference between the writers of the Greek
and Latin Churches on the whole subject of the Spirit's work,
or on efficacious grace.   From a very early period a different
view prevailed on this mysterious subject.   In the Eastern and
Western Church the relation of human freedom to the agency
of the Spirit was, in some measure, differently viewed.   The
chief emphasis was laid in the Eastern Church on the freedom
of the will or free agency (τὸ αὐτεξούσιον) ; and they spoke of
a self-determining power in man even in his fallen state.   On
the other hand, the chief emphasis was laid in the Western
Church on the extent of corruption and the power of sin.
This difference between the Oriental and Western Church was
at a very early period strongly marked ; and we connot fail
to notice the germs of that peculiar historical development
which gave such a different aspect to them both.   The Eastern
Church, neglecting to elaborate an anthropology which gave
due prominence to sin, and carried away with an airy notion
of metaphysical liberty unduly derived from the speculations
of the Greek philosophy, wasted its strength in vindicating
for man what can never be asserted in regard to him without
a misconception of the ruin occasioned by the Fall.   The
pillars of orthodoxy in the Oriental Church maintained a sort

of synergism of the human will along with the agency of the divine Spirit. They ascribe to man, in his present fallen state, a choice between good and evil, and a co-operation on man's part in the application of redemption. But in elevating human power they diminished natural corruption. The Western Church was led into a far other path, and penetrated far more deeply into the doctrine of man's corrupt and fallen condition. The Greek Fathers are defective, though it must be conceded in justice to them that the vehement urgency with which they set forth free-will, was primarily due to their dread of the determinist or fatalistic theories of the Gnostics and Manichees, with whom they were surrounded. Even where the Greek Fathers set forth man's corruption and the agency of the Spirit, as is done more or less by Cyrill of Jerusalem, Gregory Nazianzen, Basil, and his brother Gregory Nyssen, they also maintain, in terms much too strong for a Biblical theologian, the power of the free-will. Thus Chrysostom puts the matter: " God draws, but He draws the willing one " (ἕλκει μὲν Θεός, ἕλκει δὲ βουλόμενον). That defective statement was only too characteristic of the entire body of Greek theology. They never attempted to solve the question, or to remove the seeming antinomy between divine grace and free-will.

Chrysostom's opinions on the application of Christ's saving work can only be described as defective. With all his deep love to Christ and faithfulness to duty, he unduly ignores the Spirit's agency, and gives prominence to man's free-will. His view of grace to us is only grace in the objective sense, or as coincident with the salvation-work of Christ. Every reader of his homilies is aware that, in his delineation of the relation of divine grace and human choice, the tenor of his language only sets forth that God's grace offers salvation, and that man's free-will applies it; and that as no one is effectually inclined to receive the objectively offered salvation, those only are truly partakers of it, who of their own free choice are inclined to receive it. In a word, Chrysostom asserts, in the most unambiguous way, that it is in every man's power whether he shall be a child of God or not (καὶ γὰρ καὶ ἐν τῇ ἐξουσίᾳ κεῖται τῇ τούτων τὸ γενέσθαι τέκνα, Hom. 9 on John). We cannot, indeed, too highly extol the services of this truly great and holy man. But he invariably insists that those to whom the gospel comes have the decision in their own hand. He has in all his fervid appeals a practical object in view, and he would have thought that it would have invalidated the power of his warnings and exhortations, if he had listened to the further question,—if ever presented to his mind,—that human decision avails not without the subjective exercise of divine grace on the human heart, or had the supernatural work of the Holy Spirit been regarded as imperatively necessary in the effectual application of salvation.

It cannot be denied that the greatest Preacher of the Greek Church was one-sided and defective on the subject of the Spirit's work in the application of redemption. According to him, this is the result of man's free choice, and not the Spirit's work in the first instance. His mode of thought and expression, if we would correctly describe it, did not differ from the SYNERGISM which descended as a heritage to him from the early days of the Greek Church, but which since the days of Augustin has been viewed as a very faulty type of doctrine. The doctrine of special efficacious grace was never fully before him. We may describe his views by any of the three names which describe the same opinions—Semipelagianism, Synergism, or Arminianism, differing as they do from each other by only a slight shade of colouring, but really one in substance. This is the view which sound divines have always taken of Chrysostom's opinions, and in recent times they have been correctly and vividly described by Landerer [1] and Förster [2]

---

[1] See LANDERERS : das Verhältniss von Gnade und Freiheit (Jahrbücher für die Deutsche Theol., vol. ii. 549.

[2] FOERSTER's Chrysostomus in seinen Verhältniss zur Antiochenischen Schule, Gotha, Parthes, 1869.

in publications replete with erudition and sound Lutheran theology.

The discussions in the Western Church referred more to the ruin and the remedy; and they both indicated the existence of a deeper spiritual life as well as increased it. The discussions in the Western Church attest that there prevailed far more profound views as to the continued operation of the Spirit on the heart. In effecting this result Augustin was, in the course of Providence, specially trained and prepared. He rendered a great service at a critical time to the whole Church. For some time subsequent to his conversion, he was not more advanced than the writers of the Greek Church, and even less matured on the subject of grace than Ambrose. His first treatise on free-will (A.D. 388–395), which has come down to us, was meant to refute the Manichæan doctrine to which he was once attached; and it is certainly very defective. He intended it to counteract the dogma that man only acts under constraint, and from a necessity which renders it impossible for him to keep from vice and sin. He imperfectly explains himself in reference to the operation of divine grace, but by no means in antagonism to grace, as Pelagius did. About the time, however, when he received the episcopate, a decisive change took place in Augustin's opinions (A.D. 396). The Scripture text which was made the means of leading his mind to the decisive change, which he ever afterwards asserted, was: "Who maketh thee to differ? what hast thou that thou didst not receive? Now, if thou didst receive it, why dost thou glory as if thou hadst not received it?" (1 Cor. iv. 7). The conclusion to which he came was, that " in conversion God out of the unwilling makes willing ones, and dwells in those made willing;" and at a later day, when reviewing and correcting the sentiments to which he had given circulation by his pen, so far as they needed correction, we find him saying: "I have erred in having maintained that the grace of God consists only in God's revealing of His will in the declaration of truth; but that *to give assent to the preached gospel is our own work*, and that this lies in our power." And again : "I have erred in asserting *that it lies within our power to believe the gospel and to will*, but that it is the work of God to give those who believe and those who will the power of operating." Now, all was ascribed by him to the grace and Spirit of God, and nothing to man's natural power; and with marked precision the doctrine which he held was brought out in the prayer which called forth in Pelagius' mind the keenest antagonism and the greatest repugnance : "Lord, give what Thou commandest, and command what thou wilt" (da quod jubes et jube quod vis).

Augustin was thus mentally and spiritually prepared when the Pelagian error broke out. He took its measure from the first, and at once directed all the energy of a great mind to counteract every position which was laid down in vindication of the Pelagian dogma, which found only too prepared a soil both in the West and in the East, and which it was now imperatively necessary for the welfare of vital Christianity resolutely to refute and overthrow. The error which Pelagius maintained was that free-will is able by its own natural powers, *without the aid of the Holy Spirit*, to convert itself to God, to believe the gospel, and to be obedient to the law of God with the whole heart, and thus, with its own voluntary obedience, to merit the remission of sins and eternal life.

The great powers of Augustin were called forth by the Pelagian controversy. His real aim was to prove and to assert the inward operations of the Holy Spirit on the heart in conversion and in every religious act ; and the controversy, bespeaking as it does the remarkable illumination of Augustin's mind by the Holy Spirit, was accompanied and followed by results which have pervaded Western Christianity more or less to this day. Of Augustin himself, in whom we see these opinions vitally represented, we may say that subsequently to the reception of those views in which his mind found its resting-place, his whole life was a hymn of praise to the Spirit's saving grace, and a prayer for new communications of the Spirit of Life. In all that bears on man's relation to the Trinity, this remarkable man may be regarded as the meeting-place where the streams of the past united, and were sent forth anew to fertilize the future. Doctrinal truth on Roman soil reached its culminating point in him ; and whatever afterwards attained doctrinal importance, was in some way derived from the works of Augustin.

Pelagius, like all natural men, however cultured, only mistook the things of the Spirit of God. His first principle was free-will. And as to original sin, it was not in his system. He asserted that Adam's fall injured his posterity only by the ill example ; that grace facilitated that which could be done without it ; that nothing has moral significance which does not proceed from an act of free-will ; and that it was absurd to hold that an innate perversity preceded every single act. His conception of the human will was that it was always in a state of perfect equilibrium or indifference between good and evil, and that it returns as with a bound from any sinful action to the same equipoise. He deemed it self-contradictory to speak of *an evil bias or a tendency to sin, which is already sin.* And in affirming, as he did, that the will turns with equal ease to good or evil, *he made sin consist in actions merely, not in the nature.* Such views of sin obscured all due perception of the great truth that the Holy Spirit must communicate a new life and anticipate the acts of the will, and heal it of its disease and of the deep inherent ground of evil which is in it since the fall of man. In a word, there is nothing in Pelagius' utterances that gives the impression that he was a regenerate man drawn by a holy longing or aspiration towards God. The central thought of Scripture, that man was made in the divine image, and the temple of the Spirit, was reduced to a flat external ethical code that prescribes single actions. The discussions began on Pelagius' side with well-meant moral earnestness. But he had no conception of the Holy Spirit's operations on the human heart.

And when we inquire how an earnest moral nature like his, zealous against corruptions and worldly compromise, could be possessed with the pride, self-sufficiency, and elation which he betrays, the explanation is, that he was profoundly ignorant of man's natural condition, and of the indispensable necessity of the Spirit's regenerating grace. He had never comprehended Christ's words : " First make the tree good." He expected the tree to yield good fruit as it was. He had inadequate and *superficial views of sin,* having never penetrated into the true state of the heart.

It must be mentioned, as some explanation,—though it is no palliation,—that the Greek Church from which he had drawn his general culture and all his theological opinions in his earlier career, was very superficial in all that sphere of doctrine and thought. So far as the Church had expressed her views in the Creed, Pelagius had embraced all the ecclesiastical doctrines on the Trinity and the Person of Christ and the Deity of the Holy Spirit. He stood where Basil and Athanasius and the two Gregories had stood. The meaning which he attached to grace was the natural ability for good, the gift of the *posse.* He held *that the will and performance were all the man's own,* as if he had never read Paul's words : " It is God that worketh in you both to will and to do of His good pleasure " (Phil. ii. 13); and that by the right use of human freedom man merited eternal life. Only when refuted by Augustin's arguments did he allow that grace took in or was exercised about the remission of sin. He allowed *no renewing influence on the will,* nothing but an external aid. Hence, in writing to Innocent of Rome, Augustin says : " Let him be sent for to Rome, and asked expressly what he means by the term GRACE; or let him explain his meaning by letter : and if he be found to affirm the ecclesiastical and apostolic

truth, let him be fully absolved, and let us rejoice in him.
For whether he calls grace free-will or remission of sins, or
the precept of the law, he affirms none of those things which
tend to conquer lusts and temptations *by the supply of the
Holy Spirit which He who ascended to heaven has shed on us
abundantly.*" These last words show in what sense Augustin
used the term *grace*, in contrast with the opposite opinion of
Pelagius. Nothing serves more to show the defective views
of grace that prevailed in the Eastern Church, than the fact
that Pelagius was acquitted in A.D. 415 at the two Synods of
Jerusalem and Diospolis. The great Church-teachers of the
East, while admitting man's natural sinfulness and the Spirit's
agency, had continued for generations, as Augustin did in his
early theological development, to assign the ultimate decision
to the power of free-will.[1] They never attempted to explain
the two sides.

Augustin's system had become the direct antithesis of this.
Pelagius laid all stress on man's free-will. Augustin laid all
emphasis on divine grace, which he understood as the efficacious and ever-continued operation of the Holy Spirit shedding
abroad the love of God in the heart. Not that he denied
free - will, for he maintained that IT WAS ALWAYS FREE,
BUT NOT ALWAYS GOOD. His words in the clearest manner
show how free - will was admitted in ordinary things : " We
acknowledge," says he, " that in all men there is a free-will ;
for they all, indeed, have natural innate understanding and
reason ; not that they are able to act in things pertaining to
God so as to love and fear God from the heart,—but only in
external works of this life have they freedom to choose good
or evil. By good I mean that which nature is able to per-

---

[1] Kyriakos, in his interesting Church History, published at Athens in 1881,
speaks of his Church's opinions in contrast with Augustinianism as follows :
ἐν τῇ ἀνατολῇ ἐδιδάσκετο μεσάζουσα τις μεταξὺ Αὐγυστινισμοῦ καὶ πελαγιανισμοῦ
θεωρία ἀναγνωρίζουσα μὲν τὴν ἀπολυτὸν ἀνάγκην τῆς θείας χάριτος πρὸς ἀπολύτρωσιν
παραδεχομένη ὅμως καὶ τὴν διὰ τῆς ἐλευθέρας θελήσεως συμμετοχὴν τοῦ ἀνθρώπου ἐν τῷ
ἔργῳ τῆς σωτηρίας αὐτοῦ (tom. 2, p. 7).

form, as to labour in the field or not, to eat, to drink, to visit a friend or not," etc.

The point which Augustin discussed was ORIGINAL SIN AND FREE-WILL, or the free-will after the fall of man. He proved that in and by the first man the nature of all was radically corrupted (in deterius mutata), and that we were all that one man (ille unus homo omnes fuerunt); that man was left to the freedom of his will, and by an act of abused freedom precipitated the race into the bondage of sin, from which no one can be freed but by the grace of God. He held that by an ill use of freedom man destroyed both himself and his free-will. But Augustin is always careful to draw a distinction between the nature or substance of man which is good and the vitiating taint which has defiled it (*Ench.* vi. chap. 10). With the fall from God, freedom was lost. He did not assert that the will was lost or the power to will, but that the true *liberty of willing good* is lost, and in its place has come the *peccandi necessitas*, or inevitable course of sinning. Hence man can be called out of this state only by the grace of God's Spirit, which consists, according to him, not in the mere instruction of the understanding by truth, nor in the mere remission of sins, but in the renewing operations of the Holy Spirit, and in a new life of love. He describes it as creative, and as transforming the entire man (*Sp. et Lit.* iii.). He distinguishes this from everything proceeding from mere nature, and as the opposite of original sin, which, according to him, consists in evil desire (concupiscentia). Of this evil desire, grace is the antithesis, consisting in holy love to God. One of Augustin's deeply spiritual remarks is, that grace anticipates the will (gratia prævenit voluntatem), and that we do not speak of God *as having given grace*, but in the present tense, as GIVING GRACE—that is, ever giving it. Even the longing for grace is God's work (volentem prævenit ut velit, volentem subsequitur ne frustra velit).

And when we inquire how grace, or the Spirit, stands

related to freedom, we find Augustin's answer expressed in words which have constantly been re-echoed in different forms by Anselm, Bernard, Luther, and Calvin—viz. that free-will is not made void, but is healed by grace (gratia sanat voluntatem, *Sp. et Lit.* xxx.). But he allowed that still there were remains of sin in the Christian. He says, in his refutation of Julian : " The law which is in our members is put away by regeneration, and yet remains in the flesh, which is mortal. It is put away,—for the guilt is entirely remitted by the sacrament through which believers are born again ; and yet it remains,—for it produces evil desires against which the believer strives."

On the great question between the true doctrine of Christianity and the deistical religion of Pelagius, nothing can be more explicit than Augustin's testimony. Thus he says : " Neither doth a man begin to be converted or changed from evil to good by the beginnings of faith, unless the free and undeserved mercy of God work it in him. Let the grace of God, therefore, be so accounted of, that *from the beginnings of his conversion to the end of his perfection*, he that glorieth should glory in the Lord. Because, as *none can begin* a good work without the Lord, so none can perfect it without the Lord." And again : " It is certain that we will when we will, but He causes us to will who works in us to will " (*De Grat. et Lib. Arb.* chap. ii.). To the same effect all the writers speak who imbibed Augustin's sentiments. Thus Maxentius says : " We believe that the natural free-will is able to do no more than to discern and desire carnal or worldly things, which may perhaps seem glorious with men, but not with God ; but those things that belong to eternal life, it can neither think, nor will, nor desire, nor perform, *but only by the infusion and inward working of the Holy Ghost*, who is also the Spirit of Christ." Fulgentius is not less explicit : " We have not received the Spirit of God because we believe, but that we may believe."

Augustin's unanswerable polemic had so fully discredited Pelagianism in the field of argument, that it could no longer be made plausible to the Christian mind.   It collapsed.   But a new system soon presented itself, teaching that *man with his own natural powers is able to take the first step towards his conversion,* and that this obtains or merits the Spirit's assistance.   Cassian, a Scythian by birth, and a scholar of Chrysostom, holding the rank of abbot in a Marseilles monastery, was the founder of this middle way, which came to be called SEMI-PELAGIANISM, because it occupied intermediate ground between Pelagianism and Augustinianism, and took in elements from both.   He acknowledged that Adam's sin extended to his posterity, and that human nature was corrupted by original sin.   But, on the other hand, he held a system of universal grace for all men alike, making the final decision in the case of every individual dependent on the exercise of free-will.   The Massilians, as they were called from Cassian's monastery, opposed and censured Augustin for permitting himself to be carried to the opposite extreme from Pelagius, and declared that he attributed too much to divine grace. Their opinions, as we learn from the letter of Prosper to Augustin, and also from the letter of Hilary, were as follows: they held that the first movement of the will in the assent of faith must be ascribed to the natural powers of the human mind.   This was their primary error.   Their maxim was: " *It is mine to be willing* to believe, and it is the part of God's grace to assist."   They asserted the sufficiency of Christ's grace for all, and that every one according to his own will obeyed or rejected the invitation, while God equally wished and equally aided all men to be saved.   Prosper, in his theological poem, *de ingratis,* a term which he applies to these men, brings this out with much force.   Cassian held that man's moral power for good is only weakened and enfeebled, but not dead, and that he has still such a sense of his disease that he can desire a cure (voluntas medicum quærens).   The entire system thus formed is a half-way house containing elements of error and elements of truth, and not at all differing from the Arminianism which, after the resuscitation of the doctrines of grace by the Reformers, diffused itself in the very same way through the different Churches. Semi-Pelagianism represented conversion as proceeding partly from man's free-will and partly from divine grace. It puts them in juxtaposition, and the adherents of the system were some of them more inclined to the one side, or to Pelagianism, while others inclined more to the Augustinian view. It satisfied neither.

Augustin, who had triumphantly refuted Pelagianism, received intelligence of what was taking place at Marseilles from his faithful Gallic scholars, Prosper and Hilary, and proceeded without loss of time to direct attention to the new phase of error. He was soon, however, to be removed from the scene of conflict to his everlasting rest. But he had the opportunity in his treatises on "Predestination," and on "The Gift of Perseverance," to prove that this half-and-half system was untenable, and in the last degree mischievous. He showed that it must lead men back to Pelagianism, if the orthodox faith was not accepted from the heart. Cassian, with a view to secure a place for the merit of works, had affirmed *that man begins the work of salvation*, and then receives as a reward further grace and aid in the path on which he has entered. It was easy to expose this unscriptural position, which led back the mind to the Pelagian depreciation of divine grace. Augustin appeals to the text which had given rest to his own mind (1 Cor. iv. 7), and also to Paul's statements elsewhere (Rom. xi. 35; 2 Cor. iii. 5). He shows them that their position implied that they *would merit grace* by attributing to man the first commencement. He showed, moreover, the folly of a dogma which ascribed to man the most difficult thing—the commencement of a new spiritual life, and which left to God's Spirit the easier task of merely conferring an aid or assistance afterwards.

The principal error of the Semi-Pelagian system consisted in the fact that *grace was said to be given according to men's merits*—that is, according to the good use or right improvement of the natural power of free-will. But grace was often used by them to intimate nothing more than the law and the prophets. After a century of discussion the inner contradiction of Semi-Pelagianism became apparent, and at the Synod of Orange (A.D. 529) it was repudiated in a series of positions or doctrinal statements, which may be said not only to have given this heresy a decisive check, but to have exhibited the truth with a precision, accuracy, and fulness than which we have scarcely anything more condensed and valuable on this topic in the whole compass of theological literature. Though it was but a provincial Synod, *it came to have all the validity of an Ecumenical Council.* It puts together the results of the whole previous discussions on Pelagianism and Semi - Pelagianism, and has the further advantage of being specially directed to the divine operation in the matter of regeneration. I shall subjoin the first seven CANONS of this memorable Synod, as containing the soundest and most scriptural utterances on this momentous topic :—

" 1. If any man affirm that the whole man in soul and body has not been corrupted by Adam's transgression, but that the body only is subject to corruption, while the freedom of the soul remains unhurt, that man, seduced by Pelagius' error, contradicts the Scripture which says : ' The soul that sinneth, it shall die.'

" 2. If any man affirm that Adam's transgression only injured himself, but not his posterity, or that only corporeal death, the punishment of sin, but not sin itself, which is the death of the soul, passed by one man to the entire human family, he ascribes injustice to God, contradicting the apostle (Rom. v. 12).

" 3. If any man say that the grace of God is given at man's petition, but not that grace produces the supplication, he contradicts the prophet Isaiah, who says, and the apostle who says the same: 'I am sought of them who asked not after me: I am found of them who sought me not' (Isa. lxv. 1).

" 4. If any man affirm that God waits for our will that we may be purged from sin, and does not confess *that it is due to the infusion and operation of the Holy Ghost* upon us that we desire to be cleansed, he resists the Holy Ghost Himself, who says that the will is prepared by God ; and the apostle's testimony, that it is God who worketh in us both to will and to do of His good pleasure.

" 5. If any one say that the beginning or increase of faith, and the very movement of mind toward faith by which we believe in Him that justifies the ungodly, and come to the regeneration of baptism, is in us not by the gift of grace,—that is, *by the inspiration of the Holy Ghost*, correcting our will from unbelief to faith, from ungodliness to piety,—but by nature, he is proved an enemy to the doctrine of the apostles, as Paul says : 'He that hath begun a good work in you will perform it to the day of Jesus Christ ; ' and again : ' To you it is given in Christ not only to believe, but also to suffer for His sake' (Phil. i. 6, 29). They who affirm that the faith by which we believe in God is natural, describe all who are estranged from the Church as in a manner believers.

" 6. If any man affirm that mercy is imparted to us when, without the grace of God, we believe, will, desire, endeavour, watch and labour, pray, seek and knock, and does not confess *that it is of the inspiration and infusion of the Spirit of God* that we can believe, will, or do any of all these things as we ought,—who merely affirms that the aid of grace is added to the humility and obedience of man, and does not confess that our obedience and humility is a gift of his grace,—he contradicts the apostle, who says : ' What hast thou that thou hast not received ? ' and : ' By the grace of God I am what I am.'

" 7. If any man affirm that he can by the strength of

nature think anything good pertaining to the salvation of eternal life, as he ought, or choose or consent to the saving or evangelical preaching, *without the illumination and inspiration of the Holy Spirit,* who gives to all the sweet relish in consenting to and believing the truth, he is deceived by a heretical spirit, not understanding the word of God in the gospel : 'Without me ye can do nothing;' and that saying of the apostle : 'Not that we are sufficient of ourselves to think anything as of ourselves' (2 Cor. iii. 5)."

A historical succession of testimonies to the same effect might be supplied from Maxentius, Fulgentius, Albinus, Gregory the Great, and others, which would be found to be equally clear and interesting. But as the object of this sketch is only to notice the salient points of history, I shall refrain from entering into these details, and content myself with quoting a few words of the treatise " on the calling of the Gentiles," of which Leo has been supposed by many to be the author, though the writer in reality is unknown. After saying that it would be ruinous to be deprived of the Holy Spirit, the writer adds : " He [the Spirit] indeed, in the essence of the Deity, is everywhere and all-comprehensive, but is conceived in a certain manner to recede from those whom He ceases to govern. And *the cessation of His aid is to be regarded as His absence,* which that man madly thinks useful to himself who rejoices in his good actions, and thinks that he rather than God hath wrought them. The grace of God must therefore be owned in the fullest and most unqualified sense, the first office of which is that His help be felt : 'We have not received,' says the apostle, 'the spirit of the world, but the Spirit of God, that we might know the things that are freely given to us of God.' Whence, if any man think that he has any good things of which God is not the author but himself, *he has not the Spirit of God, but of the world,* and swells with that secular wisdom of which it is written : 'I will destroy the wisdom of the wise.'"

A long intervening period followed, during which ecclesiastical opinion, with many fluctuations of a downward
tendency, was still publicly controlled by the Canons of the
Synod of Orange.   That much was done in defence of the
doctrines of grace by the writers whom I have already
mentioned as opposed to Semi - Pelagianism, and tending
effectually to counteract the efforts of Cassian, Faustus,
Vincentius Lerinensis, and the like, and to discredit the
Semi-Pelagian views, cannot be questioned.   But it is too
evident that pure Augustinianism was by no means accepted
in every quarter.   We see this in the fate of Godeschalc,
and in other incidents of a like nature.

When we come down the stream of History, we are surprised to find how early the current of doctrine on the subject
of grace is found running in a wrong direction.   It is not to
the personal Holy Spirit, awakening faith and working on the
human mind, that allusion was made, but to the sacraments
as CONTAINING GRACE, and as conveying grace to the receiver,
whether faith was exercised by him or not.   The Greek
Church has only the sacraments as the means of grace ; and
the word of God, preached and received by faith, drops
out of sight.   The sacraments enlarged beyond the scriptural
number, and regarded as conveying grace, do all *ex opere
operato*.

The Church of Rome in the very same way attached all importance to the mere outward administration of the sacraments.
The Council of Trent and the clergy of the Church of Rome,
generally absorbed in the eager desire to magnify sacramental
grace as the food of the soul (cibus animæ), have fallen into
the same error, and differ from the Greek Church only in one
point, viz. that it has something to say in commendation of
PREACHING THE WORD OF GOD as an element of furthering the
religious life, but nothing to say in favour of READING THE
DIVINE WORD.   In reality both Churches, in a legal ritualistic
way, identify the mere use of sacraments with the communica-

tion of grace ; and they have nothing but an outward service (opus operatum).

We come next to Bernard, who strenuously asserted Augustin's views, and who in virtue of doing so became one of the most powerful characters that shed an ennobling influence on the mediæval Church. Bernard's treatise ON GRACE AND FREE-WILL is singularly fresh and accurate, and his age, as Neander has well pointed out, was a new spring-time of spiritual life after a long winter. At the beginning of the twelfth century a new creative epoch entered, and a new outpouring of the Holy Ghost appeared when religion, though still mingled with foreign elements, decidedly revived among the nations. Bernard was the representative of that mystic or pectoral theology which runs through the mediæval period wherever it shows spiritual elements. The stream of religious thought may be said to have divided in two from his time, the one more scholastic, the other more mystic. The definitions and distinctions supplied by Bernard are often of the happiest. Thus he says : " Simply to will comes from man's nature ; to will wickedly comes from corrupt nature ; to will well, from supernatural grace." Another passage from his treatise on grace and free-will is as follows : " You say, *What, then, is it that free-will does ? I answer briefly, It is made whole* (salvatur). Take away free-will, and there will be nothing to be healed. Take away grace, and there will be no healing influence (non erit unde salvetur). This work cannot be effected without the two—the one the cause by which it is accomplished, the other the subject on which, or in which, it is accomplished. God is the author of salvation : free-will is only capable of receiving it (tantum capax)."

The transition stage between Bernard and the epoch of the Reformation was the period of mediæval mysticism. This mystic theology, influenced as it was by vivid views of the Holy Spirit, may be said to have moved on a twofold hinge— on the sense of sin, blindness, inability, and defilement on the one hand ; and on the great deliverance from all parts of moral and spiritual ruin, which is hourly to be found from Christ's Spirit, on the other. Introverting its regards, this school of theology occupied itself with the personal Redeemer, and with the restoration of light, life, and holiness by the Holy Spirit. The centre round which this whole theology moved was fellowship of life with the Redeemer through the Holy Ghost ; and it was destined to scatter the seed, and prepare the way for the clearer views of the Reformation epoch. It may be said that the mystic element, though insufficient of itself to give rise to a general reformation, stands connected with almost every true revival or great religious movement that has ever taken place. In some cases, it goes before as an indispensable preliminary. In others, it comes in as a tribu- tary stream, or as a necessary complement when a movement threatens to decay. The labours of the older mystics— Eckart, Tauler, à Kempis, Wessel, and the author of the *Theologia Germanica*—stood in a definite relation to the full development of Christian doctrine at the Reformation. The felt distance from God, the deep solitude of their hearts, their desires for the present enjoyment of God as their proper element—these and similar feelings awakened by the Holy Spirit were uttered by these writers in mystic language, and from a mystic point of view ; but they served to some con- siderable extent to rescue a large class from the terrible infliction of ecclesiastical form and a mere dead orthodoxy. But the mystic element which limits its regards to CHRIST IN US, and which fails to give prominence to Christ's merits FOR US, never of itself produced a widespread renovation of spiritual life. It was ignorant of the liberty derived from imputed righteousness—that is, was ignorant of the true ground and indispensable condition of the communication of the Spirit, and of all filial communion with God. And it bears, when it stands alone, the elements of decay and dete- rioration in itself. But the great witnesses of free grace and

of Christ's merits and atonement, whether we think of one
period or another,—such as Luther, Whitefield, Venn, and
others,—were all moulded in their first stage by these views.

THE PERIOD OF THE REFORMATION.

The period of the REFORMATION, to which we now come,
gave a testimony to the Holy Spirit more full and explicit
than had ever been uttered since the apostolic age.[1]
Considered in its origin, the Reformation was itself a
great work of the Spirit of God, and the men who bore a
leading part in it were fully conscious of this fact. The
Semi-Pelagianism and the Pelagianism in its worst form,
which had insinuated itself into the theology of mediæval
times, were denounced in the most unsparing terms. The
Augustinian views were proclaimed with full emphasis and
with resuscitated vigour. But these doctrines, from the altered
circumstances, received a new application and a new direction
in several respects. The term GRACE, for instance, which in
Augustin's acceptation intimated the inward exercise of love
awakened by the operations of the Holy Spirit (Rom. v. 5),
and which in the scholastic theology had come to denote a
quality of the soul, or the inward endowments, and infused
habits of faith, love, and hope, was now taken in the more
scriptural and wider sense for the free, the efficacious FAVOUR
which is in the divine mind. Luther extended the meaning
according to the terms of Scripture ; and Melanchthon expressed a regret that theologians had not rather used the term
FAVOUR. The Reformers having to use the term grace or
free favour in connection with justification through Christ's
righteousness, began largely to use the phrase : " the work of
the Holy Spirit," instead of the term " grace."

---

[1] See Luthardt, die Lehre vom Freien Willen, Leipz. 1863 ; Dieckhoff's
Luther's Lehre von der Gnade Theol. Zeitsch. 1860 ; Frank, die Theologie der
F. Concordiæ ; Köstlin's Luther's Theologie, 1863.

The Reformers connected faith as the receptive organ or hand by which men receive the imputed righteousness which justifies us in the closest possible way with the operation of the Holy Spirit as its author or producing cause. While they asserted the first point, that justification before God proceeds only from faith, they asserted not less strongly the second point, *that faith in the heart proceeds only from God's Spirit.* And on all occasions they declared that if there be allowed in man any natural power or natural capacity for believing without the operation of the Holy Spirit, this inevitably overthrows at the second stage the very doctrine of grace which had been laid as the foundation of all. To show this, we need only advert to the way in which Luther expressed himself a very few years after the Reformation began. The Reformer had frequently declared that " in divine and spiritual things we have no free - will, but only in name." He said : " That any one should be represented as just and fearing God *who has not the Spirit*, would be the same as if Belial were called Christ." And when Erasmus was prevailed on to attempt a refutation of Luther, he assailed him on a point which some accounted not a central one—the doctrine of free-will, or the natural power of man. That was not Luther's opinion. " I must own," said Luther, " that you alone in this contest have seized your antagonist by the throat. I thank you for this with all my heart; for I am better pleased to engage on that subject than on all those secondary questions of the Pope, purgatory, and indulgences, with which the enemies of the gospel have teased me till now." Luther's treatise in reply to Erasmus, bearing the title *de servo arbitrio*, undoubtedly one of the most powerful treatises ever written on the subject of which it treats, overthrows the open Pelagianism of Erasmus, who knew little of theology, and the Semi-Pelagianism of men less extreme in their opinions than Erasmus ; and it proves to demonstration that the representation of free-will which he impugns, overthrows Christ's work FOR US and the Spirit's

work IN US. Almost the only thing that one regrets about
this noble production is not its vehemence, which was the
natural utterance of the writer,——nor the strong statements
about man being under the power of Satan,——nor the representation of the will as resembling the motionless inaction
or immobility of a stock or stone, for these, though lamented
by some, will not appear extravagant exaggerations to one
enlightened as Luther was, —— but the title of the book.
Had the title been *de libero arbitrio et servo*, indicating the
natural indefeasible freedom of the human being, and yet
the ground of *evil in the will itself*, both sides of the
momentous question would have been suitably recognised.
For there are times when the Church is compelled—as,
for instance, in antagonism to the stoical philosophy, to the
Gnostic, Manichæan, Pantheistic, and Determinist theories—
to lay emphasis on the freedom of the will, as well as on its
bondage.   These are the two sides, neither of which can be
unduly pressed without the other as its necessary complement.   Hence in Augustin's time the twofold question
bringing the two sides of truth to light, and running in
direct antagonism to two prevailing errors, was always put as
follows : " Without free-will, how shall God judge the world ?
Without grace, how shall God save the world ? "   These are
the two sides of truth, neither of which can ever be long
left in abeyance ; and the Church, through the whole tenor
of her history, has ever been compelled to exhibit both,
sometimes in the same age enforcing the one against
Fatalism, and the other against an arrogant Semi-Pelagianism.
It was against the latter that the Reformers had more
especially to testify.

After the allusion to Luther's treatise " on the bondage of
the will," it is not necessary to put together at any length a
collection of Luther's sayings on this topic.   A few sentences
will suffice as a specimen.   Thus he says : " We have *need of
the Spirit of Christ*, without whom all our works are only

worthy of condemnation " (damnabilia). And again : " I
reject and condemn as erroneous every doctrine which extols
our free-will, and fights against the assistance and grace of
our Saviour Jesus Christ ; because without Christ death and
sin rule over us, and the devil is the god and prince of the
unconverted world." The noble words of the Reformer
toward the close of his treatise *de servo arbitrio* are as
follows : " I confess for myself, that even if it were possible
I would not have free-will committed to me, or anything whatever left in my hand whereby I might endeavour after salvation ; not merely because I could not, amid so many adversaries and dangers, and, moreover, opposing devils, withstand
and retain it—since one devil is more powerful than all men,
and no one would be saved ; but because, even though there
were no hazards, no adversaries, no devils, I should be constrained perpetually to labour in uncertainty, and to beat the
air." Calvin is in full harmony with Luther, and constantly
appeals to Augustin's views ; and it is not necessary to do more
than refer to his *Institutes*.

We shall now refer succinctly to the doctrinal views of
the Protestant Churches, Lutheran and Reformed. Never
since the days of the apostles had anything been defined or
preached in reference to the operations of the Holy Spirit
more full, accurate, and ample than was set forth in all the
Protestant Churches under the blaze of light which shone all
around. The Lutheran theologian Hunnius thus expressed
himself : " It is most firmly believed in our Churches that in
divine and spiritual things we have no free-will, but only in
name ; " and adds, " Not a particle of what Erasmus contends
for now remains to man, and where any such ability for what
is good is to be met with, *it is to be ascribed entirely to the
Holy Spirit* " (*de Lib. Arb.*).

Without going into the vast mass of theological writing
which was produced at the period of the Reformation on the
Spirit's operations, it will be easier, as well as more com-

pendious, to refer to the SYMBOLIC BOOKS OR CONFESSIONS, and
to the CATECHISMS which the various Churches have given
forth as public documents, and which were designed to
express the Church's faith, and to serve as the rule of
teaching for the young.   It appears that on the gracious
operations of the Spirit, Zwingli, Calvin, Beza, Zanchius,
Martyr, Olivian, Ursinus, and others that might be named,
were in perfect harmony with the great writers of the
Lutheran Church.   In a word, the sun of grace shone in
the heavens, and the operations of the Spirit of grace in
that bright period of the Church's purity and zeal were
recognised with one consent on every side.   As we must
study brevity, let it suffice to say that the harmony of the
Protestant Confessions exhibits the Church - consciousness
more fully than can be found in the individual authorship of
the Churches.   Not only so ; confessional documents embodying the convictions of collective bodies have a significance
that cannot attach to individual writers, however eminent.
A few extracts here will suffice.

THE AUGSBURG CONFESSION, the Lutheran symbol, says
(Article xviii.) : " Concerning free-will it is taught that to
some extent man has freedom of will to lead a just and
honourable life, to choose between things which reason comprehends ; but without grace, assistance, and the operation of
the Holy Spirit, he is unable to become pleasing to God, or
to fear God in heart, or to believe in Him, or to cast out
of his heart the innate evil propensity ; but *these things are
effected through the Holy Spirit*, which is given through the
word of God."

THE CONCORDIÆ FORMULA, another Lutheran symbol, says
on free-will in the epitome : " It is rightly said, however, on
the contrary, that *in conversion, God, through the drawing of
the Holy Spirit, makes willing men out of the obstinate and
unwilling ;* and that *after such conversion the regenerated will* of
man does not remain inactive in the daily exercise of repent-

ance, but *co-operates in all the works of the Holy Spirit which He performs through us.*

"Also that Doctor Luther has written that the will of man in his conversion remains purely passive—that is, that it does nothing at all, is to be understood *respectu divinæ gratiæ in accendendis novis motibus*—that is, when THE SPIRIT OF GOD through the heard word, or through the use of the holy sacraments, *lays hold on the will of man* and effects the new birth and conversion. For, when *the Holy Spirit* has effected and accomplished this, *and through His divine power and operation alone* has changed and renewed the will of man, then the new will of man is an instrument and organ of God the Holy Spirit, so that it not only accepts the grace, but also co-operates in subsequent works of the Holy Spirit.

"Consequently, that before the conversion of man there are but two efficient causes found, namely, THE HOLY SPIRIT, and the WORD OF GOD as the instrument of the Holy Spirit, through which He effects conversion, and which man is to hear; he cannot, however, give credence to it and accept it through his own powers, but exclusively through the grace and operation of God the Holy Spirit."

We pass to the REFORMED CHURCH, and shall begin with THE HELVETIC CONFESSION, the most widely accepted of the Reformed Confessions. This Confession distinguishes very happily, as the CONCORDIÆ FORMULA also does, and as the WESTMINSTER CONFESSION did afterwards, between man FREE and upright before the fall, and man fallen, with *no free-will to do good after the fall*. It is then added: "In regeneration the understanding is *enlightened by the Holy Spirit* to understand both the mysteries and the will of God, and *the will itself is not only changed by the Spirit*, but also furnished with powers both to will and to do good spontaneously (Rom. viii. 5, 6)."

The TENTH ARTICLE of the CHURCH OF ENGLAND, after the admirable statement on original sin in the ninth Article, is to

the following effect : " The condition of man after the fall of
Adam is such that HE CANNOT TURN and prepare himself by
his own strength and good works to faith and calling upon
God : wherefore WE HAVE NO POWER to do good works pleasant
and acceptable to God, WITHOUT THE GRACE OF GOD BY CHRIST
PREVENTING US, that we may have a good will, AND WORKING
WITH US, when we have that good will."

In THE SCOTTISH CONFESSION (Article xii.) we read : " We
are so dead, so blind, so perverse, that neither can we feel
when we are pricked, see the light when it shines, nor assent
to the will of God when it is revealed, *except the Spirit of the
Lord Jesus quicken that which is dead*, remove the darkness
from our minds, and bow our stubborn wills to the obedience
of the blessed gospel."

In THE FRENCH CONFESSION the words are : " We believe
that *by the secret grace of the Holy Spirit* we are made partakers of the light of faith, which is the gracious gift of God,
and peculiar to those alone to whom God sees meet to impart
it."

In THE CONFESSION OF BASEL we read : " Our nature is
so vitiated, and has such a propensity to sin, that *unless it is
renewed by the Holy Spirit*, no man can do or will what is
good of himself."

In all the Catechisms of the Protestant Church, in Calvin's
Catechism, in the Heidelberg Catechism, as well as Luther's,
the testimony to the doctrine of the Spirit is definite and
ample.

We come next to a period of declension. After the
ecclesiastical confession to the doctrine of the Spirit in the
clear emphatic manner already mentioned, there followed a
period of decline and conflict, and this may be traced in all
similar epochs in history. Two phases of opinion, having
much in common with each other, broke out shortly after the
Reformation—THE SYNERGISTIC ERROR in the Lutheran Church,
and ARMINIANISM in the Reformed Church. They ran counter

to the true doctrine of the Spirit and the homage which is due to the Holy Spirit. They insinuated themselves into both Churches by conceding to the free-will or natural power of man more than the Reformers had acknowledged. They were opinions which led to disastrous consequences in both the Churches, and broke the force of the Reformation.

The synergism which broke out through the influence of Melanchthon in the Lutheran Church had everything in common with the synergistic views of the Greek Church as represented by all her great writers—Basil, the Gregories, Chrysostom, and others. Arminianism, again, in the Reformed Church, was simply a revival of Semi-Pelagianism.

To begin with SYNERGISM. The rise of this controversy, which came to be agitated shortly after Luther's death, was due to the fact that Melanchthon changed his opinion on the subject of free-will and the natural power of man. He had held, with Luther, man's natural inability, and in the first edition of his Common-places went farther in the way of denying all liberty than can be vindicated. He began to waver and vacillate after Erasmus published his polemical treatises against Luther, and by an enlarged study of the Greek Fathers, to whom he was already approximating on the subject of free-will. The change discovered itself in germ in the second edition of his *Loci Communes* (A.D. 1535), when he began to speak of three causes in conversion—the word of God, the Holy Spirit, and the human will (non sane otiosa). He next spoke of the human will *assenting* to the word of God. Then, two years after Luther's death, he describes free-will as the faculty in man of applying himself to divine grace (1548)—that is, the ability of applying himself to divine grace in some way. He began to view the human will not so much as the thing to be changed, but as a factor or concurring cause in conversion, though he only once uses the term "co-operation."

When this lamentable controversy began in 1555, the

followers of Melanchthon took up the position that man is
not merely passive in conversion, but a co-operating cause.
Strigel of Jena threw himself with all his energy into the
controversy, and openly declared himself in a synergistic sense.
Not to mention others, Flacius, the admirer of Luther, and
one of the richest as well as most erudite minds that adorned
that age, became a vehement assailant of the synergistic
opinions. The controversy, as is often the case, seemed sometimes to turn on a razor's edge, and yet truth was on one side
and error on the other. Strigel, though he continued to declare that a man could not convert himself without the Holy
Spirit, advanced, without doubt, to Semi-Pelagian views when
he maintained the human self-determination in the matter of
conversion. Flacius, again, starts with the assertion of man's
total incapacity for good, and that the divine operation of the
Holy Spirit alone gives rise to true conversion. But he
committed himself to positions on original sin which were so
extreme that they outraged the theological mind both of the
Lutheran and Reformed Church. He went so far as to affirm
that *sin had become the very substance of man*—an extravagance
which repelled every mind, and involved the fearful consequence that on such a theory man could not be a subject of
redemption.

The two parties in this controversy largely destroyed each
other's arguments, and needed the intervention of a third
party to mediate between them and readjust the balance of
truth. And this was the very issue that the course of events
brought about. Strigel contended that the Spirit's action
corresponds to the peculiar nature of the will, but not so as
to destroy the will. He held that the Spirit's action on man
as a free agent was different from the way in which power is
exercised on mere inanimate and unconscious objects, as a
stock or stone, and that co-action could not be applied to
the will (voluntas non potest cogi). No one will hesitate to
say that so far he was right. But the questionable part of

his argument begins to appear when he insists on a natural aptitude or power in the will of man for good. He would not allow that the natural man was but passive in the act of conversion. He held that man is not so much dead as sick; and he contended that the power for good is not so much lost as enfeebled, bound, or fettered by sin, so that it can do nothing without the Holy Ghost; but that when freed IT CO-OPERATES TO CONVERSION, though in a languid way. He held that the human will cannot without the Spirit begin its conversion, but that it is not a resisting or merely passive element. The affinity of this view, or rather its perfect identity with Semi-Pelagianism, cannot be doubtful. He seems to have known nothing in his own experience of a sudden conversion by divine grace; and he speaks as if it could not be without the concurrence of a divine and human cause.

Flacius, on his side of the argument, demands whence arises the will to good, the very inclination to conversion, and the prayer for it? Does this come from God alone, or partly from the synergism of man? He adds, " I demand whether you say that the will co-operates before the gift of faith or after the reception of faith?"

The Formula Concordiæ, prepared by Brentius, Andreä, and others, came in to put this matter on its right ground, and to correct extremes, when the Lutheran Church was involved in the most critical danger. It repudiated, on the one side, the error that from the human will could come the first beginnings of conversion or anything truly good till grace first apprehends it and replenishes it with new powers; and on the other side the revolting dogma of Flacius, that original sin had become the essence of man. Its admirably-balanced statements bring out that *conversion has its efficient cause only in the operation of the Holy Ghost, and that man neither effects it nor co-operates in it.* It is stated that the Holy Spirit acts on the will of man, the subject of the change,—that the operation is ON the will and IN the will by means of the word. It repudiates the active synergism of Strigel and the continuous resistance of Flacius, who contended that before and after conversion the human will does nothing but resist. It sets forth that after conversion, but only after conversion, the mind with new powers begins actively to co-operate.

THE UNITARIAN MOVEMENT, begun by Socinus and carried on by the Polish Brethren (*Fratres Poloni*), developed a bold attack on the Holy Spirit, both in regard to His personality and His work. As, however, it was only another phase of Naturalism or Deism, as well as directly anti-Trinitarian, it could not secure a footing within the Church, and was at once expelled.

But the ARMINIAN MOVEMENT, identical in all respects with Semi-Pelagianism, insinuated itself into the Reformed Churches, and became a very formidable power, which spread in all directions, and can scarcely even yet be said to have spent its force. The founder of it was Arminius, born in 1560, a man of distinguished gifts, who, by the aid of bene-volent friends, had been helped forward in his studies till he was sent to prosecute his theological curriculum under Beza in 1582. Everything in his history subsequent to this—his visit to Italy, his acquaintance with Bellarmine, the suspicions awakened by his utterances after being promoted to the pas-torate in Amsterdam (A.D. 1588), and the doubts entertained as to his opinions when called to be Junius' successor in the chair of Theology at Leyden, though he declared that he held with Augustin, and repudiated the Pelagian tenets—creates a doubt whether the doctrines of grace were ever fully accepted by him. About a year after entering upon his theological duties at Leyden, opinions were propounded by him at variance with the doctrine of the Reformed Church (1604). Then began the controversy which convulsed the Dutch Church.

Without entering into all Arminius' opinions, let me briefly notice those which referred to the Holy Spirit. He maintained that the Spirit's operation was in every case resistible, and *that there was no invincible efficacy put forth on any* to whom the gospel is preached. The assent of the will was said to decide the matter. It was held that every one could obey or resist; that the cause of conversion was not the Holy Spirit so much as the human will concurring or co-operating; and that this was the immediate cause of conversion. Let me briefly notice the points which came up in these discussions.

As to the subjects of conversion, it was a question whether the Holy Spirit exercised the same gracious operation on every hearer to whom the gospel is first proclaimed. This was affirmed by the Arminians. Not only so: they condemned it as an unwarrantable *limitation of the grace of God to hold that the Holy Spirit effectually works faith in any* by removing the resistance of the mind, and by imparting the power to believe. In a word, while nominally allowing the action of the Spirit, it came to this: that it was an inefficacious and resistible influence, little more—if, indeed, it was anything more— than external moral suasion.

They placed themselves on the same footing with the Semi-Pelagians as to everything bearing on the universality of the Spirit's grace, as to the equality which must be allowed to all men, and as to the sufficiency of grace for all alike. They took the decision of the matter *out of God's free-will*, which they challenged, and *put it into man's free-will*, which they maintained. The question was formally raised: Were all converted that the Spirit intended to convert by the gospel? and at the Hague Conference, the Arminians, without scruple or reserve, laid down the position that the Holy Spirit, when He operates on man with the intention of converting him, can be resisted (*Coll. Hag.* p. 227). Sufficient grace was strongly asserted; by which phrase they intimated that assistance was given only in such a way and measure that at his own discretion a man could take the decisive step, and that the will can help itself to the act of faith. But *they denied that the Spirit conferred the gift of faith.* That the Holy Spirit imparts the renewing of the will, or introduces a new quality into the will, rendering it certain that faith shall ensue, they denied. They allowed *only assistance*, but denied that the will is inclined by the Spirit of God. They insisted that the Holy Spirit never operates on the will of men except in such a way as could be resisted. And they openly denied that *faith* could be called *the gift of God*, as wrought by the Spirit of God.

These Arminian tenets run counter to all the invincible energy which makes faith the gift of the Spirit of God. They throw man back on himself, and make all dependent on the human will in the application of redemption, forgetting that man has AS LITTLE POWER AS MERIT. On the contrary, the Confessions all testified according to Scripture that the will —in other words, that the carnal mind—is enmity against God, and that the Spirit's operations are effectual. These are not so languid as to stop short of taking away the stony heart.

After many years' discussion on these points, in which the true life of the Church consists, the Synod of Dort was assembled [13th Nov. 1618 to 9th May 1619] to give an ecclesiastical decision on them. Representatives were invited from all the Reformed Churches, and these deputies eagerly came to that great Council, except where the Governments, from jealousy, refused permission to the deputies to attend, which was the case with France. All the topics were discussed with fairness, erudition, and zeal for truth. This great Synod, equal in importance to any of the Ecumenical Councils, is the glory of the Reformed Church. Since the first FOUR GENERAL COUNCILS, none have ever assembled with a more momentous charge or commission. It gave forth in its decrees a full and all-sided outline of the doctrines of special grace ; and nobly was its work discharged. The decrees of the Synod were not only made the fundamental articles of the Dutch Church, but continue, as part of the literature of these questions, to have a significance for all time. And it may be questioned whether anything more valuable as an ecclesiastical testimony for the doctrines of sovereign, special, efficacious grace was ever prepared on this important theme since the days of the apostles. Its great point was to show that THE SPIRIT PRODUCES ALL, AND MAN ACTS ALL.

Nowhere has the renewing work of the Holy Spirit been more correctly and fully exhibited than in the Canons of THE SYNOD OF DORT, from which I shall quote only the following articles in the division containing the third and fourth Heads of Doctrine:—

"Article VIII.—As many as are called by the gospel are unfeignedly (*serio*) called: for God hath most earnestly and truly declared in His word what will be acceptable to Him— namely, that all who are called should comply with the invitation. He, moreover, seriously promises eternal life and rest to as many as shall come to Him, and believe on Him.

"Article IX.—It is not the fault of the gospel, nor of Christ offered therein, nor of God, who calls men by the gospel, and confers upon them various gifts, that those who are called by the ministry of the word refuse to come and be converted. The fault lies in themselves: some of whom when called, regardless of their danger (*securi*), reject the word of life; others, though they receive it (*admittunt*), suffer it not to make a lasting impression on their heart (*immittunt*), therefore their joy, arising only from a temporary faith, soon vanishes, and they fall away; while others choke the seed of the word by perplexing cares and the pleasures of this world, and produce no fruit. This our Saviour teaches in the parable of the sower, Matt. xiii.

"Article X.—But that others who are called by the gospel

obey the call and are converted, is not to be ascribed to the proper exercise of free-will, whereby one distinguishes himself above others equally furnished with grace sufficient for faith and conversion, as the proud heresy of Pelagius maintains; but it must be wholly to God, who, as He hath chosen His own from eternity in Christ, so He confers upon them faith and repentance, rescues them from the power of darkness, and translates them into the kingdom of His own Son, that they may show forth the praises of Him who hath called them out of darkness into His marvellous light; and may glory, not in themselves, but in the Lord, according to the testimony of the apostles in various places.

"Article XI.——But when God accomplishes His good pleasure, or works in them true conversion, He not only causes the gospel to be externally preached to them, and powerfully illuminates their minds by His Holy Spirit that they may rightly understand and discern the things of the Spirit of God; but by the efficacy of the same regenerating Spirit He pervades the inmost recesses of the man; He opens the closed and softens the hardened heart, and circumcises that which was uncircumcised; infuses new qualities into the will which, though heretofore dead, He quickens; from being evil, disobedient, and refractory, He renders it good, obedient, and pliable; actuates and strengthens it, that, like a good tree, it may bring forth the fruits of good actions.

"Article XII.——And this is the regeneration so highly celebrated in Scripture and denominated a new creation, a resurrection from the dead, a making alive, which God works in us without our aid. But this is nowise effected merely by the external preaching of the gospel, by moral suasion, or such a mode of operation that after God has performed His part, it still remains in the power of man to be regenerated or not, to be converted or to continue unconverted; but it is evidently A SUPERNATURAL WORK, most powerful and at the same time most delightful, astonishing, mysterious, and ineffable; not inferior in efficacy to creation or the resurrection from the dead, as the Scripture, inspired by the author of this work, declares; so that all in whose hearts God works in this marvellous manner are certainly, infallibly, and effectually regenerated, and do actually believe. Whereupon the will thus renewed is not only actuated and influenced by God, but in consequence of this influence becomes itself active. Wherefore, also, man is himself rightly said to believe and repent, by virtue of that grace received.

"Article XIII.—THE MANNER OF THIS OPERATION cannot be fully comprehended by believers in this life. Notwithstanding which, they rest satisfied with knowing and experiencing that by this grace of God they are enabled to believe with the heart, and to love their Saviour.

"Article XIV.—Faith is therefore to be considered as the gift of God, not on account of its being offered by God to man, to be accepted or rejected at his pleasure, but because it is in reality conferred, breathed, and infused into him; not even because God bestows the power or ability to believe, and then expects that man should by the exercise of His own free-will consent to the terms of salvation, and actually believe in Christ; but because He who works in man both to will and to do, and indeed all things in all, PRODUCES BOTH THE WILL TO BELIEVE AND THE ACT OF BELIEVING also (*et velle credere et ipsum credere*)."

Before leaving these theories, let me briefly advert to Amyraldism, sometimes called hypothetic Universalism, which was in the last degree disastrous to French Protestantism before the revocation of the Edict of Nantes. I refer to it more especially because the phraseology which it introduced is still current in America, and is found in this country in quarters where we are surprised to find it. By those who were competent to take the measure of Amyraldism,—such as Rivetus, Maresius, and Spanheim,—it was regarded as a subtle form of Arminianism, though its author and his followers declared their harmony with the Articles of the Synod of Dort. After a long discussion of this middle way by one Synod after another, in 1637 and 1645, Amyraldus, by his protestations to the effect that he assented and consented to the Articles of Dort, succeeded in disarming further opposition, and in obtaining an acquittal from the charge of heterodoxy in 1649. But it was the death - blow of French Protestantism. The majority of the theologians and pastors soon adopted his opinions. The French Protestant Church virtually ceased to be a witness for the doctrines of grace. A scholar of Amyraldus, Pajon, went farther than his master in minimizing the extent of natural corruption and the power of the Spirit in conversion. For the gracious operations of the Spirit, he, in fact, substituted *the moral influence of the word*, or moral suasion. After this, it was rather the Jansenists—a small body separated from the Church of Rome and firmly attached [1] to all the essential points of Augustinianism—than the Protestants in France that gave any decided testimony to the doctrines of special grace.

A few years later a terrible storm of persecution broke out and scattered the French Protestants over the globe. It is not for us to call this a divine retribution, or a visitation in wrath. But few will deny that a deep declension had begun, or hesitate to affirm that the salt was beginning to lose its savour. Of those refugees who were scattered in all directions, no fewer than TWO HUNDRED PASTORS repaired to Holland, and were received with deep sympathy, and yet with due caution. They were not to be received as pastors into the Walloon Church, unless they subscribed an article binding them to accept the Articles of Dort, and never to refer in public or in private to those Amyraldist and Pajonist

---

[1] See their admirable CATECHISMUS GRATIÆ, 1650, reprinted and annotated by Maresius as synopsis veræ Catholicæque doctrinæ DE GRATIA. Groningæ 1654.

doctrines which Spanheim, Jurieu, Saurin, and others regarded as an Arminian leaven which had destroyed the French Protestant Church. These pastors consented to subscribe that article, and the Church was thus freed from the evil leaven by which it was menaced.

As to the distinction which Amyraldus drew between NATURAL AND MORAL ABILITY, still repeated both here and in America, and to which men so distinguished as Edwards, Bellamy, and Fuller gave a too ready ear, let me quote the following pointed and valuable remarks of Leidekker. " The learned Amyraldus," says Leidekker, " did no service to the cause of the Reformation by his distinction between A PHYSICAL AND MORAL POWER OF BELIEVING IN CHRIST. He supposed the sinner to have the former, but not the latter. He held that Christ died for all men according to a decree of God, by which salvation was secured to sinners on condition of faith ; which general decree, according to him, was to be considered as going before the particular decree about giving faith to the elect. When it was mentioned to him that his notion of the general decree now mentioned was absurd, as it suspended the end of Christ's death on an impossible condition, he denied that the condition was impossible. ' *For*,' said he, ' *though I do not, with the Arminians, deny the impotence of fallen man, or his inability to believe (I allow him to be morally impotent), yet I hold that man has still a physical or natural power of believing, as he possesses the natural faculties of the understanding and the will.*'

" Herein Amyraldus has given a sad example of the abuse of great parts. Shall we suppose that when Christ undertook for sinners in the covenant of grace, He considered them any otherwise than as most miserable, lost, dead in sin, utterly impotent (Rom. v. 7, viii. 3) ; or that the wisdom of God gave Christ to die for this end, that sinners might attain salvation by a natural power of believing—a power which Amyraldus confesses could never be exerted ? Further, is not faith a most holy and moral act, and, as it takes place in the sinner, purely supernatural act? And shall we allow that a principle which is not moral, but merely physical, can be productive of such a moral and supernatural act? Ought not an act and its principle to correspond with one another? Let the same thing be said of love which Amyraldus has said of faith, and the Pelagians will triumph, who used to speak so much about a natural faculty of loving God above all things. Indeed, upon this scheme there will be no keeping out of the Pelagian opinion about the powers of *pure nature*, and about *physical or natural faculties in man of doing what is morally good*. For, in confuting that opinion, our divines still maintained that the image of God was requisite in the first man, in order to his exerting such morally good acts as those of loving and seeking true blessedness in the enjoyment of Him. But Amyraldus overthrows this doctrine, while he is led, by the distinction he makes between natural and moral power, to hold that the conception of man's rational nature necessarily includes in it a power of exerting acts morally good, such as those of desiring and endeavouring to obtain the restoration of communion with the infinitely holy and blessed God. The tendency of this scheme became more manifest when Pajonius —a disciple of Amyraldus—began to *deny the necessity of the Spirit's work* in the internal illumination of sinners, in order to their saving conversion. For, said Pajonius, nothing more is necessary to that end than that the understanding which has in itself a sufficiency of clear ideas (according to the language of the Cartesian philosophy then in vogue) should only be struck by the light of external revelation, as the eye is struck by the rays of light coming from a luminous object." [1]

Church history, in one aspect of it, may be compared to a

---

[1] Leydecker, *de Veritate Religionis Reformatæ et Evangelicæ*, lib. ii. cap. 6, sect. 82. This translation, happy and spirited, is given in Dr. John Anderson's *Precious Truth*, Pittsburg 1806.

succession of advancing and receding tides. We may accordingly regard those three erratic tendencies last mentioned as the ebb-tide, after the flow of the Reformation period. Ere long, however, there appeared again clear indications of an advancing tide of spiritual influences, accompanied, as was to be anticipated, with a new testimony to the personality and operations of the Holy Spirit. To these we shall briefly advert.

I shall notice first in order THE PURITAN PERIOD, which, to a large extent, may be described as taking form doctrinally in antagonism to the Arminian teaching and to the Romish practices which were introduced and encouraged in the English Church by the influence of Archbishop Laud. The testimony to the doctrines of grace, on the part of the Puritans, was accompanied with a signal effusion of the Holy Spirit. For the manner in which they brought out the doctrine of the Spirit's operations as contrasted with the Arminian teaching, which either did not recognise His agency, or confined it to the incipient impulse given at the time of baptism, they deserve the profound gratitude of subsequent ages. Whether we converse on this point with HOWE, whose platonic mind, under the clear doctrine which he held and taught on the subject of the Spirit, loved to contemplate the beatific vision ; or with OWEN, whose study of the doctrine of the Spirit prompted him to unfold the spiritual mind and the glory of Christ ; or with T. GOODWIN, whose researches into the Spirit's operations filled him with an enraptured love of knowledge, and a singular appreciation of the least particle of that word which embodies the Spirit's revelation,—we find nothing in their spirituality false or unhealthy. Their doctrine of the Spirit was used to lead men to Christ, not to withdraw men's minds from Him.

These great divines, following in the same path with their predecessors Perkins, Preston, Bolton, and others, made it their task to prove that the Spirit's work is so essential in every system of theology and of ecclesiastical life, that without it all falls under the law of a perilous externalism; that the regeneration of the nature is not less important than the justification of the person; and that the Spirit's work is not to be represented as MERELY COEVAL AND IDENTICAL with the rite of baptism. The latter point, taking the Spirit's operations away from the mere observances of Ritualism, was one service among many which Puritan theology rendered to evangelical truth.

In this period the Christian consciousness and the Church consciousness in reference to the Spirit's operations were most definite and clear. It was a period also of great local awakenings, when villages and towns were simultaneously brought under deep religious impressions, and which were always attended with a full belief of the Spirit's personality and work. Marked revivals took place in Scotland under the earnest preaching of Welsh, Bruce, Livingstone, Dickson, Rutherford, and Blair, sometimes simultaneously, at other times more gradually. Similar effects in England accompanied the preaching of Rogers, Blakerby, Baxter, and others of that galaxy of remarkable men who lived and laboured to advance the cause of true religion. And the result was the introduction of a new phase of theology in delineating the order of salvation—*a theology of regeneration cultivated and expanded as a topic by itself.* The ample consideration of this theme by all the Puritans, such as CHARNOCK, OWEN, HOWE, convey a clear proof that a new point of view had been attained. What the previous theologians had developed was by no means repudiated or undervalued, but largely supplemented. The great theologians both of the Lutheran and Reformed Church developed the order of salvation as far as the Spirit operates, in order to justification. Now we hear more of regeneration, illumination, and the renewing of the Holy Ghost.

The first generation developed in due proportion Christ

FOR US and Christ IN US. And this was the school which of all others gave the fullest and most emphatic description of the Spirit's work. Of the Puritan theology it was the prominent peculiarity to bring out *the distinction between nature and grace*, and to enforce the new birth irrespective of the theory which identifies it with baptism. To one fact all history gives a harmonious testimony. In the ratio in which the ritualistic element ascends, the spiritual element descends; the elevation of the one being the depression of the other. And on the full persuasion of this the Puritans acted through all their history.

But they had difficulties of another kind to encounter from the extreme opinions, nay, WILD EXTRAVAGANCES, to which sects and parties pushed the very doctrine of the Spirit for which they testified. It seemed as if an enemy had done this to discredit and discountenance the great doctrine to which they gave prominence. There seemed for a time a wild war of errors contending for the mastery. There was not only the naturalism of the Arminian system, but a congeries of other errors. The Quakers abandoned the sacraments altogether, and well-nigh lost sight of the objective Christ in an all-absorbing subjectivity.

To the various classes of these enthusiasts, and to their names, it is not necessary more particularly to refer. Their great error was *to substitute the Spirit for the word*, the mischievous results of which all epochs attest. They set forth that though it was not absolutely useless to peruse the Scriptures, the mere knowledge of the latter was wholly unavailing, and could not promote the soul's salvation; that the man must learn from the Lord Himself, and be immediately instructed by the Spirit. The arrogance and presumption of such a claim was at once apparent. Though these enthusiasts had little if any learning, and a small and very inadequate acquaintance with any of the Christian doctrines by instruction from others or personal study, they claimed to be better informed than the greatest theologians who had spent their life in the humble and prayerful study of Christian truth with all the available aids of learning.   It was alleged, however, that these last were but letter-learned men, untaught by the Holy Spirit.   They proclaimed that the divine light, kindled in men by an immediate operation of God's Spirit, taught them what was needed for salvation ; that more or less of Bible knowledge was of small moment, and that man had, by sin, entirely forfeited anything like a salutary use of reason.   They claimed *spiritual illumination apart from the Scriptures ;* and they both taught and acted on the principle that they were to act as the Spirit moved them.   There were Antinomian enthusiasts professing to be mechanically acted on by the Spirit.   Rutherford, who has fully described them in his " Spiritual Antichrist," was a contemporary and a true witness of what he read and saw.

It was to defend truth thus imperilled, and to correct extravagant opinions which repelled many and drove them into antagonism to the whole subject, that Owen prepared his masterly work on the Holy Spirit.   It has long been regarded, and justly, as the most important work on the Spirit in any literature.   Without undertaking an analysis of this great work, let me simply quote what he says on the direct action of the Spirit on the human mind.   He says : " God works immediately by His Spirit in and on the wills of His saints —that is, He puts forth a real physical[1] power that is not contained in these exhortations, though He doth it by and with them."   And again, in reference to God's applications to the soul, they are, he says, " both really and physically efficient and moral also; the one consisting in the efficacy of His Spirit, the other lying in the exhortations of the word."

The Puritan movement, like other forms of spiritual life, sprang from a historical necessity, and continued to exert its energies on the foundation of the Reformation theology.

[1] It is better to say, "analogous to what is physical " (analoga physicæ).

And in their eager desire to glorify their Lord, and to display the full doctrine of the Holy Spirit, these men were scarcely conscious of that original development that they were step by step producing.

Were we to review critically the Puritan school of theology, which is not the present object, we should be disposed to say that it scarcely preserved through all its history, especially in the third generation, the equipoise of truth for which it was at first distinguished.   It must be admitted, that while it never failed to give a full testimony to the person and operations of the Holy Spirit, it sometimes forgot that the great aim and scope of the Spirit, as the Spirit of wisdom and revelation in the knowledge of the Lord Jesus, is to glorify Christ; that it occasionally gave greater emphasis to THE WORK OF THE SPIRIT WITHIN than to THE WORK OF CHRIST WITHOUT ; that it frequently gave more prominence to faith as a grace of the Spirit than to faith as the receptive action (*actio receptiva*) or uniting bond which links us to Christ as the Lord our righteousness.   The most salutary development is where Christ *for us* and the Holy Spirit *in us* are equally displayed, and where the one does not eclipse the other.

The Puritanic age may be said to have reached its culminating point, in a theological point of view, in producing those writings to which it gave origin on the doctrine of the Holy Spirit, and which depict the Christian as a new creature in Christ Jesus—a distinct existence, but never separated from the living head.   The writings of Sibbs, Gurnall, Howe, and Goodwin contain a happy delineation of the Spirit's work on the individual as well as on the Church at large, though in proportion they say less than was to have been expected on the personality and mission of the Comforter.   The English Nonconformists, the successors of the Puritans, continued for a century and a half to be the great bulwarks and defenders of the doctrine of the Spirit, and it will be an evil day for England and for themselves if, under the spell of an undue partiality for German thought, they should ever cease to regard this doctrine of the Spirit, and the spiritual religion to which right views of the Spirit can alone direct men's minds, as their badge of distinction and their glory. The work of HURRION, though a posthumous publication and never completed, may be described as a work of great value as far as it goes. The same thing may be said of the work of Dr. Guyse on the Godhead of the Spirit. They furnish two of the best specimens which our tongue possesses of the way in which the elements of truth which the ancient Church developed may be recast and blended or interwoven with the more evangelical views of Protestant doctrine. The peculiar cast of Hurrion's work, replete with references to the Greek Fathers, warrants us in saying that those writers are greatly mistaken who are disposed to affirm, as Tholuck did,[1] that on the doctrine of the Spirit the contributions of the early centuries are either barren of results or of little avail to the Church of our time.

The great writers of the English Church subsequently to the Restoration and the Revolution, such as Taylor, Barrow, Tillotson, Sherlock, South, have done less for this department of theology than for any other. The personality and deity of the Spirit have nowhere found more able and strenuous as well as erudite defenders. But on the Spirit's work they were not themselves, except Pearson and Leighton. They were in part repelled by the extravagances into which the Commonwealth sects fell. But another cause is to be found in the Arminian theology, and in the theory of baptismal regeneration to which they were wedded, and through which they, for the most part, considered the subject.

How eminent divines, in the course of another generation, treated the doctrine of the Spirit in the Church of England, appears from the work of the well-known Bishop Warburton, entitled, *The Doctrine of Grace, or the Office and Operations of the Holy Spirit*. The able writer, in fact, does not treat of

[1] *Anzeiger*, 1848, p. 571.

grace at all in any acceptation of the term. He has not in his thoughts the operations of the Holy Spirit, which are commonly called the grace by which men are converted or called to faith and holiness. With him there is no work of the Spirit in that sense, though he says that he will point out the middle way between unbelief and enthusiasm—between such as assert that no divine operation is necessary to improve man's understanding and heart, and such as boast of the personal experience of the supernatural operations of the Spirit. One expects to find that this outline will have its application to individuals in the present day, and is surprised to find that his words refer only to the extraordinary operations of the Spirit in the age of the apostles, and to the fact that these operations ceased with the apostles. No believer in Revelation will dispute his statements so far as he brings out in that connection the fact of the extraordinary operations of the Spirit. The book, however, would have corresponded with its title had he used the term GRACE as descriptive of the Spirit's operations on every true Christian. But no one in any school of theology has been in the habit of using the term GRACE with the special acceptation to which he limits it.

In a word, according to Warburton, the Spirit's office and operations were limited to the extraordinary gifts and supernatural guidance which those enjoyed who were made the chosen vessels of inspiration. He lays down as his fundamental position, that Christ's redemption could not otherwise be communicated to men ; that God sent His Spirit to enlighten their understandings and sanctify their hearts ; and that the wisdom of God appeared in the method which He condescended to employ at Pentecost in the communication of the Spirit of truth. The whole discussion is occupied with the great work of the Spirit in the inspiration of the apostles. And anything further is set down to a presumptuous and enthusiastic pretension on the part of men who cannot justify their claim, and who are only deceivers or deceived. Hence the unwarrantable violence of his denunciations of Wesley. Any claim to have the Spirit, or to be guided by the Spirit, was repudiated by Warburton as a claim to inspiration.

Before we take up the next great controversy on the doctrine of the Spirit, it is proper to notice two currents of evangelical truth and spiritual life, the result of a new out-pouring of the Holy Spirit. These were the important movement in Germany under Spener and his followers, and the great awakening which took place in this country and America in connection with Whitefield, Wesley, and Edwards. A brief allusion to these important epochs must suffice, as our object in this sketch is rather to trace the history of the doctrine of the Spirit, than to describe the reformations or revivals which His presence and operations have produced in the Churches.

Spener, in Germany, imbibing the spirit of Arnd, though a Lutheran and faithful to his Church, yet on friendly terms with many of the Reformed ministers, and appreciating true piety wherever he found it, began a movement in many respects analogous to the Puritan movement, though with complexional peculiarities which adapted it to his own land. His aim was the revival of spiritual life in the Lutheran Church, stiffened and ossified by forms ; and an extraordinary blessing from on high, or a fresh outpouring of the Spirit for at least two generations, crowned the movement. In Spener's teaching, in his lectures on Arnd's true Christianity, in his sermons on regeneration, and, indeed, in all his writings as well as in the *Collegia pietatis* which he formed, his great aim was, while ardently testifying for all the doctrines of the Reformation, to fan the spiritual life by a constant reference to the Holy Spirit. The previous theology represented by Melanchthon, Chemnitz, Gerhard, and others, had spoken of the Spirit's work in the order of salvation. Spener's constant reference to the Holy Spirit's operations introduced into theology a new set of terms. The operations of the Spirit came to be reduced under different heads, or classified in a new way. And the theologians, who had spoken in a vague, general way on the work of the Spirit in the order of salvation, were under the necessity of explaining themselves in reference to the Holy Spirit as a topic which now required to be treated independently, and in reference to Biblical terms such as calling, conversion, repentance, illumination, regeneration, renewing, holiness, which could no longer be fused together as having no distinct or separate significance, and as all meaning one and the same thing. The union to Christ, effected by the Spirit and the personal inhabitation of the Spirit, had to be treated in a different way.

The movement begun by Spener subsided in the third generation. An opposite current set in, and the spiritual decline was indicated by the question which came to be discussed, whether any SUPERNATURAL INFLUENCE was at work in conversion, or whether all was effected by the moral power of the word. Schubert of Helmstadt resuscitated Pajonism, which called forth the keen opposition of Bertling in 1753. A more formidable work appeared from the pen of JUNCKHEIM in 1775, on the supernatural in the operations of grace, which, from the reception it met with, and especially from the commendation bestowed on it by such a man as Ernesti, may be said to have given rise to a set of opinions from which Germany has never recovered. He asserted that the operation of God in men's regeneration and conversion was not to be designated SUPERNATURAL, or, if that style of language was still retained, only in so far as the Scriptures were of supernatural origin. For the rest, there was nothing that was not wholly natural. The moral power of the word effected all. This was an erratic tendency which, though it called forth less alarm than Pelagianism, or Synergism, or Arminianism, was as perilous as any of them, and proved, perhaps, more calamitous. It was a theory that recognised the Scriptures, but left the Spirit nothing further to do. The propounder of this theory did not perceive that without an inward supernatural work of grace, admitted and believed, men will not long believe in an external supernatural revelation. More than that: if the Spirit does nothing on the individual, His personality will not long be believed in, in any proper sense of the term. And both results necessarily followed, in due course, in the religious history of Germany.

Junckheim's position was, that if the operations of grace in man's soul were supernatural, conversion, faith, and holiness would be purely MIRACULOUS WORKS, and the operations of God would be irresistible. He accordingly adjusted his views to avoid these consequences, and held that the preacher must inculcate on his hearers that there are *no immediate operations* of the Spirit. He argued, with no small ingenuity and force, that the operations of the Spirit and their effects are not miraculous works, though some divines have called them so ; and all that is supernatural in these effects, said he, has one mark or criterion which no enthusiast can turn to account. It consists in this, THAT THEY ARE MEDIATE, and produced by the divine word in a manner conformable to our moral nature ; whereas the enthusiast claims immediate revelations based on feeling. He held that the operations of grace do not alter man's nature, and that they take a natural course ; that there are no mysteries connected with them, and no influences of a supernatural power which put the human machine in motion. And this he attempts to harmonize with the Lutheran position that the man is passive in conversion.

In a word, the writer, apparently ignorant of the inward experience of these gracious operations of which he ventured to treat, explains away the Spirit's operations or denies them. He concludes that these effects are not to be sought in a mode of operation on the heart, but IN THE MEANS, that is, in the word of God, of which the effect is far greater than anything effected by reason or philosophy. But plainly he reduces the word of God, acting merely in a moral way, to a philosophy.

Junckheim had nothing in common with those who affirm that the Holy Spirit immediately operates on the mind as well as the word. And he took up antagonistical ground to the Spirit's immediate operations, because he perceived that this would imply that these operations are irresistible. And he persuaded himself that this could not be proved from Scripture.

Having established, to his own satisfaction, that the Spirit's mode of operation is not supernatural, he next inquires, How does man resist grace? This is done, says he, when he suppresses good thoughts and feelings, and neglects to make a right use of them. But he further asks, Is not man, by a right use of them, a co-operating factor in conversion? And he answers no: as little as a patient heals himself by following the physician's prescription. The physician and the medicine healed him. And when he comes to speak of religious feelings, he regards all these feelings as something supernatural, in as far as they have their ground in the word of God, but not in respect of their origin; for they do not, according to him, flow from any immediate operation of the Holy Spirit, but from a comparison of their heart and life with that which the Holy Spirit, in His word, ascribes to the children of God.

With regard to the difference of nature and grace, to the exaggerated statement of which Junckheim and others traced, as they thought, many evil consequences, one is not a little startled with his conclusion. He says that this has always been an apple of discord, and therefore he wishes the term GRACE to be entirely omitted in dogmatic lectures, and not to remain in sermons where the hearers are still less in a position to form definite conceptions. No marvel that he wished the term abandoned, because he had refined away or philosophized away the thing which it expressed. He does not understand by it the supernatural operations of the Holy Spirit, by which fallen men are enlightened, converted, and sanctified. But the title of his own book, "On the Supernatural in the Operations of Grace," is, from his own explanations, a very inept and unmeaning, if not a deceptive, title.

After having explained away the true import of Scripture, we are not surprised to find that he attempts to make the symbolic books of the Lutheran Church speak in harmony with his views. Because these symbolic books affirm that the Spirit operates in us only by the word, he argues that this intimates that the operation is not immediate, not irresistible, but MORAL ONLY, and according to our moral nature. According to Junckheim, prevenient grace amounts to this, that a man cannot prevent the good ideas, thoughts, and sentiments made by the Word of God on the hearer or reader, just as it is impossible for us to open our eyes and not see.

The refutation of all this speculation is easy enough on Biblical ground. It is also contrary to the Church-consciousness of the entire Christian world from the beginning. If there was no more power or influence than this put forth, the conclusion must be that man converts himself, and that the Spirit has ceased to act since the age of inspiration. No reason could exist which demanded the immediate presence of the Holy Ghost as a divine Person. Still less could we imagine any meaning or significance attaching to the exercise of prayer for the Holy Spirit. If we accepted the doctrine laid down by Junckheim, and commended by so many in Germany toward the close of last century, that there is nothing to impress or influence the human mind but the moral power exercised by the Scriptures, the inevitable consequence must be to injure faith and to destroy all theology. The mystery of divine power illuminating, renewing, sanctifying the human mind, is merged in a moral influence or logico-moral power which the mere force of motives calls forth from the mind itself. The spiritual union of the word and Spirit—or of the word considered as "the sword of the Spirit"—ceases, and only a moral power remains. The ruin of theology must also ensue. It is too obvious to need any proof that, on this principle, all the great articles of Christianity connected with the application of redemption—calling, conversion, illumination, renewing, regeneration, and sanctification of the Spirit—must either be rejected or recast. The Church, believing in the Holy Ghost, into whom every Christian is baptized, as well as into the Father and the Son, has always maintained that there is an omnipotent SUPERNATURAL power of the Spirit exercised on every individual believer, as well as a mere logico-moral influence exercised by the word.

This theory of Junckheim was the fatal blow from which, to this hour, German Protestantism has never recovered. It has in it almost every unsalutary element that distinguished Pajonism in the Reformed French Church. And to me it has always seemed that it produced the same calamitous issues in the German Churches which Pajonism produced in the French Protestant Church previous to the revocation of the Edict of Nantes. It combined Pelagianism, Arminianism, Amyraldism, and a sort of Naturalism all in one.

It was well refuted by admirable men, but the current, of which it was but the indication, was too strong and too wide for any refutation to produce much effect. The excellent Lutheran theologian, Storr, refuted the work on Biblical grounds in two valuable Latin discussions on the efficacy of the Holy Spirit.[1] He had a comparatively easy task. His exegesis of the Scripture passages bearing on the subject under discussion was profound and conclusive, and no one can peruse them without feeling that he has scattered to the winds the special pleading of Junckheim in favour of a theory which is so far from being based on Scripture that it can only be regarded as a foregone conclusion. Tittmann

---

[1] *Commentatio Theologica de Spiritus Sancti in mentibus nostris efficientia,* Tubingæ 1788.

did the same in his *Opuscula*.[1] Wernsdorf, in his Academic
Disputations, most successfully asserted the true principles
of the Lutheran Church on the Spirit's work. And Reinhard,
in his *System of Christian Morals*,[2] maintained the efficacious
operations of the Spirit in the happiest manner and style.
But it was too late. The theological revolution was effected :
the receding tide since Spener's day continued. Michaelis,
Döderlein, and, above all, Ernesti,[3] the great name in German
exegesis, and the masterly writer on hermeneutics, by his
laudatory notice, gave Junckheim's work a passport to acceptance in the universities of Germany and among the pastors.
German Protestantism had only one step to take further, viz.
Rationalism.

The next great fact connected with the doctrine of the
Spirit, is THE AWAKENING IN GREAT BRITAIN AND AMERICA in
the middle of last century, and the theological development
resulting from it. It was undoubtedly the greatest stream of
divine life since the days of the Reformation, and imparted
mainly to the English-speaking Churches. It was an outpouring of the Spirit so powerful in its character and so
fruitful of consequences, that we are warranted to say it has
by no means spent its force ; and it deserves a passing
remark, though we are mainly occupied in tracing the history
of the doctrine. The first movement goes back to Boston and
the Marrow men, the revivers of true doctrine. Edwards and
the Tennents in America, Whitefield and Wesley in England,
Robe, M'Culloch, Maclaurin, and Gillies in the Established
Church of Scotland, Walker of Truro, Henry Venn, Berridge,
Romaine, Newton, and Robinson in the Church of England,
with others outside these Churches who zealously preached
the same doctrines of grace, may be named as instruments
with whom this great movement was identified, and who

---

[1] Tittmann, *de opere Spiritus Sancti salutari opusc.* p. 420.
[2] Reinhard, *System der Christlichen Moral*, iv. p. 251.
[3] *Neueste Theologische Bibliothek*, 1776.

were raised up to act a part in it. In the second stage we find Rowland Hill, the Haldanes, Simeon, and others at work in different ways. The progress of Christianity, and of this great movement in particular, cannot be viewed as the effect of natural development without any intervention from above. None of the theories which shut out the action of the Church's life-communicating Head can explain this great tide of spiritual influence which put a new aspect on theology and Church life. The theory of natural development, the theory of sacramental grace, not to mention the Romish notion of a vicegerent, all fail to explain such a fresh and powerful current of spiritual life ; for they proceed on the principle that Christianity has no present corresponding to its past in apostolic times. They ignore the fact that the Holy Spirit acts with omnipotent and omnipresent energy as the Comforter, Helper, or Advocate whom the Lord promised at His departure, and who frequently descends with an efficacy analogous to the Pentecostal outpouring from above to quicken and inflame, to reanimate and restore the Church ; in a word, to make all things new. The facts connected with the founding of the Church at Pentecost explode the theory of development so current in various forms in all ritualistic and sacramental Churches. These awakenings also attest the presence of the Spirit and the interposition of the Church's Head. They come in seasonably to give a practical refutation of the theology of development, though they are beyond our investigation. They are not in our power : nor will they come forth when we attempt to conjure them ; and we can only say, "It is the Lord" (John xxi. 7). While it is Christ's Spirit who ushers in these creative epochs in Church history, and while they indicate His hand who guides His Church onward to her future, they are altogether free and sovereign. We can neither tell the economy of them, nor explain why they pause. We come in only as gleaners on the field of fact, but can neither tell the laws nor estimate the momentum of that mighty and chainless force which breaks forth from the kingdom of God and sweeps over a community. Such a power at that time issued forth which could neither have been divined by human wisdom nor brought about by human power, and spread over America, England, and Scotland. At the time to which we have referred, there was a resuscitation of a Church-consciousness on the subject of the Holy Spirit such as had not been known from the days of the Reformation. It was in a large degree a restoration also of Puritan theology, though Wesleyanism attached itself to a type of theology which was more allied to Lutheranism than to the Articles of the Church of England from which it sprung. But of that revival-moment which gladdened the English-speaking Churches of last century, we may say that it was above all things Biblical; that it was not a mere revival of ancient forms, measures, and engagements; that it was not, like Jansenism, a mere resuscitation of Augustinianism, valuable as that was, but a return to the Bible, which gave it an elevation, energy, and success which it could not otherwise have had.

The effect of this memorable outpouring of the Holy Spirit was very perceptible on all the Churches. The Calvinistic Methodists, the Wesleyan Methodists, and the Welsh Methodists were the direct and immediate fruit of it. Not less marked was the effect on the doctrine as well as the ecclesiastical and missionary life of the Church of England, though not diffused through the entire mass. The *two Homilies* of the Church of England on the coming down of the Holy Ghost acquired a new significance. The prayers, replete as they are with allusions to the Spirit's work and mission, were offered with new fervour. One author treated the subject of the Spirit after another, free from the misty notions of sacramental grace and the blighting Arminian views which may be traced in all the previous period. The exposition of the subject by Henry Venn in his *Complete Duty of Man*,

by Robinson of Leicester in his *Christian System*,[1] by Romaine
in his remarkable discourse on the Holy Spirit, leave nothing
to be desired. For amplitude of statement and unembar-
rassed freeness of doctrinal view, they show how great a
change had taken place. Courses of lectures on the Spirit
were prepared and delivered. Prayers were offered for the
Holy Spirit. Haldane Stuart of Liverpool sent out a yearly
invitation to pray for the Spirit.

Of this revival the great theologian was President Edwards,
whose influence, as a thinker and leader of revival, has ever
since been powerfully felt. No man can dispute his claim
to a place among the acknowledged magnates of theology,
whether we consider his profound exposition of the high
doctrines of sovereign grace, or his view of the Religious
Affections, in which he states his doctrine of the Spirit, or
his almost unparalleled logical power. Had the theological
reading of Edwards and his acquaintance with the productions
of previous theological schools been in any proportion to his
spiritual experience and mental powers, he would have taken
his place along with Augustin, Anselm, Calvin, and Owen as
one of the greatest formers of thought for all time. But from
lack of acquaintance with the theological thought and style of
the previous ages of the Church, he does not always lay down
his premises or first principles with sufficient breadth and
caution. Thus he powerfully describes the supernatural light
immediately imparted to the soul by the Spirit of God as
giving a sense of divine things in their reality and superlative
excellency. But it is too one-sided for a high Calvinist, as
Edwards undoubtedly was. His distinction between NATURAL
and MORAL ABILITY, in which he has been largely followed by
American and English writers, was a capital mistake. Had
Edwards fully known the place which that mischievous theory
occupied in the Amyraldist system, it would probably never
have been propounded in the manner in which it is set forth

---

[1] See Robinson's *Christian System*, vol. ii.

by him in his essay on the freedom of the will and elsewhere. For the practical ends for which he appeals to it, it is safe enough ; when it is used SPECULATIVELY, it is dangerous. It was adopted in America by Bellamy, Dwight, Woods, and by the revivalists as a body. It was accepted here by Dr. Erskine, by Fuller, Ryland, Hinton, Dr. Pye Smith in England. Proceeding in that line of things, these writers thought they had gained a vantage - ground. They argued that the previous mode of representing the matter by the followers of Augustin and Calvin, left the idea of a real incapacity or natural inability ; that it was chargeable with an improper application of Scripture figures (Eph. ii. 1 ; Ezek. xxxvii.) ; that they gave a needless point of attack to Pelagians ; and that men might reasonably say that they were not responsible for not performing what was really not in their power. To obviate this, the assertors of the above-named distinction said, The proper language to be used was simply that men *would not*, not that they *could not*, repent and believe the gospel. They wished to exhibit that the entire turning-point was with the will, and they threw the responsibility on the man to make him feel that he would not come and be saved. That attempt to explain all only per-plexes all.

These expositions of inability, resolving the whole matter into an act of will, served no good purpose or end. They were not in harmony with Scripture nor with the doctrines of the Reformation, either in the Lutheran or Reformed Church. They were an attempt in words to do something, or at least seem to do something, to obviate the common objection of the Semi-Pelagians : " A man cannot be under an obligation beyond his ability; he cannot be bound to do what is not within his own power and resources." The answer to that objection, as given by Marckius and by all the divines of the post-Reformation period, was, that while God did not require of man in innocence anything for which he had not ability,

yet God DID NOT LOSE HIS RIGHT to demand obedience, though
man has forfeited his power or ability. This answer was
held to be sufficient; and it is recognised by all who have
right views either of the IMPETRATION or APPLICATION OF
REDEMPTION. The writers to whom Edwards incautiously
gave this new impulse supposed that a better answer could
be given by drawing a distinction between natural and moral
ability. They set forth that men, even as they now are,
have a *natural* power to believe in Christ and to repent, but
that they are denuded of all *moral* power to do either. There
is nothing more deceptive than the use of such nomenclature,
which really amounts to nothing. It hides the true state of
the question under cloudy terms. To show how unmeaning
that distinction is, let me notice the following points:—
(1) The inability, according to the express words of Scripture,
must be traced to THE UNDERSTANDING as well as to the will
(1 Cor. ii. 14). To the natural man the things of the Spirit
of God are foolishness, because he cannot know them, and
because he misrepresents them. But to prove that no efforts
of the natural man will avail to make a change, and that
ONLY THE SUPERNATURAL LIGHT imparted by the Spirit can
suffice, the apostle says, " because they are spiritually discerned." (2) The inability, viewed, according to the Pauline
statements, as enmity against God, as a non-subjection to the
divine law, and as an incapacity for being so subject (Rom.
viii. 7), may be called both *natural* and *moral*. That is, it is
THE LOSS OF THE IMAGE OF GOD, the loss of the Spirit, and of
the original righteousness which at first belonged to man and
was natural to him. As man's entire nature is subject to
this corruption to such a degree that he cannot think a good
thought or perform a single good act without a change of
nature, this inability may be called natural and culpable.
The act of the will is not the only hindrance. There is the
corruption of the nature and the want of supernatural grace.
If it lay all in a want of will or inclination, the frequently

repeated *cannot* of Scripture—*e.g.* cannot come, cannot please God, cannot bear fruit, and the like—would have no other significance than the disinclination of a man to do what he has within him full ability or power to do, if he were only induced to will it. There can be no greater misrepresentation or deception. (3) A common paralogism is: "If a man cannot in a true manner repent and believe, then he cannot do the opposite, disbelieve and refuse salvation." But all unbelief and impenitence have their root in natural depravity, and grow from it. The inability to repent and believe presupposes a bias or tendency to the opposite sin, and makes it natural and easy to practise it; and they are left the more to shut their eyes and ears under a peculiar induration permitted to descend on them. The true formula is that set forth by the Synod of Dort, that without the Spirit's grace men are *neither able nor willing* to return to God.

All this serves to show how mistaken Edwards was in making that distinction, which is still drawn by many of his followers, between natural and moral ability. What was really aimed at was the conjunction of two things, neither of which must be permitted to eclipse the other, viz. free agency and inability, personal responsibility and the necessary helps or aids of God's Spirit. And the true object is gained, not by magnifying natural ability and shutting men up to *will*, but by exhibiting the two sides of the incomprehensible mystery. They are both true; and all that theology effects, is to conserve the mystery.

SANDEMANIANISM.

Again, we have to trace, as in previous epochs, THE RE-CEDING TIDE OF THE SPIRIT. Before the great leaders of that revival had passed away, erratic views on the operations of the Spirit had begun to display themselves, the usual concomitants of declension. The first of these was

Sandemanianism, which we notice because its distinctive tenet—THE INTELLECTUAL ASSENT OF FAITH—was accepted by a large section of ministers in Scotland, and even by such a man as Dr. Erskine, and still holds its place. About twenty-five years after the formation of the Glasites in 1729, a dividing question was started by Sandeman on the subject of saving faith, which, according to him, was nothing but the faith of common life—ASSENT TO TESTIMONY. The letters on Theron and Aspasio, which he published in 1757, embodied a new system of doctrine. He allowed no work of the Spirit in the effectual application of redemption. He says excellent things on the impetration or purchase of redemption ; but he repudiates all inward grace as counterfeit. Under the guise of magnifying the former, he vilifies the latter, and all who preached it, with the greatest contempt and scorn. He calls any allusion to it self-righteousness and pride. One can easily see, what he himself allows, that his mind had once been troubled with convictions and contrition, and that he had solved the matter in the wrong way. According to Sandeman, faith was a mere passiveness in coming under impressions, a passive belief of the truth without doing anything but apprehending the knowledge of what he often calls the bare truth, or Christ's bare work, without any act, exercise, or exertion of the mind whatsoever. And to leave no possible misconception as to what he meant, he says, " The Spirit of God acts AS the soul, sense, or meaning of the words wherein the gospel is delivered " (p. 360). After stating that much has been said and written in defence of SUPERNATURAL GRACE, or the agency of the divine Spirit influencing the hearts of men, in opposition to those reasoners who doubt of or deny any such influence, and that many things have been said on this head, serving to give us false notions of the divine grace and Spirit, Sandeman subjoins, " The Holy Spirit is called the Spirit of truth, as also the Spirit of grace. He speaks and breathes only the grace and truth that came by Jesus Christ. When a man then comes to know the gospel, or to receive the Spirit, he thinks of no other grace but what appeared in Christ's tasting death for them ; no other truth but what was manifest in Christ, the end of the law for righteousness. This differs not a little from what the popular doctrine leads us to think of, namely, *the truth of grace in the heart.* When our systems describe faith to us as a saving grace bestowed on us, by which we make use of Christ for salvation, are we not led to think of some grace necessary to our salvation beside what appeared when Christ by the grace of God tasted death for the sins of men ? "

It is clear that the writer identified the influence of the truth and the influence of the Spirit, and that he intended to supersede every other grace but THE OBJECTIVE GRACE displayed in the atonement.   Still more unambiguously he says, " All the divine power which operates upon the minds of men, either to give the first relief to their consciences or to influence them in every part of their obedience to the gospel, *is persuasive power*, or the forcible conviction of truth." If all is persuasive power, and if the Holy Spirit acts AS the soul, sense, or meaning of the words, what have we but a position antagonistic to all that the apostle affirms when he says that the natural man cannot know the things of the Spirit of God, " because they are spiritually discerned " ? The Spirit gives all that discernment and conveys all that meaning.   Fuller, the eminent Baptist minister, and Rev. D. Wilson, London, wrote admirably against Sandemanianism. Fuller's lettters on this subject would have been more conclusive had he followed Sandeman step by step instead of turning aside to less able men.

THE DOCTRINE OF THE SPIRIT DURING THE NINETEENTH CENTURY.

It remains to sketch the doctrine of the Holy Spirit during this nineteenth century.   The revival of the British and

American Churches may be regarded as the most obvious and signal work of the Spirit during last century, though many a similar outpouring of the Spirit has taken place since. THE GREAT outstanding WORK OF THE HOLY SPIRIT in the present century is THE SUCCESS IN MISSIONS. But as our object is to trace the phases of doctrinal opinion more than Church life, I shall not turn aside from this.

In all the theological thinking on the operations of the Spirit in this country and America, the powerful influence of President Edwards may easily be detected. Its most important element appears in the various writers who, like Dwight, Ryland, and others, imbibed the views contained in the treatise on the Religious Affections. The more speculative point on the so-called natural ability, often carried to an unwarrantable and dangerous extreme, was found in all the American revivalists till Dr. Hodge and the Princeton divines withstood it, and did much to counteract[1] its spread.

Here I may add that it was a wholly gratuitous collision into which Edwards' opinions were brought with the opinions of Marshall, Hervey, Boston, and the Marrow men, by a spirit of controversy on the part of Bellamy. He represented some of the expressions of these eminent men in a wrong light, as if they did not hold the NECESSITY OF REGENERATION AS ANTE-CEDENT to the first act of faith. It was a misrepresentation of these great men's opinions, who maintained in terms the most unambiguous, that *regeneration is not effected by the word without the Spirit, nor conversely by the Spirit without the word,* and that the Spirit of light and revelation in the knowledge of Christ is the source of all spiritual affections. But the aim of Marshall, and of the others named along with him, was to set forth the supernatural work of *regeneration as the first act of faith ;* in other words, to prove that a regenerate person is never for a moment in possession of regeneration without the exercise of saving faith on its object; that regeneration

[1] See the Princeton essays *On Human Inability.*

precedes in order, but that the regenerate person is never destitute of saving faith in Christ. He held that the Spirit of God does *not work faith till we act it.* He maintained, as strongly as Edwards did, that *the Spirit produces all and that we act all,* but that there is no inoperative possession of faith as a grace of the Spirit without its active exercise on Christ as its proper object. And the design of so putting the matter was a practical one. He would have men BEGIN THE EXERCISE OF FAITH in compliance with the word of invitation, without waiting for the knowledge that the Spirit had already effected in them the saving change.

A few further remarks will suffice for what remains to be said on the doctrine of the Spirit in connection with modern American theology. If we except the peculiar views of Finney and the revivalist - school, whose tendency was to magnify human ability, and to keep the Holy Spirit and His operations out of view in all their preaching, there was little in the mode of presentation adopted either in the old or new school to which, when rightly explained, any Biblical divine could take just exception. There might be different modes of explaining the nature of regeneration. Some had their taste-theory. Dwight, for instance, following in the line of Edwards, made the change of heart consist in a relish for spiritual objects imparted by the Holy Spirit. Others explained the fact by a change of the ruling purpose or chief end. But these were only modes of exposition where the same truth was held.

The main point of discussion between those who at bottom built on the same foundation was, whether the Holy Spirit acts on the mind MEDIATELY or IMMEDIATELY. But by both the agency of the Spirit was spoken of as preceding the action of the human mind in conversion, and as the cause of the change. The human mind was considered as only concurring with the divine Spirit in turning the man from the error of his ways. The old school laid emphasis on the fact that man is passive in regeneration and active in conversion. It was held that in what is properly THE ACT OF GOD the man cannot be said to be active, because he is but the party changed, or the object on whom the change is produced. Their mode of preaching may be expressed in the formula often re-echoed to the masses in their revival sermons: "You must, but cannot. You must repent and return to God, but cannot without His renewing Spirit." As to the new school, it was sometimes alleged against it that the agency of the Holy Spirit was represented wholly as that of moral suasion. But they vehemently repelled this as an injustice.

This whole question, whether the Spirit of God acts only by the intervention of the word, is often rendered ambiguous by the mode in which it is stated. The question of the *immediate* or *mediate* operation by the Spirit is not WHETHER GOD'S WORD IS USED OR NOT. Both intend to assert that the change is effected by the word, as the instrument in the hand of God or as the sword of the Spirit. The true mode of stating the question is whether the word produces the result by mere moral suasion, or by the Spirit's direct action in regenerating the mind.

The full, well-balanced doctrine of the Spirit has long been maintained in England by the successors of the Puritans. They have handled it with an amplitude of view, a freshness of delineation, and a spiritual tone which leave nothing to desire. This is the eminent service rendered to Christianity by the English Nonconformists. Not to go back to the Baptists of former times, those eminent men who adorned their ranks at the beginning of this century, most of whom imbibed the views of Edwards in the best sense, set forth in a happy combination the operations of the Spirit with a full and free proclamation of the gospel. The circular letter of the eloquent Robert Hall gives an admirable exposition of the work of the Spirit and of the Church's duty ; and the same thing is true of Fuller's circular letter ; both prepared in order to diffuse right views on this momentous theme. The admirable work by Harrington Evans, entitled *The Spirit of Holiness*, is the work of one who had outlived the blighting influence of Sabellianism, under which he fell for some time; and who, subsequently to his restoration, continued for many years to give a more emphatic testimony to the personality and work of the Spirit than any other man perhaps has done since the time of Owen.[1]

The English Congregationalists during this century have produced several works of much value on the doctrine of the Spirit. The exposition of this topic by Williams in his *Equity and Sovereignty*, by Payne in his Lectures, by Wardlaw in several publications, and by Stowell in his admirable lectures on *The Work of the Spirit*, forms a literature with which, for its deeply spiritual and experimental doctrine, every Biblical divine must fully sympathize. This is their badge of distinction. The one exception to these important contributions is the work of Dr. Jenkyn on *The Influences of the Holy Spirit*. But as Dr. Payne has fully exposed and refuted that attempt to identify the Spirit and the word, and as it does not differ from the views of Pajon and Junckheim, already explained, it is not necessary to occupy space in further refutation of that line of thought.

---

[1] Mr. Evans, having read some of those writings of Dr. Isaac Watts which have an all too obvious Sabellian tendency, came to deny the distinction of persons in the Trinity. He published his Sabellianism in a work, entitled *Dialogues on Important Subjects*, in 1819. His history, in connection with this change of doctrinal opinion, is full of significance and warning. He had been an acceptable minister in the Church of England, and much blessed in his work. The spell of his new opinions so blinded his mind, that he did not for a time perceive all that was involved in it. As he did not deny the work of the Spirit upon the heart, he did not for a time suspect that the Holy Spirit was dishonoured. When he came to see that he denied the Deity of the Son and the real glory of the Holy Ghost in the economy of redemption, he wrote a refutation of his own work in *Letters to a Friend*, by J. H. Evans, 1826. He collected all the copies of his dialogues, and consigned them with every mark of contrition to the flames. The whole account given in the Memoir by his son is replete with interest. But the memorable fact is (p. 50) that his own soul suffered, and that there was a most manifest withering in his ministry. After his return to sound Trinitarian views, scarcely ever was there in London a more blessed ministry than his.

The work of Stowell, bating some minor points to which we have already taken exception in this volume, is a broad and comprehensive description of some parts of the ministration of the Spirit. It is limited to the spiritual life. And its object, according to a plan formed during a pastoral ministry of thirty years, was to " show that neither Church traditions, philosophical theories, nor mystical imaginations, are in accordance with what the Spirit of God has taught concerning His own work, but that Christian spiritualism is the harmony of divine revelation with the consciousness of man." Mr. Stowell begins with man rather than with the divine economy in the mission of the Holy Ghost, or with His personality and Deity. Nor could any objection against this method be sustained, if, in the subsequent parts of the volume, sufficient prominence had been given to the agent and His mission as well as to His work, which, however, we desiderate. After describing the wrong choice which is uniformly made, and which, as he happily shows, must be ascribed not so much to any other cause, as to an inward and spontaneous predisposition, he arrives at the conclusion that with man nothing becomes an actual motive, however clearly its truth may be perceived, however seriously its reason and right and authority may be responded to, until his spirit is changed ; adding that either it must remain undone, or God must do it (p. 49).

We have already referred to Dr. Wardlaw's services in connection with the work of the Spirit. As Dr. Payne and Mr. Stowell refer to the correspondence carried on by Dr. Wardlaw on the one side, and by the Congregationalist Churches, from whom he separated, on the other, it may serve, perhaps, better than any other historical facts that could be adduced, to refer to that discussion, because the important spiritual truth which he asserted in that controversy exhibited the true opinions of the Congregationalist body. In order to remain in Church fellowship with some of the neighbouring Churches, he demanded evidence that they believed in a SPECIAL INFLU-

ENCE OF THE SPIRIT, and not in a mere general influence given equally to those who believe the gospel and to those who reject it. He cut off all evasion from those who were ready to admit the influence of the Spirit in words and to deny it in fact. In taking this step, which we can only commend as a faithful act of discipline, Dr. Wardlaw declared that an agreement on the work of the Spirit in conversion was, by the body of which he was a minister, always held as equally essential with an agreement of sentiment regarding the work of Christ. And he adds that the doctrine of the special influence of the Spirit has been regarded as characteristic of that body in Scotland ever since its commencement (p. 83). The professed convert attributed his change of heart and the faith thence resulting to nothing in himself, but to the grace of the Spirit making him to differ from other men (p. 99).

The great question discussed in that correspondence was whether they who are converted to God experience any *direct inward influence or operation of the Holy Spirit on their minds distinct from, but accompanying the word.* This is emphatically affirmed by Wardlaw, and evaded but really denied by the other party, who regarded the influence of the truth and the influence of the Spirit as one and the same. What Dr. Wardlaw meant by the special influence of the Spirit was His operation *within* the mind and heart, accompanying the truth and rendering it efficacious; whereas they held no influence but that of the word, or external means (p. 124).

As the parties attached to this modern Pajonism questioned or denied any direct internal working of the Spirit in conversion, and said that the Spirit works only by His truth, His people, and Providence, the whole of their positions were fully exposed and sometimes refuted by a happy *reductio ad absurdum,* or by propounding a series of untenable suppositions which, according to their premises, must needs be held. Thus Dr. Wardlaw argues—(1) The subject of conversion must be less opposed to God than others, if the opposite view has any validity. He must have a better disposition, and have whereof to glory contrary to Scripture (1 Cor. iv. 7); or (2) the word, or means, or instruments, must have more power at conversion than on any former occasion; and who does not see the absurdity of a fact or motive having more force one day than another, when, according to the supposition, it is all external? But when we affirm the Biblical position, that the indisposition of the heart is removed by the new heart being given (Ezek. xxxvi. 26), no further difficulty remains. Dr. Wardlaw in the most cogent style of argument proves, in opposition to his opponents, that the gospel to which the heart is opposed can never change the heart *till that gospel is admitted,* and that it can never be received without the interference of a higher power (p. 140).

The following words will suffice to show the manner in which he conjoins the two things—the word and Spirit:— " To show the necessity of a direct divine agency of the Spirit in the soul of man, *accompanying the word as the instrumental means,* in order to account for its conversion would require a volume." " If the influence of the Spirit is merely the influence of the word, of evidence, and of circumstances operating on the human mind independently of any efficacious, inward, illuminating, spiritualizing energy, then there is nothing supernatural in the case—nothing beyond or different from the ordinary phenomena of the mind as affected by informa- tion with its attendant proofs, or whatever else may contribute to excite attention and command assent. You do no more than put the Spirit in the place of Providence, or of the human agent through whose instrumentality Providence works. The means are left to their own operation, there being no other influence accompanying or superadded " (p. 60). After adverting to the inadequate conceptions entertained as to the heart's alienation from God, and the historical fact that the denial of inward special efficacious grace to the conversion of sinners and the denial of the atonement have uniformly gone

together, the correspondence goes over all the points in debate.
It is one of the most valuable discussions polemically which
has recently appeared on the Spirit's work, and brings up and
exposes the present phase of Pajonism and Semi-Pelagianism.
Dr. Wardlaw exposes the avowal that when a sinner believes
he receives the Spirit! How comes the sinner to believe? he
exclaims; whence this spiritual perception?

Before passing from the Congregationalist writers, to whom
we owe some of the best parts of our theological literature on
the doctrine of the Spirit, it may not be out of place to refer
to a tendency among them to explode the distinction usually
made between the common and special operations of the Spirit.
They seem drawn to this by considerations which, whether
accepted or not, are entitled to respect. They wish apparently
to prove, against Arminian opponents, that it is only in His
testimony that the Spirit can be said to be resisted; that in
His work, properly so called, the Spirit is irresistible, and that
He who hath *begun a good work* will perform it till the day of
Jesus Christ. Of course, if that distinction can be fully established, the advantages connected with that mode of putting
divine truth are obvious. However, I am merely stating
here historically that this tendency is cropping out among
their most eminent writers. Wardlaw plainly inclines to it
in the above-named correspondence and in his system. Dr.
Pye Smith thus asserts it in his *First Lines of Christian Theology*
(Schol. iii.) : "On what is called by many *common grace* and
its essential difference from that which is *saving;* this is not
Scriptural phraseology, it is needless, and tending to embar-
rassment" (p. 568). Dr. Payne in like manner says, " I do
not believe that the influence of the Spirit of God in the
specific and proper sense of the term, *i.e.* an influence *distinct*
from the moral or persuasive influence of divine truth, is
ever exerted except upon those who were prepared unto
glory."

IRVINGISM AND PLYMOUTH BRETHRENISM.

Only two additional phenomena in this country demand a passing notice, because they claim, in a peculiar sense, to owe their origin to the Holy Spirit—IRVINGISM and PLYMOUTH BRETHRENISM. They are so vastly inferior to their pretensions, however, that they rather awaken a feeling of regret and pity.

As to IRVINGISM, with its ostentatious parade of supernatural gifts and of extraordinary offices, which have had no real existence since the apostolic age, it is after all smothered under ritualistic forms. Were there nothing more to prove its hollowness, this would suffice. Such a supply of the Spirit as this sect claims could not co-exist with its pomp of prepared liturgical and office forms. It was largely a revival of Montanism ; and the way in which it committed itself to a revival of twelve apostles for the sealing of the apocalyptic twelve thousand immediately before the second advent (Rev. vii. 4), will prove its death-blow, which cannot long be delayed or warded off in the nature of things. Professor H. W. J. Thiersch was the only theologian of note who attached himself to it.

As to BRETHRENISM, it will have a longer existence probably than the other phenomenon. It has produced a literature on the Holy Spirit of a very mixed character. Mr. Darby, Mr. Kelly, and Mr. Harris have all written on the Holy Spirit. While many excellent things have been said by all these writers on the distinction which must always be carefully drawn between Christ's work FOR US and the Spirit's work IN US, on the inhabitation of the Spirit in the hearts of Christians, and on the communion between Christ and His people by the Holy Ghost the Paraclete, there are three points where their doctrinal views on the Spirit are mischievous in the last degree. (1) They have very much resuscitated the Cocceian notions as to the alleged low plat-

form of the Old Testament saints.   They represent them all
as burdened and fettered by the Spirit of bondage, till one
hardly sees where spirituality remains.   They thus come to
divide the Church which was one from the days of Abel into
two.   (2) They make a presumptuous claim to be in their
assemblies under the presidency of the Holy Ghost, as they
phrase it ; and, accordingly, they venture to carry out the
decrees and resolutions come to under this imagination with
a confidence little less than apostolic.   (3) They take exception to what most other Churches, not swamped by
Ritualism, have always regarded as one of the most important and blessed duties—*to prayer for the Holy Ghost.*
The Church of God of all ages, according to the most explicit
Scripture examples,—the Greek Church, the Roman Church,
all the Protestant Churches, in the exercise of a deep Christian instinct,—have invoked the Holy Ghost, and expected
larger and larger supplies and communications ; and they
grieve for and confess their sin in not having more implored
His help and presence.   This sect, by an obvious misinterpretation of Scripture, objects to the practice of praying for
the Spirit, because forsooth He was given at Pentecost.

In winding up this historical survey, we have only to add
an outline of the modern views on the doctrine of the Spirit
which prevail in GERMANY, HOLLAND, and SWITZERLAND.
Germany seems to have abandoned this whole field, as if it
were no longer worthy of cultivation.   There is not a single
work in the whole compass of German literature on the office
and work of the Holy Spirit, if we except the unfinished
work of Kahnis,[1] of any value or importance.   And when
we inquire into the reason, it is traceable partly to the

---

[1] Kahnis, *Die Lehre vom Heiligen Geiste*, Halle 1847.   Having procured the
first part of this work thirty-five years ago, I eagerly waited for its continuation.
The writer had before this published a Latin tractate denying the personality
of the Spirit.   Here he asserts the opposite view, and in an able, erudite way
adduces the Patristic testimony down to Origen.   Whether the author wearied
of his subject, or Germany showed no interest in it, or whatever was the cause,

dominant Sabellianism, partly to the utterly misplaced importance attached to the sacraments, and which has produced results scarcely less calamitous, notwithstanding the evangelical preaching which prevails in Germany, than the same error has caused in the Church of Rome. The Lutheran Church system is such that it does not require the Spirit's work for the application of redemption. What other Churches ascribe to the Holy Spirit, the Lutheran Church ascribes to the sacraments and Church ordinances; and these opinions are so diffused through the community, and so dominate the minds of clergy and laity alike, that there remains in reality in the ecclesiastical or theological mind no place for the operations of the Spirit on the individual. Regeneration is identified with baptism. PRAYER FOR THE SPIRIT IS DEEMED SUPERFLUOUS, because the sacraments are always equally replenished with blessings. A new supply or outpouring of the Spirit is, according to them, an English or American extravagance.

There is A THREEFOLD STANDPOINT OF THEOLOGICAL CONCEPTION which, during the present generation, has moved the German mind. One extremely negative tendency proceeded on the supposition that Christianity had outlived itself, and that what had been regarded as the life-principle of the Church in all ages, faith in the historical Person of Jesus, incarnate, crucified, and risen, the Redeemer of sinful humanity and the source of life, must give way before another, a new and spiritualized, form which disengages the idea from the shell of the historical manifestation. Against this tendency all Christians in all lands maintained the same positive historical belief. But two other tendencies, while at one in opposing the above-named school of Baur and Strauss,

the learned author never proceeded further with his undertaking. The only other recent works on the doctrine of the Spirit in the whole compass of German literature are the two following small treatises, of no great importance : (1) Wörmer, *Das Verhältniss des Geistes zum Sohne Gottes*, Stuttgart 1862 ; and (2) *Die Bedeutung des Heiligen Geistes bezüglich der auferstehung des Leibes* (anonymous), Basle 1866.

diverged from each other in carrying out their special conception of Christianity. A *second* tendency, therefore, held firmly by the ecclesiastically given form in which Christianity had won its triumphs as a missionary power among the nations, and as a principle of reformation from the corruptions of Popery ; and they were disposed to regard this as necessary for the future as it had been powerful in the past. A *third* tendency attempted to continue at one with Rationalism in the principles of philologico-historical interpretation, and only desired a more spirited application of them. They would not break the thread of development where Rationalism began.

THE SCHLEIERMACHER SCHOOL.

This last tendency, known as the mediating school, which took its rise with Schleiermacher (A.D. 1820–34), did not recognise THE PERSONALITY OF THE HOLY SPIRIT, and consequently had nothing to say as to HIS WORK. Schleiermacher's views were in most things antagonistic to the Church doctrines. It may be said of Schleiermacher's system, though we cannot in this place completely analyse it, that it struck to the core the mind of his country, casting many in its mould, and in others setting in motion an unwonted energy of action and reaction such as nothing but the mighty impulse of a mighty spirit could create. In his system all the great doctrines connected with God as an authoritative lawgiver fall into the background. But great and glowing prominence is given to all the views which stand connected with the Person of Jesus as a fountain of spiritual influence. The centre round which His whole theology moved was, to use his own expression, the communion of life with the Redeemer (*Lebens Gemeinschaft mit dem Erlöser*).

But in reference to the distinction which obtains between the Persons of the Godhead, his views were Sabellian : Christ as the Logos, said he, apart from His manifestation in a par-

ticular Person (!), belongs to ecclesiastical conceptions ; and
instead of a personal Holy Ghost he speaks merely of " the
common Spirit of the Christian Church proceeding from God."
The Schleiermacher school, which has risen to great influence
and is still rising, bore the distinct impress of Sabellianism
or Modalism from its commencement. An ingenious essay [1]
appeared from the pen of Schleiermacher expressly comparing
the Athanasian and Sabellian doctrine, and assigning the
marked superiority to the Sabellian theory. But, ingenious
as the exposition undoubtedly was, it was highly unjust to
Biblical Trinitarianism. The entire school, so far as it abides
by Schleiermacher's principles, cannot be regarded as asserting anything approaching to sound ecclesiastical Trinitarianism. In as far as it has accepted Schleiermacher's opinions
on this point, and it has done so with a greater or less general
consent, we find nothing but the indwelling scheme or the
Sabellian view of Jesus. In every form of Sabellianism—of
the modern not less than the ancient type—there has always
been and must be a certain affinity to Pantheism. In
Schleiermacher's essay, already referred to, it was strongly
asserted that Christian faith did not expressly teach the
Deity of Christ. It was alleged that Deity was attributed
to Him only in hymns, poetical effusions, and rhetorical
addresses ; that the Church-doctrine of the Trinity arose in
Alexandria through a Platonizing tendency and in a philosophical interest; and that, but for this, the Sabellian doctrine,
which accepts no personal distinction in the Godhead, would
doubtless have become the predominant opinion. Not only
so : he goes on to affirm still further that *Sabellianism satisfies
the demands of Christian piety as well as the Church-doctrine ;*
and that it has this peculiar consideration to recommend it,
that while the Church-doctrine is transcendent, the Sabellian
view, on the contrary, refers to the order of salvation and to

---

[1] This essay originally appeared in the *Theologische Zeitschrift von Schleiermacher, De Wette, und Lücke.* Drittes Heft.

God's relation to the world. According to this Modalism, which has no tri-personal God, the name SON OF GOD means no more than God redeeming; and the name SPIRIT OF GOD means no more than the union of God with the Christian Church without distinct personality.

On the contrary, all sound Trinitarian divines have maintained that the very transcendence of the Church-doctrine which Schleiermacher depreciates is its true glory. They assert that all the Persons of the Trinity are what they are *prior to creation, prior to redemption, prior to the formation of the Christian Church.* These deeds only manifested what the Persons were essentially from all eternity. They only revealed themselves by deeds of power and of grace. They were divine Persons with a distinct subsistence prior to and irrespective of any deeds performed in creation, in redemption, or in regeneration. But we limit ourselves here to the work of the Holy Ghost. It is evident from Scripture that men were regenerated by the Spirit, and raised up by Him to do a work for God, previous to the formation of the Christian Church; and that multitudes in all the ages subsequent to the fall, and prior to the day of Pentecost, were enlightened by Him with a true spiritual knowledge, and possessed with a true spirituality of mind. All this, as we read in the Old Testament records, was going on before the Pentecostal effusion of the Spirit. The Holy Spirit dwelt in prophets and righteous men in the Old Testament as well as in the supernaturally gifted office - bearers of the New Testament Church; and the Spirit could not have so dwelt in them unless He really subsisted as a divine Person, with a distinct personality in the Godhead. Nor was that all: the Holy Spirit was the cause of all the vast variety of miracles in both economies, and the author of all Old Testament prophecy as well as of all new Testament Scripture; both of which are spoken of as the work of the same Spirit, with no difference as to their origin or authority (2 Pet. i. 21).

If all this is so, in vain do these Sabellian writers allege that the Spirit is but the union of God with the Christian Church. According to Schleiermacher's outline of the Sabellian theory, moreover, it is maintained that *the Holy Spirit is but the Spirit of the whole, the common Spirit of the Christian Church.* It is difficult to apprehend precisely what that means. But the explanation which he himself gives of the statement is in the last degree startling : " The Spirit," says he, " is only in the whole : for as the Spirit is just the God-head, *every Christian must be a Christ,* IF THE SPIRIT AS SUCH WERE IN EVERY INDIVIDUAL." The more that the reader attempts to apprehend the import of that statement, the more surprise and pain take possession of every reverent mind. But plainly, according to the meaning of the terms, the only difference between Christ and the Christian is to be traced to a more and a less of the inhabiting Godhead : and the state-ment implies that the Spirit, so understood, is RELATED TO THE CHURCH AS A WHOLE, as the Deity in Christ is related to His humanity. The writer, with all his vast powers, plainly knew not what he said, nor whereof he affirmed.

Such is modern Sabellianism as set forth by its greatest modern defender. It is fully discredited by the mere state-ment of the Scripture testimony that the Spirit's activity preceded the existence of what is known as the Christian Church.

To do justice to the school of Schleiermacher, among whose scholars there are many who have risen far above him in single points, it must be stated that it loyally adheres to historical Christianity, and maintains the foundation on which the Church has been supported from the beginning. They who belong to it, however, are (1) neither acquainted with the true distinction between the work of Christ and the work of the Spirit, nor able to put them in their proper place and due relation to each other. Of course they cannot do so, for they have no doctrine of the Spirit, and cannot make a due distinction between the work of Christ and the work of the Spirit on a Sabellian basis which denies His personality. Nor is this strange. For if the belief of a personal Holy Spirit naturally leads men to an admission of His supernatural works as something that belongs to Him in the divine economy, and especially to receive the inspired Scriptures as the standing monument of His activity, we may affirm, on the contrary, that a Sabellian view of the Spirit naturally leads men to the denial of the supernatural in any form.

(2) Another peculiarity of the Schleiermacher school is their watchword, THE CHRISTIAN CONSCIOUSNESS, OR THE TESTIMONY OF THE HOLY SPIRIT. They use both expressions, when in point of fact they, for the most part, have no personal Holy Ghost. They build on a Sabellian foundation, and yet retain the theological nomenclature in a sense entirely different from that which was usually accepted by their predecessors. What testimony of the Spirit can there be, and what Christian consciousness in any right sense of the expression can there be, without the regeneration of the Holy Ghost renewing the heart and occupying it by a true inhabitation? It can have no underlying reality, and amounts only to a figure of speech. Their whole style of thought on the Christian consciousness is a mere phrase, and a wholly unwarrantable use is made of it when it is made a test and judge of Scripture.

A few remarks will prove this. There is no Christian consciousness without a sense of SIN. But the school in question maintains tenets on the subject of sin which wholly undermine God's moral government, the nature and sanctions of the divine law, as well as the holy anger of God. This was expressed by Schleiermacher in an explicit denial of the fall and of sin. Sin was made a law of being—a dogma that undermines all reference to God's justice, as well as all necessity for a propitiation. The Lord Jesus was, indeed, depicted in glowing terms as the source of life and light, of joy and strength, but not as the Eternal Son, and only as a *person inhabited by God in a wholly unique way.* We will not deny that many pleasing views are given forth by Schleiermacher and his school on the spiritual union between Jesus and His people, and on the indwelling presence of Christ. In reference, however, to the sinner's objective relation towards God there is a total blank ; and even they who have advanced the farthest beyond their master's limits have but dim, undecided, and vacillating views on all the truths connected with man's acceptance with the Judge of all the earth. Schleiermacher's watchword was : *Religion is feeling.* And carrying out this dogma, he everywhere asserts that doctrine is only an imperfect attempt to embrace in our conceptions the true, the infinite, and the eternal ; that it is one-sided, mutable, and liable to error ; and that, while faith and religion are in all alike the same, *each one, after he has done his utmost to elaborate the truth in his own way, has merely his own individual representation of it.* Thus men, by wisdom, display the opposite of wisdom when they do not bow to the authority of the pure and perfect word of God.

Yet this so-called Christian consciousness is made the arbiter and judge of Scripture. If the Christian consciousness were definitely understood to be the sentiment of regenerate men, inhabited by the personal Holy Spirit, it would be entitled to some measure of respect. It would have much in common with Edwards' treatise on the Religious Affections, or with the subjective spirituality of the Puritans. As it is, it is natural feeling in many cases, not spiritual feeling ; a mere public sentiment, wide enough to take in the consciousness of any man who is not an atheist—a Strauss or Renan. It does not presuppose regeneration by the Spirit. The Bible does not regulate this Christian consciousness, but conversely, the latter is used as the judge and arbiter of the Bible.

Nor (3) has this school any right conception of the Scriptures as the production of the personal Holy Ghost speaking

by human agents.   This also follows from the denial of a
personal Holy Ghost.   For any amount of free-thinking on
the sacred Scriptures they are prepared, if only faith on the
personal Redeemer and vital intercourse with Him can by
any means be retained.   Schleiermacher declared his deep
conviction that faith in the revelation of God in Christ is
nowise dependent on belief in a peculiar inspiration among
the Jewish people up to a certain point ; and he affirmed that
nothing essential is lost thereby ; that Christ remains the
same, and faith in Him remains the same.   All the scholars
of Schleiermacher occupy the same unworthy relation to the
Holy Scriptures.

DUTCH AND FRENCH CHURCHES.

The testimony of THE DUTCH CHURCH in behalf of the
doctrine of the Spirit has, since the Synod of Dort, been
always more clear and effective than that of Germany.
During the last hundred years they have not contributed
anything of much importance on the doctrine of the Spirit ;
and they are beginning to lose their independence to such
a degree that they are content to register the last results of
German thought and criticism.   A few words will suffice to
describe what has been done on the doctrine of the Spirit.
At the close of last century, when Germany was beginning to
surrender the divine Personality of the Spirit as they had
surrendered His Work, we find a protest from Holland.   Professor Clarisse prepared two interesting treatises, one in Latin
and another in Dutch, in which he successfully asserted the
Biblical doctrine of the Deity of the Holy Spirit (1795).
After the formation of the Hague Society for the defence of
the Christian religion, there appeared as answers to the
prescribed subject essays of considerable merit on the Deity
of the Holy Spirit by Lotze, Corstius, and Beuzekamp.   In
1838, Heyningen published a little treatise which he kept by

him upwards of twenty years, after unsuccessfully offering it as one of the prize essays on the doctrine of the
Bible respecting the work of the Holy Spirit.   It is a useful
work, but with a very flagrant defect.   The defect is, that he
abstains from pronouncing with the firm, decisive tone
which is absolutely necessary on the point which draws the
line between Augustinianism and Semi-Pelagianism.   The
reader peruses it and is at a loss *whether the author means that
it is we or God that decisively wills the conversion of the soul.*
No one can say whether, according to Heyningen, it is God
in the first instance that works in us to will and to do.   But
the rest of the work is valuable.   He maintains, from a
Biblical evidence which cannot be shaken, that the operation
of the Spirit is *distinct from the effect of the word*, though concurrent with God's providence and the preaching of the word.
This is set forth in a clear and satisfactory light.   When we
come farther down, we trace the growing influence of German
thought on the Dutch Church, and by no means to its
advantage.   Two prize essays prepared for the Hague Society
appeared in 1844, the one by Thoden Van Velzen, the other
by Stemler the Lutheran pastor at Hoorn.   They are far from
satisfactory.   They give no testimony on the Personality of
the Holy Spirit, which they leave in such absolute uncertainty
that these writers can only be described as ignoring the
subject; and what they say about the Spirit's Work is as
vague and unmeaning as about His divine personality.   The
whole two volumes are occupied with a metaphysico-theolo-
gico-exegetical attempt to harmonize man's free agency with
a certain influence which is not the regeneration of the
Holy Ghost.

The SWISS and FRENCH CHURCHES of this century have
produced very little on the doctrine of the Holy Spirit.   Like
the Church of Holland, which we have just noticed, these
Churches are losing their independence, and coming unduly
under the spell of German theology and criticism.   There are

two interesting works, however, which have appeared in French Switzerland on the doctrine of the Spirit, one by E. Guers, Bern, another by Tophel in the form of five discourses, both written with warmth, devotional feeling, and unction. One point is very forcibly insisted on by Guers, the danger of the Spirit without the word, and of the word without the Spirit.

With reference to recent publications on the Holy Spirit in our own country, let me notice a few of the most important.

The valuable work of Dr. James Buchanan of a practical and devotional character, Hare's *Mission of the Comforter*, Winslow's work on *The Spirit*, deserved the important place which they have occupied in public estimation. An anonymous work, entitled *The Comforter*, deserves also favourable notice. Professor Candlish's interesting little book on *The Work of the Spirit* deserves attention as *a manual ;* and the useful work, entitled *The Spirit of Christ*, by Rev. Andrew Murray (London 1888, Nisbet & Co.), is well worthy of recommendation.

INSPIRATION OF THE SPIRIT AS AT PRESENT DISCUSSED.

The inadequate views of many on the supernatural action of the Spirit come to light in the current opinions on the origin and authority of Scripture. That the whole Word of God was composed by the inspiration of the Spirit, and that holy men selected as the organs of revelation spoke as they were moved by the Holy Ghost (2 Pet. i. 21), has been always held in the Church as an undoubted axiom. It is at this point that the Protestant Churches, under the influence of undue concessions made to the right of private judgment, have put themselves in the wrong in presence of the Greek and Romish Churches, which never called in question the plenary inspiration and infallible authority of Holy Scripture. And it is here that Protestantism, like Samson shorn of his locks, is already beginning to betray its weakness, and is likely to suffer a defeat, unless it ask for the old paths.   It has often been said that there are three specially momentous gifts of God—the gift of His Son, the gift of His *Spirit*, and the gift of His Word ; for it is clear that without the Word we know nothing accurately of the other gifts of God.

The Scriptures, inspired by the Holy Spirit, are the court of last appeal to every religious mind and to every Christian Church for the defence of truth and for the refutation of error.   And if the proof of this position could be invalidated, it cannot be disguised that the consequences would be in the last degree calamitous ; and that modern thought, as it is styled, could do nothing to rescue us from an invasion of the age of reason.   The favourite position of those who impugn the plenary inspiration of Scripture, from Töllner's days downward, is that we must distinguish between the Word of God and Holy Scripture.   But, in reality, the inspiration of Scripture has, in our day, been very largely given up in every sense.   This point is the burning question of our age, a point on which an immense amount of discussion has during a century been carried on.   A few words of a historical nature may here suffice.

Our best writers on this topic, such as Gaussen, Chalmers, Lee, Haldane, Jalaguier, while seeking to establish the fact of a divine Revelation, as well as the authenticity and canonical authority of the several Books, have taken nothing for granted.   Everything has been confirmed by historic proof and rational evidence.   And all this has been conclusively settled before the question of inspiration was taken up.   When all this has been completely proved on historic grounds, and only then, the Books committed to the Church as the oracles of God are next interrogated on the question of their own inspiration.   A sufficient amount of evidence from miracles and prophecy has accredited the Revelation and the divine commission of the several writers; and the same evidence accredits the inspiration to which the Apostles laid claim.

The crude German theories, finding their way into the Churches as modern thought, are the very reverse of all this. All German thinking on this subject still bears the marks of the unworthy concessions which Semler and Eichhorn, the founders of Rationalism, made to the English Deists. The Deists assailed Christianity from without; the German Rationalists assailed it dishonestly from within. The mediating theology, recently represented on this point by Rothe, Tholuck, Auberlen, allows a Revelation in historic facts, but denies the Book-revelation in any true acceptation of the term. Revelation is by them limited to the divine facts, but disjoined from any accompanying inspiration of the Books or exercised on the mind of those who composed the records. The historical revelation, in a word, is isolated from the Book, which, according to these writers, is no more than any other record or narrative digested by pious men—mere literary productions prepared at the discretion of the writers, and having no supernatural origin whatever. The Revelation, according to these theorists, is not in the records in any sense; for they are deemed correct or incorrect, just as the writers had access or had not access to reliable information; and they are not by any means supposed to be exempt from the infirmities and mistakes into which men acting from ordinary motives are occasionally betrayed.

More than that: those writers who attach themselves to the school of modern thought have recently declared that we find in Scripture instances of one man personating another,— that the book of Deuteronomy, for example, is the fictitious personation of Moses by another man, and that too in the solemn position of professing to receive a divine revelation; and that the book was not composed till many centuries after Moses' death. This fraudulent personation-theory is the lowest depth of criticism: for even the Mythical School did

not impute to the writers conscious fabrication. Such
theories are wholly inconsistent with the supposition of a
man acting under the guidance of the Holy Spirit of God ;
and if they could be endured for a moment, would render
inspiration impossible.

All this by natural and necessary consequence leads the
men who support such views to an irreverent treatment of
Scripture. Divine authority there is none on such a supposition ; certainty is at an end : conjecture reigns paramount.
These conclusions, which are styled modern thought and
modern culture, can only be regarded as profane. Such a low
view of inspiration as that to which we have referred runs
counter to the presence of the Spirit in any sense, and to the
divine authority of the Scripture in any sense.

But the fact that miracles attesting the presence of the
Spirit were performed by the Apostles in attestation of their
divine commission and of their message, remains unchallenged.
The rich supply of supernatural or miraculous gifts of the
Holy Spirit which the Apostles enjoyed, and with which the
Apostolic Churches were adorned, was a standing pledge and
sign that the Holy Spirit dwelt in them ; and that the inward miracle of inspiration was still continued wherever these
outward miracles were wrought. The cessation of these
miracles, when they had served the purpose for which they
were given, was a most significant fact. But during the
whole time of their continuance these miraculous gifts, and
especially the gift of tongues or the power of speaking the
Gospel message in actual languages which had never been
learned by the ordinary process, were so many conclusive
proofs and illustrations to the men of the Apostolic age that
the internal miracle of divine inspiration, through the presence
and supernatural operation of the Holy Spirit, was still
graciously continued in the midst of them. But the low
view of inspiration to which we have referred runs counter to
the authority of Scripture and to the finality of Scripture.

It is now time to bring this historical sketch to an end. And in doing so I have only to remark—what Church history sufficiently verifies — that without a full testimony to the divine personality and agency of the Holy Spirit, no blessing can be expected on the ministrations of any Church. He is honoured by being invoked in every prayer, and by being referred to in every sermon. Wherever religion comes in power, the presence of the Spirit as connecting the Church on earth with Christ in heaven occupies a large place in the Church's consciousness and adorations. The doctrine of the Spirit not less than the doctrine of justification by faith in Christ's merits, is THE ARTICLE OF A STANDING OR FALLING CHURCH, and without the recognition of it no religious prosperity exists or can exist.

This historical survey of past centuries, bringing successively under our notice epochs of Revival, such as the age of Augustine, of Bernard, the Reformation, and the great awakening of last century, naturally suggests a closing remark which may not be out of place. The Church of God is in her right attitude only when she is waiting for the fresh outpouring of the Holy Spirit, who comes from Christ and leads to Christ. We see combined in all successful preachers of the gospel right views of the Spirit's operations, an undiverted gaze upon the cross, and a proclamation of the fact that the Spirit comes to glorify the Son in His Person and in His offices. Thus we hear one exclaiming: "Spirit of preaching, that is, Spirit of Christ, come down upon me." [1] They have always set forth that spiritual life flows from the historical Christ the Surety through the Holy Ghost, and that though the Spirit comes not of necessity, but of free condescending love, He comes as the Spirit of our risen Lord, the organ by which He acts, the executive by whom He rules, the Comforter sent in Christ's name (John xvi. 13). And for the present sore and

[1] The missionary Macdonald.

ulcerated condition of the Church, with many marked defects and perilous tendencies, nothing but a new effusion of the Spirit will avail. Many of these tendencies would be at once obviated by the efficacious presence of the Spirit. Of many currents which might be enumerated, the following three may be named, which all too plainly argue a want of the Spirit's power, viz. irreverent criticism of Scripture, sensuous Ritualism, and spasmodic efforts put forth to produce by human appliances what can only be effected by the Holy Spirit :—

1. As to the bold criticism of Scripture, proceeding as it does on a denial of its inspiration by the Spirit, it has no significance and no attractions for a mind that has personally come under the supernatural and regenerating operations of the Spirit. Such a mind accepts on sufficient evidence without difficulty all the divine facts and prophecies—in other words, all the miracles of power and of knowledge with which Scripture is replete, but which the higher criticism, starting from a philosophy opposed to the supernatural, exerts itself to the utmost to explode.

2. As to the widespread Ritualism, it springs from a desire to substitute something sensuous for that which constitutes the true charm and glory of all religious ordinances— the presence and power of the Holy Spirit. It betrays an unrest, a want which the ritualist knows not how to relieve. To a mind replenished with the Holy Spirit, ritualistic elements have no interest or attraction.

3. With regard to the spasmodic efforts to awaken by human appliances a religious interest in the minds of others, we must distinguish two things that differ. There is, on the one hand, a noble revival spirit, burning with a pure and steady flame, which is kindled and kept alive in proportion as the Holy Spirit inhabits and quickens the Christian heart to sustained and strenuous efforts for the salvation of others. It springs from the Spirit of grace : it leads to dependence

on the Spirit's supernatural operations; and they who cherish it never forget that success is not by might nor by power, but by the Spirit of the Lord (Zech. iv. 6). But, on the other hand, there is effort of a different sort—spasmodic and fitful, FROM SELF AND FOR SELF, arguing impatience at the slow progress of the kingdom of God, and prompting measures of the earth earthy. Impure and of a mixed character, it burns itself out; and is succeeded by despondency, exhaustion, and dissatisfaction. Wholly different are those efforts which are kindled by the Spirit and done in the strength of the Spirit. The effects are blessed and abiding to the glory of the Spirit's power and grace.

Various calls to prayer for the Holy Spirit, issued by individuals and societies of associated Christian men during the last few years, must be regarded as an indication of a deep-felt want. Many have entered into such concerts of prayer for "the supply of the Spirit of Jesus Christ," as the only means of counteracting the evil tendencies of the times. All who duly consider the mission of the Comforter, and the offices which He comes to execute, can only welcome and rejoice in such UNIONS FOR DAILY PRAYER to beseech the God of all grace, for His Beloved Son's sake, to pour out the Spirit from on high, recalling the promise: "When the enemy shall come in like a flood, the Spirit of the Lord shall lift up a standard against him" (Isa. lix. 19).

THE PRACTICAL ISSUE OF THE WHOLE: BE FILLED WITH THE SPIRIT.

We close this work with a brief reference to the practical point to which all leads up: "Be filled with the Spirit" (Eph. v. 18). The apostle is writing to regenerate men who have the Spirit; and when he bids them not be drunk with wine wherein is excess, he takes for granted that he is setting before those to whom the Epistle was sent a source of joy, exhilaration, and comfort to which nothing else could be compared. In the context we find it further noticed in a series of participial clauses, grammatically connected with the injunction, *Be filled with the Spirit*, that they are further expected to be so animated with joy as to sing and make melody in their hearts to the Lord,—to give thanks always for all things to God and the Father in the name of the Lord Jesus Christ,—and to submit themselves one to another in the fear of God (Eph. v. 20, 21).

But it may be asked, Is this matter so much in our hands that it can be made an injunction or charge to us: BE FILLED WITH THE SPIRIT ? I answer, all the promises connected with the gift of the Spirit, all the titles given to Him, such as the Spirit of Faith, the Spirit of Love, the Spirit of Hope, the Spirit of Grace and Supplication, the Spirit of Adoption, the Spirit of Glory and of God, on which we have been expatiating throughout this work, and which imply an enlightening, satisfying, sanctifying, and indwelling presence on the part of the Spirit that shall be withdrawn no more, take for granted that this privilege is attainable, and that the duty can be complied with. The words do not mean that the saints are ever so filled with the Spirit that they can receive no more. It is a benefit to be attained by the divine arrangement—" to him that hath shall be given." He who says with the true fear of God, " Take not Thy Holy Spirit from me " (Ps. li. 11), shall never be unfilled. The indwelling Spirit continues to abide in the heart which is His temple, when we gratefully foster those motions which He condescends to impart. The divine rule is, that if we are faithful in a little, we shall have abundantly. Small at first were the faith, love, and hope of the Apostles; but the spark became a flame: the mustard-seed became a tree. The mode by which this is attained is expressly delineated by Christ Himself when He says: " If a man love me, he will keep my words; and my Father will love him, and WE will come to him, and make OUR abode with Him " (John xiv. 23) ; that is, my Father and I will in the fulness of the Spirit come to him, and make our abode with him. To the same purpose it is said: " If we live in the Spirit, let us also walk in the Spirit " (Gal. v. 25) ; " He that soweth to the Spirit, shall of the Spirit reap life everlasting " (Gal. vi. 8). I may also recall the language of the Psalms, which uniformly represent the Spirit-filled soul as thirsting for God, the living God, to see His power and glory (Ps. lxiii. 1, 2). All who duly appreciate the Spirit's operations and His thoughts of peace toward them, and continue in meditation, longing, desire, and prayer in the Spirit and for the Spirit, shall be filled with the Spirit according to the import of the precept which we have quoted. They receive larger and larger measures from day to day, and these are still further amplified in the course of every trial encountered in the cause of Christ, and by every arduous duty performed, as may be seen in the case of John in Patmos, and of Paul in the inner prison of Philippi.[1]

[1] Let me refer to the remarks of our excellent Scottish divine Bodius in his Latin Commentary on Eph. v. 18. Nor can I omit two other writers who write on the subject of being filled with the Spirit with peculiar point and force, viz. John Goodwin, 1670, and Finney's Lectures, although they are much more Arminian in their general doctrinal opinions than may be thought consistent with what they say on this theme.

I.—INDEX TO TEXTS ELUCIDATED.

———o———

II.—INDEX TO SUBJECTS AND WRITERS.

———o———